$1495 19

THE ANTHROPOLOGY OF MUSIC

THE ANTHROPOLOGY

NORTHWESTERN

OF MUSIC

ALAN P. MERRIAM

UNIVERSITY PRESS 1964

Material from the following books has been quoted with permission of the publisher: Louis Harap, *Social Roots of the Arts*, International Publishers, 1949. By permission of International Publishers Co., Inc. S. F. Nadel, *The Foundations of Social Anthropology*, The Free Press of Glencoe, 1951; and Routledge & Kegan Paul Ltd. A. R. Radcliffe-Brown, *The Andaman Islanders*, The Free Press of Glencoe, 1948, and Cambridge University Press. Curt Sachs, *The History of Musical Instruments*. Copyright 1940 by W. W. Norton & Company, Inc., New York, N.Y. Reprinted by permission of the publisher and of J. M. Dent & Sons Ltd. Harold Gomes Cassidy, *The Sciences and the Arts: A New Alliance*, Harper & Row, Publishers, Inc., 1962. Bert Kaplan (ed.), *Studying Personality Cross-Culturally*, Harper & Row, Publishers, Inc., 1961. Gertrude E. Dole and Robert L. Carneiro (eds.), *Essays in the Science of Culture in Honor of Leslie A. White*, Thomas Y. Crowell, 1960, p. 216–230. Frank Skinner, *Underscore*, Skinner Music Co., 1950. Melville J. Herskovits, *Life in a Haitian Valley*, Alfred A. Knopf, 1937. Melville J. Herskovits and Frances S. Herskovits, *Trinidad Village*, Alfred A. Knopf, 1947. George Davis, *Music-Cueing for Radio-Drama*. Copyright 1947 by Boosey & Hawkes, Inc. Reprinted by permission of the copyright owner. Paul R. Farnsworth, *The Social Psychology of Music*, Dryden Press, 1958. Susanne K. Langer, *Problems of Art: Ten Philosophical Lectures*, Charles Scribner's Sons, 1957. Kenneth L. Little, *The Mende of Sierra Leone*, Routledge & Kegan Paul Ltd., 1951. Geoffrey Gorer, *Africa Dances*, Faber and Faber, 1935, and W. W. Norton & Company, Inc. Charles Morris, *Signs Language and Behavior*, George Braziller, Inc., 1955. Margaret Mead, *Sex and Temperament in Three Primitive Societies*. William Morrow and Company, Inc., 1935. Copyright 1935 by Margaret Mead. Published as a Mentor Book by arrangement with William Morrow and Company, Inc., by the New American Library of World Literature.

Library of Congress Catalog Number: 64-22711

ISBN 0-8101-0178-5

Printed in the United States of America
Second Printing 1968
Third Printing 1971
Fourth Printing 1974
Fifth Printing 1975
Sixth Printing 1976
Seventh Printing 1978
Eight cloth printing 1980
First paperback printing 1980
Second paperback printing 1987

Benin bronze statue on title page courtesy of Chicago Natural History Museum. Photograph by Justine Cordwell and Edward Dams.

To the memory of MELVILLE J. HERSKOVITS

PREFACE

This book is the result of some fifteen years of thinking and of discussion with colleagues and students in the fields of cultural anthropology and ethnomusicology, two disciplines whose boundary lines are not always clear and perhaps should not be. Of anthropology little need be said by way of explanation, for its content is reasonably clear and its objectives at least moderately well-defined. Such is not the case, however, with ethnomusicology which has undergone a remarkable efflorescence in the past decade during which younger scholars, particularly in the United States, have subjected it to renewed and intensive examination. As so frequently occurs, the resulting discussion has served to blur some of the simple pre-existing concepts delimiting the field, and it is no longer easy to say precisely where it begins and ends, what its purposes are, what kinds of materials it handles or how it is to handle them. One point, however, has clearly re-emerged, and this is that ethnomusicology is approachable from two directions, the anthropological and the musicological. Given these two possibilities, it is equally clear that since we are all human, anthropologists approaching ethnomusicology tend to stress anthropological aspects, and musicologists, the musicological aspects. Both groups agree, however, that the ultimate objective is the fusion of the two taken as an ideal inevitably modified by practical reality.

When one turns to the literature of ethnomusicology, he quickly finds that this ideal has not yet been achieved, for an overwhelming number of books, articles, and monographs is devoted to studies only of music, which is often treated as an object in itself without reference to the cultural matrix out of which it is produced. Ethnomusicology has concentrated its efforts primarily upon music sound and structure, thus emphasizing its musicological component and in great part ignoring the anthropological. This, of course, is a matter of degree which does not involve absolute dominance of one approach over the other, but the result has been that the anthropological aspect of ethnomusicology has remained less developed and, most important, less clearly understood than the musicological. No matter how tentative the ethnomusicologist may feel about his tools of analysis, the fact remains that musicological techniques have been applied to a surprising number of the musics of the world with significant though certainly not final results; the questions concerning human behavior and ideation in conjunction with music have barely been asked.

Thus the musicologist may have more reason than even he knows to wonder what the anthropological approach may be and what kinds of theory and data may arise from it. At the same time, the non-ethnomusicologist anthropologist is often bewildered by the proportion of the literature which deals with technical matters beyond his ken and which is thus far too often assumed to be beyond his interest.

There *is* an anthropology of music, and it *is* within the grasp of both musicologist and anthropologist. For the former it provides the baseline from which all music sounds are produced and the framework within which those sounds and processes of sounds are finally understood. For the latter it contributes further understanding both of the products and processes of man's life, precisely because music is simply another element in the complexity of man's learned behavior. Without people thinking, acting, and creating, music sound cannot exist; we understand the sound much better than we understand the total organization of its production.

This book, then, is an attempt to fill the gap which exists in ethnomusicology; to provide a theoretical framework for the study of music as human behavior; and to clarify the kinds of processes which derive from the anthropological, contribute to the musicological, and increase our knowledge of both conceived within the broad rubric of behavioral studies. As such it is neither a complete overview of ethnomusicology nor a final attempt to fuse the two approaches to the field.

In attempting to provide a theory and methodology for the study of music as human behavior, I have drawn upon several kinds of information. One of these is comprised of studies of creative behavior and materials not concerned with music as such, that is, studies of the visual arts, oral literature, and less frequently, dance, drama, and architecture. The reason for this is that I am constantly struck by the similarities of the problems which are the concern of all students of creative behavior.

viii

The folklorist is as involved with the techniques of diffusion analysis as is the ethnomusicologist; the student of the visual arts must devote serious and detailed attention to problems of the artist. Most important, all of us are concerned with understanding why man behaves as he does, and to reach that understanding it seems evident that in the future as in the past we shall have to probe many identical problems. My feelings in this matter are due in no small part to my long association with the American Council of Learned Societies which from 1948 to 1950 granted me fellowships specifically to encourage my interdisciplinary studies in music and anthropology. It has been my good fortune, too, to have worked closely in the past several years with Roy Sieber, whose knowledge and understanding of problems of art, particularly African art, are encyclopedic. We have argued in the past and we will argue in the future, but I am richer for the experience and grateful for these arguments which I trust will continue for many years between us. I am pleased, too, to acknowledge the discussions I have had with Warren L. d'Azevedo, particularly those concerning problems of aesthetics; I have tried to resolve some of these problems in Chapter 13 of this book, and many of the ideas therein were stimulated by our exchanges. Both Paul J. Bohannan and Alan Lomax have given me permission to quote from unpublished manuscripts of theirs, and I hope I have done so with due discretion and sympathy for their views.

In writing, I have drawn upon a number of examples of music behavior from widespread areas of the world, and I should like to indicate clearly that in doing so I make no necessary implication of historic connections of similar phenomena except where this is specifically stated. The interest of these examples arises from the possibility that in music behavior, similar responses are made to like situations. This is the purpose of the comparative method: to suggest problems which are not unique to a single culture, but which have wider import in the consideration of human behavior.

Those examples which I have chosen are, for the most part, drawn from three major world areas—Africa south of the Sahara, North America, and Oceania—and as such they reflect the areas of my major interest and knowledge. Where appropriate, I have drawn from other areas as well, and I have included a number of references to music phenomena from Western culture, particularly in connection with jazz. The reader will find frequent mention of the Flathead Indians of Western Montana, and the Basongye of the Kasai Province of the former Belgian Congo. It has been among these two peoples that I have conducted my major field research in problems of ethnography and ethnomusicology, and it is a pleasure to acknowledge the support of those agencies which made my work possible. Research among the Flathead was carried out first in 1950 under a grant from the Montana State University Music School Foundation, and further work was made possible in 1958 by the Graduate School of Northwestern University. Among the Basongye, research was supported in the Bala village of Lupupa in 1959-60 by grants to me from the National Science Foundation and the Belgian American Educational Foundation, and to Mrs. Merriam from the Northwestern University Program of African Studies. Of major importance also was the close cooperation of l'Institut pour la Recherche Scientifique en Afrique Centrale (IRSAC) and l'Université Lovanium. Final typing of the manuscript of this book was made possible by a grant in aid of research from the Graduate School of Indiana University.

It seems fashionable to use a Preface to thank one's wife, who is almost inevitably pictured as long-suffering; indeed, one might be tempted to suspect either that most authors' wives lead lives of pain or that they are shrewish to a remarkable degree and must be carefully appeased. But I am as certain as any man can be that Barbara has enjoyed the writing of this book almost as much as I, and that we stand firmly together in the sharing of whatever may have been achieved by it. She has taken full part in all field research, and read and criticized this manuscript; I am grateful for all these things, and many more.

This book is dedicated to the memory of Melville J. Herskovits, who was first my teacher, then my colleague, and always my friend. My respect, admiration, and affection for Mel are a matter of written record; let it here suffice to say again that I shall always owe him debts of intellectual stimulation that can only be repaid by my attempts to stimulate others. If this book stands as an effort in that direction, then I am satisfied.

APM

Bloomington, Indiana
October 13, 1963

CONTENTS

PART ONE

ETHNOMUSICOLOGY

PART ONE

CHAPTER I

THE STUDY OF ETHNOMUSICOLOGY

Ethnomusicology today is an area of study caught up in a fascination with itself. Although its roots can be traced back some eighty years, and its origin perhaps even earlier, it is only within the past ten or fifteen years that, under the impetus of younger scholars who had brought to it new concepts of theory, method, and application, it has taken a sudden forward surge. The result has been a new awareness of its obligations and an internal probing for a real understanding of what it is and does and the purposes toward which it is directed.

Ethnomusicology carries within itself the seeds of its own division, for it has always been compounded of two distinct parts, the musicological and the ethnological, and perhaps its major problem is the blending of the two in a unique fashion which emphasizes neither but takes into account both. This dual nature of the field is marked by its literature, for where one scholar writes technically upon the structure of music sound as a system in itself, another chooses to treat music as a functioning part of human culture and as an integral part of a wider whole.

The roots of ethnomusicology are usually traced back to the 1880's and 1890's when activity in the field began with studies conducted primarily in Germany and America, and the two aspects of ethnomusicology appeared almost at once. On the one hand was a group of scholars who devoted much of their attention to the study of music sound, and who tended to treat sound as an isolate, that is, as a system which operates according to its own internal laws. To this was added the search for the ultimate origins of music, which arose partially from the theoretical thinking of the time, primarily in connection with the concept of classic

3

social evolution. As social evolutionary thinking changed gradually, and the concept of world wide diffusion began to emerge in the thinking of the British heliolithic school, and later in the Austrian *Kulturhistorische Schule*, the search for ultimate origins continued, but added to it was an equally intense search for specific origins in geographically defined areas.

At approximately the same time, other scholars, influenced in considerable part by American anthropology, which tended to assume an aura of intense reaction against the evolutionary and diffusionist schools, began to study music in its ethnologic context. Here the emphasis was placed not so much upon the structural components of music sound as upon the part music plays in culture and its functions in the wider social and cultural organization of man.

It has been tentatively suggested by Nettl (1956:26-39) that it is possible to characterize German and American "schools" of ethnomusicology, but the designations do not seem quite apt. The distinction to be made is not so much one of geography as it is one of theory, method, approach, and emphasis, for many provocative studies were made by early German scholars in problems not at all concerned with music structure, while many American studies have been devoted to technical analysis of music sound.

While ethnomusicology has inevitably been affected by the two aspects of its own study, it has also received the impact of historic event. Ethnomusicology and anthropology both began to develop as disciplines at a time when man's knowledge of man was in general restricted to Western and, to some extent, Far Eastern cultures. Anthropology emerged, partly at least, in response to a felt need of Western scholars concerned with human society and behavior to broaden their knowledge by extending the range of data available to assemble comparative information which would give them facts about the world beyond the boundaries of the classic civilizations of Europe and Asia. To anthropology was left almost the entire study of so-called "primitive" men, and the anthropologist was forced to assume responsibility for all aspects of the cultures of these people—the technologic and economic, the social and political, the religious, the artistic, and the linguistic. Early ethnomusicologists, recognizing as well the need for broader comparative materials, assumed responsibility for studying the music of all the hitherto unknown areas of the world, and thus an emphasis came to be placed upon the study of music in the non-Western world.

Partly, at least, because anthropology and ethnomusicology grew up at almost precisely the same time, each influenced the other, although the impact of the former upon the latter was the greater. Ethnomusicology tended to be shaped by the same theoretical currents which shaped

4

anthropology, and indeed there is evidence to indicate that Erich M. von Hornbostel, widely regarded as the outstanding historic figure in the field, considered the two disciplines to be in the closest sort of relationship (1905); other early scholars held the same view.

In view of the dual nature of the content of ethnomusicology, it is not surprising to find that definitions of the field, as well as more general discussions of its proper boundaries, have differed widely and have tended to take polar extremes, depending upon the emphasis desired by the individual scholar.

Early in its history, ethnomusicology, or comparative musicology, or exotic music as it was then called, was most often defined in terms which stressed both the descriptive, structural character of the study and the geographic areas to be covered. Thus Benjamin Gilman, in 1909, put forward the idea that the study of exotic music properly comprised primitive and Oriental forms (1909), while W. V. Bingham added to this the music of Dalmatian peasants (1914). This general point of view has carried forward into contemporary definitions as well, where geographic areas are stressed rather than the kinds of studies to be made. Marius Schneider says that the "primary aim [of ethnomusicology is] the comparative study of all the characteristics, normal or otherwise, of non-European [music]" (1957:1); and Nettl defines ethnomusicology as "the science that deals with the music of peoples outside of Western civilization" (1956:1).

The difficulty with this kind of definition is that it tends to treat ethnomusicology not as a process of study, but rather as a discipline which has importance only because of the implied uniqueness of the area it studies. The emphasis is placed upon *where* rather than upon *how* or *why*, and if this be the aim of ethnomusicology, then it is indeed difficult to see how its contribution differs either from musicology, in the sense that its techniques are implied to be identical, or ethnology, in that a similar area of the world is stressed.

Other definitions of ethnomusicology have tended to broaden its scope and to approach, at least, a processual rather than a static geographic distinctiveness. Willard Rhodes, for example, took a step in this direction, albeit a tentative one, when he added to the music of "the Near East, the Far East, Indonesia, Africa, North American Indians and European folk music," the study of "popular music and dance" (1956:3-4). Later, Kolinski objected to the definition of ethnomusicology as "the science of non-European music" and noted that "it is not so much the difference in the geographical areas under analysis as the difference in the general approach which distinguishes ethnomusicology from ordinary musicology" (1957:1-2).

5

Jaap Kunst added a further dimension, although qualifying the types of music to be studied, when he wrote:

The study-object of ethnomusicology, or, as it originally was called: comparative musicology, is the *traditional* music and musical instruments of all cultural strata of mankind, from the so-called primitive peoples to the civilized nations. Our science, therefore, investigates all tribal and folk music and every kind of non-Western art music. Besides, it studies as well the sociological aspects of music, as the phenomena of musical acculturation, i.e. the hybridizing influence of alien musical elements. Western art- and popular (entertainment-) music do not belong to its field. (1959:1)

Mantle Hood took his definition from that proposed by the American Musicological Society, but inserted the prefix "ethno" in suggesting that "[Ethno] musicology is a field of knowledge, having as its object the investigation of the art of music as a physical, psychological, aesthetic, and cultural phenomenon. The [ethno] musicologist is a research scholar, and he aims primarily at knowledge about music" (1957:2). Finally, Gilbert Chase indicated that "the present emphasis . . . is on the musical study of contemporary man, to whatever society he may belong, whether primitive or complex, Eastern or Western" (1958:7).

To these various definitions, I have elsewhere added my own, stating that for me ethnomusicology is to be defined as "the study of music in culture" (Merriam, 1960), but it is important that this definition be thoroughly explained if it is to be properly understood. Implicit in it is the assumption that ethnomusicology is made up both of the musicological and the ethnological, and that music sound is the result of human behavioral processes that are shaped by the values, attitudes, and beliefs of the people who comprise a particular culture. Music sound cannot be produced except by people for other people, and although we can separate the two aspects conceptually, one is not really complete without the other. Human behavior produces music, but the process is one of continuity; the behavior itself is shaped to produce music sound, and thus the study of one flows into the other.

The distinction between musicology and ethnomusicology has most often been made in terms of what the former encompasses, though what the latter encompasses is not often made explicit. Gilbert Chase suggests that the "line" between the two be drawn on this basis: "Might not these two allied and complementary disciplines divide the universe of music between them, the one taking the past as its domain, the other the present?" (1958:7). Charles Seeger makes a suggestion along the same lines, while arguing that it is only a divisive one and not to be tolerated: "But prerequisite . . . is more general recognition of the fact that continuation of the custom of regarding musicology and ethnomusicology as two separate disciplines, pursued by two distinct types of students with two widely different—even mutually antipathetic—aims is no longer to be tolerated as worthy of Occidental scholarship" (1961b:80).

While in theory Seeger's aim is both admirable and proper, the fact remains that scholarship in the two fields is divided in intent and area of concentration; even more to the point, ethnomusicology itself has seldom come to grips with its own problem of where its interests lie. Whereas the dual nature of the discipline can be, and unfortunately often is, a divisive factor, it is also indubitably a strength, and I venture to suggest that it is perhaps the major strength of ethnomusicology. Music is a product of man and has structure, but its structure cannot have an existence of its own divorced from the behavior which produces it. In order to understand why a music structure exists as it does, we must also understand how and why the behavior which produces it is as it is, and how and why the concepts which underlie that behavior are ordered in such a way as to produce the particularly desired form of organized sound.

Ethnomusicology, then, makes its unique contribution in welding together aspects of the social sciences and aspects of the humanities in such a way that each complements the other and leads to a fuller understanding of both. Neither should be considered as an end in itself; the two must be joined into a wider understanding.

All this is implicit in the definition of ethnomusicology as the study of music in culture. There is no denial of the basic aim, which is to understand music; but neither is there an acceptance of a point of view which has long taken ascendancy in ethnomusicology, that the ultimate aim of our discipline is the understanding of music sound alone.

As in any other field of study, the work of the ethnomusicologist is divided roughly into three stages, given the prior planning and preparation of the project at hand. The first of these lies in the collection of data, and in the case of ethnomusicology this has most often meant work in the field outside Europe and America, though there have been exceptions to this general rule. The collection of field data involves the complex and multiple problems of the relation of theory to method, research design, methodology, and technique, as well as other problems existing in all disciplines which follow patterns of research more rigorous than intuitive.

Second, once the data have been collected, the ethnomusicologist normally subjects them to two kinds of analysis. The first is the collation of ethnographic and ethnologic materials into a coherent body of knowledge about music practice, behavior, and concepts in the society being studied, as these are relevant to the hypotheses and design of the research

7

problem. The second is the technical laboratory analysis of the music sound materials collected, and this requires special techniques and sometimes special equipment for the transcription and structural analysis of music.

Third, the data analyzed and the results obtained are applied to relevant problems, specifically in ethnomusicology and more broadly in the social sciences and the humanities. In this over-all procedure, ethnomusicology does not differ significantly from other disciplines. Rather, it is in the use of its special techniques, and perhaps particularly in the necessity for welding together two kinds of data—the anthropological and the musicological—that ethnomusicology is unique.

Since a discipline can be defined, and since it can also be described in terms of what its practitioners do, then at least by implication it is shown to have specific aims and purposes. This question has not been widely discussed in the ethnomusicological literature, though four kinds of approaches can be discerned.

The first of these is probably the most widespread in the discipline, and it is one which is common in anthropology as well. This is the point of view, basically protective in nature, that the music of other peoples of the world is much abused and maligned; that such music is, in fact, fine and worthy both of study and appreciation; that most Westerners do not give it its due; and that therefore it is up to the ethnomusicologist to protect it from the scorn of others and to explain and champion it wherever possible. In a sense this is the outcome of the historic fact that ethnomusicology, like anthropology, takes the world as its field of study and reacts against more specialized disciplines which concentrate attention only upon phenomena of the West. This point of view has appeared frequently in ethnomusicology either through direct statement or by implication. Jaap Kunst, for example, reacts with some intensity to the Western view that the music of other peoples is "nothing more than either expressions of inferior, more primitive civilizations, or as a kind of musical perversion" (1959:1).

This kind of argument implies that the purpose of ethnomusicology is to disabuse ethnocentrics of the notion that the music of other peoples is inferior or unworthy of study and appreciation, and this must indeed be considered one of the aims of the discipline, for ethnocentrism must be attacked wherever it is found. Yet this is but one of several purposes which can be subsumed under a broader heading.

A second approach to the problem of purpose in ethnomusicology is found in the frequently expressed fear that the music of the "folk" is fast disappearing and that it must be recorded and studied before it is gone. This point of view was taken as early as 1905 by Hornbostel, and perhaps

8

earlier by others; it has been expressed over and over again in the literature. Hugh Tracey, for example, in his first real editorial in the *African Music Society Newsletter*, commented on the problems of ". . . working against time in studying the receding natural art forms of [Africa's] people," a theme which he has since consistently stressed (1949:2). Many others have taken this approach. Some have stated specifically that it is the duty of ethnomusicology to preserve materials; thus in writing about tribal, folk, and Oriental music, Curt Sachs comments:

> Such music cannot be bought in stores, but comes from faithful tradition or from personal contributions of tribesmen. It is never soulless or thoughtless, never passive, but always vital, organic, and functional; indeed, it is always dignified. This is more than we can say of music in the West.
>
> As an indispensable and precious part of culture, it commands respect. And respect implies the duty to help in preserving it. (1962:3)

While this aim of ethnomusicology is an acceptable one, the fears for the destruction of the music of the "folk" often tend to be overemphasized, and there is implied a failure to consider the inevitability of change. It has been held in ethnomusicology that music is among the most tenacious elements of culture, but those who espouse this view frequently turn in the next breath to overemphatic laments for the passing scene. Music does seem to be tenacious, though varying social and cultural situations clearly influence the degree to which this is possible. Among the Flathead Indians, whose contact with the West first took place over a century and a half ago, the traditional music system still flourishes; indeed, Western and Flathead styles have not merged but rather stand as two separate systems useful in different contexts. An even more striking example can be drawn from the Negro in the New World; in Brazil, where the first African slaves were imported about 1525, African music continues in strength and, indeed, does so in urban areas where we would expect the greatest change to take place.

So far as change as a constant factor in human experience is concerned, there is little to add to the statement itself. No matter what the efforts to retard or impede it, change does occur. This is not, of course, intended as a brief for neglecting the recording and study of any music, for what is done today will assume greater importance with the added perspective of time. But energy which is poured into lament for the inevitability of change is energy wasted. It is important that we record as widely and as swiftly as possible, but it is even more important that we study the very

9

processes of change that are being decried. The preservation of contemporary music is undeniably important, but given the inevitability of change, it cannot be the only aim of ethnomusicology.

A third viewpoint of the purpose of ethnomusicology considers music as a means of communication which can be used to further world understanding. In support of this view, Mantle Hood has written:

> In the latter half of the Twentieth Century it may well be that the very existence of man depends on the accuracy of his communications. Communication among people is a two-way street: speaking and listening, informing and being informed, constructively evaluating and welcoming constructive criticism. Communication is accurate to the extent that it is founded on a sure knowledge of the man with whom we would hold intercourse. (1961:n.p.)

Hood emphasizes the point that music is a neglected means of communication which can be used more widely for such purposes than has been the case in the past.

There is a sharp distinction to be made between music as a communicative device, which is Hood's view, and as a so-called "universal language," which is an approach ethnomusicologists have consistently rejected. As early as 1941, Seeger wrote:

> We must, of course, be careful to avoid the fallacy that music is a "universal language." There are many music-communities in the world, though not, probably, as many as there are speech communities. Many of them are mutually unintelligible. (1941:122)

Five years later, Herzog took a similar view:

> We indulge in a surprising number of beliefs that are fittingly called popular myths. One of them is the notion that music is a "universal language." . . . [But] our music . . . consists of a number of dialects, some of them as mutually unintelligible as are found in language. (1946:11)

A sharp difference thus exists between music as communication and music as a "universal language." But the question remains as to what we mean by "communication." On a simple level, it can perhaps be said that music communicates within a given music community, but if this is true, it is equally true that there is little understanding of how this communication is carried on. The most obvious possibility is that communication is effectuated through the investiture of music with symbolic meanings which are tacitly agreed upon by the members of the community. There is

10

also verbal communication about music which seems to be most characteristic of complex societies in which a self-conscious theory of music has developed. But little is known of these processes, and without such knowledge it is difficult to talk intelligently about music as communication.

On the cross-cultural level, it may be possible to say that the very fact that people make music may communicate certain limited things to members of markedly different music communities, but certainly little is known about such problems. More specifically, Meyer argues that all musics have certain things in common, though it is not clear whether he assumes that this makes music intelligible cross-culturally. He notes:

> Yet, while recognizing the diversity of musical languages, we must also admit that these languages have important characteristics in common. The most important of these, and the one to which least attention has been paid, is the syntactical nature of different musical styles. The organization of sound terms into a system of probability relationships, the limitations imposed upon the combining of sounds, and so forth, are all common characteristics of musical language. . . .
>
> But different musical languages may also have certain sounds in common. Certain musical relationships appear to be well-nigh universal. In almost all cultures, for example, the octave and the fifth or fourth are treated as stable, focal tones toward which other terms of the system tend to move. (1956:62-3)

It seems doubtful that such "universal" aspects of music contribute to cross-cultural communication through music, and in any case what evidence is available tends to stress the barriers rather than the communicability of diverse styles. Robert Morey (1940), for example, working with the problem of what he defined as "upset" in emotions, devised an experiment ". . . to learn the reactions of native West Africans to musical expressions of Western emotions . . ." Selecting pieces from Schubert, Davies, Handel, and Wagner which expressed fear, reverence, rage, and love respectively, as well as a control selection from Beethoven, chosen because it did not express a generally acknowledged emotion, Morey recorded the emotional responses of "students and teachers in the Holy Cross Mission School at Bolahun in the hinterland of Liberia." His conclusions are as follows:

> Western music is not recognized by the Loma of Liberia as expressing emotion . . . (p. 342)
> Musical expressions of western emotions do not elicit in Liberian

11

boys any patterns of responses common to all or most of the groups responding.

Forty-three answers were given by 11 subjects to four different pieces of music which express . . . typical western-civilization emotions. (p. 343)

Typical western musical expressions of emotions were not judged either as (a) signs of upset, or (b) as being produced by upset-eliciting situations by members of a society who had never previously perceived similar symptoms of western emotions.

Music, said to express emotion to an expert in music and emotion in western society, does not express emotion to auditors whose musical and social training is different from that of the composer of the music. (p. 354)

Although it is not made clear in the text, it seems probable that Morey's subjects were at least cognizant of Western attitudes and values since they were chosen from a mission school; despite this, the music did not convey Western emotions. When Morey presented his materials to twenty Zealua Loma villagers whose contact with the West was virtually nonexistent, he reports that ". . . they were restless; half of them left, especially women, during the music" (p. 338).

My own experience in introducing Western music to peoples in Africa has been similar, and I would suggest that the problem of cross-cultural music communication depends both upon understanding and, more important, receptivity to understanding. In another context, Hood has written in regard to the former point:

Today, as never before, governmental agencies of the nations of the world are recognizing the fact that international understanding and goodwill is possible only when the cultural expressions of the peoples involved are comprehended. To this end the ethnomusicologist must set for himself exacting standards worthy of his responsibility. (1957:8)

This problem of understanding has not always been well understood. Carleton Sprague Smith, for example, in 1941 called for intercultural understanding through music, but it is significant that he spoke specifically about intercultural understanding between America and Europe and between North and South America, and that he limited his discussion to popular and art music (1941). But in these musics, Europe, South and North America form what is essentially a single music community within which it is to be expected that understanding would be most easily achieved.

It is evident that another factor operates in this connection, i.e., the factor of receptivity to understanding. Whereas it is to be expected that members of an academic community in the West will be receptive, at least to a certain point, to listening to and searching for the values in the music of another culture, it is not so certain that the introduction of Chinese opera into a hillbilly bar in Kentucky will meet with enthusiastic acceptance. What is important here is the desire on the part of the potential receptors to receive the material presented, and this is a factor which seems to have been overlooked in discussion of intercultural music understanding.

The problem of understanding can be taken to a further level of analysis, however, in that it is possible that music may be useful as a means of understanding other things about other cultures. In music, as in the other arts, basic attitudes, sanctions, and values are often stripped to their essentials; music is also symbolic in some ways, and it reflects the organization of society. In this sense, music is a means of understanding peoples and behavior and as such is a valuable tool in the analysis of culture and society.

The study of music as a means of communication, then, is far more complex than it might appear, for we do not know what precisely music communicates, or how it communicates it. Communication also involves both understanding and receptivity to understanding. To view music as a communicative device is clearly one of the purposes of ethnomusicology, though it has been little investigated.

The literature of the discipline reveals a fourth approach to the question of the aims of ethnomusicology in that scholars have sometimes tended to throw all possible reasons into a common pot, leading to an approach in which catholicity is substituted for direction. Nettl, for example, speaking not specifically of ethnomusicology but rather of what he calls "primitive music," follows this pattern. Such music, he says, "is a new, rich source of experience for Western musicians" and composers. It "widens and enriches the experience of the listener as well as the composer." "Used as an educational medium, primitive music tends to make a student more tolerant of diverse styles and idioms." "The music historian may use it in his efforts to determine the origin of music." "A knowledge of primitive musical styles is . . . helpful to the psychologist of music." "The anthropologist and the historian of culture may find through examination of primitive music a substantiation of their theories; the folklorist may see its relationship to the music of rural European

13

populations and be able to trace the latter to its origins; the historian of musical instruments often finds prototypes of European forms in some of the simpler ones in primitive cultures. And the linguist uncovers ethnolinguistic materials" (1956:2-3).

While each of these statements expresses one of the aims of ethnomusicology, together they do not seem to form a coherent conclusion. Nettl adds: "In summary, then, to all people interested in music and to all interested in primitive culture, the study of this music offers new fields for exploration and a wider range for reflection" (p. 3). This is, of course, true and is a broad aim of ethnomusicology; we search for broader horizons, but we search for more than this.

Perhaps the aims of ethnomusicology can be expressed in terms of the three responsibilities which the ethnomusicologist carries to his studies. The first of these is technical; it is part of the "internal" study of the discipline. What the student wants to know is what music is, how it is constructed, what its structure is. The ethnomusicologist must be able to notate music, analyze it in terms of its component parts, and understand how these parts fit together to form a coherent and cohesive entity. This kind of study is essentially descriptive; it is, as well, highly technical and thus outside the competence of those not trained in music.

Any technical study brings with it difficulties of understanding and comprehension on the part of those who do not possess the requisite technical competence. This problem has plagued ethnomusicology from the start, for the "outsider" tends to see it only in this single light and to view its subject matter as so esoteric and technical in nature that it cannot be understood by the non-specialist. The result is that non-specialists often dismiss ethnomusicology as technical, impossible, and of no use to them because the materials can be handled only by the specialist.

The technical side of ethnomusicology, however, represents but one of the aims and responsibilities of the discipline. Equally important, and coming to be more and more understood, is the view that music involves not only sound but the human behavior which is a prerequisite for producing sound. Music cannot exist on a level outside the control and behavior of people, and several kinds of behavior are involved. One of these is physical behavior represented by bodily attitudes and postures as well as the use of specific muscles in placing the fingers on the keyboard of an instrument or tensing the vocal cords and the muscles of the diaphragm in singing. Conceptual behavior, ideation, or cultural behavior involves the concepts about music which must be translated into physical behavior in order to produce sound. Here lies the entire process of determination of the system of musts and shoulds of music, as well as the system of normative and existential concepts. Social behavior must also be con-

14

sidered. Some individuals behave in certain ways because they are musicians and because the society stereotypes musicianly behavior. Those who are not musicians are influenced in certain ways because music has emotional and even physical impact, and the behavior at one musical event differs from that at another musical event because of the conventions of the cultural system. Finally, there is the learning behavior which goes into becoming a musician, into being an intelligent listener, and into being someone who participates in musical events though not as a professional.

All these considerations are part of the study of ethnomusicology, and almost any one of them can be studied profitably by the trained social scientist without requiring an intimate knowledge of the technical aspects of music structure. Indeed, the concept of ethnomusicology as totally inaccessible to the non-music specialist, and the concomitant disregard for the behavioral problems which must inevitably be a part of music study, have been damaging to the discipline as a whole.

The third responsibility for the ethnomusicologist is one which appeared strongly in the early history of the discipline, fell somewhat into neglect, and has only recently re-emerged; i.e., the responsibility to indicate the relationships between the study of ethnomusicology and studies in the humanities and social sciences in general. This is perhaps especially important because of the prevailing view that ethnomusicology is only a highly technical discipline, but the responsibility is still wider because knowledge, unless it is broadened and shared, has only restricted usefulness. Ethnomusicology has always, tentatively at least, reached out into other fields as a source of stimulation both to itself and to its sister disciplines, and there are many ways in which it is of value in solutions to other kinds of problems. Technical studies can tell us much about culture history. The functions and uses of music are as important as those of any other aspect of culture for understanding the workings of society. Music is interrelated with the rest of culture; it can and does shape, strengthen, and channel social, political, economic, linguistic, religious, and other kinds of behavior. Song texts reveal many things about a society, and music is extremely useful as a means of analysis of structural principles. The ethnomusicologist must inevitably concern himself with problems of symbolism in music, questions of the interrelationships of the arts, and all the difficulties of understanding what an aesthetic is and how it is structured. In short, the problems of ethnomusicology are neither exclusively technical nor exclusively behavioral. Nor is ethnomusicology an isolated discipline concerned only with esoterica which cannot be understood by any save those who study it. Rather, it seeks to combine two kinds of study and to contribute the results of its research to the

15

solution of a broad spectrum of problems both in the humanities and in the social sciences.

In last analysis, the aims and purposes of ethnomusicology do not differ markedly from those of other disciplines. Music is, after all, a universal human phenomenon and thus in the Western philosophy of knowledge, deserving of study in its own right (Clough 1960). The ultimate interest of man is man himself, and music is part of what he does and part of what he studies about himself. But equally important is the fact that music is also human behavior, and the ethnomusicologist shares both with the social sciences and the humanities the search for an understanding of why men behave as they do.

CHAPTER II

TOWARD A THEORY FOR ETHNOMUSICOLOGY

The dual nature of ethnomusicology is clearly a fact of the discipline. The major question, however, is not whether the anthropological or the musicological aspect should gain ascendancy, but whether there is any way in which the two can be merged, for such a fusion is clearly the objective of ethnomusicology and the keystone upon which the validity of its contribution lies.

Neither Western musicology nor Western cultural anthropology holds the final answer. There are few musicologists, indeed, who have interested themselves in the broader study of music as a human phenomenon, as opposed to the more limited study of music in a single Western culture. Those who have been involved in such study have usually restricted themselves to very specific and limited purposes. The music of other peoples is sometimes used vaguely as an introduction to courses in the "history of music" and, more particularly, as an example of what is "primitive" in music, fitting thereby into a deductive schemata organized around invalid concepts of cultural evolution. It is also sometimes used by Western musicologists to support theories of the supposed origin of music, and on occasion it has formed the basis for melodic or rhythmic materials used in composition. But broadly speaking, Western musicology has been preoccupied with the study of the history of Western music and there has been little room either for other music of the world or for the investigation of broadly based problems which might lead to better understanding of music as a worldwide human phenomenon.

Similarly, the potential contribution of anthropology, while substantially broader in nature, has not been exploited to any marked extent.

17

While anthropologists in the earlier history of the discipline almost always included music in their ethnographies, the tradition has become steadily less practiced, particularly over the past decade or two. This decrease in attention to music has been due, partly at least, to the fact that anthropologists have recently felt a need to emphasize the "science" in their discipline and have thus come to deal more with the social than with the cultural facts of man's existence. The result is an enormous amount of attention given to studies of social structure couched in terms of science, and to economic and political studies as well. Anthropology has learned much from this relatively recent emphasis, and will continue to learn much, but in the process it seems to have forgotten that it has a foot in two camps—the social and the humanistic.

If ethnomusicologists are to develop their discipline to the point at which a fusion of the musicological and ethnological becomes a reality, it seems clear that they will have to generate their own framework of theory and method. This is not a simple achievement, for it means that the student who enters ethnomusicology from music must also be well trained in anthropology, and that he who enters from anthropology must be prepared to handle problems of music sound and structure. But it is clearly only through the fusion of these aspects of knowledge, and probably in single individuals, that the problem will be solved.

If this be the case, and if fusion is the goal, are not the problems insurmountable? Is there any hope of putting together the humanities and the social sciences, areas of study which are considered to lie planes apart? Is there any means of treating the social sciences humanistically, or the humanities in terms of social science? In order to approach a theory for ethnomusicology, this barrier must be surmounted.

The humanities and the social sciences have been differentiated in the past on five major bases: the differences between the artist and the social scientist, and those between the methods, results, activities, and content of the two fields. If the areas are to be distinguished and, more important, if the similarities between them are to be assessed, each of these points must be resolved.

Harold Gomes Cassidy (1962) argues that the difference between the artist and the scientist lies in what each communicates, and he poses the distinction in the form of a question.

> More generally, is communication of knowledge a primary function of the artist and the scientist? The answer I should like to give is, "yes," for the scientist, "no," for the artist; it is a primary function of the scientist to contribute to the body of knowledge, whereas it is *not* a primary function of the artist, though he may, incidentally, do so. (p. 12)

Cassidy draws his concept of knowledge from Bertrand Russell, and defines it as "true beliefs based on sound reasons (not on lucky guesses) and displayed in statements" (p. 13), and he continues:

> Nor would I class what is communicated by music as knowledge, even though the notes are strung out along a strand of time and certain musical phrases have come to be closely associated with a theme or message. . . . I would then say that conveyance of knowledge is not the primary concern of the nonlinguistic arts. (p. 13)
>
> In some ways it is correct to say that what the scientist communicates is primarily knowledge while what the artist communicates is primarily feelings. Both try to exclude the irrelevant, but neither has any way of knowing whether he has missed something relevant, and neither excludes the other. Yet the aspect of reality which each investigates is in many ways different from that of the other. (p. 35)

If we accept this point of view, it is clear that in ethnomusicology the basic problem is not the artist versus the social scientist, for since the artist is not concerned primarily with communicating knowledge, he is not concerned primarily with ethnomusicology. Ethnomusicology is not creative in the same sense that the artist is creative; it does not seek to communicate emotion or feeling, but rather knowledge. Cassidy, again, emphasizes this point of view:

> Of course, one can have knowledge in the restricted sense *about* painting, music, the dance, and so forth; and artists and critics . . . may contribute to this part of the body of knowledge. . . . But the artist is not, in the same sense as the scientist, *primarily* concerned with developing and communicating knowledge through the work of art. If he conveys knowledge, it comes as a bonus. (p. 14)

The artist as such, then, plays little part, so far as his creative capacities are concerned, in ethnomusicology, for it is not involved in creating works of art. Its concern lies in the problems of the artist, in how he creates the work of art, the functions of art, and so forth. Thus the process of creating art differs from the study of that process, and ethnomusicology is concerned with the latter—the accumulation and communication of knowledge about music. In this sense, its studies fall on the scientific rather than on the artistic side.

It can be fairly argued that the basic methods of investigation in the social sciences and the humanities have much in common. Both use

19

discovery, invention, experiment, isolation of variables, and other techniques, and these problems will be discussed in the following chapter. More important are the possible distinctions to be drawn between the results aimed at and achieved through the combination of basic approach and method.

It is possible to create, as Cassidy has done (pp. 72-103) a long series of dichotomies between the results aimed for in the social sciences on the one hand, and the humanities on the other. Among these dichotomies are: objective—subjective; quantitative—qualitative; presentational—discursive; theoretical—esthetic; ratio-analogy—metaphor; general—particular; assent—dissent; repeatable and general—unique and individual. While Cassidy argues persuasively that these distinctions are not really as great as is usually assumed, it is clear that, broadly speaking, they do exist.

The conclusion is almost inescapable that what the ethnomusicologist desires is not the subjective, qualitative, discursive, esthetic, and so forth, but rather the objective, quantitative, and theoretical, wherever this is possible. There is a valid distinction to be drawn between the process of creating art and the artistic outlook, as opposed to the study of such processes. The ethnomusicologist seeks knowledge and seeks to communicate that knowledge; the results for which he aims are more scientific than artistic.

A further question is whether a difference exists between the activities of the arts and the sciences, and again Cassidy argues that any such distinctions are minimal. The activity in both may be characterized as tripartite:

> . . . analytic, synthetic, and reduction to practice. Every man, whatever his vocation . . . is engaged in these activities. . . .
>
> The analytic activity involves accumulating data: increasing specific knowledge or particular experience. It is analytic in the sense that it involves making distinctions, dividing, classifying. In both arts and sciences it includes making collections, naming, observing, and reporting observations in detail. . . .
>
> The second kind of activity, the synthetic, occurs when connections are sought among data, among theories, and among theories of theories—when trends, hypotheses, theories, and laws are derived. . . .
>
> The third kind of activity . . . is reduction to practice: the activity which returns from the general or theoretical to the particular or practical, the activity which puts to use on a particular occasion the general or theoretical. (pp. 21-23)

In the study of the arts the activity processes follow this three-part division.

Let us turn now to the question of the content of the social sciences and the humanities, a problem of central concern to this discussion. The core social sciences are sociology, cultural and social anthropology, political science, and economics. To these might be added some parts of other disciplines: social psychology, social history, human geography, and perhaps some others. On the other hand, the humanities are usually held to include the arts—music, dance, drama, literature, the visual arts, and architecture—and philosophy and religion. While there may be some specific differences of opinion concerning this categorization, the distinctions made do seem to correlate with the general understanding of the two broad areas of study. Given these two fields, what are the crucial differences between them, or indeed are there any crucial differences? In order to answer this question in terms of the content of the social sciences as projected against the content of the humanities, it is necessary to turn to some basic concepts of cultural anthropology.

The central concern of cultural anthropology is with what is called "culture." Man moves in time; that is, he has a sense of the past, the present, and the future, and he is intellectually aware of himself as existing in time. From man's standpoint, so do all other animals, though it is doubtful that we can attribute an intellectual time sense to them. Man also moves in space, and this he quite obviously shares with all other living organisms capable of movement. Man moves, too, in society; he identifies himself with his fellows and cooperates with them in maintaining his group and assuring its continuity. But man is not unique in this respect either, for other organisms such as ants, bees, and the higher primates also arrange themselves into societies. In moving through time, space, and society, man is not unique, but there is one sense in which he is unique, and this is the fact that he has culture. Anthropologists have rightly given a great deal of attention to the definition of this core concept but have never come to a universally acceptable definition; for present purposes we can speak of it here simply as "man's cumulative learned behavior."

If we accept the fact that man has culture, then we should be able to account both for his culture and for its various parts. But this is not so simple a proposition as it might first appear to be. We know, for example, that certain physical characteristics man has acquired through evolution *enable* him to have culture. That is, without his upright posture, his expanded and centralized nervous system and brain, and his capacity to use language, it seems doubtful that man could have culture. But this does not necessarily tell us *why* man has culture; it tells us how man is *able* to have culture. Genetic studies have shown us how man's physical

21

characteristics are inherited and passed on from generation to generation, but geneticists have never found a gene or chromosome which accounts for the fact that man is a culture-bearing animal.

Bronislaw Malinowski has given considerable attention to the problem of why man has culture (1944), and in this search he compiled a list of seven basic needs and their cultural responses; the needs are such items as metabolism, reproduction, and bodily comfort, while the corresponding cultural responses are a comissariat, kinship, and shelter. Malinowski held that the basic needs in turn set up a series of derived needs which result eventually in a group of cultural imperatives reflected in the institutions of any and all cultures. Thus, for example, "the cultural apparatus of implements and consumers' goods must be produced, used, maintained, and replaced by new production," which leads to the response of an economic system. Working in this manner, Malinowski felt that he could account for economics, social control, education, and political organization, all of which derive ultimately from the basic needs of the human organism itself.

The difficulty of this, as well as of other similar schemes, is that Malinowski was apparently unable to account for the speculative and creative aspects of culture, for he nowhere included either religion or artistic behavior, both of which are universals in human experience. Thus, while Malinowski felt he could derive certain aspects of universal human behavior and organization from the needs of the organism as an organism, and thus account for part, at least, of culture, he did not account for man as an artistic animal.

What is most important here is that the things which Malinowski did derive from human biosocial needs are precisely those aspects studied by the disciplines we call the social sciences. He accounted for man's need of an economic organization—studied by the field of economics; for man's need of political organization—studied by political science; for man's need of social control—studied by sociology and cultural and social anthropology; and for man's need of education in order to be able to transmit his knowledge to succeeding generations—studied by sociology and cultural and social anthropology under the rubrics of socialization or enculturation. If we are willing to accept Malinowski's formulation of the derivation of certain aspects of culture from the basic biological needs of the human organism, we find that what we call the social sciences are devoted to the study of precisely these same things.

But apparently the humanistic aspects of culture cannot be accounted for through utilization of the same technique of analysis. The humanistic aspects are, by the same token as the social, universal phenomena of human existence; that is, everywhere we find men, we find not only social,

22

economic, and political systems, but also what we call artistic, religious, and philosophical systems. All men everywhere include all these aspects of learned behavior in the organization of their lives.

In sum, it appears that a crucial difference between the social sciences and the humanities lies in the fact that we can apparently derive the subject matter of the former from the basic needs of the human biosocial organism, while we cannot do the same for the latter. This indicates that the content of the two fields of investigation is of a sharply different order. But if the humanities cannot be derived from the simple fact of biosocial existence, then what remains is obviously to find what their essential nature is, and it is here instructive to turn to the words of some scholars who have approached the problem.

In an article dealing with anthropology and the humanities, Ruth Benedict speaks of "human emotion, ethics, rational insight and purpose" (1948:588), and, later, of "man's emotions, his rationalizations, his symbolic structures"; in both cases she is referring, though not directly, to what she apparently considers to be the essentially humanistic things about man. It is to the single word "purpose," however, that attention must be drawn, for there is an intimation here that the humanities may represent man's expression of the purposes he sees in his life.

Melville J. Herskovits speaks consistently about the "creative and speculative" aspects of man's existence, and groups the aspects of culture here called "humanistic" under the "creative" as opposed to the "institutional" (1948).

George Caspar Homans supports, in part at least, the view that ". . . the humanities are more concerned with human values than are the social sciences, which are more concerned with a value-free description of human behavior" (1961:4), and while this may be generally true, it returns discussion to questions of method rather than to those of the content of the fields. Still, it is important to say that the humanities by their very nature involve values, and this may be a key point.

One of the sharpest distinctions drawn between the two areas is that made by Carl J. Friedrich who, drawing upon Hegel, says: "Thus, the focus of the humanities is upon critical examination and evaluation of the *products* of man in cultural affairs (art, music, literature, philosophy, religion), whereas the focus of the social sciences is upon the *way* men live together, including their creative activities" (Parker, 1961:16). There will be occasion to return to this distinction later.

In assessing these four approaches to the content of the humanities, it is clear that the separate thinkers hold some things in common. All seem to be drawing a distinction based upon means of living as opposed to means of enriching living; all seem to indicate that the humanistic aspects

23

of culture allow man to go beyond the problems of continuing to exist. Put another way, it may be suggested that the social sciences deal with the way man conducts his life, while the humanities deal with what he thinks about it. The humanistic aspect of culture, then, is man's comment on and interpretation of his total environment, and his commentary is expressed in creative and emotional terms. Through the humanistic elements of his culture, man seems to be making pointed commentary on how he lives; he seems in the humanities to sum up what he thinks of life. In short, man lives as a social animal, but he does not live as a social animal alone, for his social life apparently brings about conditions under which he is unable to restrain himself from commenting upon himself and enunciating and interpreting his actions, his aspirations, and his values. Thus the social sciences deal with man as a social animal and the ways in which he solves his biosocial problems in daily living, while the humanities take man beyond his social living into his own distillations of his life experiences. The social sciences, then, are truly social; the humanities are primarily individual and psychological.

There is a second major difference which exists between the social and humanistic aspects of life and which is thus reflected in the content of the two areas of study. The social sciences, as we have seen, are devoted to the study of man's social institutions. A social institution exists in order to regulate the behavior of the people who comprise it. But in humanistic endeavors the aim is not to regulate behavior, but rather to produce something which is visually or aurally tangible, an art product. In these terms, the intent of the musician is sound, and it is not to organize musicianly behavior; on the other hand, society *is* behaving. We deal here with a matter of goals. The goal of man's biosocial life is the regulation of behavior to provide for biosocial needs in order to assure the continuity of existence. The goal of man's creative behavior is a product which exists to give satisfaction for other than biosocial needs. The distinction recalls Friedrich's statement that "the focus of the humanities is upon . . . the *products* of man . . . whereas the focus of the social sciences is upon the *way* men live together . . . "

Given these differences, as well as similarities between the social sciences and the humanities, is there anything which ties the two together? Can there truly be an ethnomusicology in which both function, and if so, by what means can the "scientific" and the "nonscientific," the "social" and the "individual" be considered in a single study? There are two answers to this broad problem, so crucial to ethnomusicology, which are neither particularly complex nor lost in a welter of obscure meaning.

In the first place, both social scientists and humanists are interested in what man does and why. The methods and direction of their approaches may differ, though not so much as it sometimes seems, but in the end both seek an understanding of man, and this is a clear and ever-present bridge between them.

In the second place, it is extremely important to note that although the goal of the artist or musician is a product which is visually or aurally tangible, he must behave in order to produce that product. An understanding of the product therefore inevitably involves an understanding of the behavior of the artist. Thus the social scientist and the humanist are tied together in that both must consider human behavior if they are to understand the art product.

We are faced with the inevitable conclusion that what the ethnomusicologist seeks to create is his own bridge between the social sciences and the humanities. He does so because he must be involved with both; although he studies a product of the humanistic side of man's existence, he must at the same time realize that the product is the result of behavior which is shaped by the society and culture of the men who produce it. The ethnomusicologist is, in effect, sciencing about music. His role is not to discuss the art product in terms familiar to the humanist, but rather to seek knowledge of and regularities in artistic behavior and product. He does not seek the aesthetic experience for himself as a primary goal (though this may be a personal by-product of his studies), but rather he seeks to perceive the meaning of the aesthetic experience of others from the standpoint of understanding human behavior. Thus the procedures and goals of ethnomusicology fall upon the side of the social sciences, while its subject matter is a humanistic aspect of man's existence. Ethnomusicology endeavors to communicate knowledge about an artistic product, the behavior employed in producing it, and the emotions and ideation of the artist involved in it.

Is ethnomusicology, then, a social science or a humanity? The answer is that it partakes of both; its approach and its goals are more scientific than humanistic, while its subject matter is more humanistic than scientific. Even when its studies are restricted to analysis and understanding of the product alone, the goal is not couched in primarily humanistic terms. The ethnomusicologist is not the creator of the music he studies, nor is his basic aim to participate aesthetically in that music (though he may seek to do so through re-creation). Rather, his position is always that of the outsider who seeks to understand what he hears through analysis of structure and behavior, and to reduce this understanding to terms which will allow him to compare and generalize his results for music as a universal phenomenon of man's existence. The ethnomusicologist *is* sciencing about music. If he is to do this successfully, it is clear that his prior knowledge must come from both fields. It is impossible to study the

25

structure of music without a prior knowledge of music; it is equally impossible to study music behavior without a prior knowledge of social science; and the best results derive from those studies which utilize a knowledge of both.

This problem of how to categorize a discipline is not a new one in the history of science, nor is it surprising to find that it has from time to time been a major preoccupation of anthropology. Oscar Lewis has phrased the problem clearly in noting:

> On the one hand, there are those who would underscore the kinship of anthropology with the natural sciences, would stress the need for quantification, objective tests, experiments, and a general development and improvement of techniques which might lead to a greater precision and objectivity in the gathering, reporting, and interpreting of field data. On the other hand, there are those who, though not denying for a moment the kinship of anthropology with the sciences, believe that what needs to be stressed at this time is the kinship of anthropology with the humanities, and, accordingly, they would emphasize the need for insight, empathy, intuition, and the element of art. Moreover, they are much less sanguine about the contribution to anthropology which can come from quantification, control, and experiment, and they point out that some of our most adequate and insightful anthropological monographs were written by missionaries who had had no technical training. (1953:453)

The controversy is an old one in anthropology, and equally old is the debate over whether anthropology is properly history or science (Boas 1948; Radin 1933; Herskovits 1948). The problem that has led to the debate is singularly like that which has plagued ethnomusicology; it stems from the historic fact that to anthropology, as to ethnomusicology, was left the total study of almost all mankind outside the Western stream. Faced with the enormity of the field, there was and is bound to be some ambiguity in the interpretation of what is to be done with it and what approaches are to be stressed. It is therefore perhaps of less concern than might appear to decide precisely under what rubric ethnomusicology must be classified in terms of the taxonomy of sciences. What it has done thus far indicates clearly that it is attempting to understand and communicate knowledge about a humanistic phenomenon in the terms of science.

I

In order to approach the study of music from the standpoint of scientific analysis, it is necessary to establish the bases from which the ethnomusicologist works. The most fundamental consideration involved here is the question of what music is and what relationship it has to the concept of culture.

The *Oxford Universal Dictionary* (Third Edition, 1955) defines music as "that one of the fine arts which is concerned with the combination of sounds with a view to beauty of form and the expression of thought or feeling." The *American College Dictionary* (Text Edition, 1948), says that music is "an art of sound in time which expresses ideas and emotions in significant forms through the elements of rhythm, melody, harmony, and color." It is significant to note that both definitions proceed from the premise that music need only be defined in Western terms. Music in other cultures is not necessarily concerned with beauty as such; the problem of the expression of ideas and emotions through music is definitely one which has not been finally solved; and many musics do not use the element of harmony. Neither are the definitions useful from the standpoint of the social scientist, for they tell us nothing about the element of social agreement which plays a major part in shaping sound.

More to the point is a definition whose origin is unknown to me: "Music is a complex of activities, ideas and objects that are patterned into culturally meaningful sounds recognized to exist on a level different from secular communication." Of a similar nature is a definition offered by Farnsworth (1958:17): "Music is made of socially accepted patterns of sounds." What is held in common in these two definitions, and what is of particular importance to the social scientist, is that the sounds of music are shaped by the culture of which they are a part. And culture, in turn, is carried by individuals and groups of individuals who learn what is to be considered proper and improper in respect to music. Each culture decides what it will and will not call music; and sound patterns, as well as behavior, which fall outside these norms are either unacceptable or are simply defined as something other than music. Thus, all music is patterned behavior; indeed if it were random, there could be no music. Music depends upon pitch and rhythm, but only as these are agreed upon by members of the particular society involved.

There are other social characteristics of music as well. Music is a uniquely human phenomenon which exists only in terms of social interaction; that is, it is made by people for other people, and it is learned behavior. It does not and cannot exist by, of, and for itself; there must always be human beings doing something to produce it. In short, music cannot be defined as a phenomenon of sound alone, for it involves the behavior of individuals and groups of individuals, and its particular organization demands the social concurrence of people who decide what it can and cannot be. Indeed, John Mueller points out that in our own

27

culture, even the institution of the symphony concert ". . . is not exclusively, nor in one sense primarily, a musical event." Rather, he says, "it is . . . a psychological and sociological truth, that music is often secondary to nonmusical considerations" (1951:286). Music is also a universal in human culture, though not an absolute, and the fact that it is found everywhere is of great importance in reaching an understanding of what it is and does for men.

But cultural and social factors shape music to an even greater extent than is implied in the fact that music sound accords with peoples' ideas of what is right and wrong in music. Thus Herzog, for example, writes:

> Acceptance or rejection of composition or performance may hinge much more on cultural and social matters *per se* than with us. For example: a single mistake in a single song of many hundred that form an essential part of Navaho Indian curing rituals invalidates the whole performance so that it has to be repeated, from the beginning, after due purification. The question we might like to raise—how far is it the esthetic sense and how far the ritualistic sense that is outraged—is meaningless for the Navaho and may not become clear to him at all. (1936b:8)

A far more radical and deterministic position is taken by William G. Haag, who holds that:

> Art is not free. Artists are relentlessly grasped by the strongest but subtlest force that moves the world, that is, cultural determinism. Every change in the artistic taste of the times is engendered and nourished in a realm beyond the "minds" of artists. . . . That place, of course, is the culture—the normative, stylistic, consistent behavior of which the artist is a participant and a partaker. (1960:217)

While such a position is so deterministic and simplistic that it fails to communicate usefully, it does stress the importance of the role that culture plays in shaping music.

Paul Farnsworth describes an experiment which further illustrates the relationship between music and culture.

> Some years ago a Duo-Art player-piano, made by the Aeolian Corporation, was used in an attempt to learn if college students had one specific tempo well fixed in mind for waltz time. The subjects were blindfolded and told to move back and forth a large speed lever until the playing of the composition they were hearing was at the rate they deemed proper. The lever settings given by

28

this group were generally in the neighborhood of 116 quarter-notes to the minute, just what the Aeolian Corporation regarded at that time as proper. The fox-trots were usually set at a considerably faster tempo, at approximately 143.

Further research on dance tempo was carried on six years later by Lund with a similar sample of college students. Lund found that faster speeds were by this time considered proper, 139 for the waltz and 155 for the fox-trot. (1958:69)

Such a change in "correct" tempo over time can in no way be attributed to factors inherent in the music structure or sound itself, for in taking such a position we would be forced into the attitude that music has some sort of existence by and of itself, as well as the tautology that music sound causes change in music sound. On the contrary, the factors which operate to make such a change in music are matters of taste and preference which derive from culture patterns that may have very little if any direct relationship to music tempo as such.

Yet the history of ethnomusicology sometimes seems to indicate that it has proceeded from assumptions very similar to these. The multiplicity of studies of music structure divorced wholly or to a great extent from cultural context indicates that ethnomusicologists have placed the greatest value on the structure of sound as an isolable value in itself. Indeed, music sound has been treated as a closed system which operates according to principles and regularities inherent in itself and quite separate from the human beings that produce it. But it is questionable whether music can be studied satisfactorily in this way, and indeed whether music sound is itself a system at all. A system involves a group of things or ideas whose parts fit and work together by means of their own internal logic and structure, and it implies that because of this intimate relationship, a change in part A will produce a corresponding change in part B. Thus, in music a change of, let us say, rhythm A should produce some sort of corresponding change in melody B; or an X-type melodic phrase should inevitably be followed by a Y-type phrase with the assumption that if X changes, so will Y. It may be that music does operate in this fashion, but if so we have yet to learn it, and in any case we find in our own music system that our melody B can be successfully played in rhythm A or C or D, and that the Y phrase does not at all inevitably follow the X phrase.

Even assuming, however, that music sound is a system, there is little validity for treating it as though it were divorced from social and cultural considerations for, as has been noted, music is inevitably produced by humans for other humans within a social and cultural context. The preoccupation with music sound alone means that much of eth-

29

nomusicology has not gone beyond the descriptive phase of study. We may here recall Cassidy's division of activity in the arts and sciences into the analytic, synthetic, and reduction to practice, with the analytic devoted to accumulating data and the synthetic concentrated upon seeking connections among the data; what Cassidy calls the analytic has been referred to above as the descriptive. Cassidy is extremely emphatic about the dangers of stopping with the analytic:

> *Failure to distinguish between analytic and synthetic functions, accompanied, often, by a "preference" for one or the other, is one of the chief causes of schism between scientists and humanists.* . . . This is an example of the common error of considering a part of science (analysis) to be all of science. I wish to emphasize that *analytic science and art is only partial science and art.* . . . All three activities—analysis, synthesis, and reduction to practice—must go together for science or art to be healthy. (1962:23)

Leonard Meyer speaks to the same point when he says:

> Without belittling the importance and the many contributions of descriptive ethnomusicology, the nature and limits of information it can yield need to be understood. For it has at times employed concepts and reached conclusions which were unwarranted because they rested upon unrecognized or untested assumptions of a psychological sort. (1960:50)

And finally, McAllester attempts an explanation for the high degree of emphasis upon descriptive studies in ethnomusicology:

> This insistence on the relationship of music to culture should be unnecessary and would be if it were not for a peculiar trait in our own Western European culture: the bifurcation of the concept of culture. We *can* think of culture in the anthropological sense of the total way of life of a people, but we also think of culture in the sense of "cultivated," with a particular emphasis on art forms and art for art's sake. The result of this cultural trait of ours has been a separation of art from culture-as-a-whole. We are more likely to discuss the creative periods of Picasso than Picasso as a manifestation of the social, religious and economic pressures of his times, or, in other words, Picasso as a manifestation of his culture.
>
> Similarly, in music, we are very prone to a consideration of music *qua* music outside of its cultural context. We are most likely to discuss a song as an art form, as pretty or ugly and why, and in many other ways outside its principal cultural function. (1960:468)

This reaction against studying music from the descriptive point of view alone is perhaps not so much an indictment of the approach as it is an indictment of what appears to be a faulty methodology—the substitution of a single kind of study for what must clearly be a multifaceted approach. Music can and must be studied from many standpoints, for its aspects include the historical, social psychological, structural, cultural, functional, physical, psychological, aesthetic, symbolic, and others. If an understanding of music is to be reached, it is clear that no single kind of study can successfully be substituted for the whole.

There is another objection to exclusive or almost-exclusive preoccupation with the descriptive in ethnomusicology, and this concerns the kinds of evaluative judgments which are necessarily made when the structure of the music is the sole object of study. In such a case the investigator proceeds from a set of judgments derived from the structure itself unless he happens to be working with one of the relatively few cultures of the world which has developed an elaborate theory of music sound. This means that his analysis is, in effect, imposed from outside the object analyzed, no matter how objective his analytic system may be. In itself, there is no objection to this, since any analysis involves this kind of structuring of view. But in the case of any man-made object or idea, the investigator has another available source of analysis which must not be overlooked; this is the evaluation of the object or idea by the people who created it.

Paul Bohannan (n.d.) has given us a useful set of concepts which apply directly to these two kinds of information sources; he calls them the "folk evaluation" and the "analytical evaluation." Folk evaluation refers to the fact that "when people speak or act to make something, they . . . evaluate their own statements and acts and usually . . . have an end in view. The mere assigning of words to acts and things is one form of cultural valuation. To hold moral, economic or religious ideas about them is to evaluate them further." Thus the people who create things and ideas do so for a reason and assign values to their actions. At the same time, the outside observer—the anthropologist or the ethnomusicologist— ". . . analyzes a culture not merely in order to act in it. . . . Rather, he analyzes that culture in order to classify it, understand it according to more or less scientific principles, and communicate it to colleagues, students and readers who have no experience in it and are, concomitantly, blocked to at least some degree by their own culture from understanding any other one." In other words, the folk and the analytical evaluations proceed from different premises and because of differing obligations. The folk evaluation is the explanation of the people themselves for their actions, while the analytical evaluation is applied by the outsider, based

31

upon experience in a variety of cultures, and directed toward the broad aim of understanding regularities in human behavior. Bohannan continues:

> In such a situation, the cardinal sin is to confuse the evaluation of the speaker, the actor or the doer with the evaluation of the analyst. . . .
>
> The distinction between folk evaluation and analytical evaluation is necessary because only if we know the folk evaluation can we be sure we are analyzing what is actually present in the data. Once we have determined that, the analytical evaluation can range widely and can find regularities which are unknown to the actors, without making the error of assigning the analytical evaluations to the actors in the situation. (pp. 1-3)

The specific application to ethnomusicology is clear. The folk evaluation is a necessity to the investigator, for without it he cannot know whether his analysis is present in the data or whether he has himself inserted it. This is not to say that the investigator puts nothing more into his materials than he takes out from the folk evaluation; to the contrary, it is his job to do so. But what he puts into the data must be built upon what he first learns from the culture at hand about its music and its music system, taken in the broadest sense. He is then in a position to generalize about that system from his broader knowledge of music systems in general.

II

Since all these factors must be considered in studying the music of any given people, the immediate problem is whether a theoretical research model can be constructed which will take all of them into account. Such a model must consider folk and analytical evaluation, the cultural and social background, the relevant aspects of the social sciences and the humanities, and the multiple facets of music as symbolic, aesthetic, formal, psychological, physical, and so forth.

The model proposed here is a simple one and yet it seems to fulfill these requirements. It involves study on three analytic levels—conceptualization about music, behavior in relation to music, and music sound itself. The first and third levels are connected to provide for the constantly changing, dynamic nature exhibited by all music systems.

For the purposes of convenience, we can begin with the third level, that of the music sound itself. This sound has structure, and it may be a system, but it cannot exist independently of human beings; music sound must be regarded as the product of the behavior that produces it.

The level out of which this product arises is behavior, and such behavior seems to be of three major kinds. The first is physical behavior, which in turn can be subdivided into the physical behavior involved in the actual production of sound, the physical tension and posture of the body in producing sound, and the physical response of the individual organism to sound. The second is social behavior, which can also be subdivided into the behavior required of an individual because he is a musician, and the behavior required of an individual non-musician at a given musical event. The third is verbal behavior, concerned with expressed verbal constructs about the music system itself. It is through behavior, then, that music sound is produced; without it, there can be no sound.

But behavior is itself underlain by a third level, the level of conceptualization about music. In order to act in a music system, the individual must first conceptualize what kind of behavior will produce the requisite sound. This refers not only to physical, social, and verbal behavior, but also to the concepts of what music is and should be; involved are such questions as the distinction between music and noise, the sources from which music is drawn, the sources of individual musical ability, the proper size and involvement of the singing group, and so forth. Without concepts about music, behavior cannot occur, and without behavior, music sound cannot be produced. It is at this level that the values about music are found, and it is precisely these values that filter upward through the system to effect the final product.

The product, however, has an effect upon the listener, who judges both the competence of the performer and the correctness of his performance in terms of conceptual values. Thus if both the listener and the performer judge the product to be successful in terms of the cultural criteria for music, the concepts about music are reinforced, reapplied to behavior, and emerge as sound. If the judgment is negative, however, concepts must be changed in order to alter the behavior and produce different sound which the performer hopes will accord more closely with judgments of what is considered proper to music in the culture. Thus there is a constant feedback from the product to the concepts about music, and this is what accounts both for change and stability in a music system. The feedback, of course, represents the learning process both for the musician and for the non-musician, and it is continual.

If we view music study in the broad perspective of this simple model, our attitude is not exclusively that of social science or the humanities, of the cultural and social or the structural, of the folk or of the analytic, but rather a combination of them all. Further, it leads inevitably to the consideration of such matters as symbolism, the presence or absence of an aesthetic, problems of the interrelationships of the arts and of the reconstruction of culture history through the use of music, and the

33

question of culture change. Instead of focusing attention upon a single aspect of music study, it enables and even forces the investigator to seek an integrated understanding of the human phenomenon we call music.

The proposition may be restated once more: we hear a song; it is made of sound ordered in certain ways. Human beings produce this song and in so doing they behave, not only when actually singing the song but also in their way of life, either as musicians or as people listening to music and responding to it. Since they are musicians or non-specialists responding to music, they conceptualize the musical facts of life, which they then accept as proper to their culture. And finally, they accept or reject the product because it does or does not accord with what they have learned to be proper music sound, thus inevitably affecting concept, behavior, and sound again.

The model presented here has not, to the best of my knowledge, been suggested previously in specific detail or in connection with music, although some parallels to it are found in other fields of study. Perhaps the closest parallel comes from the field of visual art, as suggested by Vinigi Grottanelli, who writes:

> Apart from its aesthetic evaluation, the study of any art object or class of objects should be carried out following three distinct though interrelated lines of analysis. The first is iconographic, i.e. at the same time morphological, technological, and historical, and concerns the nature of the objects *per se*, their formal characters, the technique of production, their distribution in space and time, and their stylistic affinities to similar productions elsewhere. The second is iconological, and has to do with the meaning of the representation, the nature of the beings it purports to portray, and the underlying system of conceptions and beliefs in which it is integrated—the world of ideas and symbols in a given culture. . . . The third approach . . . deals with the impact of those ideas and of their concrete symbols on the everyday life of the society concerned and with their influence on the ritual and social behaviour and thought of individual men and women. Only a combination of these three approaches can give us a true picture of the phenomenon we are called upon to investigate. (1961:46)

Cornelius Osgood, in investigating material culture, reached less exact but still similar conclusions in his theoretical framework for study. His aim was to work on three levels of what he called "ideas":

> 1. Ideas about objects external to the mind directly resulting from human behavior as well as ideas about the human behavior required to manufacture these objects.

34

2. Ideas about human behavior not directly resulting in the manufacture of objects external to the mind.

3. Ideas about ideas involving no human behavior (apart from speech) nor objects directly resulting from such behavior.

Category one roughly corresponds to what is apparently generally thought of as material culture. It includes all data directly relating to visible or tangible things such as tools, clothing, or shelter which a person or persons have made.

Category two roughly corresponds to what is apparently generally thought of as social culture and includes all data about human behavior which does not directly result in the manufacture of things. . . .

Category three pertains only to ideas. . . . To it one would refer the tremendous sphere of ideas which are termed religious. . . . Also all philosophy and speculation belong in category three. The principal difficulty in comprehending this conceptualization involves the definition of behavior as exclusive of the ideational content of speech. It seems quite possible, however, to regard ideas (an ego's) about a person speaking wholly from the point of view of the speaker's non-ideational behavior. (1940:26-7)

In this approach Osgood's category one closely approximates what has here been called the music product, and category three what has been called conceptualization. Category two, however, is not precisely the same as what has here been called behavior, though it appears to be somewhat similar. Since Osgood was apparently not attempting to present a dynamic model, the factor of feedback based upon learning is not present in his scheme.

Finally, there is a relationship between the model and some contemporary views of anthropology, in that the conceptual level corresponds to what might be called the cultural or ideational aspect of human organization; the behavioral to the social; the product to the material; and the feedback to the personality system and to learning theory.

It should be emphasized that the parts of the model presented above are not conceived as distinct entities separable from one another on any but the theoretical level. The music product is inseparable from the behavior that produces it; the behavior in turn can only in theory be distinguished from the concepts that underlie it; and all are tied together through the learning feedback from product to concept. They are presented individually here in order to emphasize the parts of the whole; if we do not understand one we cannot properly understand the others; if we fail to take cognizance of the parts, then the whole is irretrievably lost.

35

CHAPTER III

METHOD AND TECHNIQUE

Problems of methodology in ethnomusicology have not been widely discussed in the literature although it is apparent that one means, at least, of characterizing a discipline is through an understanding of the method of study and analysis it employs. Method depends, however, upon theoretical orientation and basic assumptions, particularly those which concern the aims of the discipline, and because such assumptions may well vary from individual to individual, it is wise to make them explicit at the outset.

My first assumption is that ethnomusicology aims to approximate the methods of science, insofar as that is possible in a discipline which deals with human behavior and its products. By scientific method I mean the formulation of hypotheses, the control of variables, the objective assessment of data gathered, and the grouping of results in order to reach ultimate generalizations about music behavior which will be applicable to man rather than to any particular group of men.

My second assumption is that ethnomusicology is both a field and a laboratory discipline; that is, its data is gathered by the investigator from among the people he is engaged in studying, and at least part of it is later subjected to analysis in the laboratory. The results of the two kinds of method are then fused into a final study.

My third assumption is a practical one dictated by what has hitherto been done in the field, i.e., that ethnomusicology has been concerned primarily with non-Western cultures and most specifically with nonliterate societies in North America, Africa, Oceania, South America, and Asia, as well as folk cultures of Europe. There have been a number of studies as well of the art music of the Near and Far East, and fewer studies we would be willing to call ethnomusicological of music in Western cultures.

The fourth assumption is that while field techniques must of necessity differ from society to society and, perhaps more broadly, between literate and nonliterate societies, field *method* remains essentially the same in over-all structure no matter what society is being investigated.

These four assumptions are essentially neutral in nature; that is, they refer simply to the background out of which all ethnomusicologists work. The three remaining assumptions, however, are essentially critical in that they refer to problems which have not been clearly understood in the past.

The first of these is that ethnomusicology has for the most part failed to develop a knowledge and appreciation of what field method is, and has thus not applied it consistently in its studies. While there are obvious exceptions to this, it seems clear that we have been beset by two major difficulties. One is that our field studies have been couched in general rather than specific terms; that is, to a considerable extent they have been formulated without precise and clear-cut problems in mind. The other is that ethnomusicology has suffered from the amateur field "collector" whose knowledge of its aims has been severely restricted. Such collectors operate under the assumption that the important point is simply to gather music sound, and that this sound—often taken without discrimination and without thought, for example, to problems of sampling—can then simply be turned over to the laboratory worker who will "do something with it."

This leads to a second critical assumption which is that ethnomusicology in the past has devoted itself primarily to fact-gathering rather than to the solution of broadly based problems couched in terms of the study of music as a part of human culture. This is emphasized in the literature of ethnomusicology, which tends to be devoted in greatest part to the analysis of the sounds of music without reference to their cultural matrix, to the physical description of music instruments as physical forms, and very seldom indeed to what music is and does in human society. Ethnomusicology has to this point been primarily concerned with descriptive materials and studies; it has emphasized the what of music sound rather than the broader questions of why and how. This has not been ethnomusicology's exclusive preoccupation, of course, but it has taken a primary role in our studies.

My third critical assumption again derives to some extent from those which have already been noted. Despite the fact that ethnomusicology is both a field and a laboratory discipline, and that its most fruitful results must inevitably derive from the fusion of both kinds of analysis, there has been both an artificial divorcing of the two and an emphasis on the laboratory phase of study. Reference is made specifically to the regrettable tendency to resort to armchair analysis. There is, of course, no objection to thinking, speculating, and theorizing from hunches, intuition, or imagination, for this is all a vital part of the development of a discipline. However, two kinds of armchair analysis are objectionable: the failure to take theories to the empiric test of the field materials, and the analysis by the laboratory technician of materials collected by others in the field. To make the latter point as clear as possible, the analysis of music materials which one has not himself collected can and does provide us with certain kinds of valuable information, but this is subject to two sharp limitations. The analyst in all too many cases has no means of knowing the kind and extent of the sample with which he is dealing; and he cannot draw upon an intimate knowledge of the broad musical scene which must inevitably be of deep concern if the formation of music sound is to be accurately understood. There have in the past been extended studies in ethnomusicology based upon a small sample of commercially issued materials; while the proof of the accuracy of such studies remains to be ascertained, it seems extremely doubtful that we can give them much credibility. Armchair ethnomusicology is, I hope, a thing of the past, at least insofar as it is not very closely controlled and used only for the limited kinds of studies where it may be useful.

In sum, ethnomusicology is both a field and a laboratory discipline; the laboratory phase must flow out of the field phase, and we must seek to achieve a balance between the two rather than exclusive or almost exclusive stress on either. Ethnomusicology has always been troubled by the dual nature both of the materials of which it is composed and the aims toward which it is directed, and there will always be some students who emphasize one aspect and some who emphasize the other. The ultimate goal, however, must be the fusion of the two into a broader understanding which encompasses both.

I

There is a valid and important difference between field technique and field method. "Technique" refers to the details of data gathering in the field, that is, to such questions as the proper use of informants, the establishment of rapport, the importance of vacation periods both for the investigator and for those he investigates, and so forth. Field method, on the other hand, is much broader in scope, encompassing the major theoretical bases through which field technique is oriented. While the two are inseparable in the actual pursuit of a field problem, they are quite different when one is considering the formulation of that problem: technique, then, refers to the day-by-day solution of the gathering of data, while method encompasses these techniques as well as the much wider variety of problems involved in creating the framework for field research.

Materials concerning field method in ethnomusicology are relatively rare. Jaap Kunst, in *Ethnomusicology*, speaks fleetingly of what one does in the field, based upon his own experience in Java (1959:14-16); the International Folk Music Council has issued a booklet concerned with problems of field collection (Karpeles 1958); and Helen Roberts (1931) makes various suggestions to the field worker; but all of these are concerned more with techniques than with method, and none makes mention of research design, problem, or any one of a number of other basic considerations. David McAllester, in an appendix to his *Enemy Way Music*, speaks briefly of his research plan, presents the questionnaire he used to give direction to his study, and comments both on the application and success of that questionnaire (1954:91-2). But field method involves much more than the techniques of gathering data, for before data gathering can proceed the investigator must face the fundamental problems of hypothesis, field problem, and research design, and in all of these, the relevance of theory to method.

To a considerable extent, it is the last—the relevance of theory to method—which is the most important and perhaps the least understood, for no problem can be designed in terms of basic hypotheses without consideration of theory. Herskovits has expressed this with great cogency in noting that ". . . the conceptual scheme of the student deeply influences not only the execution of a given field problem but also the way in which it is formulated and planned" (1954:3). Although Herskovits was speaking specifically of anthropological field method, and not of ethnomusicology, it is worthwhile to draw attention to his examples, particularly since some of the approaches utilized in ethnomusicology have been drawn directly from anthropology.

Herskovits contrasts the underlying assumptions which characterize the studies of those who are interested in trait lists as opposed to those whose theoretical orientation is shaped by the functionalist approach. For the former:

> The significant factor . . . was the hypothesis that culture is an historical phenomenon which can be understood if the contacts of peoples, as reflected in similarities and divergences in the component elements of their respective ways of life, are reconstructed, and that these ways of life consist of items sufficiently discrete to be set down separately and manipulated in mathematical terms.

On the other hand:

> . . . the theoretical position of the functionalists, which maintains that the fabric of a culture is so tightly woven that to separate

a single strand from it is to do violence to the whole, meant that the very concept of the trait was inadmissible, since the aim was to gather materials which revealed the totality of the existing patterns of behavior. Here, therefore, the aspect becomes the unit of study. (p. 4)

A difference of the same order is pointed out in the approaches of those who emphasize the concept of society as opposed to those who emphasize the concept of culture; in this case, the former ". . . will pay more attention to data obtained in response to the 'What?' questions than the one who centers his attention on dynamics and seeks answers to questions which lie in the 'Why?' category" (p. 5). Such differences do not indicate that either theoretical approach is necessarily better than the other, except in solving particular kinds of problems; what is important is that theoretical orientation inevitably affects point of view, approach, hypothesis-formation, problem orientation, and all the other considerations which go into field method, and these in turn affect field techniques.

As we look into past ethnomusicological studies, it is evident that considerations of this kind have helped to shape the discipline, and that in many cases it has been anthropological theory which led ethnomusicologists toward particular kinds of studies. Thus when Ekundayo Phillips postulates stages in the development of music from what he calls impassioned speech tone and draws examples from the contemporary Yoruba (1953), or when Balfour sees stages in the development of the African friction drum (1907), each is drawing heavily upon the classic theory of social evolution as formulated in the late nineteenth century. Or when Frobenius develops four culture circles in Africa, based partly on distribution of music instruments (1898), the *Kulturhistorische Schule* of German and Austrian anthropology in the early twentieth century has obviously been a prime source. Again, Sachs's formulation of method in constructing twenty-three strata of music instrument development on a worldwide basis (1929:1940) involves theoretical formulations both of *kulturkreis* and early American diffusion studies.

The important question is what theoretical bases at present contribute the background for the formulation of problems in ethnomusicology. This is not a simple question to resolve, for ethnomusicologists have rarely, if ever, examined their basic assumptions in this light. However, there are at least two, and possibly three, approaches implied in the literature, the acceptance of any one of which inevitably shapes the work of the field investigator. Each of these can be expressed in terms of a dichotomy, although it is my view that no single dichotomy is immutable and that all are susceptible of resolution.

The first of these involves the single most difficult problem in

41

ethnomusicology: whether the aim of our studies is to record and analyze music, or whether it is to understand music in the context of human behavior. If the former point of view is taken, then the primary orientation of the field worker will be toward recording an adequate sample of music sound in order that this may be returned to the laboratory for analysis. The basic aim is to produce an accurate structural analysis of the music taken, and the study is primarily based upon a fact-gathering, descriptive approach. If, on the other hand, the aim is to understand music in the context of human behavior, the field worker becomes almost automatically an anthropologist, for his concern is not more upon the recorded sample than it is upon much broader questions of the use and function of music, the role and status of musicians, the concepts which lie behind music behavior, and other similar questions. Here the emphasis is upon music but not upon music divorced from its total context; the investigator attempts to emerge from his study with a broad and generally complete knowledge both of the culture and the music, as well as the way music fits into and is used within the wider context. It is eminently clear that the orientation of the student in respect to these approaches will enormously affect not only his results but his field methods and techniques as well.

The second dichotomy appears in the difference of aim between what can be called extensive as opposed to intensive studies. By extensive studies, I mean those in which the aim of the investigator is to travel widely through an area, staying in no single place for any extended period of time, and recording as quickly and as widely as he can. The result of such a field design is the rapid accumulation of large quantities of relatively superficial data from dispersed geographic areas. The utility of the method is that it achieves a broad view of a given area, expressed primarily in music structural terms. The investigator can see at a relatively swift glance the outstanding characteristics of the music and the ways in which variation is manifested within the area. This approach emphasizes the general survey and can, of course, lead to future research of a more detailed nature where the most interesting problems are indicated. The intensive study, on the other hand, is one in which the student selects a particular limited area and gives his entire attention to it. This is depth study in which the aim is to exhaust the materials concerning music in a restricted area, insofar as this is possible. Again, the assumption of either of these approaches leads to the formulation and prosecution of very different research design, method, and technique.

A third kind of dichotomy, although not nearly so explicit in the ethnomusicological literature, is that which concerns the ultimate aim of any study of man. This involves the question of whether one is searching out knowledge for its own sake, or is attempting to provide solutions to practical applied problems. Ethnomusicology has seldom been used in the same manner as applied or action anthropology, and ethnomusicologists have only rarely felt called upon to help solve problems in manipulating the destinies of people, but some such studies have been made (Weman 1960) and it is quite conceivable that this may in the future be of increased concern. The difficulty of an applied study is that it focuses the attention of the investigator upon a single problem which may cause or force him to ignore others of equal interest, and it is also difficult to avoid outside control over the research project. Although this problem is not yet of primary concern, it will surely shape the kinds of studies carried out if it does draw the increased attention of ethnomusicologists.

These three sets of problems are clearly among those which can, and sometimes do, have a major effect upon the investigator's approach to his work. The relationship between theory, conceptual framework, and method is a close one; no field work exists in a vacuum, and its very nature is definitely shaped by the basic orientation of the researcher.

Given this background, it is clear that in some ways any research problem is circumscribed, but this in no way means, of course, that the field worker can simply fall back upon his general orientation and rely upon it to take automatic care of his research project. Quite to the contrary, each specific item of research requires careful planning and the formulation of an over-all research design. Raymond V. Bowers has suggested four major criteria which serve as guides to good design; although he is speaking explicitly about research methods in sociology, his criteria apply equally well in ethnomusicology (1954:256-59).

Bowers' first point is "the criterion of research feasibility," which refers to the fact that every research undertaking is a risk of time and effort and thus "should be as calculated a risk as possible . . ." Here the student must consider the relevant data already published, including materials which bear upon the particular hypothesis he has formulated and, in the case of research in cultures other than his own, the ethnographic literature. If the project is to be a team effort, questions of available personnel must be considered. Applicable research techniques are of special importance, as is the question of whether there is enough prerequisite knowledge to enable the researcher to formulate his hypotheses.

The second criterion is that of "explicit formulation of research objectives," and this is an area in which ethnomusicology has been somewhat lax, substituting undifferentiated and vague statements of purpose for precise research objectives. As has already been pointed out at some length, the statement of objectives determines in great part field method and techniques, as well as analysis of materials gathered. Bowers notes cogently that the difference between precise and imprecise formulation is the difference between scientific and prescientific investigation, and adds that "the probability is high that those who have only a vague understanding of what they are after at the beginning of a project will have an equally vague understanding of what they get at the end."

The third criterion is that of "methodological explicitness," which Bowers cites in connection with ongoing research. Two major reasons are given for keeping close track of methodology: first, that whatever results are reached have been achieved through the application of specific methodology and are thus intimately tied to it; and second, that through the recording of methodology, "research experience can more adequately be reviewed, appraised, and shared with others." To these there should be added a third: acquaintance with methodology and a clear understanding of which methods can contribute most precisely to the problem at hand contribute substantially to the achievement of significant research results.

Finally, Bowers notes "the criterion of specifying the research outcome," and says in explanation:

> Presumably results are the aim of research—a new item of knowledge, a new methodological tool, or a technique for resolving practical problems. The objective has raised questions, and the methodological design has selected and funneled empirical data appropriate to these questions. The researcher's job is not over until he has made the most of this activity. . . . His responsibility cannot end at hurried cataloguing of his results. He must come to his most considered judgment as to their significance in the light of his research operations and his professional background. He must tell what the study failed to accomplish as well as what he thinks it accomplished, and both must be stated in as precise, formal terms as the context permits. (1954:258-59)

Field method, then, is as broad and complex a problem in ethnomusicology as it is in other areas of research. It is intimately tied to the question of theoretical orientation and encompasses research design, including problem, hypothesis, objective and methodological techniques. Careful and detailed consideration of these problems is essential to the prosecution of field research in ethnomusicology.

II

What the ethnomusicologist does in the field is determined by his own formulation of method, taken in its broadest sense. Thus one project may be directed toward the specific task of recording music sounds alone, another toward problems of music aesthetics, and still another to the question of the sociological role of the musician in society. If, however, the project is conceived as a depth study in a single locale, and if the student views the study of ethnomusicology as one in which music is considered not only from its aural aspect, but from the social, cultural, psychological, and aesthetic as well, there are at least six areas of inquiry to which attention will be turned.

The first of these has been called the musical material culture, and it refers primarily to the study of music instruments ordered by the investigator in terms of the recognized taxonomy based on division into idiophones, membranophones, aerophones, and chordophones. Also, each instrument must be measured, described, and either drawn to scale or photographed; principles of construction, materials employed, decorative motifs, methods and techniques of performance, musical ranges, tones produced, and theoretical scales are noted. In addition to these primarily descriptive facts about music instruments, however, there is a further range of more analytic questions of concern to the field worker. Is there present in the society a concept of special treatment of music instruments? Are some revered? Do some symbolize other kinds of cultural or social activity? Are particular instruments the harbingers of certain kinds of messages of general import to the society at large? Are the sounds or shapes of particular instruments associated with specific emotions, states of being, ceremonials, or calls to action?

The economic role of instruments is also of importance. There may be specialists in the society who earn their living from instrument construction, but whether or not these exist, the production of an instrument inevitably involves the economic time of the producer. Instruments may be bought and sold; they may be commissioned; in any event, their production is a part of the economics of the society at large. Instruments may be considered as items of wealth; they may be owned by individuals; their ownership may be individually acknowledged but for practical purposes ignored; or they may constitute an item of village or tribal wealth. The distribution of instruments has considerable importance in diffusion studies and in the reconstruction of culture history, and it is sometimes possible to suggest or to confirm population movements through the study of instruments.

A second category of study is that devoted to song texts, and this involves the texts as linguistic behavior, the relationship of linguistic to music sound, and questions of what the texts reveal in what they say. The problem of text-music relationship is one which has long been contemplated in ethnomusicology because of its obvious significance, but it has not been until recently that specific studies have been undertaken using modern linguistic and ethnomusicological techniques.

45

Song texts reveal literary behavior which can be analyzed in terms both of structure and content; song text language tends in many cases to differ from ordinary discourse, and in some instances, as in the case of praise names or drum languages, to be a "secret" language known only to a certain segment of the society. In song texts, language is often more permissive than in ordinary discourse, and this can reveal not only psychological processes such as the release of tension, but information of a nature not otherwise readily accessible. For similar reasons, song texts often reveal deep-seated values and goals stated only with the greatest reluctance in normal discourse. This may lead, in turn, to the discernment of an available index of the prevailing ethos of a culture, or to a sort of national character generalization. An understanding of ideal and real behavior is often accessible through song texts, and, finally, texts are used as an historic record of the group, as a means of inculcating values, and as a mechanism for enculturation of the young.

The third aspect of study comprises the categories of music, envisaged by the investigator for convenience but, more important, by the people themselves as various separable types of songs. It is in this connection, of course, that the student orders his recording program, arranged to include an adequate sample of all types of music, both in controlled and in actual performance situations.

The musician forms the fourth point of interest for the ethnomusicologist. Of great importance are the training of the musician and the means of becoming a musician. Is the individual coerced by the society or does he make a free choice of his future career? What is the method of training—is the potential musician left to his own resources, does he receive a basic knowledge of his instrument or of singing technique from others, or does he undergo a rigorous course of training over a stated period of time? Who are his teachers, and what are their methods of instruction? This leads to considerations of the problem of professionalism and economic reward. A society may distinguish among levels of competence, classifying them through the use of distinct terms and reserving the highest accolade for what it considers to be a true professional; or the musician may be virtually ignored as a specialist. Forms and methods of remuneration differ widely from society to society, and in some cases the musician may not be paid at all.

Of equal interest and importance are such questions as whether the musician is considered to be an outstandingly gifted individual, or whether all members of the society are considered to be equally potentially gifted. Does the musician inherit his ability, and if so, from whom and by what means?

As a member of society, the musician may view his specialty as setting him apart from other persons, and therefore he may see both himself and society in a special light. Non-musicians also hold concepts of what is and what is not acceptable musicianly behavior, and form attitudes toward the musician and his actions on this basis. Indeed, musicians may be set apart as a class and may form associations based on their mutual skills within the society. They may own the music they produce, thus again raising questions of economics, in this case in respect to intangible goods.

It is in this connection, too, that cross-cultural tests of music ability enter; although no culture-free tests seem to have been developed, their formulation would be of exceedingly high interest in assessing latent and manifest abilities of musicians and non-musicians, both as these are judged by society and in terms of the individual.

A fifth area of study concerns both the uses and functions of music in relation to other aspects of culture. The information we have at hand suggests strongly that in terms of use, music cuts across all aspects of society; as human behavior, music is related synchronically to other behaviors, including religion, drama, dance, social organization, economics, political structure, and other aspects. In studying music, the investigator is forced to move through the total culture in search of music relationships, and in a very real sense he finds that music reflects the culture of which it is a part.

The functions of music in society are of a different level of investigation from that involved in determining use, for here the search is directed toward much deeper questions. It has been suggested that one of the primary functions of music is to aid in the integration of society, a process of continual concern in human life; another suggestion is that music is primarily a means of release of psychological tension. The distinction between use and function has not often been made in ethnomusicology, and studies in this general area have tended to concentrate on the former to the exclusion of the latter, but studies of function are potentially the more exciting of the two since they should lead to the deeper understanding of why music is a universal in human society.

Finally, the field investigator studies music as a creative cultural activity. Basic here is the phase of music study which concentrates on the concepts of music held in the society under investigation. Underlying all other questions is that involved in the distinctions made both by musicians and non-musicians between what is considered to be music and what is considered not to be music, a subject little touched upon in ethnomusicology. What are the sources from which music is drawn? Is music composed only through the agency of superhuman assistance and sanction, or is it a purely human phenomenon? How do new songs come into existence? If the composer has a recognized status in the society, how does he compose, and what does he say, if anything, about the process of composition? The standards of excellence in performance are of great importance, for through the understanding of such standards the investigator can throw light on good and bad music and on the ways in which the standards are enforced in the society. Such problems lead both to folk and analytic evaluation of a theory of music in the society at hand, to the specific problems involved in the extent to which form is visualized as something which can be manipulated, and to whether such aspects of form as music intervals or particular core rhythm patterns are reified in the thinking of musicians and non-musicians.

The answers to such questions lead to still broader problems. Is music conceived to be an aesthetic activity or is its main orientation toward the functional? Is it seen as intimately related to other artistic activities in graphic and plastic arts, in literature, dance, or drama—or, conceptually, does it stand alone?

These then are some of the things the ethnomusicologist looks for in the field phase of his study. That there are other specific problems is obvious, but in general outline the field phase of study must lead the student through all aspects of the culture at hand, for the objective of the ethnomusicologist is to understand music not only as structured sound but as human behavior as well. Thus music must be approached in terms of the tools used in its production, the expressive language employed, the kinds of music produced, the musician as a member of society, the uses and functions of music, and its creation, as well as in terms of its aural sound.

III

If, again, we assume that ethnomusicology originates in field study, that music is a part of culture, and that the societies which ethnomusicologists study have historically been those outside the Western stream, we are led almost inevitably to the further assumption that field method and field technique must be derived from cultural anthropology. Although this has seldom been specifically acknowledged by ethnomusicologists, it is in fact the case. Perhaps more precisely, field method in ethnomusicology has derived from the social sciences in general, while field technique is borrowed most widely from the particular social science of anthropology.

As is the case in ethnomusicology, anthropologists began to discuss specific aspects of field technique rather late in the history of the discipline, but much material is now available. It is generally conceded that the first concrete and detailed discussion of field technique to accompany an ethnographic field report in anthropology was contributed by Bronislaw

Malinowski as the Introduction to his *Argonauts of the Western Pacific*, the first volume of his monumental study of the Trobriand Islanders published in 1922. In this Introduction, Malinowski laid down three criteria of field work:

> . . . First of all, naturally, the student must possess real scientific aims, and know the values and criteria of modern ethnography. Secondly, he ought to put himself in good conditions of work, that is, in the main, to live without other white men, right among the natives. Finally, he has to apply a number of special methods of collecting, manipulating and fixing his evidence. (1950:6)

The first of these criteria is as clearly applicable today as it was in 1922, and it subsumes broadly the questions discussed here under the rubric of "field method." The second precipitated considerable controversy in anthropology, which continues to the present day; the question is how far, how long, and to what extent the ethnographer can be a participant observer, and whether the rewards outweigh the disadvantages. The third point concerns precisely what has here been called "field technique," and Malinowski continued his discussion to include various specific techniques which he considered most rewarding.

Since Malinowski's initial formulation, many other anthropologists have written on general problems of method and theory (Radin 1933), on field method and technique in particular investigations (Mead 1940b), on specific suggested techniques (Herskovits 1950), and on various other problems. The most detailed discussions of field method have probably been those contributed by Paul (1953) and Oscar Lewis (1953), although others could be cited.

Benjamin Paul, for example, organizes his contribution under a series of headings and sub-headings which deal with such problems as introductions, establishing a role, ethics of role-playing, types of participation, the informant, interviewing, taking notes, and so forth. Herskovits, on the other hand, divides the problems of field research into those of duration, communication, rapport, comparison, and historic depth, of which the first three are considered to be common to any field project, while the two latter depend upon the particular problem and approach (1954:6). There is no need to enter here into details of field technique, for these are discussed at length in the various writings noted above. There are, however, some special problems which have not been widely considered in ethnomusicology and which bear some discussion here.

The first of these is the problem of what in anthropology has been called "ethnographic truth." This refers to the fact that within any given culture there is what often seems to be almost infinite variation in the

49

details of any given behavior or belief, and this applies as well to music as to any other aspect of culture. Given the fact that the investigator cannot possibly consider every minute variation because of the simple limits of time, how can he ever know what is the "proper" or "correct" version of a song? The answer lies in the distinction to be made between an absolute correctness and an understanding that such an absolute probably does not exist. What is important is not the search for a single truth, but rather "the limits within which a culture recognizes and sanctions variations in a . . . given mode of behavior" (Herskovits 1948:570). That is, the ethnographic or ethnomusicological "truth" is not a single fixed entity, but rather a range of entities within a particular distribution of variation, and it is the limits of the variation, rather than a supposed absolute, which lead to an understanding of the phenomenon.

This problem of variability and ethnomusicological "truth" has been considered infrequently in ethnomusicology. Helen Roberts was aware of it in her study of variations in Jamaican folk song (1925), and A. M. Jones makes an extended analysis of two versions of the same Ewe song (1959:234-45). One of the most interesting discussions, however, has been contributed by John Blacking, who proposes the use of transcriptions which are syntheses of several performances. His argument is that,

> Unless we are specifically studying interpretation, we want to know what a musician sets out to do each time he plays a certain piece of music, not *exactly* what he did on one particular occasion. "Time-pitch" graphs and other mechanical devices may be helpful and necessary for the ethno-musicologist in the course of his analysis, but the final transcription should, if possible, be as straightforward and as easy to read as a standard musical score, which in any case is only a guide to musical performance and an approximation of the sounds produced.
>
> The four musical transcriptions in this paper do not represent the exact sounds that are made every time two Venda boys play ocarina duets, but are a synthesis of several performances of the same duets. Detailed transcriptions of every performance that I heard or recorded are not given, since I do not consider that the early stages of an analysis need be printed any more than the field-notes of an anthropologist. The transcriptions are intended to represent the musical patterns desired by any two Venda who set out to play the duets. (1959:15)

Blacking, then, considers two aspects of the problem. On the one hand, for purposes of analysis the ethnomusicologist must use his detailed, individual transcriptions, while on the other, an exposition of what is striven for in sound and structure can be represented adequately by a synthesis of several performances. In this point of view, Blacking is indeed reflecting ethnographic practice, for the anthropologist, although careful to record the range of variation of any given phenomenon, seeks in his reporting to give a balanced synthesis of that range. The ethnographic or ethnomusicological "truth," then, results from the gathering of the widest possible range of data concerning the given question, and the reporting of the consensus of behavior with equal attention given to the limits of variation within that consensus.

A second problem of special concern lies in the use of what have been called "spot" studies, a technique of investigation which adds further reliability to the search for ethnomusicological truth. Quite simply, the spot study refers to the checks, made usually toward the end of the field stay, of the validity of data gathered to a wider context. That is, in a small undifferentiated society, the investigator may spend the bulk of his time in one village, but in the last few weeks travel to neighboring areas to check the information gathered with "outside" informants. In a larger, differentiated society, a spot check may be made in different classes or levels of society, and in a certain sense the cross-checking of information with different informants in the same class of the same society falls under the rubric of spot checking. The kind of information obtained through this technique is not primarily intended to reveal new facts, but rather to check facts already garnered and, particularly, to discover the extent to which the observer can generalize the information he already has on hand. The spot check technique has apparently not been widely used in ethnomusicology, or if it has, the results have not been reported in the literature.

A third point of particular importance concerns restudies, in which an area or a problem is checked a second time either by the same or by a different investigator. Oscar Lewis has given particular attention to this problem (1953:466-72) as it applies to anthropology, and he finds it possible to distinguish four types of restudies:

(1) those restudies in which a second or third investigator goes to a community with the express design of re-evaluating the work of his predecessor; (2) those in which the same or an independent investigator goes to a community studied earlier, to study culture change, utilizing the first report as a base line against which to measure and evaluate change; (3) those in which one returns to study some aspect of the culture not studied earlier; and (4) those in which one studies more intensively and perhaps from a new point of view some aspect of the culture studied earlier. There is,

51

of course, some overlapping between these types. All restudies are additive in a sense. However, it is a matter of emphasis in research design. (pp. 467-68)

Lewis gives a number of examples of restudies in the anthropological literature, but the point here is that ethnomusicology does not seem to have given adequate consideration to the importance of the restudy. The restudy can help to provide checks on, and a better understanding of, methodology in ethnomusicology. The objective is not, of course, to point out the mistakes made in earlier studies, but, as Lewis puts it, to find out ". . . what kind of errors tend to be made by what kind of people under what kind of conditions. Given a sufficiently large number of restudies, it might be possible to develop a theory of observation which would help to evaluate the role of the personal equation, personality, and ideological or cultural variables" (p. 467). A second value of the restudy is the light it can cast on culture change.

There are, of course, some compelling reasons for the lack of restudies in ethnomusicology. One of these is the simple lack of available personnel, and another is the limited funds available for field research. Further, a certain pressure has been felt in ethnomusicology to study the music of peoples whose culture is changing rapidly, and of course there is a greater appeal in breaking new ground than in working with music which has already been the object of study. But ethnomusicology has already approached the point at which restudies would be extremely important and revealing, for we now have a time depth in published work which makes restudy feasible. The research of LaFlesche or Densmore among the American Indians, Hornbostel's analysis of songs from Ruanda, Herzog's early studies in the music of the Pacific are all base lines from which restudies could make significant contributions to the understanding both of methodology and of music change.

Finally, although it lies more in the realm of analysis of materials gathered than in the question of field technique, mention must be made of the comparative method, for if comparison is to be an aim of analysis, it must be considered in the research design. At the outset, a distinction must be clearly drawn between the comparative method as used by those who espoused the theory of social evolution in anthropology, and the comparative method as envisaged at present. The older comparative method was based essentially on a deductive theory which espoused stages of culture, the concept of the contemporary ancestor, and like formulations. Here, cultural facts were applied more or less indiscriminately to "prove" the already deduced theory; thus given the concept of stages of culture, the investigator had only to look around the world for facts that would fit into and support the conclusions already reached.

The comparative method as presently used, however, eschews the application of fact to support deductive theory, and instead aims at controlled comparison which, through inductive application, will lead to generalization on an ever-wider basis. In order to make such comparison, it is clear that the approach must be cautious, that like things must be compared, and that the comparisons must have bearing upon a particular problem and be an integrated part of the research design. It is assumed here that one of the aims of ethnomusicology is to produce data which can be compared and that therefore the broader aim is generalization about music which can be applied ultimately on a worldwide basis.

Thus comparison for its own sake is not the goal to be sought, for there are many ways in which a comparative method can be used. Herskovits has summed up some of the possible approaches:

> Are we concerned with items of culture, perhaps in the tradition of the classical "comparative method"? Are we comparing cultural institutions, as in studies of totemism, or the market, or magical practices? Do we wish to draw comparisons between whole cultural aspects, as in general treatises on art, or social organization, or economics, or folklore? Or, as in the case of those concerned, for example, with national character, do we take a holistic approach and attempt to compare total cultures? Again, we may ask what we hope to achieve through our comparisons. Do we wish to establish the boundaries of cultural variation, so as to assess these in terms of limiting biophysic and ecological factors? Or, in philosophical terms, are we seeking to discern the universals in human behavior that give mankind a common basis for the differentials in perceptive and value patterns that guide action in each society? Are we attempting to establish contacts between peoples, and analyse the historical implications of these contacts? Is our aim to understand the dynamic processes which underlie cultural change? Moving to the methodological plane, we ask how we go about making our comparisons. Here classification is of the essence. Shall we draw our comparisons in terms of a particular phenomenon, or by historic stream, or by area?
>
> All these, and others that could be indicated, are questions which must employ the method of comparison in some form, if they are to be answered. (1956:135)

Although Herskovits is speaking of the comparative method in anthropology, it is clear that his questions apply equally well to ethnomusicology. Ethnomusicology has more or less taken it for granted that comparison is one of its major aims, and indeed its early name, "comparative musicology," stressed that conclusion, but there has been little awareness of the problems involved in comparison. Anthropology has paid more attention to the matter, and studies such as that of Herskovits, cited above, or Lewis (1961) can be of considerable importance in resolving the problem for ethnomusicology.

IV

It has been noted above that ethnomusicology is both a field and a laboratory discipline, and it is therefore clear that within the broad area of its method two kinds of techniques must be used. While it is not the intention here to describe in detail ethnomusicological methods of transcription and analysis of music sound, there are several problems which must be considered.

Cutting across the two areas of field and laboratory techniques is the extremely difficult question of what constitutes an adequate sample of the music of a community, tribe, or larger grouping. Theoretically, at least, the number of songs in any given song community is infinite, because it is hardly possible to know the total sample and because, so far as we know, creativity is a never-ending process under whatever cultural rules it is carried out; thus what might be conceived as a total sample one day may be lacking the next. What percentage, then, of an infinite sample constitutes reliability? The answer is that there is no answer.

It is obvious, however, that ethnomusicology must reach some workable definition of what constitutes an adequate and reliable sample, and there appears to be one reasonably simple solution. This consists of taking a single given song, chosen at random from a large song body, transcribing it, analyzing it, and scoring the results on an objective, arithmetic basis. This process would then be repeated, using a sample of five different songs from the same song body, and averaging the results. A further sample of perhaps twenty-five songs, and possibly a final sample of one hundred songs would probably be sufficient to complete the basic work. The results obtained for the different-sized samples could then be compared and subjected to statistical analysis with an aim toward assessing the significance of difference in the arithmetic figures obtained. It should be possible, then, to determine the sample point at which the results obtained do not differ significantly from one another, and this point may be found to occur at ten songs, or twenty-five, or perhaps even one hundred. In order to validate the results, it would be necessary to run the same kinds of tests on different song bodies, since the range of allowable variation in music may vary markedly from style to style. To the best of my knowledge, no such procedure has been applied to ethnomusicological studies, and yet it seems imperative that some certification of what constitutes an adequate sample must be undertaken, for at present there is no assurance that our studies are reliable in giving us an accurate idea of the constituent parts of a music style.

This general problem of sampling is further complicated by the fact that we do not as yet understand clearly the extent to which the characteristics of the music of a single group can be generalized, or whether, conversely, sub-styles of a markedly different structure exist in any or all music groups. That is, given an over-all sample of the music of any group, do war songs differ significantly in structure and style from love songs, or from funeral, play, drinking, hunting, or other types of song? Again, the answer to the question seems to lie in a practical experiment in which the songs of a given group are subjected to analysis couched in comparable arithmetic terms, and the results compared.

George Herzog raised this problem in connection with North American Indian music as long ago as 1935, when he suggested that four kinds of songs seem to cut across tribal styles regardless of the "major" style of any particular group in which they exist; these included Ghost Dance, love, Hiding Game, and animal story songs. He says:

> In the light of such findings, we have to reconsider the current notions of tribal or national styles as integrated, homogeneous pictures which tend after due time to assimilate new additions to their background, maintaining or restoring their "original" integrity.
> . . . Suffice it to say that often the description of a musical "style" is merely the enumeration of the traits of single disparate styles representing different categories of songs; or else of divergent types each of which offers numerous examples. (1935:10)

Herzog went on to suggest three possible reasons for the phenomenon of "style within the style," which he took as a given fact, and these were the possibility of an older stratum of music overlain by more recent additions, borrowing from another group, or ". . . psychological preferences which shape musical form to accord with psychological attitudes" (p. 10). Unfortunately, although a few music examples were appended to the article, Herzog apparently did not follow out the full implications of his suggestion, i.e., the submission of proof that styles within the style do actually exist. There seems to be very little question, however, that such is the case, and Nettl's study of the Shawnee, though perhaps not couched in sufficiently abundant detail to be finally conclusive, is certainly corroborative (1953a). Equally suggestive is Herskovits' discussion of Dahomean song:

> It would be strange if a variety of types of songs such as has been indicated did not carry with it a variety of musical styles, and, as

55

a matter of fact, it is impossible to speak of "Dahomean music" as though it were a unit. Not only do the occasions vary for different types of singing, as do the songs sung on these occasions, but the forms of the songs, their duration, and the musical treatment of them show a wide range of variation. (1938b:II,321-22)

Herskovits describes the songs "which glorify the names and deeds of the dead kings and living chiefs" as highly polished in performance through rehearsal; these are contrasted with the songs for "dances in the market-places or certain songs of the ancestral and Sagbata ceremonies" in which the music "is less complex; its rhythms are more regular, its range narrower, its melody simpler. Indeed, the style of such improvised songs is in the main much more a unit than in the elaborately composed songs. . . ."

If it be the case, then, that some music styles are made up of a number of identifiable sub-styles, how does the analyst present the results of his research? Does this mean that any study of a music style must be presented in terms of sub-styles, or can the sub-styles in turn be lumped together into a single over-all style? If we assume the latter is feasible, it must be kept in mind that to seek an over-all style may distort specific portions of the more detailed picture and that the result may not conform at all to any single sub-style.

Such questions as these lead, in their turn, to further problems involved in the analysis of music, among the most important of which is determining what, precisely, are the points of structure which characterize a style. Ethnomusicologists consider a large number of stylistic elements in making their analyses, among them melodic range, level, direction, and contour; melodic intervals and interval patterns; ornamentation and melodic devices; melodic meter and durational values; formal structure; scale, mode, duration tone and (subjective) tonic; meter and rhythm; tempo; vocal style, and others. But which of these elements characterizes a music style? Is melodic range of equal importance to, or more or less important than, durational values? And further, is it not possible that one aspect may be of differing importance in different styles?

Again, the answers to such questions are difficult to make, but there does seem to be at least one way in which the validity of regarding certain elements as characterizing can be established, and this is through the application of tests of statistical validity. In 1956, Freeman and Merriam attempted to make exactly this kind of application, using Fisher's discriminant function in connection with a single structural measure, the relative frequency of occurrence of major seconds and minor thirds in two bodies of African-derived music in the New World, that of the Ketu cult of Bahia, Brazil, and the Rada cult of Trinidad. The conclusion was that this simple measure alone serves to distinguish between the two styles with only a .09 error, and that had more variables been considered, the error would have been substantially reduced. In effect, then, the study indicated that the frequency of occurrence of two kinds of intervals in these song bodies is statistically significant to a remarkably high degree, and that this particular aspect of music structure is characterizing (Freeman and Merriam 1956).

This study does not give a final answer to the general problem, for its sample was limited to but two cultures, and only two simple measurements were employed. But there is a logical, though unproved, assumption that if the simple criterion of relative frequency of but two intervals gives such remarkably precise results, there must be other elements of structure that are equally diagnostic, and further, that the more elements considered in combination, the higher the accuracy of the result will be.

Underlying the problems discussed thus far is the assumption that the laboratory analyst has available to him accurate methods of transcribing music sound to paper, but this is a question that is far from resolved. Ethnomusicologists are agreed that the ultimate aim of translation to paper is to obtain an accurate picture of a song which can then be analyzed to reveal elements of structure and style. How this can best be done, however, and to what extent the details of sound must be faithfully recorded, is open to question.

Early in the history of ethnomusicology, transcriptions were made by ear in the field, but this method has long been eschewed because of its unreliability. Not only does song usually go too fast for the transcriber, but if repetitions are demanded, it is likely that variations may occur to such an extent that the transcriber receives a mottled version of the singer's efforts. Moreover, recorded material can be played over and over and the accuracy of transcription checked repeatedly in detail.

At least one student, however, has argued for the advantages of transcription by ear in the field. Helen Roberts notes:

> Longhand notation is, of course, very much slower than record making, and requires patience in all concerned. On the other hand, it has many merits. It affords excellent opportunities to the recorder for observing the musical intelligence and ability of the singer, his variability from repetition to repetition in melody, form, text, etc., as would not be noted under the rather more strenuous and rapid recording by phonograph. It also affords an excellent chance for conversation by the way, for questions are bound to arise which would never occur to the collector in the more perfunctory process of making records, and would only too late be put by the transcriber. Moreover, in this more leisurely pursuit, an informant may

appeal to a bystander for assistance in recollecting, or arguments may arise which, to the alert collector, may furnish valuable additional data. Longhand notation is the best method possible for checking up on impromptu composing and frauds. Phonograph records and longhand notations of the same song may be compared with advantage.

Apparently any singers take almost as great an interest in the process of notation as in that of making records, and are particularly delighted when the collector, reading from the music, is able to reproduce, not only the text, but the melody of their own songs on so short an acquaintance. (1931:111-12)

Despite these arguments, ethnomusicologists are agreed that there is no substitute for recording, though a combination of techniques might prove rewarding. The development of recording apparatus—first disc, then wire, and finally tape, which is by far the most versatile—enables the ethnomusicologist to make a permanent record of music sound and to bring it back to the laboratory where much more precise transcription can be made. Even here, however, transcription itself depends upon the human ear, and accuracy varies from individual to individual.

It has normally been assumed that every transcription must be as precise and detailed as possible, but the advent of certain mechanical and electronic equipment seems to suggest that precision is a relative matter which can be interpreted in many ways. For example, the early development of such devices as the monochord coupled with the cents system (Kunst 1959:2-12, 231-32) made it clear that it is possible to ascertain measurements of pitch with a precision far exceeding the possibilities inherent in the human ear, and this is further borne out by the development of devices such as the Stroboconn (Railsback 1937).

More recently, Charles Seeger has developed a fundamental frequency analyzer known as the melograph which gives the most detailed graphic analysis yet possible of a single-line melody (1951: 1957: 1958). It is Seeger's contention that the conventional symbolic-linear music-writing used in Western notation, and by ethnomusicologists in general, is at best a relatively crude prescriptive tool which is not accurate for descriptive purposes.

It does not tell us as much about how music sounds as how to make it sound. Yet no one can make it sound as the writer of the notation intended unless in addition to a knowledge of the tradition of writing he has also a knowledge of the oral (or, better, aural) tradition associated with it—i.e., a tradition learned by the ear of the student, partly from his elders in general but especially from the precepts of his teachers. For to this aural tradition is customarily left most of the knowledge of "what happens between the notes"—i.e., between the links in the chain and the comparatively stable levels in the stream.

In employing this mainly prescriptive notation as a descriptive sound-writing of any music other than the Occidental fine and popular arts of music we do two things, both thoroughly unscientific. First, we single out what appear to us to be structures in the other music that resemble structures familiar to us in the notation of the Occidental art and write these down, ignoring everything else for which we have no symbols. Second, we expect the resulting notation to be read by people who *do not carry the tradition of the other music.* The result, as read, can only be a conglomeration of structures part European, part non-European, connected by a movement 100% European. (1958:186-87)

Seeger contends that the melograph, used in conjunction with conventional notation, gives us a better understanding of those aspects of music which are not necessarily perceived by the ear, that is, elements of music which may characterize a style but which, because of the conventions of present music-writing, go un-notated.

The graphs produced introduce the ethnomusicologist to a level of analysis which differs markedly from that to which he is accustomed, and it is clear that if such "notation" is to be used, there will have to be an accompanying new system of analysis. Whereas a note in conventional notation presents a concrete entity which can be handled in a variety of ways, the melograph "note" is a continuous jagged line which may flow on virtually without interruption. Thus the question involves the nature of the unit which can be separated for study, or perhaps most accurately, whether units can or should be isolated. What the melograph appears to show us involves a level of interpretation markedly different from that achieved through the use of conventional notation.

This raises a whole new series of questions revolving around the central problem of how accurate a transcription should, can, and must be. The melograph is the most accurate transcription device presently available, and Seeger argues that such accuracy is necessary because conventional notation represents music through a screen of ethnocentrism and because it does not indicate certain very important aspects of the music. On the other hand, the question arises whether conventional notation does not tell us enough about music structure to allow a reasonably precise description and analysis of outstanding structural patterns. In other words, it may be that conventional notation simply gives us one kind of information

59

while the melograph gives us another, and that each of these is equally important.

If we accept this view, it still remains important to know how accurate conventional notation must be. Bartok and Lord (1951) have used what is perhaps the most elaborate system of descriptive accuracy in transcribing Serbo-Croatian folk songs, but the system is so detailed that it is sometimes difficult to read. Most ethnomusicologists use a much simpler system with fewer added markings, but is this accurate enough to delineate a music? And if two ethnomusicologists, as is so often the case, transcribe the same song and achieve slightly different results, how much does this alter the understanding of the over-all system? Is it a question of taking refuge in quantity in the hope that data numbering in the thousands will cancel out whatever errors may be made? And if so, we are led inevitably back to questions of sampling and, particularly, to what constitutes an adequate sample of the music of a given people.

Ethnomusicology, then, is faced with a large number of problems concerning method and technique. Solutions, or even partial solutions, to them will do much to strengthen the discipline and give it a wider and firmer grasp both of its aims and of the theoretical problems it wishes to pursue.

PART TWO

CONCEPTS AND BEHAVIOR

CHAPTER IV

CONCEPTS

Every music system is predicated upon a series of concepts which integrate music into the activities of the society at large and define and place it as a phenomenon of life among other phenomena. These are the concepts which underlie the practice and performance of music, the production of music sound. Many of them are not verbalized directly, though some are, and thus they must be approached through analytical evaluation based upon an understanding of the folk evaluation. Taken together they constitute the framework upon which music is ordered in the society and upon which people think about what music is and should be. There is a distinction between this kind of underlying concept, and those which directly concern music structure. Our interests here are not directed toward the distinctions people may make between major and minor thirds, for example, but rather toward what the nature of music is, how it fits into society as a part of the existing phenomena of life, and how it is arranged conceptually by the people who use and organize it.

One of the most important of such concepts is the distinction, implied or real, made between music on the one hand, and noise, or non-music, on the other; this is basic to the understanding of music in any society. It is logical to assume that if no distinction can be made there can be no such thing as music, for either all sound will be music or no sound at all will be music and thus music cannot exist. Further, what is considered to be music or non-music sound determines the nature of music in any given society. If one group accepts the sound of the wind in the trees as music and another does not, or if one group accepts the croaking of frogs and the other denies it as music, it is evident that the concepts of what music is or is not must differ widely and must distinctively shape music sound.

63

The difficulty of the problem is emphasized by the lack of complete accord as to what constitutes the distinction in our own society. Western theoreticians tend to use acoustic criteria, citing as music "sounds with regular and periodic vibrations" (Culver 1941:4-5), or as noise, "pitchless sounds" (Seashore 1938b:20). Bartholomew says that "a sound either so complex or so irregular, or both, that it seems to have no tone when heard by itself, is called a noise," but adds, "there is, of course, no definite boundary between tone and noise" (1942:159). This difficulty is further emphasized when we realize that the acceptability of certain sounds as music varies both individually and in time; the piano was not always accepted as a musical instrument (Parrish 1944), Beethoven's music was at one period rejected, and current controversy rages over the various forms of electronic music.

Distinctions of an acoustic nature are not, of course, commonly made in most societies; rather, the differentiation is achieved along other lines. Among the Congo Basongye, for example, there is a broad concept of what music is, although it is not expressed directly. In speaking of this question, the Basongye tend to respond with aphorismic statements such as the following:

When you are content, you sing; when you are angry, you make noise.

When one shouts, he is not thinking; when he sings, he is thinking.

A song is tranquil; a noise is not.

When one shouts, his voice is forced; when he sings, it is not.

Using statements such as these, as well as detailed questioning and observation, it is possible for the outside observer to construct a three-part "theory" of noise and music as held by the Basongye.

In the first place, music for the Basongye always involves human beings; the sounds which emanate from non-human sources are not, and cannot be, considered music. No informant classifies the sound of "singing" birds as music, nor does the wind "sing" in the trees. The consistency of this point of view is emphasized by the fact that only certain kinds of supernatural or, more accurately, superhuman manifestations are capable of producing music. The *mulungaeulu*, which are purely non-human beings, not only do not make music but are entirely mute. However, the *bandoshi*, or witches, have their own songs which they sing together at periodic conclaves; this is explicable in terms of the fact that witches *are* human beings pursuing an evil course in life and are not considered to be anything but human, though they do have extra-normal powers. There is some difference among the Basongye as to whether the *bikudi*, or ancestral spirits, sing, but this is more a question of whether the singing can be heard rather than of whether music is produced. The elders say that on exceptional occasions the ancestral spirits can be heard singing in the bush at night, and this is consistent with the theory of music since ancestral spirits are conceived to be human and thus capable of making music. Younger men, however, say that the elders are foolish and that the night noises ascribed to the ancestral spirits are really the crying of the jackal and thus not singing at all; this again is consistent since animals cannot produce music of any kind. Finally, song is not a part of myth or legend; although the ability to sing or play a music instrument comes directly from Efile Mukulu (God), Efile Mukulu is not conceived as a music producer in the sense that he sings himself, nor do the culture heros involved in the creation of the earth and man sing in the course of their creative activities. Thus the idea that music is created only by humans is consistent within the framework of Basongye conception.

Although information is extremely limited, it is clear that this view of music as produced uniquely by human beings is not universal. In speaking of the xylophone in Sierra Leone, J. T. John records the following origin tale:

> According to stories handed over to succeeding generations by word of mouth, "balanji" music was introduced by a small boy of about ten years of age. It is said that while he was going to his father's farm early in the morning, he heard a little bird whistling in the woods, and, greatly impressed by the melodious voice of the bird (as small boys always are), he stopped and listened to a song. After carefully listening, he went on his way, cut some sticks and shaped them flat. He cut another two sticks, and, after arranging the former on his lap, he began to strike them with the latter. By constantly practicing, this lad succeeded in playing the song which he picked up from the mouth of the bird. This song is known and played by every "balanji" player. (1952:1045)

The unnamed group or groups about whom John is speaking quite clearly accept bird song as music, or at least as the basis for music, and this is in sharp contrast to the Basongye who could not support an origin story of this kind because birds do not make music. Thus the acceptance or rejection of certain sounds as music has ramifications beyond music itself.

The second point in the Basongye "theory" of what constitutes music sound is that such sound must always be organized. A random tap on the xylophone or the drum, for example, is not considered to be music. But organization alone is not enough to fulfill the criteria, for if three

65

drummers make a single tap together on their drums, it is still not music even though it is organized. The third criterion, then, is that to be music the sounds must have a minimal continuity in time.

By these three criteria—music is produced exclusively by human beings, it must be organized, it must have continuity in time—the Basongye do define the boundaries between music and non-music. Not surprisingly, however, there is an intermediate area between the two in which some disunity of concept is expressed, and in which the context of the sound determines its acceptance or rejection as music.

Whistling is one of these areas, and Basongye informants simply disagree as to whether this is or is not music. But there are different kinds of whistling. One can whistle as a signaling device in the course of the hunt, and here the Basongye are unanimous in saying that this is not music; differences of opinion appear when one is discussing the whistling of a recognized tune. The Basongye also produce sound by blowing into the cupped hands and into various devices such as the ocarina (Merriam 1962a). The latter, called *epudi*, is again a signaling device used in hunting; it is also blown as sporadic accompaniment to certain hunting songs, but in neither case is it considered that the sounds are music. On the other hand, blowing into the cupped hands can be done as a melodic and rhythmic accompaniment to certain dances, and in this case it fulfills the criteria for music and is accepted as such. The same is true of *epudi* playing. Finally, although singing is differentiated from singing in nonsense syllables, both are accepted as music, while humming lies in the borderline area and is accepted as music by some and rejected by others.

Nketia makes somewhat similar points in generalizing about African music, particularly in respect to the importance of context in determining the acceptability of sound as music.

> Thus the sound of a flute or rattle, the sound of an iron bell, the concussion of rocks . . . the clatter of sticks, the noise of seeds in the shell of a fruit, the sound of stamping feet—all these provide potentially musical sounds that may be utilized by the creative performer under specific circumstances. That is to say, sounds that enter into the concept of music include not only sounds with definite pitch but also those with indefinite pitch. They include sounds that can be sustained as well as those that cannot be sustained. . . .

> This breadth of concept does not mean that all sounds that may be heard in African society have the same value or that any sound is regarded as music or musical. On the contrary, there are discrimination and evaluation. Different reactions are shown to what may be physically the same sound according to where and how it is used. . . .

In Akan society if someone scraped mud off a bottle with the lid of a cigarette tin, he would produce noise as a by-product. If he performed this act of scraping in the performance of ahyewa music, the sound, though similar, would have a different meaning. It would be purposeful in a musical sense. (1961b:4-5)

The problem of the distinction between music and non-music is one of high importance in the understanding of any music system. It delimits what is musical in the society, and it shapes not only music itself but even stories about music and concepts of the origin of music. Although there has been some theoretical attempt to differentiate speech from song, for example (List 1963), there is virtually no information available in the ethnomusicological literature concerning this important folk evaluation which lies at the root of all music systems.

Of equal importance among the concepts which underlie music in all societies is the question of music "talent." Does the society conceive of ability as being possessed to a greater degree by some individuals than by others, or is talent equally shared throughout the society? Is it inherited by the individual from his parents or from other relatives, or does any concept of inheritance exist at all? This problem might be approached by the outsider through the application of tests of music ability, but unfortunately such tests seem clearly to be culture-bound, designed for music as it is known in the Western world and thus of definitely limited value. At the same time, what little information is available shows that folk evaluation of the question does exist. Messenger has found that the Nigerian Anang consider all individuals to be born with equal inherent talent for aesthetic activity, and that it is subsequent training which is believed to make one person more skilled than another. In connection with woodcarving, Messenger writes:

> Once an individual commits himself to this occupation by paying the fee and participating in a religious ritual, he almost never fails to develop the skills which will enable him to enjoy success as a professional. It is simply taken for granted by all concerned that he will become an accomplished and creative artisan. The Anang do recognize that a very few carvers exhibit talents that are somewhat superior to their fellow craftsmen, but at the same time they will not admit, as we tried so hard to get them to, that there are those who lack the requisite abilities. This same attitude applies to other esthetic areas. Some dancers, singers, and weavers are considered more skilled than most, but everyone can dance and sing well, and those who choose weaving as an occupation learn to excel in this activity. (1958:22)

This Anang point of view, which emphasizes equal potential at birth, contrasts strongly with the Basongye view, which holds that music ability is definitely inherited unequally. Although Basongye society is strongly patrilineal, inheritance of music ability can come either through the father or the mother. If either of the parents is a musician it is considered likely, though not definite, that the child will inherit ability and will become a musician. Negatively, some individuals are recognized as lacking music ability, and these can be explained by the Basongye on the grounds of their not having had musical ancestors. Thus for the Basongye there is a definite concept of the "gifted" individual whose talents come through inheritance; the concept is very similar to our own in the Western world.

The concept held in this respect is clearly of considerable importance for music in the given society, for it helps, at least, to determine who will or will not become a musician, and who will or will not be encouraged along these lines. Further, it affects the potential for music within the society; among the Anang, it may be presumed that the potential resources from which the society can draw to provide musicians are substantially greater than in Basongye society where the number of possible musicians is sharply restricted by the concept of individual inheritance of "talent." Societies, then, differ markedly in this respect, and it seems logical to assume that the concept has direct and substantial bearing upon the general music picture in any single group.

While the ethnomusicological literature bearing on this subject gives us more leads than that devoted to the distinctions made between music and non-music, it is not extensive, and what is available seems to concern Africa more than any other world area outside the West. Thurow, for example, says of the Baoule of the Ivory Coast, that "although individuals are recognized as having special talent for a given artistic technique, virtually every male member of the society practices some special religious or artistic skill" (1956:4). Alakija, speaking generally for Africa, says that "the African is a born musician. . . . I have often watched African children at play, and I have discovered that each and every one of them has the gifted capacity of becoming a composer" (1933:27), thus perhaps echoing the Anang concept. Basden, for the Ibo of Nigeria, reports that "talent is recognized" (1921:190), and Gbeho says of the master drum on the West African coast that "its complicated rhythm is beyond description and the man to play it is born rather than made" (1951:1263). On much the same level, Sinedzi Gadzekpo reports that among the Ewe of Ghana, "the skill in playing the principal drum appears to be hereditary, though at times an individual from a non-drumming family may also be a skillful drummer" (1952:621). Nketia gives us more precise information concerning the drummer in Akan society:

The duties of a drummer are passed on from father to son, for it is believed that if a person's father is a drummer, he inherits his father's skill and he is able to learn the art with ease. As the Akan maxim goes: "the bird is never the offspring of the crab" . . . That is to say, offsprings are like their progenitors. "The son is like the father" . . . and owes his spiritual nature and discipline to him, . . .

There is also a common belief about drum progenies. It is believed that a person could be born a drummer. Soon after birth, it is stated, such a person shows his inherited trait, for when he is carried at the back, he drums with his fingers on the back of the person carrying him. (1954:39)

Aside from Africa, information seems to be very scanty. Melville and Frances Herskovits report that in Trinidad "improvisation is not considered a specialized gift, a talent of the few, but its molds are at hand for any ready wit, any alert mind" (1947:276), and Quain notes for Fiji that "aside from the general abilities of Toviya's ancestors, some of them have special talent for singing to him which he can't teach to other men" (1948:236). Although we can only assume it applies equally to music, Margaret Mead writes of the Mundugumor:

Only an occasional Mundugumor woman plaits the little vase-shaped creel that the fishing women wear suspended from the back of their necks as they go fishing. These basket-makers are the women who were born with the umbilical cord twisted around their throats. Males so born are destined to be artists. . . . They it is who can carve the wooden figures that fit into the ends of the sacred flutes, embodiments of the crocodile spirits of the river. Men and women born to arts and crafts need not practice them unless they wish, but no one who lacks the mark of his calling can hope to become more than the clumsiest apprentice. (1950:124)

The nature of Mead's comment re-emphasizes the differential that exists in various societies as to the potential number of artists that can be expected. If the Mundugumor must rely upon persons born with the umbilical cord twisted around the neck for their supply of potential artists, and if the Basongye must draw from children of musicians, as opposed to the Anang concept which makes every child born a potential artist, the effect must be substantial.

It is difficult to assess the importance of this question because of the lack of requisite information, but it seems reasonable to assume that beliefs concerning inheritance may well be correlated with the extent to which the general public participates in music as well as the general importance of music in the society. In respect to the former only a few statements are available; thus Best says for the Maori that "almost all natives are singers" (1924:142), and Burrows reports for Uvea and Futuna that "characteristic of all the singing of the two islands is its social character. Solo singing is confined to leading off a chorus, or to reponsive or interspersed passages" (1945:78). Other statements of the same nature could be cited, but they are equally general in nature and, more important, those societies for which some information is available are also those for which we have no evidence concerning inheritance of musical ability.

The problem of the general importance of music in a given society is not widely discussed in the literature, though again some tantalizing clues can be found. Nicholas England (personal communication) reports that in an African Bushman camp there is almost always some music activity going on, and this is also true of my own experience in a pygmy camp in the Ituri Forest of the Congo. On the other hand, the impression one gains among the Basongye is quite different, despite the generally held notion that music is a constant ongoing activity in all African societies. Among the Basongye, literally days can pass without music activity of any kind, and there is but one event which occurs periodically over relatively short periods of time requiring music performance: at the first appearance of the new moon a ceremonial is practiced in connection with the village fertility figure and protector. Although the incidence of practice of music cannot be taken as the exclusive indicator of its importance to the society, it does at least give us some clues.

Speaking of the Plains Ponca, Howard and Kurath note that "the importance of dance and ceremony in Plains Indian life has been greatly underestimated by most American anthropologists. Dancing and ceremonial activity [including music] occupied most of the Plains Indian's spare time, and it would probably be safe to say that a third or more of a Ponca's year was taken up preparing for or participating in such activity" (1959:1). Although speaking of a music instrument rather than music sound, Mead's report of the New Guinea Mundugumor is apropos:

> About these sacred flutes, the hereditary possession of a rope, the almost-equivalent of a woman, these flutes upon which all the artistic skill of the best carvers and the cherished shell valuables of a whole group of men have been lavished, is centered the pride of the Mundugumor. Of their lands, of their houses, of their loose possessions, they are careless, prodigal, and often generous. They are not an acquisitive people, interested in piling up possessions. But of their flutes they are inordinately proud; they call them by

kinship terms, they offer them food with a great flourish, and in a final burst of shame and anger, a man may "break his flute," that is, take it apart and strip it of all its lovely ornamentation and take away its name. (1950:151)

Mead has also contributed information on the Tchambuli of New Guinea, speaking of the arts in general:

As the Arapesh made growing food and children the adventure of their lives, and the Mundugumor found greatest satisfaction in fighting and competitive acquisition of women, the Tchambuli may be said to live principally for art. Every man is an artist and most men are skilled not in some one art alone, but many; in dancing, carving, plaiting, painting, and so on. Each man is chiefly concerned with his role upon the stage of his society, with the elaboration of his costume, the beauty of the masks that he owns, the skill of his own flute-playing, the finish and *élan* of his ceremonies, and upon other people's recognition and valuation of his performance. . . .

But the Tchambuli value primarily their intricate, delicately patterned social life, their endless cycles of ceremonies and dances, the shining surface of their interrelations. . . . The description of this ideal of an impersonal artistic Utopia. . . . (1950:170, 183)

Mead reports, too, upon the arts in Bali, relating them to the culture at large and to personality patterns, but also to the relative amount of attention given them.

But in societies like Bali, where an unusually large part of human energy goes not into eating and drinking, sleeping and making love, but into the arts, children are brought up differently. Each need of the developing child is not satisfied simply and inevitably, as it appears, but instead there are areas of understimulation and areas of overstimulation which so pattern the developing organism as to make it demand other satisfactions than food and drink and sex. One of these special needs which is developed in Balinese children is the need for symbolic activity—playing a musical instrument, cutting out offering designs, . . . or watching a play . . .

. . . man may shape his culture, as the Balinese have done, so that there is a symbolic answer for every need which is patterned in the growing child. The young child may be taught to know terror and frustration, bitterness of rejection and cruel loneliness of spirit

very young, and yet grow up to be a gay and light-footed adult because, for every tension of the threads which have been twisted or
double-woven in the delicate mesh of the child's spirit, the culture
has a symbolic relaxation ready. (1940a:343, 346)

A somewhat different emphasis on the arts of Bali is given by Colin Mc-
Phee, who stresses a kind of concept about music in the culture which
differs considerably from that in the Western world. He writes:

> The primary utilitarian nature of this music . . . emphasizes
> a conception rather different from ours,—that music may be some-
> thing which is *not to be listened to in itself*. . . . Never will it
> become personal, or contain an emotion. At a ceremony its pres-
> ence is as necessary as incense, flowers and offerings. . . . Here a
> *state of music* is required for a certain length of time, nothing more.
> (1935:165-66)

This view seems to be corroborated by Mead when she adds that "this
delight in the art of acting rather than in the play, in the way in which
music is played rather than in the music, . . . is essentially Balinese and
depends of course upon the Balinese character, with its preoccupation
with activity for its own sake and its studied avoidance of climax and of
identification" (1941-42:83).

These are but glimpses into a general problem which has barely been
touched upon in ethnomusicology. Yet the importance of how a society
regards its music, the extent of participation, how much time and
attention is given to it, and the degree to which it is important, are all
concepts which inevitably shape music-making in every society.

Closely related to these problems are concepts about the optimum size
for the performing group. Again the literature is meagre, but it can be
discerned that such concepts are held and that reasons are given for
holding them.

Among the Basongye, concepts differ depending upon the kind of
music being performed. The core music group is always conceived to be a
combination of three men: one playing the *lunkufi*, or slit drum; one
playing the *lubembo*, or double bell; one playing the *esaka*, or rattle; and
depending upon the particular music, one, two, or sometimes all three
singing. Truly fine music emanates from this group, which is optimum for
the Basongye, and of a fixed nature. Even in those cases in which the size
of the group is allowed to vary, for example in young men's songs or in
social singing, informants are rather closely agreed on what group size
makes for the best performance. Basongye give the following repre-
sentative figures:

7 minimum and optimum	15 maximum
5 minimum	8 maximum and optimum
5 minimum	7 maximum and optimum

As the figures for the optimum group tend to agree very closely, so do the reasons given for it. The Basongye say that if there are fewer singers than the minimum, the group cannot be clearly heard; on the other hand, if the maximum is exceeded, the song will be muddled because there will always be some people included who are not good singers. The question of loudness figures as prominently as that of a muddled sound; both seem to be definite values in Basongye group singing. But musicians almost always make a further qualification, and this is that the optimum number would always be *singers of their choice*.

The Flathead Indians make a contrasting judgment on the proper size of a singing group, for their concept is "the more singers, the better." There are several reasons for this. There is the practical point of view that when there is a substantial number of singers, mistakes are not heard. "Yes, it would be better to have more people. Then the song goes fine; it works better. Maybe just one or two people would get mixed up. The song would sound better." Further, singers note that singing is a demanding physical activity: it is "pretty hard when you are alone; you need help to keep it up." Finally, there is some thought on the part of the Flathead that in singing those songs which give the singers the power to achieve some desired end, the more singers, the more efficacious the song.

Fletcher and LaFlesche reach somewhat similar conclusions about the singing group among the Omaha, noting:

> Few Indian songs were ever sung solo. Almost all were sung by a group, many by a hundred or more men and women. The volume not only strengthened the tone but steadied the intervals. A single singer frequently wavered from pitch, but when assisted by a friend or friends the character of the tone at once changed and the pitch was steadied by the union of voices. (1911:374)

Speaking of a specific kind of Apache song, McAllester writes:

> [Healing] is performed at a large gathering, the larger the better, by the medicine man, and all who know the chant even partly join in. There are drummers, dancers and many on-lookers. The whole community, men, women, children and dogs are present, all participating, if only being there. (1960:469-70)

And finally, Handy notes for the Marquesas Islands:

> Most of the chanting was done in groups, sometimes mixed, or sometimes entirely of one or the other sex—in other words, the

73

native's singing . . . was communal. The only individual singing of which I know, aside from occasional solo parts by leaders of group singing, was the chanting of personal spells . . . done by the ceremonial priest. . . . (1923:314)

The size of the performing group is apparently a concept of importance in most if not all societies. It varies according to the kind of music being performed, and it may well correlate with other aspects of music such as its importance and efficacy to the society; it may also reflect the organization of the society as a whole.

If distinctions are made between music and non-music, between individual and generalized talent, and regarding the number of people who comprise the optimum singing group—and if music is of varying importance from society to society—it is evident that there is a connection between all these concepts and the ideas concerning the sources from which music is drawn. A distinction must be made at the outset between the ultimate source from which music originates and the sources from which the individual draws his specific music material. That is, the ultimate origin of music or of specific kinds of music may be held to be the creation of the gods, for example, while individual songs in the same society may be obtained through borrowing.

It is somewhat surprising to find that there seem to be almost no available accounts of beliefs concerning the ultimate origin of music, though the origins of specific kinds of music, music instruments, or individual songs are frequently encountered in the ethnomusicological and ethnographic literature. Among the Basongye, there exist different points of view which correlate rather clearly with generation differences and beliefs. The younger men say they simply do not know; although their fathers and their fathers' fathers had music, its ultimate origin is unknown. Older men are more definite, saying that music came from Efile Mukulu (God), although there is difference of opinion concerning whether it came directly from Efile Mukulu or indirectly through the agency of the culture hero, Mulopwe. The Flathead Indians ascribe all music ultimately—at least in the "old days"—to the vision quest, but this is more a matter of individual songs than it is music as a genre. Speaking of the Pueblo of Sia in New Mexico, Leslie White reports that "the songs and rituals for each creation were provided as they were made" (1962:115-16), thus indicating a supernatural origin.

More evidence is obtainable in respect to the origin of specific kinds of music or music instruments; we have previously noted J. T. John's account of the origin of the xylophone and the standard xylophone tune in Sierra Leone from the song of a bird. Similarly, the Ashanti attribute the origin of drumming to a particular bird. Rattray notes:

The *Kokokyinaka* is a beautiful dark bird that frequents the forest. . . . Its call is not unlike the notes of the drums. It is every drummer's totem, they claim clanship with it and would not eat or kill it. Its call is something like *Kro kro kro kro ko kyini kyini kyini kro kyini ka ka ka kyini kyini kyini kyini ka.* The Ashanti say it taught them to drum. (1923:279, Note 2)

Most accounts, however, direct origins to supernatural or at least superhuman sources. Thus Mockler-Ferryman's account in 1892 attributed one kind of music among the Asaba of Nigeria to forest spirits.

The Asaba people say that music was first brought into the country by a hunter named Orgardié, a native of Ibuzo, upon his return from an expedition in search of big game. Orgardié having lost his way in a thick forest, was surprised at hearing sounds of music; he accordingly concealed himself and discovered that the music proceeded from a party of forest spirits that were approaching. From his hiding-place, Orgardié managed to hear and observe sufficient to enable him to remember the steps of the dances, and the music of the songs sung; and upon his return to his village he taught his countrymen this music, which was called *Egu olo*. From Ibuzo music was imported to Asaba land. . . . every fresh dance or song is believed to have been first heard by hunters during their expeditions in the jungles, and attributed to forest spirits. (1892:274)

Adele Madumere reports that "the Ibo believe that some of the music is the true reproduction of the voices and plays of their grand forefathers and dead heroes' spirits. With this in view, many songs are sung and played with entire concentration and humility" (1953:67).

From the Wagawaga area of former British New Guinea, C. G. Seligman gives the following rough translation of a tale concerning the origin of drums.

Once upon a time there were no drums in Wagawaga. But the people who lived beneath the ground had good drums, to the beating of which they danced.

Once a man went hunting and strayed a long way from home. He was about to return when suddenly he heard a muffled sound coming from beneath the earth. He found a way into the earth, and followed the sound until he came upon two men beating drums, so he went up to one of them and asked him to lend him his drum. The drummer consented and the Wagawaga man slipped

75

away quietly, and ran with the drum as fast as he could towards Wagawaga.

Soon the men noticed that their drum was gone, so they came above ground and saw the Wagawaga man a long way off. They followed him but could not overtake him, and so turned back before they reached Wagawaga. Now when the man got home, he hung up the drum in his house, and next day, while the men of the underworld were asleep, he went back and stole some more drums and brought them to Wagawaga.

So men copied them and have used drums for dancing ever since. (1910:385)

A very similar story is noted by Walter Ivens for the Lau people of the Solomon Islands.

The panpipes are of Tolo origin, and are said to have been made originally by the Gosile, the children of women dying *enceinte*. The Gosile live after their mothers are buried, and they are to be found in the hills. They are of short stature, and have long hair and nails like claws. They live in holes in the deep forest and wander about looking for food which they eat raw, being ignorant of how to make fire. They are also said to be cannibals. One of them was caught and his pipes taken from him by human beings and copied. (n.d.:214-15)

Somewhat similar tales are found among the North American Indians. George A. Dorsey, in reporting upon the origin myth of the Arapaho Sun Dance notes that the Creator ". . . took another small heap of this dried clay, faced the southwest, held the clay up in the air, [and] carefully sang four songs with clear voice, . . ." (1903:199). In this creation, the Creator constantly sings songs, though it should be noted that his songs apparently are more the mechanism whereby certain actions are effected than they are the creation of songs as such. In respect to the Arikara, Dorsey reports the origin of the Mother-Corn ceremony, and says: "Mother-Corn then made a bundle, made songs, made the ritual, and gave the people the ceremonies" (1904:16). In fact, literature concerning North American Indians is full of similar situations in which origins of specific ceremonies are accounted for, and song almost always plays a major part. Thus Kroeber reports on the origin of the Cheyenne Fox Company (1900:164), Dorsey on the origin of the Pawnee Eagle Dance (1906:402), Densmore the origin of the Mandan and Hidatsa Little River Women Society (1923:98-9), and so forth. The origin of specific ceremonies, types of songs, or music instruments seems to be credited to events happening in and from the supernatural world in many if not most societies.

The conception of a close relationship between music and the supernatural may be extended to include the musician. Nketia informs us that:

> The drummer of the talking drums is called the Creator's Drummer . . . or the Divine Drummer. . . . He is closest to the spirit of the Ancestor chiefs whom he addresses. . . .
>
> The creator's drummer is close to Nature. In accordance with the world-view held by the Akan, he exercises to the spirit of the objects of creation from whom the components of his drums are obtained. . . . He also calls on the Supreme Being, to all lesser gods, witches, Ancestor drummers and so on, capable of interfering with his work or his well-being. . . .
>
> The drummer of the talking drums calls himself the Creator's Drummer because as he says on his talking drums, he is among the first important people "to be created": . . . (1954:36, 39)

The close connection between the musician and the supernatural is similarly emphasized by Rattray in speaking of the Ashanti: "Many Ashanti think that the 'man in the moon' is a drummer; children are warned not to watch him too long lest they should see him lay his drumsticks upon his drums, when it is thought they would die" (1954:282).

When we turn from the ultimate origin of music to the origin of individual songs as related to the individual singer, the picture broadens somewhat. There are three major sources by which music material can be created: from the supernatural or superhuman, through individual composition, and by means of borrowing. It appears that most if not all societies recognize all three as at least potential sources, although emphasis is put upon one or the other of them.

Among the Basongye individual composition is not an important acknowledged source of music, for in fact no individual will admit to such creativity although it is accepted as being hypothetically possible. One of the reasons which lies behind this attitude is a general idea which can perhaps be labeled the concept of "normalcy." That is, no Musongye wishes to stand out as an individual in the group situation which characterizes Basongye life. One of the most suspicious activities in which a person can engage is eating alone; not only is this considered bad manners, inhospitable, and abnormal, but the individual who does so is suspected of having extranormal powers, probably those of a witch. On the positive side, the principle of normalcy accounts for the strong Basongye attitude that marriage partners should "match"; that is, a fat man should marry a fat woman, or a tall man a tall woman, but a short man and a tall woman should not marry. In fact, Basongye society offers but few acceptable roles which allow the individual to differ markedly from his fellows; among them, as will be noted later, is the role of musician, but not the role of composer. If, however, any approach is made toward attributing composition, it is always said to have been a musician who did the composing—musicians of course deny it.

Given the fact that there is no admitted individualistic music composition, songs must stem from the two other possible sources. The Basongye are sanguine about borrowing, and can indicate through some few formal devices of music structure which songs in the current repertoire have been borrowed. These are attributed almost exclusively to the Batetela, the Basongye's nearest neighbors to the north, and they make up but a small recognized proportion of the total repertoire. It seems likely that these borrowed songs are more frequent than the Basongye conceive them to be, but that they tend to lose their foreign identity through time.

This leaves the supernatural as the final possible source of music, and indeed this is the ultimate source for the Basongye, though the actual compositional process remains in question. The Basongye say that all songs come ultimately from Efile Mukulu (God), and that the reason for their new existence is simply that Efile Mukulu wills it so. The Basongye believe in *kwelampungulu*, translated best as "fate," and this includes a strong component of predestination. Thus when one is born, Efile Mukulu writes down in a book (clearly a European intrusion) everything that will happen to him during his lifetime, and this record extends to the most minute details of life. When one's fate declares that a new song is to be created, the individual simply sings that song; the process is explained as an action of Efile Mukulu through the medium of the individual. This means of creation applies to outsiders as well as to Basongye; when the author sang songs which he claimed to be improvised on the spot, the Basongye explained his ability to do so by saying that Efile Mukulu had willed it for that precise point in time. It must be re-emphasized, however, that despite this mechanism the individual Musongye not only refuses to admit to personal composition, which would be contrary to his beliefs, but refuses as well to admit having been the agent of Efile Mukulu in the creation of a song. Thus, in effect, although a mechanism for composition is part of Basongye belief, the only manifest possibility for the absorption of new songs into the repertoire is through borrowing. Other mechanisms must of course be operative; it is inconceivable that musicians, especially, do not create any new music, and one of the ways this may be accomplished is through improvisation which is an important part of xylophone music, for example. But what is important is that the Basongye concept of the sources of music allows what appears to be an extremely

78

restricted amount of acknowledged creativity. The implications are substantial, for in a society which holds such beliefs change in music must tend to be less than in those societies which place emphasis on individual creativity. Thus the concept of the sources of music is of considerable importance in the broad music picture of any given society.

The Flathead Indians accept the possibility of all three sources, and their concepts are arranged in such a manner as to allow for more flexibility in music than among the Basongye. Individual composition for the Flathead is not of particular importance, at least as a recognized process, although some individuals do admit to making up new songs. Borrowing is a rich and recognized source of new music materials, and the Flathead pinpoint songs borrowed from a variety of neighboring tribes, the Blackfeet, Kootenai, Coeur d'Alene, Cree, Chippewa, Shoshone, Nez Perce, and Snake. Such songs are sometimes recognized by stylistic peculiarities, but more often because the time and place of borrowing is known. As among the Basongye, songs borrowed by the Flathead tend to lose their identity and become absorbed into what is considered Flathead music.

The third source of music for the Flathead is felt to be by far the most important and the most "natural"; this is from the supernatural through the agency of the vision quest. All songs held to be "true" Flathead songs are considered to have originated from this source. We will speak further of this problem in connection with discussion of the composer and the processes of composition, but suffice it to say at this point that Flathead visions tend to be standardized in respect to music, with the songs learned in certain specific ways from supernaturals who appear at given times and in given ways in the vision.

The matter of the vision quest in Plains Indian culture has been summarized by Benedict (1922) and need not be described here, save to note that song always seems to play a prominent part. Thus Densmore, for the Northern Ute (1922), Pawnee (1929), and Teton Sioux (1918) reports on song experience from the vision quest, and similar reports are made, among many others, by Flannery for the Gros Ventres (1953), Fletcher and LaFlesche for the Omaha (1911), Lowie for the Assiniboine (1910), and Wissler for the Blackfeet (1912). A similar situation, though not in the vision quest as such, is reported by Elkin for the Songman in Australia (1953), and other examples are found frequently in the literature.

Actual instances of borrowing are not so frequent, though one or two may be cited. Generalizing for all of Melanesia, Albert Lewis says: "New songs are also introduced from other regions, and travelers frequently bring back foreign songs, which they teach to their fellow villagers"

(1951:169). Charles Lange reports for the New Mexico Pueblo of Cochiti that "to obtain new songs, a person may go to another village or tribe and memorize songs that he hears there" (1959:311). Further instances will be cited in connection with mechanisms of borrowing as they affect processes of diffusion and acculturation.

One further concept concerning the sources of music must be noted here; this concerns the Yirkalla of Arnhem Land in Australia, as observed by Waterman (1956). The Yirkalla interpret some babies' "inept attempts to mimic speech" as "revelations of secret and sacred song-words," and this is coupled with the concept of "finding" songs. Waterman comments that ". . . there is no invention or creation of songs at Yirkalla, only discovery. A sacred song based on infantile babbling is considered a song as ancient as any other. The implied idea that all possible songs exist and have only to be found is in complete harmony with Aboriginal attitudes in general toward time and innovation" (p. 41, Note 1). In this case, then, as among the Basongye, individual creativity is negated, for the existence of the individual song is accounted for in terms other than those relating to human activity. While the Basongye hold that Efile Mukulu is constantly creating songs, the Yirkalla draw upon a pre-existing body of music which has only to be discovered.

The concepts which people hold concerning the sources from which their music stems are of major importance in shaping a music system. The most common alternative sources—the supernatural, individual human creativity, or borrowing—are emphasized to greater or lesser degrees, and the particular emphasis given affects not only the potentiality of sound sources for music use, but forms of creativity, change in style, and other aspects of music as well.

A further concept of particular interest has to do with whether music is, in itself, an emotion-producer. We shall have further occasion to discuss this question in considering music as an aesthetic phenomenon, but it must also be touched upon here. Reference is not made to the function of music as such, but rather to what extent music producers conceive of music as something which can arouse emotion either in the producer or the listener. Almost nothing can be gleaned from the ethnomusicological literature concerning this problem, for wherever emotion is discussed in connection with music, it is considered from the standpoint of the observer rather than from that of the participants.

A. B. Ellis, for example, speaking of the Tshi of the then-Gold Coast, wrote of ". . . this known emotional influence of music . . ." (1887:326) but without making his remarks specific. Elsdon Best notes for the Maori: "For these people made much use of song in order to express their feelings and thoughts" (1924:II,135), and Burrows, speaking of the people of the Polynesian island of Futuna, remarks that "singing is used in Futuna to express any sacred emotion" (1936:207).

More directly to the point, Burrows, in discussing the functions of music in the Tuamotus, noted:

> Some of these functions are clearly established by the data already given; others are inferred.
>
> 1. Stimulating and expressing emotion in the performers, and imparting it to the listeners. The emotion may be religious exaltation, as in the creation chant and song of the sacred red bird; grief, as in the laments; longing or passion, as in the love-songs; joy in motion; sexual excitement, and a variety of other emotions, in the dances; exaltation of the ego in the chants of glory; stirring to new courage and vigor, as in the enlivening chants; and doubtless others. . . .
>
> Underlying all of these in greater or less degree is the general function of stimulating, expressing, and sharing emotion. . . . According to the native way of thinking, something more than emotion—namely, mana or supernatural power—is conveyed in the incantations; but from the European point of view the function actually performed is still that of imparting emotion. (1933:54, 56)

In another context, Burrows wrote: "In sum, the collected songs indicate that singing in Uvea and Futuna may express and stimulate any emotion that is shared by a group, be it household, working gang, or entire kingdom" (1945:79).

Among the Basongye, it is stated that music itself, abstracted from its cultural context, has the capacity to stir the emotions, but as will be discussed later in some detail, this is in fact a questionable assumption. However, musicians in particular agree unanimously on three things concerning the emotions when the individual is performing. First, the act of making music causes the musician to feel happy. Second, the musician must always think hard about what he is doing, both individually and in connection with what the other musicians of the ensemble are doing, and this may override any specific emotion other than that of general well-being. Third, musicians are much aware of the fact that while the state of making music is a happy one, conflicting emotions may be induced by the situation in which music is taking place. Thus at a funeral, the musician is happy to be performing his music, but at the same time sad because it is a funeral.

Statements of this sort can contribute to our knowledge both of the musician and of his audience's reception of his music; discussion of the

81

concept is so rare that nothing further can be suggested except to re-emphasize the obvious importance of gaining further information.

Closely related to this question about emotions and music is that of why people make music, but again, the general point must be separated from the specific responses devoted to the functions of music. The Basongye give three reasons for making music, of which one is stressed more than the others. First, people make music in order to be happy. Second, they make music in order to make money. Third, they make music because "Efile Mukulu told us to do so." Of these, happiness is stressed most often and seems clearly to be most important; even those who are concerned with acquiring wealth fall back upon the happy qualities of music-making in the last analysis. On the other hand, the Flathead Indians tend to say that people make music in order to help themselves: "In my time and in my mother's time, people sang because they were poor and the songs helped them." Neither the pleasure nor the financial advantage of music is stressed, and these are seldom mentioned. Although generalization on such incomplete information is hardly to be attempted, the contrast between Basongye and Flathead in this matter is striking. The nature of the responses indicates quite different attitudes toward music, and it is safe to assume that further information would be of considerable use in understanding the place of music in the thinking of other peoples.

Once music is produced, it becomes property of one sort or another—property of an individual, of a particular group, or perhaps of the society at large. Jaap Kunst has given some attention to this problem (1958), and speaks of three major categories of ownership of songs: "compositions belonging to certain personalities, compositions which should be per-formed only by a given individual, [and] compositions which should be performed only by one given group (caste, tribe)" (p. 2).

It is clear that individuals have rights to specific music compositions in many parts of the world. Speaking of the Melanesian Tanga, with particular reference to the money-token, *amfat*, Bell comments:

> A dance master on Tanga has the inalienable right to his own compositions, and to such other songs and dance arrangements as he has seen elsewhere and introduced to the island. Although a dance is a public affair . . . no other village would dare to plagia-rize an original composition. A fee of several *amfat* is paid to the master, and he spends weeks in the other villages teaching the in-habitants the new dance. There was not a dance on Tanga the name of whose composer was not known. (1935:108)

Elkin (1953:93) reports equally inviolable ownership for the Australian Songman, and perhaps best known in the literature is the ownership by North American Indian individuals of personal songs obtained in the vision quest. Somewhat less known is the strict ownership of music by specific groups. Speaking of Tikopia, Norma McLeod comments:

> . . . certain kin groups are said to "own" certain songs or dance types. . . . One person, usually the head of the kin group involved, will supposedly hold the "true" version of the song in his memory. Thus the rights in the song are vested in the head of the group. . . . This right of the "true" version is linked with the concept of expertness. . . . (1957:130)

Still less known is the fact that ownership can often be transferred both from individual to individual and from group to group. Wissler reports upon the transfer of medicine bundles, including the songs that go with them, from one man to another among the Blackfeet (1912), and Benedict extends the concept of sale of the bundle to the Crow, Arapaho, Hidatsa, and Winnebago (1922:18). Similarly, Elkin reports that the Songman "owns his series of songs, but will give permission (in return for gifts), or 'trade' the right to sing his songs, to Songmen in other tribes. This occurs at inter-tribal gatherings for ceremonial and 'trade' purposes. He also passes the ownership on to a younger person, when his own powers show signs of failing, . . ." (1953:93). Margaret Mead tells us of the sale of dance-complexes from group to group among the New Guinea Arapesh:

> All of these importations from the beach are grouped into dance-complexes, which are sold from village to village. Each village, or cluster of small villages, organizes through a long preliminary period to collect the necessary pigs, tobacco, feathers, and shell rings (which constitute the Arapesh currency) with which to purchase one of these dances from a more seaward village that has wearied of it. With the dance they purchase new styles of clothing, new bits of magic, new songs, and new divining tricks. (1950:19)

Gladys Reichard reports that among the Navaho "songs are a form of wealth. Individuals own songs for increase and prosperity, songs belonging to the fetishes of domestic animals and the bundles of the simple domestic rites devoted to family or group welfare. . . . Songs, like other forms of wealth, may be exchanged" (1950:I, 289, 290).

Music, then, is conceived as wealth in the form of intangible goods in many societies. As such, it is of economic importance within the society

83

and, if conceived in this fashion, takes on an aspect of primary importance to the investigator who seeks to understand the position of music in the minds of the people who make and, in this case, own it.

Concepts about music, then, are basic to the ethnomusicologist who searches for knowledge about a music system, for they underlie the music behavior of all peoples. Without an understanding of concepts, there is no real understanding of music.

CHAPTER V

SYNESTHESIA AND INTERSENSE MODALITIES

The problems of synesthesia and intersense modalities fall under the general rubric of concepts which underlie a music system, and the highly involved questions they raise lead to consideration of further problems of music and language, aesthetics, and the interrelationships among the arts. Although direct studies of synesthesia and intersense modalities do not seem to have been carried out cross-culturally, these topics introduce problems of major interest to ethnomusicologists, problems which are particularly susceptible to attack through ethnomusicological research. One of the key articles in the field, which stimulated a considerable amount of further speculation and experimentation, was contributed by an ethnomusicologist, Erich M. von Hornbostel (1925, 1927), but his colleagues do not seem to have followed his lead.

Synesthesia falls broadly within the field of psychology and has been studied primarily by psychologists; it is, of course, a phenomenon of perception. Historically, it has been the Gestalt psychologists with their emphasis upon patterns of organization of experience who have given the phenomenon the most attention, and this is not surprising in view of the fact that synesthesia involves, theoretically at least, the interrelationships among all the senses.

Synesthesia has been defined in a number of ways. Tiffin and Knight, for example, refer to it as "the mistaking of the stimulation of one sensory organ as the stimulation of another" (1940:388), but the use of the word "mistaking" does not seem apropos, for the phenomenon does not depend upon error but rather upon an interresponse of the senses. Morgan couches his definition in somewhat different terms: "A phenomenon

85

experienced by some individuals in which certain sensations (such as color) belonging to one sense, appear regularly whenever a stimulus (such as a certain sound) from another sense field is received" (1936:111). More economical of words is Carl Seashore, who defines synesthesia as ". . . the experience of an associated sensation when another sense is stimulated" (1938a:26). Seashore segregates two further and more specific manifestations: "*Chromesthesia* is the experience of color when any other sense organ other than the eye is stimulated. *Colored hearing* is the seeing of color when the ear is stimulated." Although we shall have to return to the problem later, it must be noted here that there appears to be a necessary distinction between "true" synesthesia, in which such sense transfers are actually experienced by the individual, and an associated synesthesia in which such transfers can be made artificially but are not truly experienced.

These definitions, as well as the caveat cited above, indicate that there are a number of aspects to the study of synesthesia, and this conclusion is borne out by an examination of the various experimental approaches which have been taken in the past. Indeed, there seem to be at least six kinds of approaches, although all clearly fall under the general rubric.

The first of these is synesthesia proper, which occurs when one is exposed to a stimulation in one sense area but receives and experiences that stimulus in association with another sense area. The best known examples of this classic synesthesia occur when the subject hears music and at the same time sees color; this has been reported on, among others, by Karwoski and Odbert (1938), Riggs and Karwoski (1934), and Vernon (1930). In all cases the subject's visual sense is stimulated by auditory reception; the evidence points to the fact that this is a natural phenomenon experienced and felt without conscious association of one thing with another. Somewhat less known, and perhaps less frequent, is a similar process reported by Reichard, Jakobson, and Werth (1949) in which phonetic rather than music sound stimulated the same kinds of color experience. In this case, a student in one of Reichard's classes was discovered quite by accident to have this kind of synesthesia, and further investigation disclosed a few other cases; both vowels and consonants were found to have color synesthesic connections. In a more general way, Whorf has commented on language synesthesia, pointing out, for example, that "the vowels *a* (as in *father*), *o*, *u*, are associated in the laboratory tests, with the dark-warm-soft series, and *e* (English *a* in *date*), *i* (English *e* in *be*) with the bright-cold-sharp set. Consonants also are associated about as one might expect from ordinary naive feeling in the matter" (1951-52:186).

A second kind of synesthesia occurs when the addition of a second sense stimulus, B, to an original sense stimulus, A, increases the acuity of perception of A. Classic experiments of this phenomenon have been carried out by Hartmann (1933a, 1933b). In the second of these, Hartmann designed an experiment in which the subject looked through one eye at brass squares so arranged that they initially appeared to be a single square. By moving one of the squares, a separation was effected visually, and it was the subject's task to tell the investigator the precise moment at which the squares separated in his vision under given conditions. After obtaining a distribution of response under these conditions, Hartmann introduced stimuli from senses other than the visual; these included musical tones at 2100 vps and 180 vps, the "pleasant" smell of citronellol and the "unpleasant" smell of sylenol, pressure from a bar placed on the extended left hand, and pain from pin pricks. Each of these was introduced separately into the experiment as an additional stimulus to vision, and Hartmann found that visual acuity inevitably increased when the visual stimulus was accompanied by any of the other stimuli: "There is a definite and consistent improvement in visual performance in every instance where auxiliary excitation occurs" (1933b:396).

In another experiment, Hartmann (1934) administered the Seashore test of music ability to a number of graduate students, using the factors of pitch discrimination and intensity. The test was given under conditions of varying degrees of light intensity in the room; these were changed from a maximum of 510 watts to as complete darkness as possible. Hartmann concluded that "the statistical treatment here followed shows that the mean auditory efficiency . . . is definitely better by about three percent in the light than in the dark. In absolute amounts these differences are small but they meet the conventional tests of reliability" (1934:819).

It appears, then, that there is a definite correlation between performance achievement level and auxiliary stimulation from senses other than that being tested. This particular phenomenon, which clearly belongs within the general rubric of synesthesia, can perhaps be called "intersense stimulation" in order to differentiate it from synesthesia proper, discussed above.

A third kind of synesthesia, which I would venture to call "intersense transfer," occurs when the presentation of a stimulus from one sense area can be represented in a second sense area with the relationship acknowledged. This phenomenon can in turn be subdivided into two different types, the second of which has one further subdivision.

In the first place, intersense transfer can be carried out creatively, that is, when a subject is given a stimulus in one sense area and deliberately asked to represent it in another. Such an experiment was designed by Willmann (1944), who sent a series of four visual figures to an unspecified number of "Standard" (i.e., art music) and "Popular" composers in the United States and asked them to compose themes suggested by each. The four designs sent to the composers were as follows (p. 9):

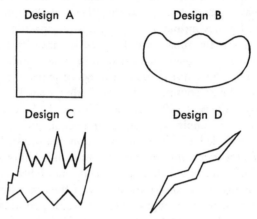

Design A

Design B

Design C

Design D

Willmann summarized his results in this way:

Certain characteristics were found generally to be predominant in the themes to each design and these predominant characteristics were different and distinct from each other according to the designs to which the themes were written. The results were essentially the same whether they were ascertained from the statements by an authority after an inspection of the themes, from observations made from the scores, from a catalogue of elements found in the themes, or from a check of the characteristics heard in the themes by expert auditors. The characteristics in the themes to each design were: for

Design A:

Generally duple and regular in rhythmic pattern, moderate or slow in tempo, medium or loud in dynamics, even in melodic pattern, and decisive in character.

Design B:

Generally triple and regular in rhythmic pattern, moderate in tempo, soft or medium in dynamics, even and flowing in melodic pattern, and quiet in mood or character.

Design C:

Generally duple and syncopated in rhythmic pattern, moderate or fast in tempo, loud and accented in dynamics, jagged in melodic pattern, and agitated and quite frequently decisive in mood or character.

Design D:

> Generally duple and syncopated but also quite frequently triple in rhythmic pattern, fast in tempo, loud and climactic in dynamics, rising and/or falling in melodic pattern, and impetuous or decisive and restless in mood or character. (p. 45)

Willmann makes some further distinctions between the thematic responses of the Popular versus the Standard composers, and concludes:

> There is a carry-over from an abstract design to the resultant musical theme when the theme is composed to the design. This provides an indication that the creative product is influenced by an abstract design or possibly some other visual object when the design or object is used as a stimulus by the creative worker. (p. 47)

In this case, the subjects worked from a graphic representation to music sound, but the process can be reversed as well, as in the case of a woman reported by Paget (1933:363-82) who expressed Beethoven's C Minor Symphony in a group of four sepia paintings.

These results, particularly Willmann's, are indeed striking, but they raise two problems which, again, will be discussed below: 1) whether these are really synesthesia or are, rather, associated phenomena which fall more clearly into the realm of symbolism and thus eventually into aesthetics; 2) the extent to which the results are culturally determined, or, on the other hand, cross-culturally applicable.

Intersense transfer occurs in another context besides the creative, and this we can perhaps call "perceptive matching." In this case, experiments are carried out through the presentation, for example, of a range of tones and a range of colors, with the subject charged with the responsibility of matching the two sets of stimuli.

A classic experiment of this type was carried out by Omwake (1940), who presented a series of tones played on the piano to five hundred and fifty-five fourth-grade through high-school children. As each tone was played, she showed the children a large card divided into red, blue, black, and yellow segments, and asked the subjects to note on a form which color went with the particular tone being played. The tones she used were, in order, as follows:

1. E—second E above middle C
2. G—third G below middle C
3. F sharp—below middle C

4. C—second C below middle C
5. G—below middle C
6. C sharp—second C sharp above middle C
7. D—second D above middle C
8. A—second A above middle C

Calling the experiment "synesthesia," she reached the following conclusions:

> The tendency to associate a certain color with a piano note was definitely greater than chance, and the agreement of response increased with the age of the subjects. . . . Black was usually suggested by a low note, yellow by a high one, red by a relatively high one, and blue by a relatively low one. (p. 474)

A similar kind of experiment was carried out by Cowles (1935), who asked Princeton undergraduate students to match eight Western art music selections and eight Western paintings of mountain scenes. He concluded:

> . . . pictures with represented content capable of motor activity were nearly always selected with the musical selections of prominent dynamic changes; and likewise, pictures of slight content were nearly always selected with music of relatively weak dynamic qualities. . . . Formal elements of the pictures, however, were but rarely noted. Rhythm, tempo, and changes in loudness were most frequently noted in the music. (p. 469)

Finally, an analogous but not precisely similar experiment was carried out by Krauss, as reported by Werner (1948:70), in which the three following designs were to be matched with "gold," "silver," and "iron." The indicated correspondence of response amounted to some eighty per cent for the entire group of subjects.

A subdivision of this same kind of experiment is found in those cases in which a range of tones is presented and the subject is asked to give color responses with no choice prescribed by the investigator; in other words, while the situation is artificial, the subject is given a free range potential for expression. Such an experiment is that of Odbert, Karwoski, and Eckerson (1942), who played ten selections of Western art music and asked their subjects to describe the moods represented; on a second playing of the same selections in the same order, the subjects were asked to ascribe what they considered to be fitting colors to the moods. The investigators concluded:

1. Subjects who are forced to relate colors to music give responses very similar to those of subjects who react readily to music with vivid visual imagery. . . .
2. Subjects who disagree on the mood of a selection tend to report different colors for the selection.
3. The colors named with a selection are systematically related to the named mood of the selection.
4. When subjects are asked to name the color best fitting the same mood-words, the results are very similar to those obtained with the use of music. (p. 172)

At this point we begin to approach rather closely the final division of synesthesia, i.e., intersense modalities, but before considering this matter we must return to a discussion of some of the problems raised in the preceding paragraphs.

The first of these is whether there is a difference between what we may call at this point a "true" as opposed to a "forced" synesthesia, and this clearly does seem to be the case. Kerr and Pear (1932-33), for example, conducted an experiment designed to *force* the subject to evoke imagery, and they draw a clear-cut distinction between this experiment and occasions in which synesthesia is actually felt or sensed rather than evoked.

Whereas earlier students of synesthesia tended to ascribe its "true" presence to large percentages of the subjects tested, later investigators, differentiating between true and forced synesthesia, were reluctant to ascribe more than a very small percentage of cases to the former category. Thus Seashore holds that true synesthesia is "very rare," and explains other synesthesia-like effects as deriving from:

. . . the continuous color activity of the retina which normally goes unobserved but can be seen whenever attention is directed to it, the normal tendency of associating musical sounds with objective situations in which color may play a vivid role, and a wide range of normal habits of association by analogy in which one sense experience suggests another. (1938a:26)

If the distinction between true and forced synesthesia is acceptable, then we must conclude that examples of the latter are culturally determined and are perhaps more a symbolic than a synesthesic phenomenon *per se*. Some further evidence along this line is cited by Farnsworth (1958:90-3), who charts key-color relationships visualized by Rimsky-Korsakov and Scriabin, as follows:

Key	Rimsky-Korsakov	Scriabin
C major	white	red
G major	brownish-gold, bright	orange-rose
D major	yellow, sunny	yellow, brilliant
A major	rosy, clear	green
E major	blue, sapphire sparkling	bluish-white
B major	somber, dark blue shot with steel	bluish-white
F♯ major	greyish-green	bright blue
D♭ major	dusky, warm	violet
A♭ major	greyish-violet	purple-violet
E♭ major	dark, gloomy, bluish gray	steel-color with a metallic lustre
B♭ major	- - - - -	Steel-color with a metallic lustre
F major	green	red

It is not necessary to have a practiced eye to see that these key-color ascriptions differ in many respects, though they do coincide at three or four points. Two major problems are raised. In the first place, do we operate here on a more symbolic than true synesthesic level, since the ascriptions do differ? On the other hand, is there any reason to suppose that true synesthesic experiences duplicate themselves from one individual to another, or in the same individual at different times? Despite the high percentages of like results obtained in many of the experiments cited above, there is no clear-cut evidence, to the best of my knowledge, which either confirms or denies these questions. A further problem arises in connection with the different kinds of symbolism, individual and group, as well as with the mechanisms whereby forced synesthesia is learned. In respect to the latter, the unanimity of individual experimental results points toward the learned nature of the responses.

The second problem arises from these questions and is concerned with the cross-cultural validity either of true or forced synesthesia. One interpretation has been given by Masson, who suggests that there are different kinds of synesthesias. He notes:

> . . . alphabetic, day-of-the-week, and number synesthesias are for the most part private, depending on individual experiences, fantasies of infancy, and cultural conditions. . . . On the other hand some, though not necessarily all, synesthesias even in one individual for seasons, months, hours of the day and night, are

likely to be dependent on natural symbolism for experiences and emotional atmospheres which are common to most persons in a given part of the world. . . .

A third group . . . includes some of the true acoustic synesthesias, due to music or speech sounds. (1949:39)

Reichard, Jakobson, and Werth add that "the ethnologist asks whether the color-hearing is culturally determined. Certainly the interpretation of letter form connected with sound must be so interpreted, particularly since visual memory in the system of education is so dependent upon writing" (1949:230). Thus we seem to be faced with two major types of synesthesia, true synesthesia and culturally-derived synesthesia. While it is obvious that the latter concept may well be cross-culturally applicable as a general phenomenon, we apparently do not really know whether either kind of synesthesia exists among peoples outside the EuroAmerican stream, though a few possible examples are afforded us. Cushing, for example, in a description of the Zuni creation myth seems to indicate, though none too clearly, that the Zuni make the following correlations between directions and colors: North-yellow; west-blue (?); east-white (?); and south-red (1891-92:442). More clear-cut are the Hindu and Chinese examples. In the former, the correlation between the musical mode, or *raga*, and visual portrayal, architecture, color, times of day and night, and so forth, are well known (Raffe 1952). In Chinese music, similar correlations are made between the five basic scale tones and considerations of politics, season, element, color, direction, and planet (Picken 1954). But we do not know whether such associations are true synesthesia or culturally-conditioned synesthesia. And further, we are clearly faced with a shading into the symbolic without knowing where, or even whether, a line can be drawn between synesthesia and symbolism.

It is clear, then, that one of the pressing problems in the study of synesthesia is cross-cultural research carried out in a variety of cultures. While I do not regard my own tentative efforts as being "experimental" in any sense, it is apropos to report that no informant among the Basongye either admitted to synesthesic experience or, indeed, even considered questioning along this line to fall clearly within the bounds of normal sanity. Those questioned included males, females, professional musicians, non-professional musicians, and non-musicians. In one instance a professional musician indicated some possibility of a sound-vision relationship when he held xylophone sticks in such a fashion that the ends formed a series of four stair-steps, and indicated that this was analogous to relationships between tones. The same informant also reported that while playing the xylophone he kept the keyboard in his mind's eye and saw it as "white"; unfortunately, in Kisongye, the same term, *itoka* (pl. *bitoka*), translates either as "white" or as "natural colored" which applies to the color of raw wood, and further questioning made it clear that what he visualized was the shape and color of the keyboard itself.

A similar lack of response to such questioning occurred among the Flathead who admitted no color-sound relationships, and the most frequent single response to such questioning was "That's silly!" While the sample is, of course, too small to allow for any sort of generalization, the apparent absence of the phenomenon among two non-Western peoples argues for the high interest of carrying out controlled research in much wider areas.

The final aspect of the general problem of synesthesia falls into the area of what has been called "intersense modalities." This refers specifically to the linguistic transfer of descriptive concepts from one sense area into another, and is simply illustrated by the variety of terms used in Western culture to describe music sound, such as "cool," "rough," sharp," "smooth," "blue," and so forth.

One of the early approaches to this problem was taken by Hornbostel (1927), who noted the apparently equal applicability of the term "brightness" to sound, color, and odor. Hartmann, working from the leads suggested by Hornbostel, added further applications of the term: "This is the characteristic shared by most high-pitched tones, 'loud' colors, penetrating but pleasant odors, sharp 'pointed' tactile stimuli as opposed to dull, blunt surfaces, etc." (1935:142). This led him to further exposition in which he moved from intersense modalities as such into the broader area of synesthesia in general.

> If one produces upon the color wheel greys resulting from five different proportions of black and white and presents with each a definite tone, there is considerable agreement—with the interesting exception of color-blind observers—that one and only one of the greys has a "brightness value" most like the sound. . . . The really startling demonstration, however, appears when one finds that a given odor can similarly be equated with a specific grey, and that this can be indirectly checked by equating the odor with the tone originally used! . . . Consequently, there must be something sensory in nature which is not restricted to a single receptor. (p. 143)

Thus Hartmann was led from language usage, i.e., intersense modalities, into the wider area of synesthesia and this, as we shall later see, is one of the important applications made of the phenomenon.

Probably the most detailed, and in a certain sense most incredible, report of experimentation in the area of intersense modalities is that given by Edmonds and Smith in 1923. These experimenters presented their subjects with various intervals and instructed them to "find adjectives which shall characterize or describe them" (p. 287). Of the various subjects, four responded "well" to the instructions, with the following reported results.

> *Octave:* A, "smooth, like the surface of window glass;" *Ba,* "smooth, like polished steel;" *Bi,* "smooth, a unitary experience like one note;" *M,* "smooth, like the feel of ice-cream in the mouth, or the touch of polished glass." *Major Seventh:* A, "astringent, like the taste of a persimmon;" *Ba,* "gritty, like the feel of small sharp granular objects;" *Bi,* "astringent, like strong vinegar or alum;" *M,* "harsh, a nippy, biting effect like a strong astringent." *Major Sixth:* A, "sweet, satisfying, with no sustenance;" *Ba,* "astringent, intermittent puckeriness associated with roughness;" *Bi,* "rich, a lusciousness;" *H,* "luscious, like a juicy mellowness;" *M,* "sweet, like the flavor of fruit, softly rich in the sense of flavor." *Perfect Fifth:* A, "hollow, like a hollow tree, no body to it;" *Ba,* "hollow;" *Bi,* "hollow, empty, has no body;" *M,* "hollow, like a hollow tree or a cave," "like a sound produced by tapping on a hollow wooden box." *Perfect Fourth:* A, "rough, like the feel of coarse sandpaper;" *Ba,* "harsh, like the feel of a coarse granular surface;" *Bi,* "harsh, with a little astringency, thick and heavy;" *M,* "a certain coarseness, rich, oily, hard, lumpy." *Major Third:* A, "mellow, like biting into a very ripe apple;" *Ba,* "thick, like bean soup;" *Bi,* "luscious, like peaches to the taste;" *M,* "mellow, like sweet fruit or a soft diffused light." *Major Second:* A, "gritty, like the feel of small pebbles in the hand or grapenuts in the mouth;" *Ba,* "rough;" *Bi,* "gritty, like sand in one's teeth;" *M,* "gritty, like sandpaper." (p. 288)

The authors went on to summarize the terminology of the results:

> We may, therefore, summarize the characteristic qualities of these intervals as follows: the octave smooth; the seventh astringent, sharp-rough, hollow-astringent; the sixth luscious, juicy-mellow, succulent; the fifth dilute, hollow, harsh; the fourth rich, harsh, coarse; the third mellow, sweet (no taste); the second gritty, grating.

It will be observed that the terms employed belong to three different categories. We may, first of all, characterize the various intervals by reference to taste-touch fusions. Taking the intervals in order from octave to second they would be smooth, like smooth ice-cream or smooth molasses; astringent, like the feel of a green persimmon; luscious, like a juicy succulent fruit; dilute, like a clear soup; rich, like whipped cream or like ripe cantaloupe; mellow, like a ripe but not juicy fruit; gritty, like corn flakes or other coarse substance in the mouth. Or we may characterize them in terms of touch fusions, in which case we should have, taking the intervals in the same order, smooth, like polished glass; harsh, like fine sand-paper; no term for the sixth; coarse, like tweed suiting; harsh, like crushed paper or crash; no term for the third; gritty, pebbly, like pebbles in the fingers. Finally, the interval of the fifth was most frequently described as hollow. We believe that this term had reference to the sound of the experience. It is the only descriptive term in our series which belongs to an auditory category. (p. 290)

It is not necessary to indicate the problems raised by the amazing unanimity of the subjects' response as reported by Edmonds and Smith. What is important here is the experimental establishment of the fact of intersense modalities, at least in Western culture. The variety of linguistic response to sound, drawing upon terms borrowed from senses other than the aural, is almost bewildering in its heterogeneity, and yet it is apparently a common part of our descriptive terminology.

But what of the question of the cross-cultural applicability of the concept of intersense modalities? C. F. Voegelin (personal communication) has pointed out that in searching for the presence of a concept in another culture, one can approach the question by searching first for the parallel utterance. If we find, for example, the term "blue" applied to music sound in another language, we are probably justified in searching further for the underlying concept in the culture which would provide the connection between the two kinds of sense experience.

The difficulty is that information is almost totally lacking, though there are some few hints that can be cited. Nketia, for example (personal communication), indicates that the Ashanti refer to music as "hard," but the context of this reference is unknown. Among the Bashi (Merriam 1957), reference is commonly made to what we call a "high" tone as a "small" or "weak" tone, and to what we call a "low" tone as a "big" or "strong" tone, and Tracey (1948:107) reports a similar usage for the Chopi. Walter Ivens notes for the Lau of the Solomon Islands that: "In singing, a low note is called *bulu* (black), and a high note *kwao* (white). These names are taken from charcoal marks made on a plank to indicate the tune: heavy down-strokes being 'black,' and light up-strokes 'white' " (n.d.:98). Nikiprowetzky, speaking of Mauritania in general, adds a color association with styles of music:

. . . within the different styles there are two "manners of performance"—the "white" and the "black". The latter, called
"Lekhal", is preferred by the Griot people since it allows more
spectacular effects—the voice spanning a wide range and the notes
being held longer, etc. . . .

The "white" manner—or Lebiadh is favoured by educated
people. It is closer to the Arab tradition, and produces a smoother
performance and more subtle singing.

It is possible in performance to move gradually from one "manner" to the other. (1961:n.p.)

Among the Basongye, with whom I paid particular attention to the
problem of intersense modalities, high tones are "small" (*lupela*), and low
tones are "big" (*lukata*). Some other intersense terms are also used by the
Basongye, but these seem to be individual rather than widespread group
usages. Thus one informant was willing to apply the term "hard" to the
sound of certain music instruments, including the rattle, the slit drum,
and the double bell. Another informant grudgingly applied the term
"smooth" to singing, saying, "if the music is not 'smooth' the dancers
cannot dance well"; but the difficulty here is that the term used, *kutala*,
does not translate really accurately as "smooth." Still another informant
used the term "hard" in respect to music "because it is always moving,
never still." And finally, one professional musician described a musical
group that is playing and singing really well, as "boiling" (*akisakila*), but
his ascription of the term was decidedly tentative and was flatly
contradicted by a number of other musicians.

Leonard Meyer (1956:262) indicates rather tentatively that he believes
the phenomenon of intersense modalities is common in musical cultures
throughout the world, but it is not clear whether his reference is
specifically to linguistic transfers or rather to associations of a general
nature between musical and non-musical experience. Certainly the meagre
evidence we have at hand seems to indicate that language transfer to the
remarkable extent reported by Edmonds and Smith for our own culture is
not present elsewhere, a point of considerable importance in its application to other problems.

The presence of intersense modalities in our own cultural vocabularies
has led observers to four kinds of speculation concerning its importance.
Kerr and Pear (1932-33:167) state specifically that what they call "the
use of simile or metaphor" may be "regarded as the entrance door to
synaesthesia." We are reminded here, too, of Hartmann's use of
Hornbostel's concept of "brightness" as a key to the introduction of a
great variety of synesthesic occurrences and experiments. In other words,
these students regard the presence both of synesthesia and intersense

97

modalities as indicating a connection between the two, although it is not clear which is evidence of which. Do we use intersense modalities in our language because of the knowledge of true synesthesic experiences, or does the presence of intersense modalities in such profusion indicate that "forced" or "culturally induced" synesthesias really fall into the broader realm of the symbolic experience? We do not have the answers to these questions.

Charles Stevenson has approached the problem in a different way. He argues that music itself is not really "square" or "rough," but rather that we use such terms in an extended sense, borrowing from one sense to another, because we lack an adequate vocabulary:

> We are not tempted to say that a square melody, heard in any usual way, leads us to take account of the geometrical square; for we there realize that we are calling that melody "square" in the lack of any other appropriate adjective. And perhaps we should not be tempted, with Mrs. Langer, to say that a sad melody leads us to take account of sadness. Instead of supposing that the melody symbolizes an emotion, we have the alternative of saying that it merely resembles an emotion—and resembles it, perhaps, in a rather imperfect way. In that case there will be only one symbolic relation that requires attention: that between the word "sad" and the music, where the word is used in an extended sense. And this symbolic relation will not be an unusual one. It will be just another of the many instances in which the poverty of our language forces us to borrow a term. (1958:212-13)

If we are to accept this view that intersense modalities arise simply from the poverty of language, then it would seem that we are forced to accept the opposite as well, i.e., that in those cultures, such as the Basongye, where intersense modalities are not used, we must be dealing with a language which is not impoverished. This, in turn, leads us to the conclusion that the Basongye must then have a different terminology which can be and is applied to each sense, and we would expect that the words used to describe music as a generic unit would differ from those used to describe visual art as a generic unit. Such is not in fact the case. Not only do the Basongye use intersense modalities in a very sparing way, but the general and specific terms tend to be applicable both to music and the visual arts, for example, and specific to neither. Both music and art may be described as *bibuwa*, a term which refers to the inherent quality of goodness in an inanimate object. Neither does Stevenson explain why particular terms are chosen for particular descriptions. The idea that intersense modalities are to be referred to in terms of language poverty as a cause may, however, have merit when coupled with a third approach.

This approach has to do with the extreme elaboration in our own culture, and perhaps that of some Near and Far Eastern cultures as well, of the idea of the aesthetic. Around this concept we have built up an extraordinarily complex system of speculative and philosophical thought which is manifested in the literally thousands of books and articles devoted to the subject. We argue over the purposes of the arts, their symbolic content, the differences between "pure" as opposed to "applied" art, the functions of art, and, above all, what the concept of the aesthetic really means. We have created a verbal jungle around the aesthetic, and it may well be that a part of that jungle is represented in the use of intersense modalities. The aesthetic has become such a complex subject that we have perhaps been forced to stretch our language to cover what we wish to say about the aesthetic experience, and it is here that Stevenson's "poverty of language" idea may come into play. There remains the question of whether this should be referred to as "poverty of language" or "complexity of idea," but it may be suggested that our inter-artistic use of language may have been forced upon us through elaboration of our concept of the aesthetic.

To the best of our knowledge, cultures other than our own and those of the Near and Far East simply do not concern themselves with the aesthetic to anything approaching this same extent. Working among the Navaho, McAllester found it impossible to separate what he felt he could call the aesthetic from what he called the functional (1954), and in a shorter study he reached much the same conclusion for the Apache (1960). My own work with the Basongye and among the Flathead Indians has led me to conclude that the concept of the aesthetic is very slight, particularly when compared with our own elaborate ideas. We shall return to these problems in our discussion of the aesthetic as such.

The final application suggested by some in dealing with synesthesia and, perhaps particularly, intersense modalities is to use these phenomena as an illustration of the unity or interrelationships of the arts. It will be recalled that Hornbostel's early article was titled "The Unity of the Senses," and his summary point stressed this:

Since the sensuous is perceptible only when it has form, the unity of the senses is given from the very beginning. And together with this the unity of the arts. Art unfolded into the variety of the several arts. In the mask-dance, music and painting, sculpture and poetry, are not yet separated from one another; colours and

99

forms are still drawn into the sounding whirl of human action and its cosmic meaning. (1927:89)

Moving from precisely the principle of intersense modalities, Curt Sachs also argues for the interrelationship of the arts:

> Melody is often said to describe a "line" or a "curve," which might be "smooth" or "jagged"; orchestration gives "color," and the orchestrator has a more or less well-assorted "palette." Painters, on the other hand, have or have not "tone"; a painting with much light is "high" in "key" or "pitch," and one with little light is "low." To such metaphors, which liken and unify the worlds of music and painting, language has added a number of semimetaphors which, making one forget that they have been transferred from art to art, bear witness to the existence of a common stock of qualities from which all arts are built, as: form and structure, symmetry, rhythm, color, clearness, movement, and numberless others. (1946:18)

In our culture, this assumption of the interrelatedness of the arts can lead to enormously elaborate assumptions of parallelisms. Strechow, for example, in speaking of Schumann's "transmutation of Cologne Cathedral," writes as follows:

> It constitutes one of the most amazing transcriptions of architectural structure—not only architectural mood—into music. I am speaking of the fourth movement of Schumann's *Third* ("Rhenish") *Symphony*, opus 97. An analysis of this astounding piece, which was conceived during a high mass celebrated in Cologne Cathedral, shows that the somber mood, announced by the pianissimo trombones at the very beginning and only momentarily brightened by a ray of sunshine in the fanfares at the end, provides us with an underpainting only, and that the structure of the composition is inspired by principles analogous to some main principles of Gothic architecture. The thematic material of the entire movement consists basically of the one motif of a rising fourth which appears in ever varying combinations. It is comparable to Gothic architecture in two decisive respects. First, it shares with the Gothic church the essentially *rising* quality which impresses itself at once on spectator and listener, although naturally, in each case, it again "returns to earth." Second—and from the structural point of view equally important—it fully partakes of the principle of homology, which is the other main characteristic of Gothic architecture. . . . Some of the basic means to achieve this end

were repetition, assimilation, entwining, augmentation, and diminution, just as Schumann's movement is based on developments of a simple fourth by way of repetition, contrapuntal interlocking of parts, augmentations, and diminutions. It is true that this parallel does not cover *all* structural aspects of the architectural and the musical organization; but it did not seem inappropriate to apply the term "structure" to what it does cover. (1953:325)

Elaborations such as these are not uncommon in our discussions of the arts, but our assumption of and search for illustrations of the interrelatedness of the arts may well be the function of our concept of the aesthetic. Again a crucial point is whether similar ideas are found among other peoples, and again our information is extremely scanty if not, to all practical purposes, nonexistent. The question remains open because of the paucity of evidence, but it would seem wise to extend our inquiries to the cross-cultural level before we generalize further on the "fact" of the interrelatedness of the arts.

The problems raised here far outweigh any solutions which have been suggested, but it should be reasonably clear that this is a vast area of research to which ethnomusicology can make an extremely fruitful contribution. We need to know, first, what the difference is between a "true" and a cultural synesthesia, and in this connection it would be of substantial significance to know whether the phenomenon exists among peoples outside Western culture. Such evidence would cast some light upon the relationship of culturally conditioned "synesthesia" to the whole symbolic structure of a given people. Reichard *et al*, for example, have pointed out that of their subjects who showed language synesthesia, ". . . three of the individuals . . . are trained in the imaginative arts. All deeply appreciate art forms, literary, plastic and musical; . . ." (1949:230), and this seems to argue that "synesthesia"—other than those cases in which there is clear evidence of a felt correlation—is a culturally determined matter which involves not only a patterned arrangement of connections but a deep-lying and culturally induced symbolism.

The problem of synesthesia has led us, further, into speculations about language, and particularly about the concepts of the aesthetic and the interrelationships among the arts. Cross-cultural perspective, such an integral part of ethnomusicology, is needed here, as is the ethnomusicological approach which stresses not only the sound of music but the concepts out of which that music arises.

101

CHAPTER VI

PHYSICAL AND VERBAL BEHAVIOR

The concepts held about music and accepted as cultural facts by individuals and groups of individuals underlie both the sounds of music and the attitudes and values associated with them. But concepts alone do not produce music; they must be translated into various kinds of behavior which result in culturally acceptable music sound. Four major kinds of behavior can be isolated in respect to the production and organization of sound; these include physical behavior, verbal behavior about music sound, social behavior both on the part of those who produce music and those who listen and respond to it, and learning behavior which enables the musician to produce the appropriate sounds. The first two of these will be discussed in this chapter.

Physical behavior refers to the fact that in order for sound to be produced, people must flex their fingers and use their lips and diaphragm if the sound is to be produced on a music instrument; or they must manipulate the vocal cords and the diaphragm if the sound is to be vocal. Techniques of playing music instruments have been rather widely discussed in the ethnomusicological literature, and but two or three examples will suffice here. Among the Bashi people of the Eastern Congo (Léopoldville), the *mulizi* is a notched, end-blown flute played primarily by cattle herders.

In performance the *mulizi* is held to the center of the mouth with the notch away from the player and with the lips covering approximately half the diameter of the tube. The second finger of the left hand is used to cover the upper hole; the first finger is

THE ANTHROPOLOGY OF MUSIC

placed on the instrument above the hole in order to hold it steady. The second finger of the right hand covers the lower hole with the first finger above it again providing support for the instrument. Before placing his fingers on the instrument the musician invariably wets his finger tips. The flute tone is produced by blowing an air stream across and down the open end of the instrument and through the notch. . . .

In addition, good and poor *mulizi* players are differentiated on the basis of their ability to produce a larynx tone coterminously with the flute tone. This tone, while akin to humming, is considerably more forceful and much rougher than the normal humming sound. Not all musicians are capable of producing it, and those who cannot are relegated to secondary status. It will be seen that the production of the two melodic lines, each of which has recognizable and changing pitch, is not a simple matter, since the lips must be kept relatively relaxed in order to produce the flute tone, while the larynx and diaphragm must be taut in order to produce the forceful "throat tone." It is a real criterion of musicianship among the Bashi *mulizi* players and lay public; and a difficult method of performance by any standards. (Merriam 1957:144)

The physical behavior involved in playing a particular type of musical bow among the Hottentots is described by Kirby:

The player, having tuned the instrument, . . . seats herself upon the ground, and takes the bow in her hands. The lower end, where the string is knotted, she places upon a bag of skin . . . or a dish of willow wood, which acts as a resonator . . . and is placed to her right. The right foot holds this end of the bow in position, while the upper end rests against the left shoulder. Taking the beater between the first finger and thumb of her right hand, she strikes the string with a clean *staccato* action, comparable to that used in side-drum playing, and a ringing tone is produced. This is the fundamental tone of the string. By lightly touching the middle point of the string with the second phalange of the forefinger of her left hand, and at the same time striking the string, the first harmonic, one octave above the fundamental, is produced. Again, by pressing upon the string with the chin at the appropriate spot, a second fundamental, a tone higher than the original one, is obtained, and by touching the string at the new middle point, the octave of this second fundamental is heard. (1953:211-12)

Descriptions such as these are frequently found; indeed, the mass of information is so great that it is impossible for present purposes to attempt to correlate and compare it. However, the physical behavior involved in the production of sound from music instruments is of high technical importance and may well figure prominently as well in consideration of culture complexes, particularly as applied to diffusion problems.

Vocal techniques are less frequently discussed in the literature than instrumental techniques, and yet recent studies by Lomax seem to indicate that such knowledge would be advantageous both in widening our studies and in providing ethnomusicology with a more precise set of descriptive techniques. In the past, Nettl, for example, has used vocal style as one of the characterizing criteria for differentiating music areas in North American Indian music (1954a) but, like those of most of us, the descriptions tend to be tentative and imprecise in respect to terminology, and differentiating only in the broadest terms, such as the implied contrast between "relaxed" and "tense." In another source, Nettl summarizes vocal tension as follows:

> . . . most primitive singers use a tenser vocal technique than we are accustomed to, although there are exceptions. . . . The tensest known technique was found among some North and South American Indian tribes, whose method of sound production gives rise to a great deal of ornamentation. . . .
>
> The African Negroes sing generally with a tense, slightly hoarse-sounding vocal technique, which is also used by some American Negro singers. . . . Sometimes unusual vocal technique, like Alpine yodeling, can be traced to the attempt of singers to imitate instruments. In many parts of Negro Africa, singers alternate falsetto with ordinary tone production to produce a sound reminiscent of yodeling. The Nayaho Indians use falsetto in a clear, non-ornamented way. Other specialized forms of sound production exist which are characteristic of individual areas. (1956:58)

While it is clear that vocal technique does provide an important criterion for differentiating music styles, the problem is to find more precise terminology or more precise measurements which can be used in place of such terms as "tense," "more tense," and the like.

Alan Lomax has recently made some tentative approaches to this problem, as well as to others involved in vocal techniques, but his research has not as yet been carried far enough to give us the precision of descriptive terminology needed. Thus in describing vocal style, Lomax is also forced back upon a wide variety of adjectival terms, some of which,

105

incidentally, again illustrate the operation of intersense modalities. For American White folk singing, he describes the voice as "rigidly pitched, somewhat higher than the normal speaking tone, confined to a limited range of vocal color—it is often harsh, hard, nasal—the ideal being a pure violin-like tone with which the singer can make ornaments on the melody" (1959:930). American Indian singing is described as follows:

> The manner of Indian singing is strikingly muscular in character. . . . Indians characteristically sing at full volume. Their singing tones are throaty, husky, sometimes grating, rich in nasal overtones, and produced at the normal speaking pitch. Some North American Indians punctuate their throaty chanting with high-pitched hunting yells, war cries, yelps, or other animal-like sounds, and it is out of this material that the electrifying Plains style of singing in a high-pitched, liquid, almost yodeling tone may have developed. (p. 933)

Eurasian singing is described as ". . . ordinarily high-pitched, often harsh and strident, delivered from a tight throat with great vocal tension, frequently with an effect of being pinched or strangulated" (p. 936); Old European as ". . . produced from a relaxed throat" and, in comparison with the Eurasian, ". . . generally rounder, richer in timbre, fuller; a liquid or yodeling tone is sometimes found . . ." (pp. 936, 937). In southern Spain, Lomax reports, singing comes from a "tense throat" (p. 939), while in northern Spain ". . . the throat is not distended with strain" (p. 943), and in Italy ". . . the throat is distended and flushed with strain . . . in a voice as pinched and strangulated and high-pitched as any in Europe" (p. 942). While the utility of the concept of vocal quality is apparent, the distinctions are made in purely linguistic terms of essentially imprecise application.

In order to obviate this difficulty, Lomax has turned to the analysis of vocal timbre as indicated by visible records of sound, and although he has not as yet reported upon his findings in detail, he has remarked that from a sample of six hundred such records, ". . . I feel that I have been able to isolate eleven qualities whose presence or absence characterize the voice production in song style families around the world" (1962a:13-14). Some criteria of vocal timbre apparently form the basis as well for several points in the system Lomax calls "cantometrics" (1962b:426-31). In addition to these problems, Lomax has postulated certain correlations between vocal quality and other characteristics and behaviors:

> In relation to the latter correlation—permissive sexual mores and vocal relaxation—I refer the reader to my paper which has

now been confirmed by an additional year of research. Many specialists in the field of laryngology . . . make the point in detail that vocal tensions of various types, including vocal dysphonia, are of psychic origin. A recent and wide-ranging study of the structure of song performance carried out by Victor Grauer and myself this year showed that there is a tight correlation between vocal relaxation and openness and the occurrence of well-blended choral and polyphonic singing. (Lomax and Trager 1960: Pt. III, p. 1)

Finally, Lomax finds a correlation between vocal tension and vowel usage and movement:

(1) High frequency of front vowel and front vowel movement are regularly associated with vocal tension and with sources of psychic tension and social tension.

(2) Conversely, high frequency of back vowels, especially low back vowels, and movements to and in the back, are regularly associated with vocal relaxation and with sources of psychic relaxation and the social patterns that produce them. . . .

(9) A given vowel pattern seems to bear a tight relationship to its accompanying musical structure, to go hand in hand with it, and to express the same over-all states. In one or two cases . . . it has been possible to show that song form, singing style and vowel patterning move together in the same situation.

(10) Styles with a high frequency of front vowels and narrow movement seem to be solo or monophonic in nature. (Pt. III, pp. 2-3)

An understanding of problems of vocal quality may contribute not only to refinement of stylistic description, but also to a clearer cognizance of the possible correlation of vocal quality with other aspects of human behavior. In the latter connection, it is significant to note that Lomax, while approaching the problem from a different model than that used here, deals directly with the translation of concepts into behavior in speaking of the problem of vowel usage. Thus he notes that "as independent elements of various constructions, the occurrence of back and of front vowels within any system seems not to be a product of the system but of unconscious psychic factors of an aesthetic character" (Pt. III, p. 2), and summarizes as follows:

If all or most of the preceding conclusions are correct, there can be no doubt that one aspect of tradition is concerned with the stylization of vowel choice. It is probable, therefore, that all

107

texts within an oral tradition are constantly being revised and refined so as to conform to the vowel aesthetic of the culture. This steady wearing-away process, which . . . has been thus far thought by scholars to be due to faulty folk memory, on the contrary represents the action of an aesthetic sensibility at the folk level. This aesthetic . . . can change its demands as the general situation or culture of the people changes. . . . Thus the phonotactics of folk singers alter a new song to fit old needs or revise an old song to fit a newly emerging emotional pattern. (Pt. III, pp. 4-5)

As there are specific kinds of physical behavior concerned with the manipulation of voice and instruments, there also seem to be characteristic bodily attitudes, postures, and tensions, and it is possible that such bodily characteristics can be correlated with other behavioral elements to reveal significant facts about music making.

In a useful review of posture as such (without specific reference to postures taken in music performance) Gordon W. Hewes lists five "levels of relevance" for the organization of data (1955:232-33). The first level is that of applied physical anthropology, or biotechnology, which refers to the study of postural habits in relationship to technology. The second concerns the "functional interrelations of postures and non-postural cultural phenomena" such as the relationship to terrain and vegetation, clothing, status and role differences, and so forth. The third level relates to the psychological and psychiatric implications of postural behavior; the fourth, to the relevance of postures to culture history; and the fifth, to phylogenetic implications. Hewes deals only with standing, sitting, and kneeling postures in discussing these levels of relevance, but it seems clear that some, at least, of the five apply equally well to body attitudes in connection with music performance.

Descriptions of such body attitudes are not easy to find. In speaking of men's evening singing in Polynesian Futuna, Burrows notes that the "singers sit mostly in little circles, with their heads together. Whatever the emotional content of the song, their faces remain perfectly impassive. They often stare upward or close their eyes" (1936:208). Wachsmann reports a particular performance form among the Nyole of Uganda in the following terms: "The choruses, men on one side, women on the other, lined up facing each other, and the soloist-leader stood between them. The soloist remained static, but the chorus groups moved and danced, and I had a strong impression of two forces setting up some vital tension between them" (1953:55). It is again Lomax who seems to have paid the most specific attention to this question as a problem for ethnomusicology, and he describes characteristic performance postures for a number of peoples. In contrasting American White folk and American Negro folk singers, he charts the following:

American White Folk	American Negro Folk
The body is held tensely, as the singer sits or stands stiffly erect. The head is often thrown far back.	The body of the singer moves sinuously or in relaxed easy response to the beat. He dances his song.
The singing expression is mask-like and withdrawn, normally, and agonized on high notes.	The singer's expression changes with the mood of the song, line by line; there is a great deal of smiling and even laughing in many performances. (1959:930)

In other passages, Lomax notes the following characteristics of facial and body posture for various groups. Old European: ". . . the facial expression is lively and animated, or at least relaxed." Southern Spain: ". . . a tense throat and . . . an expression of agony on the face." Northern Spain: "The singer's body is relaxed, the throat is not distended with strain and the facial expression is often composed and lively and, though not always animated, neither melancholy nor mask-like." Northern Italy: "Singers stand with arms round their cronies' shoulders, or, leaning across a wine-soaked table, blend their voices, smiling at one another benignly. . . ." Southern Italy: "The singing expression is one of true agony, the throat is distended and flushed with strain, the brow knotted with a painful expression" (1959:*passim*).

Both Thuren and Holm have given us information concerning body responses to music among the Eskimo; their descriptions tally very closely. Thuren writes:

> . . . the East Greenlander by no means keeps his body at rest whilst singing. He bends the knees at regular intervals, takes at times a step forwards, or backwards, turns half round or twists the upper part of his body. In contrast to the men the women while singing stand still in the same spot, moving the hips from side to side in a figure of 8. The singers always stand with half-closed eyes and with a quiet smile on their faces. (1923:11)

Holm notes:

> The singer stands before the entrance in the middle of the floor with his legs apart and his knees slightly bent. If the singer is a man, he does not remain stationary in his place, but bends his knees more or less in time with the song, and occasionally takes a

step forward or back, or makes a half turn. Now and then the upper body is twisted in a great number of different contortions. . . . The singer stands with half-closed eyes and with a stereotyped grimace on his face, though every now and then he breaks into a laugh or giggle.

If the singer is a woman, she stands quite firm on her legs, but keeps moving her hips in a figure that forms an 8. . . . The head is either bent or held straight up. The eyes are half closed and the face wears a stereotyped smile. (1914:125-26)

There is enough information here to indicate both that body attitudes do differ from singing style to singing style, and that problems of descriptive terminology again make delineation difficult. Further, Lomax restricts his discussion of the implications of body attitudes to the third level of relevance suggested by Hewes, namely, the psychological and psychiatric, thus making it somewhat difficult to grasp the broader implications of such study. Within this framework, however, he argues for a close relationship among body attitude, vocal tension, emotional tension, and singing style, and summarizes the possible relationships in the following passage:

When a human being, especially a female, is given over to agonized grief, she emits a series of high-pitched, long, sustained, wailing notes. Even grown men sound like little children when they howl in sorrow. Then the head is thrown back, the jaw thrust forward, the soft palate is pulled down and back, the throat is constricted so that a small column of air under high pressure shoots upward and vibrates the hard palate and the heavily charged sinus. An easy personal experiment will convince anyone that this is the best way to howl or wail. Then, if you open your eyes slightly (for they will automatically close if you are really howling), you will see the brows knitted, the face and neck flushed, the facial muscles knotted under the eyes, and the throat distended with the strain of producing this high-pitched wail. (1959:947)

While my own experience in Africa does not indicate that this pattern is always the case, it may well be that the description applies as a broad generalization to which some exceptions exist. In any case, this appears to be an extremely fruitful line of investigation concerning relationships between bodily attitudes and other aspects of music performance.

While physical behavior is manifest in the manipulation of parts of the body to produce sound, and in the general bodily attitude in producing sound, there is yet a third dimension to the problem—the response of the

110

organism to music. We have previously discussed the question of whether music is held to produce emotion in the listener, but in the present context it is the actual physical response to music which is relevant. In this case, information concerning non-Western cultures is almost nonexistent. Nettl (1955a) has discussed in very general terms possible music therapeutic practices among non-Western peoples, and Densmore suggests that healing songs as a class among the American Indians are marked by irregular rhythm "produced by frequent changes of accent" which are indicated by "changes in measure lengths" (1954a:109). The fact that music very often accompanies healing ritual in nonliterate societies is well established, but the exact nature of the influence of music, either as verbalized by members of the culture at hand or as observed by the investigator, is seldom reported except in the most general terms. In our own culture, the healing aspects of music have been suggested for literally thousands of years; it is known that some four thousand years ago, the Egyptians called music the "physic for the soul." The ancient Hebrews used music in cases both of physical and mental disturbance, and perhaps the most familiar passage quoted in this context is that which pertains to King Saul:

> And it came to pass when the evil spirit from God was upon Saul that David took up a harp and played with his hand; so that Saul was refreshed and was well and the evil spirit departed from him. (The Old Testament, I Samuel, Chap. 16, verse 23)

In 600 B.C. Thales is purported to have cured a plague in Sparta by means of music, and Pythagoras directed that music be used to cure mental disorders. Thus from the earliest history of our own culture there is ample record that music has been held to have a direct influence on the individual biological organism.

In more specific reference to the effect of music and non-musical sound on the individual organism, a number of experiments have indicated that, in Western culture at least, there is a definite physiological response. Thus, in 1830, J. Dogiel published the following experimental results, as summarized by Diserens:

> 1. Music exhibits an influence on the circulation of the blood in man as in animals.
> 2. Blood pressure sometimes rises and sometimes falls. These oscillations of pressure depend chiefly on the influence of the auditory stimulus on the medulla oblongata which is in relation with the auditory nerve.
> 3. The action of the musical sounds and of the whistles on

111

animals and man expresses itself for the most part by the acceleration of cardiac contractions. . . .

4. The variations of the circulation as a result of musical influence agree with the respiratory changes, although they can be observed independently of the latter.

5. The variations of the circulation depend on the pitch, intensity and timbre of the sound.

6. In the variations of the blood pressure, the idiosyncrasies of the individual, whether man or animal, are plainly apparent and even the nationality in the case of man has some effect. (Diserens 1926:131)

It is significant to note, of course, the last statement regarding differences in the response of peoples of different "nationalities," for this is precisely what would be expected, i.e., that people of different cultures respond physiologically in different ways to the same music or sound, depending upon its cultural significance. What is important, however, is the establishment of the fact that the organism does respond physiologically.

Music affects the organism in other ways. In an experiment carried out in a plant in "an Eastern city" of the United States, the effect of music on attitudes, production, and industrial accidents of employees was studied by Henry Clay Smith. In general, he found that production increased while accidents remained about the same on "music" as opposed to "no-music days." He summarized the results of the study as follows:

Music during working hours will generally improve production where repetitive work is common. Properly administered in such situations, it not only will increase production but also will provide widespread employee satisfaction. Music probably produces its major direct effect when the individual's capacity for attention is not absorbed by his work; in this circumstance, music appears to divert unused attention from brooding, talking, or off-the-job activities. Although music, on the average, had no influence on the accident rate, the relation of music to accidents was not entirely clear in the present study. (1947:58)

Although not applied to a specific problem, Diserens indicates comparable findings in his own laboratory experiments.

1. Music tends to reduce or delay fatigue and consequently increases muscular endurance.

2. Music has no definite effect on precision or accuracy of movement, if the rhythm is not adapted to the rhythm of the work. . . .

3. Music speeds up such voluntary activities as typewriting and handwriting. It also accelerates respiration.

4. Music increases the extent of muscular reflexes employed in writing, drawing, etc.

5. Music reduces normal suggestibility, except in the case of direct suggestion involving color in which case suggestibility is increased.

6. Music influences the electrical conductivity of the human body as manifested by increased fluctuations in the psychogalvanic reflex. (1926:205)

Finally, Diserens summarizes the physiological effects of music as determined experimentally in Western culture.

Music:

1. increases bodily metabolism (Tarchanoff, Dutto)

2. increases or decreases muscular energy (Fere, Tarchanoff, Scripture)

3. accelerates respiration and decreases its regularity (Binet, Gunibaud, Weld)

4. produces marked but variable effect on volume, pulse, and blood pressure

5. lowers the threshold for sensory stimuli of different modes.

6. It thus affords the physiological bases for the genesis of emotions according to the James-Lange theory and consequently influences secretions according to the researches of Cannon and others.

7. The precise influence of different modes and types of music has not been determined, and waits upon an adequate classification of musical selections, which must probably proceed at first by introspective and statistical methods. (1926:154)

While the effect of music on the human organism has here been taken in its entirety, that is, music has been regarded as a functioning whole, there have also been some attempts in Western culture to discuss the effects of various components of the musical composition. Thus pitch, intensity, timbre, and duration have been considered individually by Heinlein (1928), while rhythm, melody, mode, and key have been discussed by Licht (1946), rhythm and sonority by Hanson (1942, 1944), and tempo by Hevner (1937). In each case, discussion has centered around the effect of the particular aspect of music on the human organism.

The problems involved in understanding the responses to music of the

113

group and the individual are many, but there is reason to believe that further study would elicit extremely interesting results. The most obvious unknown factor stems from the lack of any significant cross-cultural information. Although it is clear that music produces physiological effects on individuals in Western culture, and that it also affects the behavior of groups, no comparable information exists for other cultures. While we would expect that Western march music would produce different physiological effects when heard by Western and African peoples, for example, we still apparently do not know whether it would produce any effects on Africans at all. Nor have we information concerning physiological effects of African music on Africans, either from the standpoint of whether the phenomenon is human or cultural or whether different kinds of African music produce different effects on Africans. There is no evidence, in other words, to answer the simplest kind of question, i.e., whether the physiological effect of music is a human response, though we may be tempted to assume logically that it is. Similarly, we seem to have no information concerning group response in general to music. How does the African crowd respond, as opposed to the American Indian or Chinese crowd, and in what ways to what kinds of music? It has already been pointed out that even in the matter of the physical behavior of the musician, relatively little is known, and certainly what information is available has not been arranged into meaningful studies. Yet it is apparent that studies of the physical production of sound, the bodily attitudes of the musician, and the physical response of the listener are all of high interest in understanding music behavior as a cross-cultural phenomenon.

The second kind of behavior which exists in respect to music is verbal behavior, to whatever extent it may be used, about music sound. This, too, of course, is a reflection of underlying concepts of music, but in this case applied specifically to what people say about music structure and the criteria which surround it.

Perhaps the most obvious verbal criteria are those which are applied to judgments of the performance of music: these are the standards of excellence in performance. Such standards of excellence must be present, for without them, as has been noted in another context, no such thing as a music style could exist. If we take our definition of style in music from Schapiro, this point becomes obvious: "By style is meant the constant form—and sometimes the constant elements, qualities, and expression— in the art of an individual or a group" (1953:287). Further, style has continuity, as expressed by Haag when he notes that "the important point is the continuum in music; each musical style is drawn from the idiom of the preceding period. . . . Music teachers . . . draw their standards of

114

excellence from the preceding generation" (1960:219, 220). All groups must emphasize certain music values above others, and these values tend to be continuous in time, though change can and does occur. The question here, then, is not whether criteria of excellence exist, but rather whether and how they are verbalized.

Verbalization of standards is emphasized by a number of points in the ethnomusicological literature. Elsdon Best, speaking of the Maori, says: "Europeans complain that native songs are tuneless, but no Maori will agree to this, and he will decline to render a song if he be unacquainted with the *rangi* (air or tune) thereof" (1924:II, 137). Densmore says that among the Teton Sioux, "certain men are generally acknowledged to be 'good singers' and certain songs are said to be 'good songs.' This implies the songs and the singers satisfy some standard of evaluation" (1918:59).

More specifically, certain criteria are verbally pinpointed and, for vocal music at least, some of these criteria seem to be the number of songs known, memory for words and music, tempo, voice quality, accuracy of rendition, and the necessity for group or solo singing. Speaking of the Blackfeet, for example, Wissler reports that men are considered to be better singers than women because, partly, they "learn more songs, though the women could do as well, if they had the chance, for women are not supposed to try to learn all the different songs like the men" (1912:264); and Fletcher and LaFlesche note for the Omaha that "men with good voices and memories are the music teachers, who . . . frequently have at their command several hundred tribal songs. . . ." (1893:241). In fact, the number of songs at one's disposal seems to be a very widespread criterion of the "good singer" among North American Indian tribes, and perhaps in other parts of the world as well.

Memory for words and music is emphasized by Densmore for the Chippewa and Sioux when she says ". . . they stated that a good singer must be able to sing a song correctly after hearing it two or three times, he must have a retentive memory. . . ." (1930:653); and for the Maori, Mc-Lean emphasizes the point, reporting that "foremost amongst the qualities demanded of a leader are memory for words. . . ." (1961:59). According to the same source, the leader must "have the ability to maintain an inflexible tempo and to enunciate in rhythmically accurate fashion" (*loc. cit.*).

Accuracy of rendition, both in words and in music, seems to be an especially important verbalized criterion. Among the Flathead Indians, it is agreed that a single error in the course of a song is enough to render the entire song incorrect, and we have previously had occasion to note Herzog's remark that a single error in a single song is enough to invalidate

115

an entire Navaho ceremony. Fletcher and LaFlesche remark that Omaha singers take "great pride in the accuracy of their singing" (1893:11), and McLean discusses the point in some detail for the Maori:

> Associated . . . is an extreme concern for the accurate transmission of the chants. This concern showed itself in recording sessions by a notable reluctance to record without practice . . . and by an outright refusal to record when any uncertainty existed in text or tune. Sometimes a group of singers would practice a song for a long time—perhaps twenty minutes—and then abandon it in favor of another after mistakes had been discovered which could not be put right. . . .
>
> That this concern for accuracy has always been a characteristic of the performance of Maori chants . . . can be seen from the tapus which have traditionally been placed upon memory lapses. A lapse is still widely regarded as an omen of death or disaster for the singer or someone very closely associated with him. . . . Concern . . . can also be seen in the long discussion of the historical background of each song which typically preceded recording and in the detailed announcements which were invariably made concerning the songs by singer or leader immediately before recording. . . . Once singing began, the aim was always to sing both the words and music as near to the original as possible. . . .
>
> Accuracy is ensured by strict and comprehensive rules of performance, the governing principle of which is known as "whakaeke." Whakaeke is a word used primarily for the practice governing the maintenance of strict tempo and accurate rhythm in performance. It can, perhaps, best be briefly defined in this sense as "rhythmic unison." (1961:59, 60)

Another kind of criterion has been expressed by Densmore:

> . . . there must be a convincing quality in a singer's rendition of a song. It has frequently been said to the writer, "So-and-so knows the old songs, but he is not a good singer; he can give you the melody, but it will not be well sung." Into this "convincing quality" there enters another element—the personality of the singer. It is required that a good singer among Indians . . . shall carry with him full confidence in himself, and do his work with authority. (1918:62)

Vocal quality is also sometimes verbalized. Densmore reports that among the Chippewa ". . . a vibrating, or wavering tone, is especially pleasing to the singers. This is difficult for them to acquire and is con-

116

sidered a sign of musical proficiency" (1910:4). Nettl notes that "on the Great Plains of North America a singer with a high voice is considered admirable: in the Pueblos of Arizona and New Mexico a low, growling voice is preferred; . . ." (1956:20). McAllester, speaking of the Apache, contributes still another criterion, that of loudness: "Anyone who can make himself heard is considered to have a good voice. A bad singer is one who does not know the song" (1960:471). Among the Flathead Indians, the following criteria are verbalized:

> In answer to direct questioning as to the attributes of a good singer it was most often stated that such a musician must have "a good voice," and that his lungs and throat must be "good and strong." Considerable emphasis was also placed upon a long and reliable memory; that is, the good singer is one who can recall a great number of songs. Another informant gave the following qualities of a good singer: "A good singer must be long winded. He must be able to sing together with other singers. He must be able to sing loud. A singer must also have good helpers, two or three, to sing the various parts." (Merriam, 1955:11)

The importance of the group is also stressed by Fletcher and LaFlesche for the Omaha (1911:374).

It is difficult to generalize about the standards of excellence in performance on the basis of these varied responses taken from the ethnomusicological literature. We may repeat, however, that some standards must be held by all peoples if there is to be a music style, or even a music system at all, and that enough examples are available to indicate that some, at least, of these standards are verbalized. It is also to be expected that cultures differ in the extent of such verbalization, but at the same time it is very doubtful that any people have nothing whatsoever to say about their music style.

Indeed, the literature of ethnomusicology reveals a good deal of verbalized information on the part of nonliterate peoples about technical details of music structure. Handy reports that in the Marquesas

> . . . three voices are distinguished: *a'o*, deep; *vavena*, medium; and *mauna*, high. Registers between these are designated descriptively as *mauna o te eo i vavena*, just above the medium voice; and *mauna a'e*, very high. There were these three voices for both men and women. . . . Every chant had its established pitch. . . . Thus the *pu'e*, or chant of the creation of the land, was intoned *i a'o oa*, in very deep bass; while the graceful *pipine* for the young maiden was sung in a high register. (1923:314)

117

The Flathead Indians make a distinction between War Dance songs borrowed from other tribes and those considered to be "true" Flathead War Dance songs; the differentiation is based upon the presence of a short coda to the song in borrowed materials and its absence in true Flathead songs.

Among the East African Chopi, Tracey found that the *Hombe*, or xylophone central tone, was a matter much discussed among the musicians and thus a highly conscious, and technical, musical point. Of special interest, however, is the fact that the musicians argued among themselves as to the proper pitch, and the basis for the various claims was not musical but social. Thus, "Katini maintained that, as the Paramount Chief's musician, his was the one and only correct pitch, his was the 'king's note,' vouchsafed to him by his father, grandfather, and ancestors who had been hereditary leaders and composers of the king's music for generations. . . . The other musicians had equally good claims to hold the norm, but they were based upon the patronage of somewhat lesser chiefs" (1948:124). Tracey's list of musical terms (pp. 149-52), as well as his discussion of the extremely complex *Migodo* throughout his book, indicates the probability of a considerable complexity of verbalization of music structure among the Chopi.

In an article dealing with drum-signaling among the Jabo of Liberia, Herzog comments that there is a definite technical terminology for signaling known primarily to musicians.

> Higher and lower registers are called by the terms ke^{22} and Do^3lo^2, respectively. These are unanalyzable stems, said to be the names of two birds which "keep company together and answer each other's calls," the first being a smaller bird with a higher voice, the second a larger bird with a lower voice. In signaling as in music the metaphors are not our "high" and "low;" occasionally "large" and "small" voice is used. The four registers are designated by expressions which combine ke^{22} and Do^3lo^2 with the regular words for "large" and "small.". . .
>
> The terms . . . are applied also to the registers representing higher and lower speech-tones on the horn, the musical bow, the xylophone, the dance-drums, and in signal-calling with the voice; and they are also applied to musical usage, for instance on the native harp. . . . Finally, the terms are used in connection with the device of transposition on the horn and on the musical bow. . . .
>
> Partial as these native theories are, they are not without interest. They indicate a degree of intellectual and technical sophistication

118

which is not rare in "primitive" Africa. They demonstrate how terminology and technical theory may well develop where there is an object or instrument on which an otherwise abstract system can be observed in visible operation; . . . (1945:230-32)

Among the Basongye, there is a variety of terminology used and a considerable range of verbalized attention paid to aspects of music structure. Relatively little attention, however, is given to vocal quality so far as specific terms and discussion are concerned. Singers recognize that there are different vocal sounds, but the distinctions they make are, in our terms, between soft and loud, and high and low. Some singers also see a connection between pitch and muscle tension, but this is not clearly or regularly verbalized. In general, a good voice has the following characteristics: it can be understood; it can be understood over a long distance; the singer can speak the words quickly; the singer can name names correctly in his song. In terms of theoretical discussion, then, the Basongye do not pay a great deal of attention to voice quality or production.

Matters of pitch are treated in approximately the same way, although all musicians recognize the problems involved in reaching the proper pitch for beginning a vocal song. Some singers say there are different starting pitches for different classes of song, but pitch tests simply do not bear this out. A major problem is how a song leader begins his song on a pitch which will conform to his own voice and to those of his chorus. In the case of a xylophone song, the problem is simple, for pitch is taken from the *fumu edimba*, or xylophone central tone. If there are drums, there is some slight evidence that drum pitch provides a reference point, but if this is true, it is not consistent to the point that a song always begins in a given pitch relationship to the drums. If there is no possible reference to a fixed pitch, then the song leader must make a selection on his own, and the Basongye verbalize several possibilities here. First, the musician has his own past experience to draw upon, and the individual musician tends to stress this. Again, some connection is made between pitch and muscle tension; the musician becomes accustomed to the muscle tension which he knows to be correct. One Basongye musician expressed this by saying that he chooses a pitch "which does not make me sweat," and the same musician very logically noted that he comes to know the voices of the people with whom he sings and thus chooses a starting pitch "in the middle" which he knows will suit all the voices. The problem of song starting pitch, then, is recognized by the Basongye, and there are logical explanations for the solutions to it.

In respect to the over-all structure of various kinds of songs, the

Basongye exhibit a certain degree of formal understanding. The derivation of some kinds of xylophone-vocal songs is fixed by a formalized

opening, and thus

rrrrr   ah. . . .

as an introduction indicates that the song is distinctly Bala-Basongye

and modern in terms of time, while

rrrrr   ah   ah

is exclusively Batetela and therefore introduces a song borrowed from the Bala's nearest neighbors to the north. These introductory formulae are seen as strict musical identifications.

The Basongye *mashina* is not, strictly speaking, a song, but is rather a praise name sung to accompaniment of double bell, rattle, and slit drum. However, the singer whose duty and privilege it is to sing these praise names in the village of Lupupa conceives a structure for all such "songs." The *mashina* begins with a falling slide demonstrated as approximately a Major third, to which the person's name is sung. This is followed by the song proper, or *lono*, which closes with the praise name repeated on a falling minor third beginning on the lower tone of the introduction.

Finally, xylophone songs are generally agreed to have a distinct structure of their own. In Basongye xylophone playing, two instruments, pitched differently, are always used together; the instrument of lower pitch plays one of four standard patterns, while the higher pitched instrument carries the song. The Basongye estimate that there are about eight standard xylophone songs, and each can be played with any one of the four bass patterns. A xylophone song begins with the *mitashi* or "starting," which is a patterned introduction played on the upper xylophone in free rhythm against the lower pattern which has already begun; it consists of one of six short patterns, all of which emphasize the *fumu edimba* (literally, "chief of the xylophone") or central tone. After the *mitashi* has been played, the upper xylophone moves to the *lono*, or song proper, and at this point picks up the rhythm already established in the lower xylophone pattern. This is a definite theme which is stated clearly once and then improvised. Finally comes *kuchiba* ("cut"), a very short pattern which consists of playing the low *fumu edimba* once, followed by the *fumu edimba* octaves three or four times. Of these three parts to the xylophone songs, by far the most clear-cut in performance is the *kuchimba*, or closing formula.

Intervals as such are simply not conceptualized by the Basongye, at least in terms which are at all analogous to Western terminology. There is, however, a perfectly good ability to hear different intervals; what

120

complicates the problem is that intervals are not conceived as "distances between tones," and the differentiation between intervals sometimes rests upon what is or is not considered to be musical significance. Thus while every musician recognizes by ear that a Major and minor third are not the same thing, xylophone tuning can use either a Major or minor third at any given specific point where a third is required. Major and minor seconds seem to have the same musical performance value, though musicians are completely capable of distinguishing the two *in abstracto*. Thus what is important is musical significance rather than absolute differences between two intervals, and this, coupled with a lack of concept of intervals as such, makes it extremely difficult to compile accurate information.

Rhythm, on the other hand, is important in Basongye musical thinking, and three major classes of rhythm are differentiated. *Mukwasa* are the rhythms played with a stick, striking either the side of a wooden drum or the highest xylophone key; such rhythms are not meant to have pitch as such, but are simply a rhythmic part of music performance. *Komba* are the rhythms played by the hands on a drum. *Musodiya* are the rhythms made by clicking the tongue against the roof of the mouth, and these are distillations of the combined rhythms of drums and stick. In general speech about rhythm as an over-all concept, the Basongye used the term *mukwasa*.

A pattern related to verbal behavior, but not quite the same thing in music, is the matter of cueing in performance. This refers to the signaling means on the part of a song leader or a drummer, for example, which tells other performers—other musicians or perhaps dancers—what is going to happen next, when the end of a piece is approaching, and so forth. The Flathead use such a signal in the War Dance; when the end of the music is imminent, the drum beat is halved in tempo and greatly increased in volume as a signal to the dancers, who respond perfectly to the cue. In speaking of Ewe drumming in Ghana, Cudjoe points out the great importance of cueing for the proper continuity of the dance:

> The real art of master-drumming does not consist merely in playing beautiful contrasting themes, but in the drummer's ability to introject his themes before the dancer shows obvious signs of waning vigor. A true master must time his utterances to replenish the dancer's physical and aesthetic energy at the right psychological moment. (1953:288)

Discussion of the complex forms of signaling on the part of the West African master drummer has been contributed by A. M. Jones (1959) and King (1961), among many others.

There is, however, another kind of cueing which has received very little attention and which is quite certainly of major importance in many, if not all, cultures. This concerns the devices used to indicate the level of performance which is being introduced, and this has been noted most clearly by Devereux and LaBarre:

> It is seldom recognized that the artist habitually uses certain formal devices for signalling that his product is "art," . . . A very simple example of this is the traditional way of beginning a tale: "Once upon a time" in England, "Cric-crac" in Haiti, and the like. A symphony does not start like a jazz tune. A pornographic novel does not open with the lyrical description of a landscape. . . . An, alas, very common device of signalling that "This is serious art," is to be simply dull, just as the device of countless footnotes and references and an even greater dullness often seek to signal: "This is scholarship." (1961:376)

The two kinds of behavior discussed here—physical and verbal—make up important parts of a music system taken in broadest perspective. Both grow, as does all music behavior, out of the concepts which underlie them. Of the two, we know least about physical behavior; for verbal behavior we have a great deal more raw information, but it has not been put together in a meaningful way. Physical behavior must by its very nature exist to approximately the same degree in all cultures; verbal behavior clearly lies on a continuum which ranges from very little conscious discussion to elaborate theoretical and technical verbalizations. Both are a part of music, but neither has received the attention it deserves.

CHAPTER VII

SOCIAL BEHAVIOR: THE MUSICIAN

A third type of behavior in the music process is that of the musician who, no less than any other individual, is also a member of society. As a musician, he plays a specific role and may hold a specific status within his society, and his role and status are determined by the consensus of society as to what should be proper behavior for the musician. Musicians may form a special class or caste, they may or may not be regarded as professionals, their role may be ascribed or achieved, their status may be high or low or a combination of both. In nearly every case, however, musicians behave socially in certain well-defined ways, because they are musicians, and their behavior is shaped both by their own self-image and by the expectations and stereotypes of the musicianly role as seen by society at large.

The initial problem in assessing the social behavior of the musician is whether he is or is not a specialist. The prevailing view seems to be that musicians in nonliterate societies are not specialists; this has been explicitly stated by Nettl, who writes:

> The typical primitive group has no specialization or professionalization; its division of labor depends almost exclusively on sex and occasionally on age; and only rarely are certain individuals proficient in any technique to a distinctive degree. All women do the same things each day, possess approximately the same skills, have the same interests; and the men's activities are equally common to all. Accordingly, the same songs are known by all the members of the group, and there is little specialization in composition, performance, or instrument-making. (1956:10)

Nettl excepts "some parts of Negro Africa" from this general statement, but his position as stated seems to be accepted by many ethnomusicologists. There are, however, two major objections to this view.
The first is that it is not clear what is meant by "specialization" in this
context, and the second is that the information available to us about
musicians around the world simply does not seem to bear out the contention.

Viewed in broadest perspective, the amount of labor which must be
performed in any given society can either be performed by all members of
the community indiscriminately or it can be divided, with specific kinds of
tasks assigned to specific groups of individuals. There seem to be no
societies in which labor differentiation is absent. The most common
division of labor is made upon sex and age lines, for women's work differs
from men's, and the work of the young differs from that of the old. Labor
may also be divided along lines of caste or guild, membership in associations of other kinds, hereditary position, affiliation with a particular social
group, and so forth. Herskovits assigns the term "division of labor" to
those situations in which ". . . we speak of the splitting up of the total
amount of effort needed to keep the economy of a given society operating
at its customary rate of efficiency" (1952:124-25).

In this situation, "each of the sub-groups whose members perform a
particular aspect of the work may be regarded as specialized in its particular calling, and the kind of labor each performs in achieving this can be
denoted as its 'specialization'" (p. 125). Thus the potter, the palm-nut
cutter, the shaman, or the musician is an economic specialist, performing
particular tasks to which he is assigned by the society, and producing a
particular kind of good, whether tangible or intangible, which contributes
to the total labor necessary for the economic requirements of the society as
a whole. In this sense, the musician is a specialist. Further, he is a
specialist whether paid regularly, given gifts, or simply acknowledged as a
musician, for his labor does differ from that of others in the society. It
seems clear, too, that in all societies individuals exist whose skill at making
music is recognized in some way as being superior to that of other
individuals so that they are called upon, or simply take their "rightful"
place, in musical situations. It is doubtful that there exists any group in
which absolute equality of music performance among all members is either
a fact or a supposition.

If every group holds the music abilities of some of its members to be
greater than that of others, it follows that in some groups such individuals
must stand out more sharply than in others. Here we begin to approach
professionalism, which is usually defined in terms of whether the musician
is paid for and supported economically by his skill. If our criterion be

economic, however, there must be a number of degrees of professionalism; in fact, professionalism seems to run along a continuum from payment in occasional gifts at one end to complete economic support through music at the other. It is difficult to know at what point professionalism begins and ends, and the problem of precise definition is as apparent in our own society as it is in others. Is the student who works his way through the university as a card-carrying member of the musicians' union a professional? In one sense he is, since union membership in Western society is usually considered a major criterion of professionalism; on the other hand, this is not the student's full-time occupation, nor is it necessarily the total means of his support. If we were to assume that professionalism means total devotion to the profession of music and the receipt of total economic income from music, there would be few individuals in any society who could truly be called "professional."

All musicians, then, are specialists, and some musicians are professionals, though the degrees of professionalism vary. There is, however, another criterion of major importance, and this concerns the acceptance of the individual as a specialist or professional. In other words, the "true" specialist is a social specialist; he must be acknowledged as a musician by the members of the society of which he is a part. This kind of recognition is the ultimate criterion; without it, professionalism would be impossible. Although the individual may regard himself as professional, he is not truly so unless other members of the society acknowledge his claim and accord him the role and status he seeks for himself.

Such acknowledgment may be forthcoming in a number of ways. Most visible, of course, is payment—either in the form of the abstraction of wealth represented by money tokens or in the form of basic economic goods—which, if sufficient to support the musician totally, acknowledges complete professionalism. "Payment" may also be in the form of gifts given to the performer, in which case total economic support may not be forthcoming; and in some societies, the musician's contribution may be acknowledged only by recognition of ability unaccompanied by any form of emolument. Complete acceptance, however, depends upon public recognition of the musician as a musician, whether or not this is accompanied by any sort of payment, and the granting by society of the privilege of behaving as a musician is expected to behave.

The ethnomusicological literature reveals examples of all these kinds of acknowledgment. In some societies, the musician seems to be entirely supported by, and because of, his musical activities. Although Nketia speaks of Akan drummers as "unpaid," it seems clear from his account that in former times, at least, they were supported as artists by the political leaders of the state: "In the state, drummers are supposed to live on the bounty of the chiefs for whom they drum, and to remain at the courts of those chiefs as much as possible. . . . In the past . . . most of their time was spent at the court in readiness for any emergencies. Drummers explain . . . : 'In the past you gained something by staying with the chief. You got something to eat . . .'" (1954:40-41). Nketia reports that this situation has now changed, and is changing further, but in the past the drummer seems clearly to have been a sort of political dignitary attached to and supported by the state.

Although the literature is not precise, the *griots* of Senegal are apparently entirely self-supporting through music (Gamble 1957; Gorer 1935). A similar lack of specificity applies to Elkin's discussion of the Songman in Australia (1953), and to Handy's description of the *hoki* of the Marquesas (1923), but in both cases it appears that at least the major portion of the income is derived from music activities. Among the most specific descriptions of a professional role for musicians is that given by Nadel for performing companies in the Nigerian city of Bida.

> Each group is, economically, a closed unit. All earnings are divided equally among the members. This division of the income has no bearing on factors of family or household organization. Individual group-members may contribute to the expenses of their own families; but the "company" is purely a professional association . . .
>
> Drumming in Bida is a full-time occupation (sometimes a drummer practises a little farming besides, but this is very infrequent). . . . The free competition of talent and individuality rather than family tradition determines professional success, and thus the professional association in which the craft organizes itself. Indeed the profession of Bida musicians and drummers represents the only instance in the economic organization of the country of a free association purely on a business basis, and without the support of the framework of kinship and hereditary tradition. (1942:303)

The question, then, of full support for the musician is not answered clearly in the literature, although the evidence, particularly from the griots and from Nadel's description of Bida musicians, indicates that some musicians do depend upon their music activities for total economic support of their way of life.

Much more substantial information exists in respect to partial payments made to musicians, although detailed figures are seldom encountered. It is somewhat surprising to find reports of direct payment for music among North American Indian groups, but Densmore notes several such instances among the Teton Sioux. Thus, "the ceremonial

126

songs must either be composed by the man who sang them, or purchased from some one who had previously held the office and instructed him in its duties. A large amount was paid for the instructions and songs" (1918:101-02). Again, a member of the Elk Society stated that the song for that Society was ". . . still sung at dances and must always be paid for by the man who asks that it be sung" (p. 293). In speaking generally of North American Indians, Densmore also notes that "songs are taught to one person by another, and in the old days it was not unusual for a man to pay the value of one or two ponies for a song" (1926:60). Although it is not clear whether she is speaking for North American Indians in general or for the Cherokee specifically, Fletcher says that "men and women having clear resonant voices and good musical intonation compose the choirs which lead the singing in ceremonies, and are paid for their services" (1907:959). In respect to Cochiti, Lange says "no payment, as such, is involved for teaching songs to another person or tribe. . . . However, when a specific song is taught to a person upon request, it is customary to give a present to the teacher. This is voluntary, and it is considered more a matter of courtesy than a formal business transaction" (1959:311).

In Polynesia, Firth reports "ceremonial presents of bark-cloth, *ufi,* 'coverings' " to the *purotu* who are experts in "the chanting of songs . . . and in dancing" (1939:229), but there is some question as to whether this is to be regarded as payment or as gift exchange in view of McLeod's remark that *ufi* is "not a payment but rather an exchange of goods, whereby a person honoured with a song will offer bark-cloth to the composer, the expert, and the beater of the measure in return for the song. These 'gifts', however . . . tend to be immediately returned in kind, so that the net result is an exchange balance which serves as a public recognition of service or honour on the part of the person to whom the song is directed" (1957:127). Speaking of a company of pipe-players among the Lau in the Solomon Islands, Ivens says: "Fees are paid to the pipers, and the leader might receive a going-away present; even a wife is given him if he asks for one" (n.d.:215). For the African Nupe in village life, Nadel says:

> Drumming in the village thus moves in the framework of a close organization on guild lines. In every larger Nupe village we find a special group of drummers and musicians . . .
>
> Today . . . the drummers, like so many other Nupe craftsmen, complain bitterly about the bad times. Formerly, they told me, they used to be paid 6s. to 8s. a night; to-day they receive 3s. for the night or, for one "song" . . . one kola nut. . . . The drummers, who once devoted only their spare time to farming, are

127

to-day mainly farmers and carry on their old profession only as a sideline. (1942:301-02)

While some musicians thus seem to be full-time professionals, and others receive some payment in the form of money tokens or ceremonial gifts, still others apparently practice music for no payment whatsoever, though they are still acknowledged as musicians. This seems to be most evident among North American Indians. Herzog says: "We seldom find the figure of a singer or musician as a member of a specialized profession, though his skill or good memory may be among the indispensable prerequisites for the office of priest or a curing doctor" (1942:204). Much the same point of view is taken by Roberts:

> So far as I know at present, no Indian group recognizes a special musician class unless it is the Southern Indians mentioned by Fletcher. Gifted individuals are recognized, and may lead the choruses or compose most of the songs which eventually become part of the tribal heritage and ceremonial equipment. (1936:9)

More specific is Richardson, speaking of the Kiowa:

> Proficiency in special skills might heighten distinction. Lacking the aspects previously mentioned, [wealth, war record, kindred, etc.] no profession not even curing skill, could put one in the ranks of the really great. No skill was a specialized profession, for every man in the tribe did his own hunting and probably went on the war path. The following sample skills are listed roughly in decreasing order of distinction: curing powers, deer-surround power, composer and singer of songs, orator, storyteller, surgeon (no power involved), artist, dancer, eagle-catching, arrow-making, jockey, and horse breaker. (1940:14)

Among the Flathead Indians, much the same sort of situation exists. "Good singers" are known, recognized, and appreciated, but they are not celebrated for their abilities, nor are they paid for their performances unless it is by outsiders. The best musicians are simply expected to lead the singing and play the drum, and these same musicians are consistently named outstanding by other members of the society. Not only are the musicians unpaid, but neither do they receive gifts for their services; informants are unanimous in making this assertion. Thus the Flathead musician remains acknowledged, and so a specialist in the broadest sense, but he is not a professional or economic specialist supported by his music.

Information from other world areas concerning specialization without payment is meagre and in most cases can be cited only in default of specific information. Thus Peter Buck speaks in some detail of specialists in music and dance in Mangareva but omits mention of payment (1938), while Rout speaks of "the making of musical instruments" as a "skilled profession" but does not inform us whether compensation is forthcoming for the specialist (1926:75).

While payment to musicians ranges from full economic support to no support at all, very little detailed information is available on the subject, and it is probable that within any given society there exists a range of customary behavior at any given time. Among the Basongye, five classes of musician are differentiated. The highest class, reserved for the male professional, is *ngomba*, followed by the *ntunda* who is an acknowledged male professional player of the slit drum. The *mwiimbi* is a male rattle and double-gong player, while the *nyimba* is a song leader, and the *abapula* are members of a singing group. The *abapula* are never paid, though in an exceptional case they may divide a gift given by a stranger or certain notables, and the *nyimba* shares in a like manner in any such windfall. The *mwiimbi* and *ntunda* are paid for their services but are not full-time economic specialists, while the *ngomba* is considered to earn his full living from music. Among women only the *kyambe*, the female professional of highest classification, earns any substantial sum of money from her music activities.

In the Basongye village of Lupupa in 1959-60, there were four out-standing musicians: of them, two were *ntunda* and one a *mwiimbi*; the fourth, a xylophone player, held an unrecognized status, for the xylophone is of relatively recent reintroduction and the players have not yet been admitted into the classification of "true" musicians. In addition to these musicians, the village was visited from time to time by an *ngomba* who traveled throughout the area. Although it is not possible to give total figures for the income of these musicians during the year, special occasions call for special payments. Thus at a major funeral, the presence of an *ngomba* is an absolute requirement; he is hired at a flat fee (in 1959, about 400 francs, or $8.00) and in addition receives gifts of money from all those involved in the funeral, i.e., the entire village. In the seven-day ceremony of a major funeral in late September and early October of 1959, the *ngomba* had a gross income of approximately 1400 francs ($28.00) plus two chickens (valued at about 20 francs apiece) and one piece of cloth (valued at about 120 francs), for a total of 1560 francs, or about $31.20. The significance of this figure gains emphasis from the fact that the average income for a male Lupupan is about $100 per year, and thus the *ngomba* realized almost a third of this amount from a single funeral. At the same time, one *ntunda*, whose role was less significant in the funeral, received 120 francs, one piece of cloth, and one chicken for a

129

total of about $5.60, and the *mwiimbi* received one chicken and one-half piece of cloth for a total of approximately $1.60. In addition to these direct economic benefits, all the musicians involved received the customary free food aand drink dispensed by the family of the deceased.

Of most importance to the present discussion, however, is the fact that none of these musicians, including the *ngomba*, felt free to depend entirely upon his musicianship for his living. The *ngomba* and the four lesser musicians all kept fields for cultivation, tilled by their wives or other family members and themselves, and in addition two worked regularly for me, one worked at raffia basketry, and the fourth had an additional economic skill. Indeed, except for the *ngomba* and one of the *ntunda*, the major source of income derived from non-musical activities; yet all were accorded the respect of some title in the professional scale. Thus in this particular village, at least, and including the one true professional, none of the musicians could be called full-time economic specialists, for none depended exclusively upon his musicianship to support himself and his family. The *ngomba* came closest to professionalism, the other four far less close. Yet it should be repeated that all were considered to be professionals of one degree or another.

The problems of specialization and professionalism are difficult ones primarily because of the lack of information concerning this important aspect of music behavior. Yet its effect is clearly of major impact; the role and status of the individual, as well as the highly practical matter of means of gaining the essentials for sustaining life, depend to a considerable extent on the degree of professionalism attained and particularly the concepts held by society about it. Complete professionals seem relatively rare in nonliterate societies, but it is not always easy to judge what is or is not complete professionalism, for specialization may not always depend upon the presence or absence of economic gain. The Basongye example indicates the possibility that other societies may also contain within the ranks of musicians some who approach full-time specialty, some who may be complete specialists, some who gain additional income from music, and some who are rewarded in no other way than perhaps a slightly increased prestige in the society.

If we can assume that the role of musician is to some extent singled out in every society along with other roles, there must be ways in which society assures that the requisite number of people is recruited to fill the role. To some extent, we have spoken of this problem in discussing folk evaluations concerning the inheritance of "talent" and the way in which this influences the potential supply of artists in a given society. The question of "talent" impinges closely upon the concept of ascribed and achieved

130

statuses and roles suggested by Ralph Linton, who defines the terms as follows:

Ascribed statuses are those which are assigned to individuals without reference to their innate differences or abilities. They can be predicted and trained for from the moment of birth. The *achieved* statuses are, as a minimum, those requiring special qualities, although they are not necessarily limited to these. They are not assigned to individuals from birth but are left open to be filled through competition and individual effort. (1936:115)

In these terms, and judging from the literature, it seems that the role of musician is often ascribed rather than achieved. The Basongye concept that children of musicians are more likely to become musicians than are children of non-musicians is essentially a means of ascribing a role. Even the Anang concept which holds all individuals to be equally talented at birth is a broad means of ascription, for it makes potential artists of all children. It is interesting to note that Dennison Nash, in his excellent study of the composer (1961), gives considerable space to ascription of the role of composer and none to achievement as such. Among the Basongye, in addition to the general concept of individual inheritance of ability, a young man is occasionally chosen by the council of notables to fulfill the role of *ntunda,* and there is relatively little area for objection on his part. For the Akan of Ghana, Nketia points out that ". . . the office of drummer and drummer-chief is usually apportioned to 'households' of commoners or 'households' of kings' sons. It is the duty of these households to provide the artists and the servants. Accordingly duties like drumming or the blowing of horns are passed on from one generation to another within the 'household' " (1954:39).

On the other hand, among North American Indians the role of musician seems often to be achieved rather than ascribed. Among the Flathead, not only are musicians not ascribed in any known way, but it is made quite difficult to achieve the role. Youngsters who wish to sing and drum are given no training and must be extremely persistent in their efforts to join an established singing group. The outstanding Flathead musician at present details a chronicle of his efforts as a youth to join the singing, his rejection by the singers, and his return time and time again until finally he was accepted through his own efforts to learn songs.

Blacking has discussed this problem among the Venda, though he does not use the ascribed-achieved terminology. He says:

Whereas in our own society, an individual's role as musician and dancer is generally voluntary, in Venda society almost everyone is

131

compelled to fulfill some musical role or series of roles; and only when the accompanying social role is acquired by personal choice, can the musical role be chosen because of a taste for music. Some Venda would even go so far as to say that there is no musical role which can be filled as the result of personal choice, since even personal choice in these matters is controlled by external factors such as dreams. This is tantamount to saying that Venda musicians are born, not made; but there are certain qualifications of this statement that must be mentioned. (1957:45-6)

Among these qualifications Blacking notes that there is evidence to indicate that "the accident of noble birth" increases the chances of a person's becoming a musician. Further, "self-confidence and lack of inhibition are important factors in the development of a dancer or singer in Venda society," and Blacking sees a connection between these characteristics and membership in "privileged classes." While these factors apply more to women than to men, the latter "seem to thrive as musicians as a result of being social misfits." Good male musicians "are often rather sad, lonely, introvert characters," and "one might almost go so far as to say that in Venda society, the outstanding musicians are often people who depart from the innate nature of their sex, that the best female musicians are aggressively masculine, and the best males are rather apologetically feminine." Blacking concludes: "At any rate, the original dictum, 'musicians are born, not made,' might be modified to suit Venda society:—'Musicians are made according to their birth' " (p. 46).

Finally, some mention must be made here of the ascription of the role of musician to the blind. This seems to be a common event in Africa where many blind persons make their way as professional musicians, but so far as is known, no specific study of the phenomenon exists for this area. Both Harich-Schneider (1959) and Malm (1959) speak briefly of the role of the blind as musicians in Japan, and Elbert gives some attention to a blind musician, Moa Tetua, in writing of music in the Marquesas (1941). The problem is an extremely interesting and suggestive one, but too little is known to allow us to postulate any kind of correlation between the blind and the ascription of the musician's role.

The question of ascribed versus achieved status and role is intimately related to the learning process which will be discussed in the following chapter. The difficulty of treating it is again referable to the lack of documented information in the literature, a lack which must be remedied if we are to understand the ways in which societies provide for a supply of musicians.

Our information concerning the requirements for becoming a

musician, the duties of the musician, and the expectations of the musician by others is equally limited, though the fragments of knowledge which can be gleaned are of substantial interest.

Thus Cudjoe reports that among the Ewe, "all would-be drummers must possess an exceedingly sensitive ear, a good memory and sense of timing, as well as considerable powers of observation" (1953:284), and Nketia notes that among the Akan, "drumming . . . is the business of a few individuals in various communities holding the office in the state, or appointed by common consent of a band or an association to perform for all because of the skill, knowledge and reliability they have shown" (1954:34). The expectations of society for the drummer are also noted by Nketia:

> These drummers and indeed all others who drum in Akan societies, perform not when they feel like it, but rather when directed by custom and tradition or by corporate interest—the interest of bands, associations, village and town communities or states and chiefs for whom they drum.
>
> The different organisations of drumming make varying demands on their drummers in skill and service. . . .
>
> All drummers, whether of bands or states, are expected to know their art and the duties required of them, to maintain a reasonable standard of performance and to be ready to perform whenever called upon to do so. (1954:35)

These expectations shade into the specific duties of the musician in Akan society; similar kinds of information are given for Polynesia by Firth (1939:229) and McLeod (1957:120). But in general, answers to questions of this nature are not to be found in the literature.

Among the most complex and fascinating aspects of the behavior of the musician is the problem of his social status, both as seen by himself and as judged by the rest of society. Again, the ethnomusicological literature seems to contain relatively few careful studies of this question, but what is available indicates that the status of the musician can best be placed upon a continuum running from high to low status. The problem, however, is more complicated than might appear, for in some societies at least—and probably in more than the literature indicates clearly—status of the musician is not a simple and clear-cut proposition of either high or low. We have already called attention to the remarks of Richardson, Roberts, and Thurow, all of whom report that the musician in the particular society of their interest has very little determinable status, retaining rather what might be called respect of a limited tangible nature on the part of the people for whom they sing or play.

There are, however, some very definite reports of the ascription of high status to musicians. Among the Ibo of Nigeria, Basden says:

> Instrumental soloists of any reputation, especially performers on the awja and ekwe, are treated with great respect, their services are in demand and their reward is generally liberal. Talent is recognized and many artists become very popular. . . . The leader of a chorus is accorded much the same honour amongst the Ibos as that granted to the minstrel in ancient days in England. (1921: 190)

Gbeho, speaking of Ghana in general, says that "musicians are treated with reverence, and they have a tremendous influence over the rest" (1952:31). Rattray (1923, 1954) and Nketia (1954) both comment on the status and privileges of the Ashanti drummer and note that he is considered to be close to the gods and therefore a person to be treated with dignity and respect. In the cults of Bahia, Brazil, Herskovits says that the drummers are "respected" (1944:477), and Albert B. Lewis, generalizing for Melanesia, reports that "the recitatives with humming accompaniment and chorus are often improvised accounts of recent events, and a skilled singer of this kind is held in high honor" (1951:169). Roberts and Swadesh note that the Nootka master singer role is considered "very honorable" (1955:203), and other similar examples could be cited. From such descriptions, however, it is often difficult to tell precisely what is meant by "respect" or "reverence," and it is to be suspected that the picture is much more complicated than might appear.

Instances of musicians holding a low status in society are far less frequent in the literature, and in such cases there is a definite question as to whether the attitude toward musicians is not ambivalent and whether musicians may not in fact occupy a special situation in which behavior not tolerated in others is considered acceptable, or is at least tolerated, for them. That is, the musician may be assigned a special status in society which allows him certain privileges not given to others because of his importance to society at large. We can approach this hypothesis through Malinowski's report on the behavior, and its consequences, of a Trobriands singer:

> Mokadayu, of Okopukopu, was a famous singer. Like all of his profession he was no less renowned for his success with ladies. "For," say the natives, "the throat is a long passage like the wilu (vulva), and the two attract each other." "A man who has a beautiful voice will like women very much and they will like

him." Many stories are told of how he slept with all the wives of the chief in Olivilevi, how he seduced this and that married woman. For a time, Mokadayu had a brilliant and very lucrative career as a spiritualistic medium, extraordinary phenomena happening in his hut, especially dematerializations of various valuable objects thus transported to the spirit land. But he was unmasked, and it was proved that the dematerialized objects had merely remained in his own possession.

Then there came about the dramatic incident of his incestuous love with his sister. She was a very beautiful girl, and, being a Trobriander, she had, of course, many lovers. Suddenly she withdrew all her favours and became chaste. The youth of the village, who confided in each other their banishment from her favours, decided to find out what was the matter. It soon appeared that, whoever might be the privileged rival, the scene must be laid in her parental house. One evening when both parents were away, a hole was made in the thatch and through it the discarded lovers saw a sight which shocked them deeply; brother and sister were caught in flagranti delictu. A dreadful scandal broke out in the village, which, in olden days would certainly have ended in suicide of the guilty pair. Under present conditions they were able to brave it out and lived in incest for several months till she married and left the village. (1925:203)

There are a number of striking points in this passage. In the first place, the musician has obviously indulged in behavior which is not normally acceptable to the Trobrianders—he is a thief, a charlatan, an adulterer, and, worst, guilty of secret and then open incest. But at the same time, the society apparently has ready-made excuses for his behavior: "the throat is a long passage like the *wilu* (vulva), and the two attract each other," and thus it appears, at least, that the musician is expected to behave in certain ways which are outside that sanctioned for other people. Most important is the fact that Mokadayu was apparently allowed to escape punishment for his transgressions; at least Malinowski does not make mention of any penalties. Although it is not possible to generalize from this single brief passage, it appears that the role of singer, in this case, carries with it certain privileges to behave in ways not normally tolerated by the society, and with impunity. Thus the hypothesis may be advanced that the musician, in view of the license allowed him, seems to be of such special importance that he must be retained in the society even at considerable social cost.

This general situation concerning the musician's role, status, and behavior is strongly echoed in the practice of the Basongye. Basongye

135

informants—both musicians and non-musicians—present to the stranger a stereotype of the musician and his behavior which indicates a low status. Musicians are the butt of jokes in the society; they are considered to be lazy, heavy drinkers, debtors, impotents (an extremely disgraceful and humiliating state), hemp smokers, physical weaklings, adulterers, and poor marriage risks. The Basongye feel that musicians exist only for music and that other aspects of life are not important to them. Of all individuals questioned—male and female, professional and non-professional musicians, musicians and non-musicians—but a single individual reported that he wished his child to become a musician. The reason for this negative attitude is that musicians are considered to be people who can be ordered about; they work for other people and not for themselves, and thus they are often equated with the *lukunga*, or village messenger, whose status is lowest among the notables.

Stereotypes are notoriously inaccurate, but in the case of the four village musicians the attributed characteristics were remarkably apt. All four were definitely considered to be lazy, heavy drinkers, and poor marriage risks. One of the musicians was the outstanding debtor of the village and at the same time the single known impotent; another was the constant butt of jokes about his physical weakness, and it was often suggested to him that he let his wife do some job which demanded physical strength. At least one, and probably two of the musicians were hemp smokers, and at least two were known adulterers. Thus the facts fit the stereotype to a considerable degree.

The question, then, is that given this behavior, which violated Basongye standards for the normal man, why should the villagers tolerate the presence of the musician? In fact, the reaction to the facetious suggestion that these ne'er-do-wells should be banished was one of extreme seriousness and even real horror. Life in a village without musicians is not to be considered, and people spoke of leaving the village were no musicians present. This reaction cannot be taken lightly, for the bonds of kinship and economics which tie an individual to his village are extremely difficult to break. The fact of the matter is that without musicians a village is incomplete; people want to sing and dance, and a number of important village activities simply cannot be carried out without musicians. The villagers are unanimous in stating that musicians are extremely important people; without them, life would be intolerable. Thus the attitude toward musicians among the Basongye is ambivalent: on the one hand, they can be ordered about, and they are people whose values and behavior do not accord with what is considered proper in the society; on the other hand, their role and function in the village are so important that life without them is inconceivable.

136

There is considerable evidence to indicate that the implications of this situation do not escape the Basongye musician. It often seemed difficult in the field situation to understand why the villagers continued to lend money to one particular musician, for the chances of repayment were extremely slim, and everyone knew this; yet the debtor calmly and confidently went on approaching people for loans and receiving them. True, he was constantly berated, and what money he did earn was often forcibly removed from his pockets, but he had no particular difficulty in obtaining further loans. He was, however, the only man in the village who could sing the praise names of the male villagers in the esoteric linguistic combination of Kisongye and Otetela required. Whether consciously or unconsciously, he was aware of this fact and so were the villagers—he was a musician, and a special one at that, and therefore his behavior was tolerated.

In fact, the role of the musician, at least in this Basongye village, was conceived as deviant, and in a society which lays much stress upon normality there was but one other comparable role. This was the *kitesha*, somewhat analogous to the *berdache* in Plains Indian society; among the Basongye, the *kitesha* is a man who avoids male responsibility by taking the female role, although homosexuality is not a part of the associated behavior. Both the musician and the *kitesha* play roles in the society which allow them to behave in ways not tolerated from an ordinary citizen. The musician, though low in status, is in the last analysis a person of very high importance, allowed to follow a role which puts him outside the requirements of normal behavior, and allowed to capitalize upon it. Even in those cases when he goes too far, punishment may be waived, as in the case of a visiting professional musician who committed adultery with the wife of one of the high village notables but who was forgiven by the outraged husband and allowed to continue on his wandering way.

There is some evidence, at least, to suggest that this pattern of low status and high importance, coupled with deviant behavior allowed by the society and capitalized upon by the musician, may be fairly widespread and perhaps one of several which characterizes musicianly behavior in a broad world area. In the pattern noted for the Basongye there is more than a casual echo of the jazz musician in the United States, who is often considered to be lazy, a heavy drinker, a debtor, a user of narcotics, a physical weakling, an adulterer, and a poor marriage risk. Although this stereotype, as is almost always the case, exceeds actuality, and although the situation in respect to the jazz musician is at present in a state of flux, studies in the past have tended toward confirmation of this behavior as a way of life. There is reason to believe, as well, that the jazz musician is aware of his social status, and that he capitalizes on it to indulge himself

137

in certain kinds of deviant behavior. Within what has been called the jazz community (Merriam and Mack 1960), which is comprised of the jazz musician and his admirers, such deviant behavior is not only tolerated but also admired, and the importance of the musician is high. In this case, however, the society at large is not so impressed as is Basongye society, and the jazz musician has suffered considerable punishment, for example, for narcotics addiction. This may well be due to differences between a small undifferentiated society and a large differentiated one. If we use as a standard of comparison the jazz community itself, which forms a group much more comparable to Basongye than American society as a whole, the attitude toward musicians and the general musicianly pattern are of a very high degree of similarity.

Other examples of a similar nature found in the ethnomusicological literature include the griot or gewel caste of the Senegambia in Africa. Those who have written on the griots are unanimous in assigning them to a low status in society, though the precise designation differs. Gamble, for example, speaking of the "hierarchical system of social classes" among the Wolof, divides the society into three major groupings: the freeborn, which is subdivided into royal lineages, nobles, and peasants; the "low-caste groups," including smiths, leatherworkers, "praisers," musicians, and so forth; and slaves, a class also subdivided into two further groups (1957:44). Bodiel speaks of five classes among the Wolof, including the freeborn, the jewelers and blacksmiths, the shoemakers, the weavers, and, finally, the griots; he considers slaves to be outside the class system (1949:12). Both Gamble and Bodiel list the classes in descending order of importance, and no matter what the precise division these and all other authorities are agreed that the griots are part of the lowest caste, with the exception of slaves. This position is emphasized by burial customs for griots imposed by society at large; according to Gamble, among others, it is believed that if a griot corpse is buried in the ground, "crops would fail or the fish die" (p. 45), and therefore griot bodies are "buried" in the hollowed trunks of the baobab tree. Considerable amounts of skeletal material recovered from baobabs, and presumably of griot origin, have been the subject of investigation in Senegal in recent times (Mauny 1955).

There is also considerable evidence for the high importance of griots in Wolof society. Gorer writes:

> Griots are by tradition attached to families; they are family
> jesters and buffoons . . . whose duty it is to keep the company
> amused; they are the family bards, who learn and recite the family
> and national history . . . ; they are family magicians, who must

be present at all ceremonies and whose advice must be taken; they are the first to hold the newborn baby and the last to touch the corpse; they are the actual recipients of most gifts given to their patrons; they are the spiritual mentors and guides of the young . . . ; they console the mourner and comfort the downcast with music and song; they are the family's official boasters, singing their merits, triumph and wealth on public occasions; they are lower than the meanest servants and often richer and more power-ful than the master. (1935:55-6)

The griots also are allowed to behave in ways not permissible for others in the society. Gamble writes that "in the old days gewél had the right to mock anybody and could use insulting language without any action being taken against them. If a reward for their praises was not forthcoming or was considered insufficient, they were liable to switch to outspoken abuse, in consequence of which they were greatly feared and normally amassed considerable wealth. In the past they had a reputation for drunkenness and licentiousness and were long resistant to Islam" (1957:45). In another context, Gamble adds that the gewel "have the utmost freedom to behave and speak as they want. The women of low-caste groups can act in an outrageously flirtatious manner, make risque remarks, and when dancing, perform the indecent actions and postures for which Wolof dancing is notorious" (p. 75). Writing in 1882, Bérenger-Féraud notes:

On devine que le Griot use et abuse de ce qu'il est bien recu partout pour soigner ses intérêts et accroître ses bénéfices; il a l'étrange licence de pouvoir passer partout; d'aller en temps de guerre d'un camp à un autre sans rien craindre; et de chaque côté, lorsqu'il est entre deux peuplades ennemies, on le comble de faveurs pour s'attirer sa bienveillance; . . . Il fournit aux uns et aux autres, mais surtout à celui qui sait le mieux le récompenser, les renseignements qui souvent font que c'est l'ami du Griot qui est le plus fort dans la paix comme dans la guerre. (1882:276)

Bérenger-Féraud also points out the high political importance of the griots, as well as re-emphasizing the power held over the population at large through ridicule.

The griot pattern is clearly a variation upon those behaviors which characterize both the Basongye and the American jazz musician, although most of its aspects seem to be more heavily accentuated. Thus the griots form a definite caste, which is not true of Basongye or American jazz musicians, although the general status of the latter groups is low. The importance of the griots also seems to be higher, their deviant behavior

139

perhaps more pronounced, and their power in daily life stronger. These, however, are matters of intensity rather than kind; in general the patterns are very similar.

A final example, somewhat less clear than those noted above, concerns the Arioi society of Polynesia. Early writers such as William Ellis (1833) described the Arioi as "a sort of strolling players, and privileged libertines, who spent their days in travelling from island to island, and from one district to another, exhibiting their pantomimes, and spreading a moral contagion throughout the society" (I:182). Later writers, such as Williamson have tended to de-emphasize the "objectionable" aspects of the Arioi company and to stress the religious foundation on which the group was based. It is difficult to ascertain whether the Arioi society was held in low esteem, but there is much evidence to indicate that the behavior of its members fell outside what was considered normal. They apparently had little respect for the property of others and took what they wished without opposition (Williamson 1939: 127), and their deviant sex behavior was constantly remarked upon by chroniclers (pp. 130-32). At the same time, they seem to have been of considerable importance to society at large, and Williamson writes that "they played a part in great feasts and festivals, at birth ceremonies and marriages, at the inauguration of a king, and at certain ceremonies connected with war" (pp. 126-27). The Arioi seem, then, to fall into the general pattern, though the evidence in this connection is not so strong as in other cases.

This pattern of low status and high importance, deviant behavior and the capitalization of it, cannot be said to characterize the musician in all societies, but it seems to be a basic organization for a number of groups in a rather remarkable world distribution. While it is to be expected that other patterns will emerge, this one is clearly of considerable importance. It is to be hoped that further research will disclose its actual geographic extent, as well as its social significance.

Further evidence concerning the behavior of the musician is gained through an understanding of his position in those societies in which he forms a definite social group with his fellow musicians. We have previously had occasion to note that such social groupings are not found in all societies; thus among the North American Indians there seems to be little evidence of any kind of special social grouping for the musician. In other parts of the world, however, special groups are formed and are distinguished from the society at large through a number of devices.

Among the Basongye, there is little evidence for a social group as such, simply because the number of musicians in any given community is too small. Yet it is clear that the musician is distinguished from his fellow villager by his behavior and through the stereotypes of him as a musician

140

held both by himself and by the society at large. Thus the Basongye musicians do form a distinct social group, but because of its size it is not one of high importance. It should be pointed out, however, that one of the attributes of an organized smaller group within a larger society is a hierarchy of distinctions made within the membership; this the Basongye musicians do, as evidenced by the grades of "professional" musicians recognized within their ranks.

A more clear-cut example of a distinct social group is provided by the griots who, as we have seen, are consistently referred to as a "caste" within the larger society. This grouping is emphasized by what appears to be an endogamous marriage situation imposed by those outside the caste: Gorer says, for example, "the griots form a special caste and never by any chance marry with anyone except another griot. They are outcasts from all religions and can never be buried in consecrated ground. The position is a hereditary one, and unless the child of a griot emigrates he can find no other occupation. They are looked down upon by the rest of the population as slightly untouchable" (1935:55). Gamble adds that "no one other than a gewel would play a traditional musical instrument" (1957:45), and Nikiprowetzky emphasizes the isolation of the griots in noting that they "have always aroused feelings of fear or contempt" (1962:n.p.). Bérenger-Féraud remarks, too, that the griot caste is subdivided into three groups, including the singers, the players of "guitar" or "violin," and the drummers, and indicates that these internal groups in themselves form a hierarchy in descending order of importance and prestige (1882:268-69).

Among groups of musicians for whom detailed information is available, American jazz musicians have in the past formed what is perhaps as tight and closed a group as is known in the literature. What sets the jazz community apart is that not only do the professionals constitute a group, but their public is included in it in varying degrees. The distinctive behavior patterns which characterize the group seem clearly to revolve about a central theme—the isolation of the group from society at large, an isolation which is almost equally psychological, social, and physical. Jazz musicians and their public tend to cluster together, to hold antisocial attitudes, and to segregate themselves physically; this general behavior stems from three major sources: "(1) the rejection of jazz and the jazz musician by the general public; (2) the fact that the jazz musician, whether by choice or not, is isolated from the public by the nature of his occupation, as is his group of admirers as well since it is associated with the musician; and (3) by the nature of his occupation, the musician (and his public by association) is faced with a dilemma regarding the nature of his art and, in his own view, is expected to be both a creative artist and a commercial entertainer, contradictory roles which lead to confusion in

141

respect to status" (Merriam and Mack 1960:213). The jazz community is further marked by a number of observable characteristics, most of which serve as further manifestations of the isolation of the group. Among these are the use of special language, greeting rituals, titles, and dress; folk plots in stories which are traded among members; a lack of race prejudice, in former times, at least, although this has changed in the past few years; the reinforcing jam session, although this, too, has tended to change; and other characteristics. It is partially the nature of the special social group itself which contributes to the values held by its members:

> . . . while from the standpoint of the outsider, the members of the jazz community appear fearful and withdrawn, leading an abnormal life which deliberately rejects many of the things popularly considered "good" in our culture, to the jazzman and to his devoted followers it is a good and satisfying life filled with many rewards. And the fact that these rewards come from his own group is perhaps most satisfying of all, since it is their judgment which he considers valid and their terms which shape his life. To himself and to his followers, the jazz musician is a creative artist, and he participates fully in the satisfactions and thrills of creativity. In his own terms, then, his life is rich and fullbodied, for creativity of his own special kind is, in his judgment, the most important thing in life. (Merriam and Mack 1960:220)

It is germane to note in connection with the jazz community that Kolaja and Wilson have also stressed the isolation of the artist and poet in American society, emphasizing that "both pictures and poems, whatever their differences, may be evidence of a position of specialization in which American painters and poets find themselves today. It is our opinion that this specialization also brings about the feeling of isolation that is so significantly projected into contemporary American painting and poetry" (1954:45).

According to Williamson, the Arioi Society is strongly marked by differentiations from society at large. Evidence is provided by the behavior of the members and the special roles they fulfill, as well as the strong internal structure of the group. Seven distinct ranks or grades are isolated, and the candidate is required to pass a very definite set of entrance rituals based upon specific criteria of eligibility (1939:114-21).

In less detail, evidence from other parts of the world points to similarly exclusive or at least socially-recognized groupings of musicians. Thus for the Afro-Bahian drummer, Herskovits reports that "Drummers form a group of their own, and regard each other with the friendly respect of professionals who acknowledge one another's competence" (1944:489-

90), and adds that they have their own special personal names as well as musicians' games, and that they are drawn together through their sharing of a special knowledge, i.e., the intricacies of music. Besides the particular behavior and status which mark off drummers in Akan society, Nketia notes that they may live in special quarters:

> The traditional quarters of drummers, that is, the section of the town in which the households of drummers live is called akyerɛ made, and people who live in those quarters . . . are identified as akyerɛmadefɔ, the drummer-group, though in the modern set up, the quarters are occupied by non-drummers as well. Not all drummers, however, live in those quarters. In many states, drummer-groups live in village satellites of the principal towns; these villages come to be associated with the particular groups. (1954:39)

As musicians may be set apart as a group, so may music and music behavior be used to identify specific groups in the society. Crowley points out, for example, that "Trinidad is probably the only place in the Western world where a teen-ager's position in his gang is determined by his musical skills. As a result, well over half the urban Trinidadian young men can play the steel drums skillfully enough not to be criticized by their peers" (1959b:34). Coleman speaks frequently of music as a part of adolescent society in the United States:

> As if it were not enough that such an institution as today's high school exists segregated from the rest of society, there are other things that reinforce this separateness. For example, adolescents have become an important market, and special kinds of entertainment cater almost exclusively to them. Popular music is the most important. . . .
>
> Rock and roll is most popular with both boys and girls. . . .
>
> The hedonism of popular music, for example, is found nowhere to such a degree as among adolescents. . . .
>
> . . . music and dancing provide a context within which they may more easily meet and enjoy the company of the opposite sex. . . . (1961:4, 22, 126, 236)

The formation of a sub-culture based on music, as well as the identification of a sub-culture partially through music, seem to be fairly widespread both in nonliterate and Western societies, and particular kinds of roles and behavior for the musician are equally widely distributed. Such problems are of high importance if we are to understand the behavior of the musician as a human phenomenon. To what extent and in what areas of the world is the musician a specialist? What constitutes professionalism in given societies? Is the role of the musician ascribed or achieved, and what are the requirements for being a musician? What is his social status, and do the patterns of role and status discussed here apply more widely than we may at present be led to believe? Who the musician is, how he behaves, what society thinks of him, and why these patterns emerge are questions of vital importance to a thorough understanding of music as human behavior.

It remains to be noted that as the musician is distinguished by certain kinds of social behavior, so is his audience. We have previously discussed the physical response of the listener, but his behavior is also shaped by the nature of the social event in which music occurs. Thus Blacking, for example, makes the following remarks concerning audience behavior among the African Venda:

> Reactions to the music of initiation, therefore, differ considerably according to the age, sex, and social status of the listener. At the end of *tshikanda*, for instance, there is much singing, dancing, and playacting: some of the little girls who sit with their mothers may be interested enough to imitate some dance steps, or even to play the drum when there is an interval in the proceedings: the older women and especially those in charge, dance and sing loudly and enjoy every moment: in marked contrast to their enthusiasm are the reactions of the initiates, for whose instruction and edification the performance is held; when not singing or dancing, which they do with expressionless faces, they crouch on the ground, perhaps doodling aimlessly with a piece of stick. Their indifference to the music is of course partly conditioned by the role which they are playing; as initiates they are expected to be without personality or feelings—except at certain moments, as when the older women sing a song which is supposed to induce them to shed tears. . . .
>
> There are, too, cases where people of different sex, age and social status have the same reactions to the same music. (1957: 44-5).

Thus the listener responds socially in different ways to music, depending both upon the situation and his role in it. The primary question here is whether it is the music or the entire situation which shapes the listener's behavior, and we shall have occasion to return to this matter in speaking both of symbolism and of the problem of aesthetics.

CHAPTER VIII

LEARNING

In viewing music sound as the end result of a dynamic process, we have pointed out that underlying concepts lead to actual behavior which in turn shapes structure and presentation. It is obvious, however, that concepts and behaviors must be learned, for culture as a whole is learned behavior, and each culture shapes the learning process to accord with its own ideals and values. Further, learning represents the last step in the model presented in Chapter II of this book, for music sound is judged in terms of its acceptability to society as a whole. Thus music sound feeds back upon the concepts held about music, which in turn alters or reinforces behavior and eventually changes or strengthens music practice. Learning, then, is vital not only in the sense that music behavior, taken as a unit, must be learned, but also because it forms the link that makes the process of music-making dynamic and ever-changing.

To speak about the entire process of accumulating music knowledge is patently impossible, for it would involve an understanding of all the mechanisms of learning in all societies. We can, however, discuss with profit what information is available to us concerning those processes whereby music as sound, as well as musicianly behavior, are transmitted from generation to generation, or between individuals of the same generation.

In order to describe the process of cultural learning and to distinguish it from the more specific social learning, Herskovits has suggested the term "enculturation." Other terms such as "culturation" and "culturalization" have also been proposed, and some anthropologists simply use the sociological term "socialization," but for present purposes "enculturation"

145

has the highest utility. It is defined as "the aspects of the learning experience . . . by means of which, initially, and in later life, [man] achieves competence in his culture" (Herskovits 1948:39). In other words, enculturation refers to the process by which the individual learns his culture, and it must be emphasized that this is a never-ending process continuing throughout the life span of the individual.

If enculturation is to be regarded as the broad and continuing process of learning one's culture, it is also useful to isolate some of its more specific aspects. Socialization is one of these, at least as normally used by sociologists, for it refers specifically to the process of social learning as it is carried on in the early years of life. A second special subdivision of enculturation is education—which may be defined as the directed learning process, both formally and informally carried out, for the most part during childhood and adolescence—which equips the individual to take his place as an adult member of society. Finally, the most restricted aspect of cultural learning is schooling, which refers to "those processes of teaching and learning carried on at specific times, in particular places outside the home, for definite periods, by persons especially prepared or trained for the task" (Herskovits 1948:310).

It should perhaps be noted that while some nonliterate societies lack formal educational institutions, this in no sense means they have no educational system. Obviously culture persists, and since culture is learned behavior, learning must take place. The confusion for most Westerners lies in the distinction between education and schooling; the lack of formal institutions in no way suggests that education, in its broadest sense, is absent.

When we turn to the processes of learning connected with music behavior, it is clear that all of the terms discussed above are applicable. Learning music is part of the socialization process; it may take place through education, as when, for example, a father teaches his son how to perform on a music instrument; and schooling may be operative in an apprentice system. All these are, in turn, part of the enculturative process.

Perhaps the simplest and most undifferentiated form of music learning occurs through imitation, which tends to be limited to early learning, though this is not always the case. But music is a specialized branch of learning, at least as it applies to the musician. While we might expect that members of society who take part in singing only as members of a larger group may learn their music through imitation, musicianship, seen as a special skill, usually requires more directed learning. It may be added that in any society an individual learns only a small portion of his cultural habits by free trial-and-error, for in this way he would learn only those habits which were most rewarding to him and to him alone. Such

146

indiscriminate and selfish learning cannot be allowed by society; the individual must learn behavior which is specified in the culture as being correct or best. Such behavior is, of course, the result of the learning process as carried on by previous generations. Behaviors which are successful have persisted in the form of customs, while those which are unsuccessful have either suffered extinction or passed out of existence with the untimely deaths of those who tried them. This accumulation of adaptive habits is passed on to the child; he does not simply learn through imitation how to get along in the world; rather, he is enculturated.

There is, however, considerable evidence to indicate that imitation forms an important part of music learning and that it may well be a universal first step in the process. Densmore, for example, writing about the American Indians in general, says:

> . . . the only mention of learning songs is that, in the singing for dances, the young men "sit with the singers at the drum and learn the songs in that way." They are allowed to pound on the drum with the others, and they sing softly until they learn the melodies. If a man has learned a song in another tribe, he may teach it to the other singers in the same manner, allowing them to sing with him until they learn the tune, pounding meantime on the drum or, in tribes that use a rattle, shaking the rattle as they gradually learn the song. (1930:654)

This account is reminiscent of the Flathead situation previously cited. Less specific is McAllester's reference to the Apache in which he notes that "there is little conscious musical training of children. There seem to be no special inducements offered to teach them to sing" (1960:471). Thus, in this case, learning by imitation can only be inferred.

A more precise statement concerning musical imitation is given by Mead in discussing the New Guinea Manus:

> Whenever there is a dance there is an orchestra of slit drums of all sizes played by the most proficient drummers in the village. The very small boys of four and five settle themselves beside small hollow log ends or pieces of bamboo and drum away indefatigably in time with the orchestra. This period of open and unashamed imitation is followed by a period of embarrassment so that it is impossible to persuade a boy of ten or twelve to touch a drum in public. . . . (1930:34)

McPhee says of Balinese children that "their early life is based upon imitation of the elders; their play is partly reproduction in miniature of various adult activities, carried out with a careful regard for detail. They

147

are enthusiastic patrons of the arts, and never seem to miss a musical or dramatic performance" (1938:2). In Bahian cult life, Herskovits remarks:

> Boys are encouraged by tradition to learn the drum-rhythms, and are often to be seen thumping boxes or calabashes. At ceremonies, before the skilled drummers take over, the older boys and young men of the house begin beating out rhythms. . . .
>
> Wherever drums are played, a group of boys is invariably found standing close by, listening, watching, learning. (1944:489)

Among the Venda of the Northern Transvaal, Blacking says:

> From the earliest age, Venda children have every opportunity to imitate the songs and dances of adults, as most music is performed publicly and children generally follow their mothers everywhere until at least the age of three. Their efforts to imitate adults and older children are admired and encouraged rather than hushed up, and spectators often comment when a small child begins to clap or jump about in response to music. . . . Although the melodies are there to be imitated, small children make little or no attempt to sing, and are at first content to imitate only the motor movement. (1957:2)

Nadel says that among the Nupe "you may see small boys practising drumming on little toy-like instruments under the eye of the father. They will go with him wherever he is called to perform, watching him, and when they are sufficiently advanced, accompanying him on their own drums" (1942:301). Imitative behavior or drumming among the Ewe is commented upon at some length by A. M. Jones, who describes the "toy" instruments made by children, and adds:

> There is no direct teaching or school of instruction: it all happens spontaneously. You start as a boy and if you are seen to be musical, your father or musical relations will unostentatiously encourage you. In fact the art is acquired to start with through play, during which one graduates through mastery of two play-drums. . . .
>
> Boys form gangs for practice and, quite contrary to adult custom where each different drumming belongs to some separate and particular occasion or ceremony, they have a shot at playing any drumming which they fancy. . . . In this way are the principles and practice mastered till a lad at last has an opportunity to take part in a real drumming. He will still be only a beginner. (1959: 70-71)

Nketia adds that among the Akan, "secondary or minor state drummers did not have to undergo long training. Often they picked up the art in the situations by watching others play. When they felt sufficiently able, they attempted to play with the master drummers" (1954:40).

One of the more detailed descriptions of early imitative learning has been contributed by Blacking in a further passage dealing with the Venda:

> By learning these songs, children are gradually acclimatized to singing the heptatonic melodies and more complex rhythms which are so common in traditional Venda music. Nevertheless, it would be wrong to say that Venda children learn tetratonic songs before embarking upon pentatonic and hexatonic songs. Other factors must be considered. First, there is the factor of rhythmic complexity: some pentatonic songs are better known at an earlier age than tetratonic songs, probably because their rhythms are simpler. Then there is the sociological factor: *ngano* are better known than *nyimbo*, probably because they are sung when children and adults of both sexes are together in the evenings, whereas the transmission of *nyimbo* depends upon more voluntary associations during the daytime. Finally, there is the factor of taste, which is always hard to explain: the hexatonic *"Ndo bva na tshidongo"* is everywhere very popular, so that in spite of certain musical and linguistic complexities, it appears to be one of the first songs that children learn, simply because they hear it more often. There are too many exceptions to make any hard and fast rule; but generally speaking it may be said that Venda children learn the simplest songs first, and by degrees graduate to those that are more complex. Certain social factors tend to direct this process of learning, but on the whole Venda children elect to learn those songs which are *musically* within their grasp. Failure to understand the meaning of the text is not a hindrance to learning a song: it is in fact rare to come across children, and even adults, who can explain the meaning of what they sing. It is particularly important to remember that the learning of these songs is a matter of personal choice; children are never taught them systematically. Thus in considering the growth of their musical consciousness, it is significant that Venda children tend to reject songs which at the time of hearing seem too complex. . . . Venda children . . . hear almost every kind of traditional music from the earliest age, and yet they too can only absorb simple rhythms and melodies. (1957:4)

In addition to these more detailed descriptions, Basden for the Ibo (1921:190), Cudjoe for the Ewe (1953:284), John for Sierra Leone

149

(1952:1045), Lange for Cochiti (1959:311), and Thalbitzer for the Eskimo (1923b:607) all stress the importance of having a "good ear" and the ability both of children and adults, including musicians, to pick up songs by hearing and by simple imitation.

There is, then, considerable evidence to indicate that children begin their musical training, and that in some cultures adults continue to expand their musical knowledge, through imitation. If, however, young children begin their music enculturation through this kind of learning process, there is equal evidence to indicate that more formal training is required if the youngster is to become a real musician in the society. A distinction must again be drawn between the casual music performer whose interest is limited to singing as a member of a non-specialized group and the individual who undertakes training which will make him a specialist in some form of music. There is reason to believe that in most societies the casual performer receives relatively little training of a direct nature and instead learns almost entirely from imitation, while the future specialist must almost always undergo some sort of instruction, for special skill requires special training.

We move then from the more casual kinds of learning, which fit broadly into the enculturation process, to special aspects of it, and, at this point, most particularly to education as such. Education involves the interaction of three factors: technique, agent, and content. Of these, we can eliminate the third, for the content of any music training is specific to the society at hand, that is, what is taught is how to behave musically in order to produce music sound acceptable to the members of the society. Matters of technique and agent are, however, of specific importance to an understanding of the learning process. Thus, where the essentials for learning are not already provided by the interaction of the individual with his environment, they must be supplied by a teacher. In order to change the habit structure of the individual in the desired manner, the teacher must employ certain techniques, and these have been classed under the three major headings of motivation, guidance, and reward. Examples of all these techniques with respect to music learning can be found in the literature of ethnomusicology.

The area of motivation is usually subdivided into a number of specific techniques, and thus in some cultures punishment is used when the instructor is dissatisfied with his pupil's performance. Nketia notes for the Akan that "drumming instructors were not always patient with their pupils. Master drummers have memories of the smacks they received when they faltered and of other hardships" (1954:40). Herskovits adds that young men attempting to join the cult drumming in Bahia, Brazil are not only "put to public test before the gods themselves, but any deviation from the strict rhythm will be punished by a sharp rap over the knuckles, administered by the player of the large drum, who uses his drumstick for the purpose" (1944:489).

Novices may be threatened as another technique of motivation: among the Maori, where any deviation from the correct was regarded as a serious offense, tapus were placed upon memory lapses, and students were informed that any such lapse would bring death or disaster to himself or someone closely associated with him (McLean 1961:59). Similar kinds of threats are reported by Handy for the Marquesas:

> When a father desired to have his son or daughter taught the sacred chants he employed a teacher for the purpose. . . . The *tuhuna a'ono* (master of chanting) having been employed, he commenced his instruction. The work was begun in the common dwelling house. During instruction the boy or girl was under strict *tapu*. (1923:318)

Elbert adds further information for the Marquesas:

> Music was in constant demand among these festival-loving people. . . . Music students worked under a rigid *tapu*. Painting with saffron, smoking, . . . spitting, conversation, sexual play, and all unrelated activity were strictly prohibited. Food was brought to the students so that they would not need to leave the *tapu* house. (1941:59)

A further motivating technique is to incite the student to effort; this may be achieved indirectly, through the traditions of the society, which encourage music learning (Herskovits 1944:489), or directly, as noted by Gbeho in West Africa when he says that "African mothers can, and sometimes do, play a great part in this early training, keeping the children occupied by singing, and clapping, providing the rhythm for them to dance to" (1951:1263). In at least one case in the ethnomusicological literature, deprivation and imitation are combined as a part of motivation. McAllester, speaking of the Apache, notes that:

> Instead of being learned by ordinary memorization, healing chants are learned by ordeal and supernatural help. Putting himself under the tutelage of a ceremonial practitioner, the student listens to the songs for four nights without sleep. Then, perhaps several years later, the songs come to him in his sleep, and he is ready, himself, to become a practitioner. (1960:470)

Other motivating techniques include scolding, warning, ridiculing, the use of sarcasm, and so forth, and although no examples of these

151

techniques seem to be described in the ethnomusicological literature, it is safe to assume that they are used in connection with music in societies around the world.

A second class of techniques used by teachers falls under the general heading of guidance, and this too can be subdivided to include, among others, leading, instructing, and demonstrating. Leading refers to the process in which the teacher tries to limit physically the random responses of the pupil so that he makes the correct responses more quickly or is prevented from making the wrong responses. It is sometimes difficult to differentiate between leading and demonstrating in the music learning process; the following description of a Balinese music teacher includes elements of both:

> The method of the teacher is strange. He says nothing, does not even look at the children. Dreamily he plays through the first movement. He plays it again. He then plays the first phrase alone, with more emphasis. He now indicates that the children are to commence. Two or three make a tentative attempt, following him, and watching every movement. The phrase is repeated, and they try again. Another joins in. Those instruments which do not play the melody are ignored for the moment, for the melody must be learned first; . . . Bit by bit the children who are learning the melody go from phrase to phrase, forgetting, remembering, gaining assurance. The teacher remains silent, unless to point out a repeated mistake; generally he is gazing off into space. At the end of an hour, however, several can play through the whole melody. (McPhee 1938:7-8)

In describing this teaching process, McPhee gives some further information concerning the personalities of various of the children and how these personalities inhibit or hasten the response to the teacher's technique. Working three hours a night, the children in question required five evenings to learn the first piece and, working on approximately the same schedule, five weeks to learn nine pieces. McPhee comments further on the teacher's technique:

> . . . the teacher does not seem to teach, certainly not from our standpoint. He is merely the transmitter; he simply makes concrete the musical idea which is to be handed on, sets the example before the pupils and leaves the rest to them. It is as though, in teaching drawing, a complex design were hung on the wall and one said to the students, "Copy that." No allowance is made for the youth of the musicians; it never occurs to the teacher

to employ any method other than the one he is accustomed to use when teaching adult groups. He explains nothing, since, for him, there is nothing to explain. If there are mistakes he corrects them; his patience is great. But he plays everything far too fast, even from the beginning, and it is up to the children to follow him as best they can. (1938:11)

McPhee postulates that because the learning process is a group activity, it is both a pleasure and a recreation rather than a chore. At the same time he emphasizes the concept that Balinese music is so constructed that it is the group rather than the individual which is of primary importance:

> The peculiar technic of the modern Balinese gamelan is an important factor in producing such satisfactory results in so short a time. No heavy demands are put on any individual; each instrument is a single voice in the ensemble; . . . in every case it presents a single problem, to which the player can give his undivided attention. When each part is played alone it is . . . simple enough; when all are played together the result is rich and dazzling. The formulae which go to make up this polyphonic texture are those which have developed through a long tradition. . . . They are so sound, so practical, and based upon such simple and natural principles that the general effect does not depend so much upon the excellence of the individual as upon the unity of the group. (1938:11-12)

Thus McPhee suggests that the group nature of the rehearsal is especially conducive to learning music, while at the same time the nature of the music structure is such as to emphasize group rather than individual activity and excellence. This is a very interesting concept, and one on which it would be most stimulating to have comparative materials.

Methods of demonstration in music learning are sometimes reported in the literature. For the Ewe of Ghana, Cudjoe reports that:

> Less talented persons are made to lie on the ground barebacked and face-downwards, while the master sits astride them and beats the rhythms into their body and soul. There is a less drastic method which consists of imitating the rhythms orally. A third method consists in allowing the pupil to repeat on his own drum what the master plays. (1953:284)

These methods are echoed by Gadzekpo (1952:821) and Nketia (1954:40). Among the Basongye, musicians speak of their teachers'

153

having held and guided their hands on the xylophone or slit drum, and other like examples could be cited.

Demonstration, of course, implies some definite mode of instruction, and there are a number of available examples of such instructive techniques. Elkin reports for the Songman in Australia:

> Passing on songs or giving permission to sing them involves teaching them. The process is simple: the new owner or user sings with the Songman. Indeed, the latter often faces the other and sings the song almost into his mouth, until caught up in the rhythm, the learner finds himself singing the words and tune even before he has grasped the meaning. (1953:93)

Other techniques are recorded by Roberts and Swadesh for the training of the master singer among the Nootka.

> The period of training is hard and involves much prayer, fasting, and memorizing. Someone in the family, already a master singer, trains the younger new ones.
>
> The children are given medicines for the voice so that it will not become hoarse. They take medicines (swallow them) to make for a good voice and a good memory. . . . There are no set vocal exercises except that called *pile·* that Alex knows, and this is in reality a breathing exercise. A pile of sticks is strung along and all those undergoing training . . . try to say *pile·* for each one of as many sticks as possible before the breath is exhausted. This is done after the bathing and rubbing down in the morning.
>
> . . . Ordinarily the singing and training are family affairs and family competes against family for the skill of its master singers, and is self-contained in this respect. (1955:203)

A third class of techniques used by teachers falls under the general heading of providing rewards, but a distinction must be made at the outset between two kinds of rewards. On the one hand, there is always the assumption that the ultimate reward for undergoing training in music is the achievement of requisite skill which then allows the musician the recompense of his profession whether this be in economic or social terms, or simply in the knowledge of accomplishment. We are speaking here, however, of the rewards that stimulate the learning process specifically, although acknowledging that the ultimate rewards contribute to this process as well. Provision of rewards has been further subdivided into helping, giving, praising, and allowing. In helping, teachers take advantage of the fact that the pupil can satisfy only a few of his drives without the aid of another person or persons, and thus being helped is a reward in itself. The significance of giving is that the teacher has done the work of producing or otherwise obtaining the gift for the pupil, thus relieving the pupil of the necessity of doing so for himself. Praise, of course, is self-explanatory, and allowing refers to the granting of permission to carry out a certain action as opposed to giving, in which the reward is a specific thing. Examples of these reward techniques in the process of teaching are difficult to find in the ethnomusicological literature, although accounts of rewards to established musicians are commonplace. It should not be assumed from this that such rewards are lacking in nonliterate or other societies, however; rather, the assumption is that close attention has not been given to teaching techniques.

These, then, are some of the techniques of music training used in various societies around the world. As there are techniques of education, there must also be agents of education; these are the teachers, and in discussing some of the techniques used we have already had occasion to mention specific instructors. These include the family (Nootka), established musicians (Australia, Ewe, Basongye, Bali, Maori, Marquesas, Bahia), the ceremonial practitioner (Apache), mothers (West Africa), other children (Ewe, Venda), and the father (Nupe). It is to be expected that other agents of education are also present, though unreported in the literature. In those societies in which the mother's brother tends to take a leading social role in respect to his sister's family, it is quite possible that he may perform special music duties in his approved role. Both casual bystanders and the community as a whole often act as educational agents in respect to other kinds of learning, and there is no reason to suppose that they do not function in music learning as well. The question of the variety of agents of music teaching, then, is far from answered.

Aside from those individual teaching sessions, which may or may not be sporadic according to the culture in which they take place, two major kinds of training indicate the presence of music schooling in nonliterate societies. The first of these occurs in what has come to be known as the bush school, organized usually in connection with puberty rites and initiation. Among the Mende of Sierra Leone, for example, initiation into Poro begins with an intensive bush school session in which the initiates remain in isolated camps for several weeks (and, formerly, for considerably longer periods of time). The kind of training received in the Poro bush school is summarized by Little:

> In general, the training provided varies according to the length
> of time the boys are able to remain in the bush. It may include
> a certain amount of natipe law and custom, exemplified by the hold-
> ing of mock courts and trials, in which the boys enact the roles of

their elders. Boys who can afford to stay for a length of time learn a good deal about native crafts as well as the ordinary duties of a grown man, such as "brushing" and other farming operations, and cleaning roads. Individual specialists at making raffia clothes, basketry, nets, etc., sometimes go into the bush with the boys and help them to become proficient in the particular craft they choose. Bridge-building, the making and setting of traps for animals and fish, are also taught. On the social side, the boys learn drumming and to sing the special Poro songs. They practice somersaults and acrobatics, and altogether their experiences produce a strong sense of comradeship. (1951:121)

Although no details of music training as such are given, it seems reasonable to assume that the instruction is important, organized, and direct.

More specific information is given for the Venda in East Africa by Blacking, who speaks of boys' and girls' initiation schools and the role that music plays in them. He notes, for example, a particular kind of singing called *muulu*, and points out that it is first learned in the girls' puberty school (1957:10). In the *domba* initiation school, which usually lasts for a year, but which may continue for as long as two years or be stopped after three months, a special instructor is in charge of music. Blacking writes:

Nyamungozwa is responsible for all the music, drama and ritual at *domba*. He must organize and prepare the models and costumes for the *dzingoma* symbolic representations, which are designed to teach the initiates certain lessons in a graphic way. There are special *domba* songs (*nyimbo dza domba*) to accompany both the *dzingoma* and various other items of ritual which occur at certain stages of *domba*. Some of these songs are taught by *nyamungozwa* in the evening and are sung for the sake of variety in between performances of the great *domba* songs; others are little more than jingles to accompany some ritual action, and the initiates pick up the chorus almost immediately: some of these songs are performed in public, so that initiates remember them from previous *madomba* of which they may have seen a little as children. . . .

There is therefore a large amount of music performed at *domba* in addition to the ritual *domba* song, and its performance and organization is all in the hands of the *nyamungozwa*, who must be considered an outstanding figure in the musical and dramatic activities of the Venda. (1957:15)

At another point, Blacking indicates some differences between girls' and boys' initiations in respect to music; in the latter schools:

Initiates learn special songs from the *midabe:* many are obscene, and even today they contain a number of Sotho words which mean nothing to the initiates. There is a song called *"Hogo,"* which initiates sing when the school is burnt and they are welcomed back to their homes, and this is known and sung by people of both sexes and of all ages: it is the only *murundu* song that is heard outside the confines of the school, as all initiates are severely warned not to disclose any of the songs and secrets of the school. (1957:18)

Similar examples could be cited (Richards 1956), but it is clear that the bush school, functioning as a definite schooling situation, particularly in Africa south of the Sahara, provides a setting in which music is consciously and directly taught to the initiates.

A second music schooling situation is found in the system of apprenticeship used to teach music in a number of societies, particularly in Africa. Among the Nupe, Nadel notes:

Sometimes boys from other families desire to become drummers. Their father will then get in touch with the head of the drummers, and give him his son as an apprentice. The young apprentice will visit the drummer's house every day for his lesson. In the beginning he will be allowed to use the drums in the house; later he will buy himself a drum of his own. No payment is taken for the tuition; but when the novice later performs at ceremonies or feasts, he will send his former teacher a small gift of money or food. (1942:301-02)

A somewhat similar situation is described by Nketia for the Akan.

Because the post of the master drummer of the state was in the past never to be vacant, boys were trained to assume the pose in the event of the death of their fathers. Fathers, however, did not always show a willingness to teach their children because they feared that they would be hastening their own departure from this life if they trained people to succeed them. Accordingly some drummers delayed personal instruction until late in life, or else got some other people to teach their children. . . .

In the past, however, the training of the state drummer was seriously undertaken. Early in the morning he was taken to the drums and instructed in the art together with other prospective drummers. He was always in attendance when master drummers played, and gradually gained the experience that he needed to step

157

into the shoes of his father in the event of illness or death. (1954:39-40)

Nikiprowetzky says that the training of the Senegalese griots was "exclusively oral," involving "a long apprenticeship with an older man— mostly a father or an uncle. Several years are needed to master the technique of an instrument or to learn all the songs which are indispensable to a griot's profession" (1962:n.p.). Among the Basongye, there is a definite system of apprenticeship under a recognized performer. When a young person wishes to learn a particular music instrument, for example, he approaches the established musician who decides whether he will accept the student. If he does, instruction takes place over a period of several months depending upon the quickness and understanding of the neophyte; the teacher works with his pupil at stated and regular times, if possible, explaining his role, teaching him basic rhythmic and melodic patterns as well as song texts, and sometimes using the definite technique of guiding his hands on the instrument. Payment is made to the instructor in chickens, which have a ritual significance in the culture, and when the teacher considers the neophyte ready, he gives him permission to play in public. All proceeds of the first three or four performances are given to the teacher, and throughout the teacher's lifetime some share of the proceeds may be given him. It is clear that some students learn more quickly than others, and different kinds of instruction are apparently given for different kinds of instruments, with some, such as the xylophone, not included in the apprentice system.

Schooling, then, at least through the initiation school and the apprentice system, is used for music teaching in some societies along with less formalized systems of education and the universal learning technique of imitation. However, no matter what the system used, learning does not cease once a particular instrument, song, or style has been mastered initially. We have previously had occasion to call attention to the fact that learning must be a continuing process since the response of the listener to music sound determines, ultimately, the form which that sound must take. If the product is rejected, the musician must "re-learn" his music in order to satisfy his audience, and thus it is through the continuing learning process that a link is formed between the product on the one hand and the concepts and behaviors of the musician on the other. Acceptance or rejection of the product is, of course, phrased in cultural terms, but the canons of correctness and taste in any society can and do change both internally and externally; the musician must be constantly alert to the rest of society if he is to retain its respect. Music performance, as well, requires constant practice if techniques are to be kept at maximum flexibility and skill; while we recognize this fact for our own society, we do not seem to have acknowledged the fact that it is a requisite of the musician in all societies.

Accounts of practicing are encountered fairly frequently in the ethnomusicological literature, though they tend to be primarily descriptive of the fact rather than providing accounts of how practicing is carried on or what proportion of the musician's time is given to it. Among the American Indians, Dorsey speaks of practicing among the Cheyenne: "Shortly after the Dew-Claw warriors entered the tipi, where they spent the greater part of the night in informally rehearsing songs" (1905a:95). In somewhat more detail, Mooney reports on rehearsal for the Ghost Dance among the Sioux:

> The leaders, both men and women, frequently assembled privately in a tipi to rehearse the new or old songs for the next dance. . . . Rehearsals were held in Black Coyote's tipi almost every night . . . , each session usually lasting about three hours.
>
> On these occasions from eight to twelve persons were present. . . . The prayer ended, they consulted as to the song to be sung first. . . . From time to time explanations were made where the meaning of the song was not clear. . . . Finally, about 10 o'clock, all rose together and sang the closing song . . . and the rehearsal was at an end. (1896:918)

In Cochiti, Lange recorded the rather extensive preparations made through rehearsal:

> In preparation for the July 14 Feast Day, the kiva mayorli reminds the chorus members as early as May to begin thinking of songs. He makes the final selections, and the choruses begin to practice about June 15. For about two weeks, they meet in their respective community houses every evening to work out words and melodies. . . .
>
> After July 11, practices are held every other evening until the last four evenings before the Feast Day. For the last four practices, the choruses meet in their kivas with the dancers. (1959:351)

Roberts and Swadesh describe rehearsals among the Nootka in some detail.

> The singers are summoned to practice . . . the night before the potlatch is to occur. For the practice the people go to the house of the man who will give the affair. He has prepared food for them as part of the practice entertainment. Some practices are

formal and some very informal. . . . In the formal practices the leader has to be obeyed; he scolds and may be very stern when things do not go well. Troublemakers and incorrigibles are put out of the rehearsal.

While they are drilling the master singer stands on something, such as a box, which elevates him so that his baton may be seen. The men singers stand on one side of him and the women on the other. He begins by yelling "whoo" four times, to limber up his voice and attract attention, and then the rest join in singing "whoo" and clapping their hands.

The master singer raises his arm and indicates the beat before he sings; that is, what it will be. . . .

After a moment of beating, the master singer starts to sing and sings through a stanza or verse. Then he makes a motion with his hand that holds the "baton," the drummers and singers all start with him, the clappers keep time with the "baton," and they recommence the song. (1955:204)

Roberts and Swadesh also indicate special kinds of songs which must be rehearsed because of their particularly difficult nature.

For Oceania, McLeod notes the importance of practicing for the Tikopia (1957:138), and Burrows remarks that in Uvea and Futuna, "I heard it only when a group was trying over a song *sub voce* to refresh their memory in a rehearsal before the real performance" (1945:91). In Southern Lau, Fiji, Laura Thompson says:

Meke learning provides entertainment for the whole village. Two or three months before an important event . . . *meke* are practiced on the ceremonial ground almost every afternoon and, if the moon is bright, in the evening. The dance is repeated innumerable times until each individual has mastered every detail. The rehearsal is a social event attended by all women and children of the village. (1940:76)

Mead speaks of practicing among young boys of ten or twelve in New Guinea, and indicates that "girls practice less, for only one drum beat, the simple death beat, falls to their hands in later life" (1930:34).

Mead also points out that the rehearsal process in Bali tends to be almost of more importance than performance, thus stressing an attitude toward music which differs from our own.

When the young men or the young men and girls or the small children of a Balinese village decide to form a club to play some particular types of music . . . the interest of the rest of the village fastens not on the final performance, as it does in America . . . , but on the rehearsals. . . .

This delight in the art of acting rather than in the play, in the way in which the music is played rather than in the music, . . . is essentially Balinese and depends of course upon the Balinese character, with its preoccupation with activity for its own sake and its studied avoidance of climax and of identification. . . .

Round about the group that is rehearsing will sit other men, who also play musical instruments. They will be listening, enjoying the nuances and the changes, with hands cupped in readiness for the moment when some player tires or slips away for a rest and some one of the audience can take his place. For every Balinese man is, for part of his life, if that be only once a month when the orchestra of his temple plays for its special temple feasts—a professional musician. (1941-42:80, 81, 86)

Descriptions of rehearsals in Africa are very difficult to find, though we have had some occasion to mention practicing in connection with various techniques of teaching. This apparent lack in the ethnomusicological literature is certainly not present because African musicians do not rehearse, but rather because the problem of practice has not been widely noted. Among the Basongye, practice is a known and accepted fact of the musician's life, and all musicians say they practice, if not every day, then at least once a week. It is difficult to determine the duration of such practicing, but in theory, at least, it is fairly substantial, amounting to three or four hours a week at the minimum, according to the musicians.

The questions which surround the learning of music are very important ones, for they provide us with a knowledge of how music is produced, as well as an understanding of techniques, agents, and content of music education in a given society. It is through the learning process that the relationship between product and concept is established via the response of the musician to the criticism of his performance by his listeners. Musicianship is maintained through practicing, and this too is a form of continuing learning which allows the musician to follow the perfection of his craft as well as to change his concepts of music performance through time.

But the concept of learning is even more closely related to culture in general, and specifically to the problem of change and stability. Gillin has emphasized four points in this connection which are helpful in understanding the learning process in general and music learning as well (1948:248-49). The first is that "culture provides the conditions for learning." At birth, the human infant enters a man-made environment

161

which acts as a buffer between him and the raw habitat. He is surrounded by a number of artifacts characteristic of that particular culture, as well as by older human beings who have learned to act in given ways in given situations. Thus the artifacts and behavior of people provide a series of stimulus situations which are continually presented to the child as he matures, and the child must learn to make specific responses.

Secondly, "culture systematically elicits appropriate responses." While a certain amount of the child's behavior is learned by trial and error, every society makes special efforts to elicit responses which are considered appropriate to certain situations. The child is weaned, toilet trained, taught to use particular songs on particular occasions, and so forth. While the responses desired vary from culture to culture, as does the amount and intensity of the direction, in no society is the individual allowed to grow up discovering everything by trial and error.

Third, "culture, through its products or agents, provides reinforcements." In all cultures, appropriate stimuli are presented and appropriate responses elicited, and there is also a constant press of rewards and punishments which hastens the learning process and extinguishes undesired habits. "Thus we may say, not only that culture *is* learned behavior; it is also a setup for *learning* behavior of very complex and specific types."

Finally, "the culture of a society therefore has certain self-perpetuating tendencies, so long as the human population which manifests the culture does not die out." In other words, it is through learning, enculturation, that the culture gains its stability, for members of one generation teach to members of succeeding generations what the culture is and does.

At the same time, since culture is learned, when the stimulus and response situations change culture also changes, although the members of the older generation feel that the form of culture when they were growing up was best, and teach it that way. But if the situation has changed, the children are being raised in different circumstances, and they attempt to modify the culture to their own liking and pass on the result, in turn, to succeeding generations. Changes of this type are usually minute and gradual, although sudden, revolutionary changes in culture can and do occur. But revolutionary changes are infrequent in man's history, while the small and gradual changes growing out of enculturation are always present. Culture is stable, but it is never static: it is, on the contrary, dynamic and ever-changing. It is this that accounts for the fact that enculturation persists throughout life, since each elder generation must adjust, as best it can, to the changes introduced by the younger generation. It is this fact also that accounts for the reaction of the older generation all over the world that "the good old days are gone," that "things ain't what they used to be," and that "the younger generation is going to the dogs."

Thus it is through education, enculturation, cultural learning, that culture gains its stability and is perpetuated, but it is through the same process of cultural learning that change takes place and culture derives its dynamic quality. What is true for culture as a whole is also true for music; the learning process in music is at the core of our understanding of the sounds men produce.

CHAPTER IX

THE PROCESS OF COMPOSITION

Composition is part of the same learning process we spoke of in the preceding chapter, shaped by public acceptance or rejection, learned by the individuals who practice it, and contributing to music change and stability. It is not the intention here to concentrate on the composer as an individual, as excellent guidelines for further study have been laid down by Dennison Nash (1956-57, 1961). Rather, the question of primary interest is that of composition as a process—how new songs are brought into being.

Bruno Nettl has discussed three points in connection with composition among nonliterate peoples that can be restated here with profit (1954b:81). The first is that any music composition is ultimately the product of the mind of an individual or a group of individuals. This statement is in opposition to that proposed by the Grimm brothers in the nineteenth century and still occasionally cited today with respect to folklore items. It was argued by the Grimms that folklore is the expression of an entire people and that the group of reference as an entity is the creator of each folklore item. While the theory is credible if one accepts it within the framework of the differences between individual creations and style in its broadest sense, it is not really plausible in direct application. For it argues that there is no individual creation and that any item of folklore is created from bits and patches contributed by all the people and put together into a cohesive entity at the time of creation. Viewed in this way, the theory foreshadows some of the concepts that hold culture to be the creator of culture. As we shall note in more detail later, there are group contributions to style, and there are also known processes of composition

165

in which a group of individuals work together, but in all cases these are individuals working creatively. Items of culture do not simply appear out of nowhere; there must be contributions from specific individuals, whether these contributions can or cannot be pinpointed after the fact of composition.

The second point noted by Nettl is that ". . . no generalizations can be made about composition techniques in primitive music which contrast it with the music of high cultures, with the exception that it is, in contrast to the latter, composed without written (or otherwise preserved) records" (*loc. cit.*). Generally speaking, this seems to be true, with perhaps the added comment that in nonliterate societies there is less conscious discussion of techniques and processes of creativity than exists in the West.

This brings us to the third and final point discussed by Nettl, which concerns what he calls "conscious composition" (1954b:86; 1956:16). This refers to the deliberate and planned process of creating new music material, carried out by individuals who are aware of their specific and directed actions to the desired end. While the phrase is understandable when contrasted to those compositional techniques in which inspiration is derived directly from, for example, the supernatural, it seems to have two implications which are not necessarily desirable. The first is that, given the nature of the English language, it implies a dichotomy—that is, if there is conscious composition on the one hand, its opposite must be unconscious composition, and unless one is willing to hold that the supernatural does invest individuals with new songs at one gulp, as it were, no composition can be unconscious. The second point derives from the first in that although we know relatively little about the process of composition as carried out in a state of trance, for example, there is evidence which points to a definite structuring not only of the music composed but of the process whereby the composition is achieved. Therefore, although the use of the phrase "conscious composition" is understandable, it will not be a term employed here except in reference to Nettl's use of it.

Despite Leonard Meyer's contention that "the primitives themselves do not make musical creation a self-conscious endeavor" (1956:239), there is a good deal of evidence to show that nonliterate peoples know composition, recognize it as a distinct process, and are in a number of cases quite able to discuss it. Composition is affirmed for a number of cultures, among them the Ibo (Basden 1921:190), Gros Ventre (Flannery 1953:91, 98, 99), Omaha (Fletcher and LaFlesche 1911:319), Solomon Islands (Douglas L. Oliver 1955:36); Baoule (Thurow 1956:10), Mafulu of British New Guinea (Williamson 1912:216), Tikopians (Firth 1940:passim), and so forth. In all these cases, and in a

166

number of others, composition is recognized as a definite technique of making new music. Indeed, in several societies it has been noted that there is direct pressure to compose: Basden says of the Ibo that "the musician must learn all tunes by ear, or compose his own, which he frequently does" (1921:190). In Mangaia in Polynesia, Andersen quotes Gill as saying that in so-called death talks "each adult male relative must recite a song. If unable to compose one himself, he must pay some one to furnish him with an appropriate song" (1933:155). Densmore says of the Teton Sioux that "the ceremonial songs must either be composed by the man who sang them, or purchased from some one who had previously held the office and instructed him in its duties" (1918:101-02). In these cases it appears that not only is composition recognized by the society but that individuals are expected to be able to compose and thus contribute to the music corpus of the culture.

We have had occasion in Chapter IV of this book to discuss concepts concerning the sources from which music is drawn in various cultures, and these included composition by individuals, music drawn from the supernatural, and borrowing from other peoples. In returning to the second of these sources—the supernatural—it need only be said by way of introduction that the phenomenon of the vision quest among the Plains Indians has long been recognized as the ultimate source of songs considered to be the "true" as well as the "powerful" music of the culture. In considering the compositional process in connection with the vision quest, however, we have but two choices: first, we can assume that songs do come to the supplicant in a flash of supernatural or other inspiration, and that the process is therefore practically instantaneous. The second and more likely possibility is that the weakened condition of the petitioner, who has usually fasted and gone with little water over a period of several days, contributes to hallucinatory activity, and that in this sense the visions seen are "real." In any case, the point to be emphasized is that the vision quest, particularly in respect to certain aspects of the songs included in it, tends to be standardized in a given culture; in the case of the Flathead Indians, this standardization may well indicate in certain of its parts a symbolic reflection of the actual compositional process. In order to indicate what this process may be, let us cite a few vision quest and other supernatural experiences among the Flathead.

> When I was about six years old, my father lost my horse in the stick game. The man who won the horse took it and led it away; I followed, crying. I saw a woman coming toward me in a buckskin dress singing this song. She told me to turn back, that I would have better horses. "Don't cry over one horse."

There was a man who was out hunting. He was sneaking up on the game by sitting at a spot on the game trail when he heard somebody singing. He thought, "There must be people around." So he stood there and waited to see who was coming. Pretty soon, a spike bull elk came out from the brush and told him, "This is your song. If you really need this song, sing it." It was a love song. So he didn't kill the spike, and never killed an elk again.

There was a guy who was looking for power once, and he heard a guy coming from a long way off, singing a song. He finally met the guy, and the guy was singing a stick game song. He told the young feller, "When you get to be a certain age, you can use that song for the stick game." The young man remembered the song until the time came to use it.

One time long ago EBS and her husband attended a war dance near where PP's cabin is now. They were coming home and crossed the creek below the present BS house. They decided to camp there for the night. It was just dawn and as they lay down to sleep they heard a flute playing from a long way off. It came closer and closer, but when they rose up to see who was playing, it went away again a long distance. They did not know who it was and never found out.

This kind of supernatural experience can be objectified by some Flathead, at least, who see a set of distinctive patterns in the experience. Thus one informant spoke of such experiences as follows:

When somebody is discouraged or he doesn't know what to do, he may be sitting around his tipi and a spirit comes to tell him what to do. Sometimes he can hear the singing from way far off, and hear it approaching. Before daylight he hears the spirit coming, always from the East. The tipi always faces east, with its ears up. [The ears refer to the open smoke flaps of the tipi.] The spirit comes from afar and hits the ears; then it comes down the ears and stands in front of the person. It tells him what to do, and it sings the song. As it comes toward the tipi it has been singing the same song many times as it comes.

In these various experiences, as well as the objectification of the experience quoted above, one aspect of the process seems to be repeated again and again. This is the fact that the song, which the petitioner will later learn, is first heard from far away; the being who is singing it comes closer and closer, singing constantly, until it finally actually appears. Without desiring to stretch a point too far, it seems quite likely that this formalized supernatural-song pattern refers symbolically to the process of composition. That is, the song is dimly heard (dimly formulated) at first, and then becomes clearer and clearer as the supernatural being approaches (as the petitioner gains a stronger sense of the structure of the song he is, in fact, composing). There is almost no such experience involving the supernatural and song among the Flathead in which this pattern fails to appear, and while the people would hotly deny the interpretation presented here, it seems likely that hallucination and composition are closely connected in the manner suggested. This is further borne out by other facts about music and the vision quest. Thus in the following quest report, it is significant to note that although the pattern of slow approach is not suggested, there is substituted a type of situation in which the individual is subjected to a number of repetitions of the songs he will learn. The informant recalls that he was "eight or nine" years old at the time. His parents had left him and his sister alone in the wilderness while they were investigating some aspects of a placer mine. His sister looked up suddenly and saw a "great big grizzly bear" coming toward them; she caught her brother's attention and then, he says,

> I went out of my head. I was way up on top of a mountain. People were dancing, singing, playing stick game, cards. I looked around and it was me singing. Then I went out again. I was on another mountain and the same people were there doing the same thing. The grizzly bear took me back each time, and this happened on four mountains. The people all had otter skins around their heads. All the animals were singing and dancing in there. It was always me singing.

The magic number four is of course part of the pattern, but, as noted above, the significance of the citation is that the boy, who later became an important shaman on the basis of this and other visions, "heard" the songs four times at least. It seems logical that, given the expectation of success in obtaining a song or songs in the supernatural situation, four times would be enough to fix a new song in the composer's head.

A further part of the relationship of quest to composition may be found in the fact that there is difference of opinion among informants as to how the song is learned. Some say that the supernatural being has to sing the song but once; others admit that learning the songs was a difficult process achieved only after numerous repetitions. The translated expectation would be that those who learned after a single rendition are those whose skill at composition is relatively quick, while those who had difficulty in "learning" the song were those who had the lesser skills at composing a new song. Unfortunately, it is impossible to match informa-

169

tion concerning slow learners among the Flathead with their subsequent music "careers," but it seems likely that the slow learners do not become outstanding musicians.

This interpretation of the relationship of the vision quest or other supernatural experience to the compositional process seems logical, at least in the case of the Flathead. Whether it can be extended to other tribal groups is not known, but there are some indications in the literature which suggest a similar kind of process. Speaking of the Pawnee, for example, Densmore recounts a song-learning experience in which it is implied that the same process of long-distance hearing is operative:

> A young man received this song in a dream, while mourning for his parents who had died. He saw a woman coming toward him and said, "Mother is coming." The woman said, "You have seen me, now you must learn this song." The young man learned the song, lived a long time afterward, and took part in the Bear Dance. (1929:37)

More significant is the statement made by Wissler concerning the manner in which one individual among the Blackfeet obtained a song in the quest:

> We are convinced that the deliberate composing of new songs is going on at the present time. One individual asked the writer to let him hear songs from the distant tribes. Having at hand such a phonographic record, his request was complied with. After several repetitions he was able to follow accurately and went away humming it over and over. Some time afterward he reluctantly admitted that he had now arranged words for this song and "expected to dream something." (1912:104)

In his autobiography, Crashing Thunder, a Winnebago Indian, tells us that he falsely claimed a visitation from the supernatural during a vision quest (Radin 1926:26). Since he does not say so specifically, we can only speculate on whether he also composed a song or songs to go with the false vision. From these illustrations it seems quite possible that at least some composition was prepared before the vision quest, or perhaps as the aftermath of an unsuccessful petition.

In any case, the learning of songs in the vision quest or in other supernatural experience is clearly a process of composition, and the implied dichotomy between "conscious" and "unconscious" composition seems to impose an unnecessary distinction upon the compositional process. It is of course probable that from the standpoint of the individual involved, differences do occur, thus emphasizing again the folk rather than

170

analytical evaluation; but it is to be suspected that in a substantial number of cases the process is more conscious than the individual is willing to admit, given the dictates of his culture.

Similar processes may operate in those cases in which the individual composes while in trance or possession, though descriptions are so infrequent that no conclusions can be reached. Gbeho, writing of music in the former Gold Coast, notes that:

> Many years ago it was not unusual to see a man "possessed" by music; he would be found in the forest singing to himself or composing new tunes, and when he felt he had satisfied himself he would return to his village, singing. The villagers would all go out to meet him and join in singing with him and a few musical ones would be selected to learn his new tunes and they would teach them to others. (1952:31)

For the American Indians, Mooney has written the following:

> The Ghost-dance songs are of the utmost importance in connection with the study of the messiah religion, as we find embodied in them much of the doctrine itself . . . together with such innumerable references to old time customs, ceremonies, and modes of life long since obsolete. . . . There is no limit to the number of these songs, as every trance at every dance produces a new one, the trance subject after regaining consciousness embodying his experience in the spirit world in the form of a song. . . . (1896: 953)

There is little to be learned from such brief citations save that trance or possession form the framework within which composition does take place; what the process of composition is under such circumstances can only be ascertained through further investigation.

Further understanding of composition can be gained through a knowledge of who the composer is in his society; at least three kinds of composers are identifiable from the literature. The first of these is the specialist composer, a man who may or may not gain recompense from his activities but who is socially recognized as performing this specialized function. Among the Tanga of New Ireland, writes Bell:

> A dance master . . . has the inalienable right to his own compositions, and to such other songs and dance arrangements as he has seen elsewhere and introduced to the island. Although a dance is a public affair . . . no other village would dare to plagiarize an original composition. . . . There was not a dance on Tanga the name of whose composer was not known. (1935:108)

171

For the Maori, Best writes that "the facility with which natives compose songs is quite remarkable, . . . In former times some specialists appear to have spent much of their time in song making; such as Mihi-ki-te-kapua, a woman and Piki, a man of the Tuhoe district, who have a large number of songs to their credit" (1925:111). Peter Buck says that "some individuals could compose and instruct, as well as sing, and so became regarded as experts" in Mangareva in southeast Polynesia (1938:305), and Thurnwald notes the existence of paid composers in Buin, Solomon Islands (1936:6). Douglas Oliver, also speaking of the Solomon Islands, writes that "leaders sometimes commission composers to create music and the lyrics for songs to be sung at feasts and pay them with pork or shell money, but just as often these composers voluntarily contribute their creations for the feast of kinsmen or friends" (1955:355), and Elbert speaks of a specialist composer in the Marquesas:

> Moa Tetua was a blind leper who died about 1900. He could neither read nor write. He was so popular as a composer and musician that natives gathered illegally every night outside the leprosarium to listen to his concerts. . . . They have an individuality of style and richness of imagery which distinguish them from all other *rari*. Moa Tetua sang his compositions to the music of beating *fau* sticks. (1941:76)

There also exist composers whose contribution is apparently sporadic or even consists of a single song composed on a particular occasion; such persons are not celebrated as composers, and their contribution seems to be unique. Speaking of the Gros Ventres of Montana, Flannery cites a number of such composers:

> The song was composed by the husband of one of the captured Gros Ventre women. Another song, classed as a victory song, was composed by an old man whose faith in a young man was justified. . . . Still another song was composed on the occasion on which a Piegan, who had survived a partial scalping, was killed by the Gros Ventres. (1953:99)

Demetracopoulou, speaking of a Wintu song, says: "This is, to my knowledge, the most popular Wintu song. It is said to have been composed by a lover rejected for his poverty, when he found his old love in circumstances so reduced that she had to live on a diet of clover" (1935:493). Similar casual composition could be cited from a number of other sources, and the pattern is particularly significant from two points of view. In the first place, there is clear indication here that it is by no means only the specialist composer who contributes to the formation of the

172

musical corpus in a given culture; to the contrary, it appears that casual "one-shot" compositions are contributed by what is probably a considerable variety of non-specialist individuals. In the second place, it appears that specific occasions can be the stimulus for composition; thus the rejected lover or the killing of an enemy may be the cause for the expansion of the music repertoire. Again generalization is impossible, but a roster of the kinds of occasions which bring forth compositions might be very revealing of the types of stimuli required for particular kinds of composition.

Aside from individual composers, whether they be specialists or not, there are a few descriptions in the literature of group composition in which the song is the product of all those participating. Speaking of the Sioux, Densmore reports as follows:

> In this connection the writer desires to record an observation on musical composition among the Sioux. A song was sung at a gathering and she remarked: "That is different from any Sioux song I have ever heard, it has so *many* peculiarities." The interpreter replied, "That song was composed recently by several men working together. Each man suggested something, and they put it all together in the song." This is the only instance of cooperation in the composition of an Indian song that has been observed. (1922:26)

Densmore alludes to what is probably the same occasion in writing about the Teton Sioux (1918:59). At a considerably earlier date, Richard Dodge remarked on a similar phenomenon, though he did not name the people among whom his observation was made:

> A party of warriors returning from a successful foray must embalm their exploits in song. They have decided on the music, but the work before them is to fit words to it. . . . One man will propose a line; all try the effect by singing it in chorus. . . . So also in other songs. One man will adapt a set of words, whose appropriateness to some situation or personal peculiarity will make them popular for a while, or until another set of words displaces them. (1882:351)

The only other case of group composition known to the present writer comes from Trinidad, where Melville and Frances Herskovits report that "a song may be the collaboration of several persons, and there are, of course, at any given time, some men and women who excel as song makers" (1947:276).

There are, then, three "kinds" of composers noted in the ethnomusicological literature: the specialist composer, the casual composer, and group composers. How widely each type is distributed in the world, or what proportion of songs each contributes; whether every society contains some representatives of each type; or whether groups of societies could be distinguished on this basis, is not known. However, it is suggested that the composer base in any society may be much wider than is usually believed.

No matter who the composer may be, it is evident that his composition must be approved, either formally or informally, by the people who are to sing it. Informal approval simply consists of singing the song; what the exact mechanisms of this process are we do not know. Similarly, formal acceptance of a music composition has apparently not been described frequently in the literature, although there are two exceptions. The first of these, a report by Lane on the Tiv of Nigeria, refers to a very formal pattern of acceptance or rejection and, incidentally, calls attention again to the non-specialist as composer.

> The most important type of song is called the Icham; this is sung by a soloist with chorus, frequently the soloist being the composer. A new song is submitted to the tribe by its composer for approval, even new words to an old setting can prompt a "Royal Academy Sitting"! One of the most popular songs in Katsina Ala at the moment was composed by an agricultural labourer. . . . (1954:13)

A slightly less formal situation is described by Fletcher and LaFlesche for the Omaha; in this case, it is emphasized not only that songs must be accepted by society, but that certain standards in composition are required.

> They [the songs] all conformed to the rhythmic standards peculiar to the society or the ceremonial. . . . This custom has restricted freedom in musical composition and thus has retarded its development among a remarkably musical race. It has tended to make the songs of the tribe monotonous and this tendency has been enhanced by certain beliefs concerning the function and power of music entertained by the native peoples. Every member of the Hon'hewachi was required to compose a song which had to conform to the rhythmic standard of the Hon'hewachi initial song. The song had to be an expression of the man's personal experience, and frequently though not invariably, it referred to a dream or vision that came in answer to his supplications. (1911: 502-03)

Radcliffe-Brown describes the care with which the Andamanese composer prepares his song for public performance:

> Every man composes songs, and the boys begin to practise themselves in the art of composition when they are still young. A man composes his song as he cuts a canoe or a bow or as he paddles a canoe, singing it over softly to himself, until he is satisfied with it. He then awaits an opportunity to sing it in public, and for this he has to wait for a dance. Before the dance he takes care to teach the chorus to one or two of his female relatives so that they can lead the chorus of women. He sings his song, and if it is successful he repeats it several times, and thereafter it becomes part of his repertory, for every man has a repertory of songs that he is prepared to repeat at any time. If the song is not successful . . . the composer abandons it and does not repeat it. Some men are recognized as being more skillful song-makers than others. (1948: 132)

We should expect patterns of this nature to occur in respect to composition as well as within other behaviors; the fact that so few references are available does not mean that patterns of social acceptance of music do not exist.

Having discussed various kinds of composition, as well as the identity of the composer and the pressures generated by society to insure acceptable composition, we can now turn to some of the actual techniques used in composing a new song. In order to initiate a composition, it is evident that the composer must engage in some thought processes about what he is doing. Although very little information seems to be available concerning this question, considerable evidence is given by various authors for the Eskimos. Speaking of a Netsilik hunter, shaman, and poet named Orpingalik and his "views of how a song is born in the human mind," Rasmussen cites his informant as follows:

> Songs are thoughts, sung out with the breath when people are moved by great forces and ordinary speech no longer suffices.
>
> Man is moved just like the ice flow sailing here and there out in the current. His thoughts are driven by a flowing force when he feels joy, when he feels fear, when he feels sorrow. Thoughts can wash over him like a flood, making his breath come in gasps and his heart throb. Something, like an abatement in the weather, will keep him thawed up. And then it will happen that the words we need will come of themselves. When the words we want to use shoot up of themselves—we get a new song. (1931:321)

175

That the process of composition is a conscious one is evidenced by three songs composed by Piuvkaq, another Netsilik:

A wonderful occupation
Making songs!
But all too often they
Are failures.

A wonderful fate
Getting wishes fulfilled!
But all too often they
Slip past.

A wonderful occupation
Hunting caribou!
But all too rarely we
Excel at it
So that we stand
Like a bright flame
Over the plain.

It is lovely, a bit of song
To put together.
But I often do it badly avaya!
It is lovely (to hunt)
But I myself seldom shine like
  a burning wick (as being lucky)
On the ice avaya!
It is lovely to have wishes (fulfilled)
But they all slip past me!
It is all so difficult avayaya.

Ayaiyaja
This why, I wonder
My song-to-be that I wish to use
My song-to-be that I wish to put
  together
I wonder why it will not come to me?
. . .

(Rasmussen, 1931:511, 517)

Similar discussion, with text samples, of Eskimo speculation on the compositional process is given by Boulton. She notes:

There are many songs about song-making. Some of them are conjurer's songs, many are hunters' songs. Some are ancient, others very recent. Often they begin with something like this:

> "There is no song about it
> Words being far away (hard to find)."

or "I am going to get a song now,
> Because they want me to sing."

or "I hooked this song
> Last night."

or "He loves to make up words
> When singing to his dancing companion,
> Being a man
> Who loves to compose songs."

The text of this song follows:

> "All songs have been exhausted.
> He picks up some of all
> And adds his own
> And makes a new song." (1954:4-5)

While such evidences of the composer's thoughts are seldom presented save for the Eskimo, some further information about the processes of composition can be gleaned from the objectified ways in which new songs do appear.

One of the most frequently mentioned techniques of composition is that which involves taking parts of old songs and putting them together to make new ones. This technique is mentioned by Best for the Maori when he says that "songs of modern composition are often largely composed of selections from old ones" (1924:II, 142). Somewhat more specific are the Herskovitses in speaking of Trinidad: "various molds shape the songs emerging from the local scene. Some are newly improvised for ritual occasions, . . . For each group there are melodies that have come down from one generation to the next. To introduce a new song, an old melody, to which new words are put, might be used, or two melodies might be combined, or a melody might be reworked" (1947:276-77). Speaking of Washo Peyote songs, Merriam and d'Azevedo note:

> Most songs seem to have been embellished, consciously or unconsciously altered over time, combined, improvised, forgotten and "caught" again in new form as one's own. The last are thought of as "new" or "my" songs, but the singer has no inclination to hide

177

the fact that he was influenced by another song, and that "I just changed it a little." Nevertheless, it does become a "new" song. (1957:623)

Nettl reports a similar tendency for at least one informant who was speaking at the time of Arapaho Peyote songs:

In the second method discovered, a man may take one song and change it, shorten, or lengthen it, until it has become a new song. Evidently not much change is required for a song to change its identity. Example 4 contains a song which, like many Peyote songs, consists of a series of isorhythmic units. It is followed by the beginning of another song which was evidently composed with the first one as the basis. All that has been done is to add two notes at the end of each isorhythmic unit. The change is not due to a change of text, because the syllables of both songs are meaningless. The informant considered these songs as separate, but admitted that they were similar. (1954b:87)

A somewhat different aspect of the same matter is reported by the Herskovitses for Trinidad:

But not all melodies are rephrasings of old ones. Sometimes a tune heard, a European tune, can be "swung" into a desired rhythm, with perhaps a change of a few measures, or no change at all. In this case the words to a traditional song might be joined to the new melody, or a proverb might be used and to it added lines from older songs. Many times this is done half-consciously, or un-knowingly. (1947:277)

Perhaps the most clear-cut example of this kind of borrowing from old material to create new is found in McPhee's description of the process in Bali:

So also the music; retaining its traditional melodies and phrase formulae it receives new treatment by successive generations of *gurus* (teachers) who take the place of the composer. The present tendency . . . is to break up the old composition and weld frag-ments or episodes from these into new works which, though they may lack the unity of the older music, glow with fresh life and vitality. Only the most sacred and ceremonial music remains static and archaic. . . . Thus one may say that in Bali music is not composed but rearranged. . . . (1935:165)

Margaret Mead, writing about the same materials as McPhee, tends to stress other aspects of the matter:

178

Colin McPhee has described how, in the Balinese treatment of music, the contribution of the individual leader or the local club lies in the manner in which the music is played rather than in the composition of new music. So much freedom is left to each orchestra to improvise, to embroider and to alter the emphases of a traditional piece of music that in a sense each composition, beautiful in its basic conformity to an exacting tradition, *is* new after any group has rehearsed it for several months. The peasant, the vendor, the potter who has worked all day . . . comes to his evening rehearsal, not to learn how to do something that has already been done a thousand times, and much better than he could do it . . . but to change, to add, to recreate a piece of music. . . . (1941-42:86)

Two further means of composition are added to our list here, improvisation and communal re-creation. Improvisation is unquestionably a rich source of new compositional materials, but so little is known of the process that it can hardly be discussed intelligently. Nettl speaks of on-the-spot improvisation among the Eskimos, its restriction among American Indian groups in general, and its encouragement among various African groups, but nowhere is it clear precisely what is improvised or how (1956:12-14). While it is clear that there must always be limits imposed upon improvisation, we do not know what these limits are, nor do we know how much of what appears to be improvisation really is. Among the Basongye, improvisation in xylophone music definitely follows clear-cut and predetermined patterns, and the xylophone player standardizes his "licks" to such an extent that he can isolate and play oft-repeated phrases for the outside observer. But improvisation is a difficult question, and it is not possible to say to what extent it contributes to the compositional process, though it seems obvious that wherever it does occur it must involve composition as such.

A similar degree of difficulty surrounds the concept of communal re-creation. This idea, credited to Phillips Barry, holds that each singer who performs a song changes it to a certain extent and that therefore any song present in a repertoire built from oral tradition is the end result of almost infinite changes since the original version was composed (Barry 1939:passim). Further, through this process the song has become the property of the group rather than of any one individual. There seems to be no question but that songs are altered in this way; the difficulty comes in observing the process, although we do have some indication of the end result (Roberts 1925).

Still another process of composition is that of creation arising out of

179

emotion. In this case, there is re-emphasized the importance of a particular situation in generating new music material, but the individual's personal reaction to emotion as evidenced by his composition is stressed. Gladys Reichard speaks of such emotional situations as triggering songs among the Navaho, singling out times of emotional stress brought about by loneliness, contemplation of natural beauty, grief, or situations interpreted as warnings or signs (1950:284-86). Among Washo Peyotists, some specific examples can be cited. Thus, "the songs made up by individuals seem also to involve dramatic learnings; the singers say that when one 'catches a song' it is learned all at once in a moment of great emotional intensity" (Merriam and d'Azevedo 1957:623). A Washo informant described such a point in his own experience in these terms:

> When I was a child in Carson Valley I used to go out in the fields at night during a thunder storm to listen. Lightning and thunder had a special fascination for me, and I still dream about it. I remember how the sound of thunder seemed to strike against Job's Peak and then glance off and go rolling northward like the sounds which had followed and swallowed up "the old lady and the old man" (mythological creatures in the Washo creation tale). While the thunder was rolling away I could hear him singing a song; his voice was that sound thunder makes when it echoes among the mountains. I can remember that song, and I can sing it. I have sung it ever since I was a child. It is my song. The words went *li wa . . . li wa na*. That *li* sound was a kind of white man's language sound, kind of hard and rolling along . . . *li wan*. (p. 624)

While this composition is also tied to supernatural forces, the informant clearly felt the song to be one he composed, and it is equally clear that his response to thunder and lightning was a strongly emotional one.

Two other techniques of composition can be briefly mentioned here. The first is transposition, which refers of course to the internal structure of song; it is a technique which Nettl has found to be widespread in a belt of " 'transposing cultures' stretching from Western Europe across northern Asia into North America. Some peoples outside this belt, such as the Torres Straits Islanders, are represented in our examples as well, but on the whole the area given includes those cultures most obviously characterized by transposition" (1958b:61). The second technique may well signal only an individual peculiarity, but it is a direct example of new composition based upon the desire of an individual for something different. This is a case among the Wintu in which ". . . the tune of a song was revised consciously. A singer of some note altered the tune to suit his taste, and it is his version which is known and sung now" (Demetracopoulou 1935:485).

A final problem which arises in connection with the process of composition is whether it is alteration in words or in music which results in a new composition. To this point, we have been concerned primarily with changes in melody or rhythm, but there is considerable evidence to suggest that the words of a song are often more important than the sound structure and that new compositions are measured by changes in text set to old music. In certain ways this violates our own attitude toward composition; although we would agree that new words are, indeed, something new, we would be equally quick to point out that they were sung to an old, recognized tune. Thus for us the song would be only half new; among many other peoples, it appears that such a song is considered to be entirely new.

We have already cited Lane's remarks concerning the Tiv (1954:13) and Dodge's reference to the group composition of new words to what is apparently an established melody (1882:351), but there are other examples as well. On June 6 and 7, 1919, a dance was held in honor of those Pawnee who had served in World War I, and Densmore reports:

> Old war songs were sung with new words appropriate to the occasion. For example, one man had composed words which mentioned airplanes and submarines, these words being sung to an old tune. A woman had composed two similar songs, and crossing the circle, she stood in front of the chief . . . and sang them alone, without the drums. (1929:65)

Flannery reports that "most of the songs sung during the victory celebration had words which referred to encounters wherein the Gros Ventres had been successful. New words were often made up to commemorate a particular incident" (1953:98). Much more detailed is Thurnwald's description of the process of verse composition in Buin, Solomon Islands.

> I met a number of young and aged men who had composed songs. . . . The method of their work has always been the same. The poet very often not only composes for his own purposes but works on behalf of others. . . . Sometimes the author mentions himself in the poem or even complains about the honorarium. . . .
>
> The composer, together with his pals, will sit at the fire in the evening, or he may go into the forest and hide there in order to be undisturbed. He hazards some phrases and tries to sing them to the melody he has chosen. The adjustment of the words selected to the melody involved rhythm . . .

The composer will test how the words meet the melody and try over and over again. Playing with fancy and imagination accompanies this work until, after three or four weeks or more the new song is considered to be completed. (1936:6)

The important point here is that the composer apparently is not interested in making up a new melody, but rather concentrates upon words; yet Thurnwald speaks consistently of this as a "new song." While there is some question of interpretation here, it seems reasonably clear that new words constitute a new song and that sound structure is not the major consideration.

A very similar situation is described by Buck for Mangareva:

The *pou-kapa* as a composer had to be versed in traditional lore in order to select suitable themes for new compositions. . . . In the course of time such wealth of *kapa* was composed and learned that the *pou-kapa*, as song leader and instructor, simply selected songs already composed. The song expert, besides having a good memory, had to have a sense of rhythm of appropriate words and the selection of movements and gestures to go with the words, as most songs took the form of a combined song and dance. . . .

If the composition did not fit easily with action, it was termed *maro* (hard). If a leader introduced such a new composition, he met with criticism and opposition from his company. . . . A new composition was also criticized by other experts as to whether or not it complied with the established literary standards. It was necessary that quotations from tradition be accurate. The words must have a smooth swing that not only suited the voice but that would blend readily with appropriate movements of the hands, feet, and body. (1938:305-06)

In another context, Buck notes some of the techniques used by composers of texts:

Parallelism is a favorite form of composition. The first verse is repeated with just the change in the names of the characters who figure in the story. . . . The people delighted in singing refrains after each verse; composers purposely lengthened some songs by enumerating details.

A favorite form of parallelism was the use of question and answer. If the theme deals with a number of historical characters and their wives, the first and alternate verses ask the name of the wife of a character, and the following verse answers it. Thus the song is lengthened and the singers have the pleasure of repeating the refrain.

Metaphor and simile . . . are frequently used. . . .

The language used is cryptic at times. . . .

Grammatical construction in songs is apt to cause trouble to students who attempt to translate according to the rules of prose grammar. It must be remembered that the compositions are meant to be sung, and if a grammatical particle interferes with the rhythm, it is simply left out. Similarly the last syllable of a word may be drawn out, and in the singing rhythm, it may appear to be joined with the first syllable of the following word; . . . Sometimes a vowel may be drawn out. . . .

Words occur in songs which are seldom or never used in prose, usually exclamations of joy or distress. (1938:384-85)

Thurnwald also gives some excellent insights into the process of composing song verse:

Composing a new text implies a careful selection of words as pointed out above. Consequently, the language of these songs does not exactly correspond to the tongue used in daily conversation, but becomes "elevated speech." This is demonstrated by a number of peculiarities. Arm-chair expressions are employed, such as koro'kua for urugito (pig); ta'nćina for a'buta (shell money); bana'uku for opo (sleeping house on piles); ro'bana for ro'ikene (men, people), etc. Foreign expressions are particularly favored, in order to demonstrate snobbishly the author's vast experience. In the old times Alu words were used, since the Alu people were treated with reverence as the origin (together with Mono) of the aristocratic chiefs. Thus la'gara is found for kaikai (speech); ta'iga for ko'ci (garden); and so on. In more recent days the contact with white men has been instrumental in bringing into use a host of English words. However, these cannot always be easily discerned, because of their "Buinization." Bainim will be revealed as "find him," or "find it;" a'sikim as "ask him," for ask him or ask her; ba'lata as "brother;" bi'bo as "before;" abimu'item as "afternoon-time;" ro'kuta as "doctor," etc. These words moreover are often equipped with suffixes of the Buin language. Thus, in bere'ćige, ge is the local suffix and be'rećí, "place," meaning "on the place." The call to assemble for cleaning the road, uàká'bèle, originates from ua ka, "work," plus be, "go," and le or re, the local suffix. A difficult problem is le'si te'ngere, 1 stands for a misinterpreted the, ng is interchangeable with m, and re is the local suffix, therefore it means "at this time."

183

Combinations of words are sometimes hard to disentangle, such as niumo'nio, "when new moon [is];" tu'maniboi, "two man boy," i.e., two boys; tuda kau, "when too dark," i.e., fully dark or at night, etc. The deformation of English words is, of course, due to the peculiarity of Buin pronunciation which cannot be discussed here. . . .

The most essential deviation from the colloquial speech lies, however, in the rhetoric of the songs which is a deliberately chosen thing. It is not so much the phrasing itself as the ideas rendered. The poet wants to appeal to his listener's emotions not only by carefully picked expressions but by adducing special observations, touching situations, and striking imagery. The composer searches his memory and his creative faculty for whatever he can find to direct his hearer's emotions toward the desired end. Therefore he offers legendary and mythic allusions as well as anything else from "far away" and from the enigmatic accomplishments of the whites. . . . As he accumulates these references the artificial character of the song will be realized, distinguishing it from ordinary speech. (1936:7-8)

Although some question exists, then, as to whether a song is adjudged to be new because of its text or its sound structure, or both, there is no question but that the setting of words to music constitutes a form of composition.

Composition seems clearly to be the product of the individual or a group of individuals and not to differ radically between literate and nonliterate peoples save in the question of writing. All composition is conscious in the broadest sense of the word when viewed from an analytic standpoint. Composers may be casual individuals, specialists, or groups of people, and their compositions must be acceptable to society at large. Techniques of composition include at least the following: the reworking of old materials, the incorporation of borrowed or old material, improvisation, communal re-creation, creation arising out of particularly intense emotional experience, transposition, and composition from individual idiosyncrasy. Composition of texts is quite as important as the composition of the sound structure. Composition involves learning, is subject to public acceptance and rejection, and is therefore a part of the broad learning process which contributes, in turn, to the processes of stability and change.

PART THREE

PROBLEMS AND RESULTS

CHAPTER X

THE STUDY OF SONG TEXTS

The first two sections of this book have been directed toward the development of a definition and theory of ethnomusicology, a model for its study, and illustrations of the kinds of problems involved in and suggested by that model. It has been stressed that ethnomusicology involves much more than the structural analysis of music sound, for music is a human phenomenon produced by people for people and existing and functioning in a social situation.

We turn now to some of the major problems ethnomusicology must approach if it is to fulfill its promise as a discipline which attempts to make scientific analysis of its subject matter. We shall be searching not only for the motivations which lie behind music behavior as such, but also for the means of expanding knowledge of music to knowledge of other and wider human behavioral processes. What *do* we learn from music? What can we learn from the broad study of ethnomusicology viewed as a discipline which treats music as one further aspect of human behavior taking its place beside man's other multiple activities?

One of the most obvious sources for the understanding of human behavior in connection with music is the song text. Texts, of course, are language behavior rather than music sound, but they are an integral part of music and there is clear-cut evidence that the language used in connection with music differs from that of ordinary discourse.

It is a truism to say that music and language are interrelated, and that the study of this interrelationship is thus a task for the joint energies of the ethnomusicologist and the linguist. The exact nature of the problem, however, tends to be technical and structural in nature and is not of

187

primary concern here, although some aspects of it may be noted briefly. Language clearly affects music in that speech melody sets up certain patterns of sound which must be followed at least to some extent in music, if the music-text fusion is to be understood by the listener. Bright comments that "languages display regular patterns of high-pitched and low-pitched syllables, loud and soft syllables, long and short syllables; and different languages give different emphases to these factors. Since patterns involving these elements of pitch, dynamics, and duration are also among the basic elements of music, it is at least a reasonable hypothesis that there may be some cultures in which features of spoken languages have played a part in conditioning the musical patterns of song" (1963:27).

Music also influences language in that musical requirements demand alterations in the patterns of normal speech. Thus language behavior in song is a special kind of verbalization which sometimes requires special knowledge of the language in which it is couched. We have had occasion in the preceding chapter to comment upon some of the linguistic changes in song texts in connection with the processes of composition, but some further discussion may be entered into here.

In speaking of the Maori, Best notes that "a serious difficulty encountered in the translation of these songs is found in alteration of word forms for the sake of euphony. Thus vowels may be inserted, elided, or altered, or an extra syllable may be added to a word. Again, not only do song makers employ archaic expressions and resurrect obsolete words, but they also sometimes coin a word" (1924:139). In another work, he continues;

> In order to render a line euphonious, words are altered in form to the confusion of the translator. Thus vowels may be inserted or elided, thus producing word forms which render the translator help-less. Thus, in one song, we find the phrase *te ahua o te kupu* (the aspect or character of the remark) is altered to *te ehu o te kupu*, and ehu means "turbid," and to bail out water, and to exhume, as bones of the dead. . . . In this case the desire was to shorten vowel sounds. *Kua* is sometimes lengthened to *koua*, all for the sake of euphony. In other cases a single vowel sound is drawn out, as in the *huatau*. In the legend of Rata occurs a charm that commences:
>
> Rata wărě, Rata wā . . a . . a . . re
> In the word *wărě* both vowels are short, and it is so pronounced in its first occurrence; but in the second the *a* is drawn out as shown. (1925:107)

Such technical details of changing linguistic structure appear to be a common feature of song texts, and there is the further difficulty of the use of special kinds of language in song. Best points out that the Maori also use "metaphor, allegorical expressions, mystic and mythopoetic phrases and aphorisms" in their texts, and that "for these reasons the translation of native songs is almost invariably a difficult matter, unless one can obtain enlightenment from one who is acquainted with the figurative expressions, sacerdotal terms, old sayings, allusions to old myths, and cryptic utterances that they contain" (1924:136). Indeed, Best was particularly concerned with such problems of translation and devotes considerable discussion to them (1925:107-14).

Special language use is apparently a common feature of song texts. Migeod, speaking of the Mende of Sierra Leone, comments that "words are often slightly modified in pronunciation as well as shortened, and a further complication is that the singer is himself very commonly unable to give meaning. . . . The many meaningless words they will describe as 'song-words' . . ." (1926:289). Firth notes for the Tikopia:

> As in the uru and other pivotal chants of the festival, the language of the taume is of a different character from that used in everyday conversation, and contains a number of words which are said by the natives to be of archaic form. Thus of some phrases it is said "speech of former times; it has disappeared." The absence of any very precise meaning for individual words and phrases, however, is not detrimental to them in native eyes. Their value is essentially symbolic and lies in the correct recital and conjunction of them, not in their individual significance to the people who sing them. (1940:II,264)

Titiev adds that the Mapuche of Chile ". . . employ a highly figurative style, full of nuances and subtle turns of expression. Then, too . . . they like to use phrases that are markedly elliptical and laconic, with very few words serving to suggest complete thoughts. Moreover, most of the references . . . derive so much of their significance from close familiarity with Mapuche culture, that outsiders are apt to find them meaningless or enigmatic" (1949:1).

The widespread difficulty of translation of texts due to linguistic change, particular forms of language, the insertion of archaic expressions, and so forth, is further emphasized by the statements of a number of writers concerning a number of widely separated cultures. Such comment is made, for example, by Birket-Smith for the Eskimo (1935:156),

189

Douglas L. Oliver for the Siuai of the Solomon Islands (1955:369), Voth for the Oraibi (1903:passim), LaFlesche for the Osage (1925:passim), and others. And this, of course, takes no consideration of the very special cases afforded by tonal languages (Marius Schneider 1961) and by drum signaling (Carrington 1949a&b).

We can say, then, that not only are music and language interrelated in the formation of song texts, but also that the language of texts tends to take special forms. Therefore we should expect that the language of texts would have special significance and would function in special ways, and this seems to be the case.

One of the most striking examples is shown by the fact that in song the individual or the group can apparently express deep-seated feelings not permissibly verbalized in other contexts. This phenomenon has been commented upon most frequently for Africa, although it apparently operates in other world areas as well. Hugh Tracey in speaking of the African Chopi says: "You can say publicly in songs what you cannot say privately to a man's face, and so this is one of the ways African society takes to maintain a spiritually healthy community" (1954:237). Margaret Green reports for the Nigerian Ibo that the women of the village occasionally come together in order to judge a woman suspected of stealing from another member of the group. In doing so, they gather at the home of the accused; Green notes that in order to summon all the women to the judging the group sang a song on a particular occasion she witnessed: "Women who will not come out in this place, let millipede go into her sex organs, let earthworm go into her sex organs." Green comments that "such things would be said on no ordinary occasion to a woman, but were used here to induce the women strongly to turn out in force" (1947:199-206). From a different part of the world, Devereux and La Barre report that "a Sedang Moi girl . . . once improvised a little song to tell me that they were tired and wished to go home. Asked why she did not tell me this in ordinary language, she replied that to do so would have been rude. Apparently, by expressing her wish in the form of a song, she left me free to decide whether to hear it only as a bit of vocal music, or to take cognizance also of its conceptual content" (1961:369).

Similar freedom in song is illustrated by an occasion witnessed by the author among the Bashi people of the Congo (Léopoldville). The songs were sung by a group of girls working at the time on a coffee and quinine plantation in the Kivu area. "The owner of the plantation was acting in the capacity of interpreter . . . and thus could not fail to follow the song texts; due to advances in prices he had recently stopped giving the workers a ration of salt and, particularly peanut or palm oil." The first song of the series spoke of a girl who was working on a plantation; it was made abundantly clear that the Plantation was Bwana X's. In the second song, a mother says to her daughter:

"Go work in my fields."
The daughter refuses, saying:
"No, I want to work for Bwana X. I want to work for the white man where I have a task, for when it is finished I can leave."
The mother is angry, but the girl goes to work for X. One day while going to work, she comes to the edge of the Nyaberango river which is in flood stage.
"What shall I do? How can I cross the river and get to work? And if I cross and work all day then perhaps it will rain some more and I won't be able to get back again. But I will go, work quickly, finish soon, and come back before it has a chance to rain any more."

In the third song, the girls said:

"We don't work for Bwana Y. On that plantation, they just work taking out the bad coffee. They don't work with the fork. But here we work for Bwana X with the fork. Why do we come here to work when we could work for Bwana Y just picking out the bad coffee? It is because Bwana X is a good man. He gives us a task and we can do this task, and when we finish, we may go home. So we are good girls who are able to work like men."

In the fourth song, the point began to emerge more clearly.

"We come to work for Bwana X. We finish our tasks and we do good work. When it is pay day, Bwana X gives francs to all of us. We say: 'Well, that is good, but Pedro (Bwana X's headman) said that Bwana X said that if we worked well and finished our tasks, he would give us salt and oil.' Here we are, and we have the francs, but where is the salt? Where is the oil? We don't understand it because Pedro does not tell lies. But here it is. Why?"

And in the final song, the point is driven home.

"We have finished our work. Before, we used to get oil; now we don't get it. Why has Bwana stopped giving us oil? We don't understand. If he doesn't give us oil, we will all leave and go to work for the Catholic Fathers. There we can do little work and have plenty of oil. Be careful! If we don't get oil, we won't work here."

191

These five songs, of course, represent an organized plan to inform the plantation owner of the desires and intentions of the working girls. The discontent was unknown to the planter; while the girls were unwilling to express their doubts directly to him, they seized the opportunity which presented itself to inform him indirectly of the situation. The melodic lines of the songs were well established as Bashi melodies; the words were improvised on the spur of the moment, save for the last song which had been given the new text at the time X stopped giving oil to the girls (Merriam 1954).

Given the apparent freedom of song lyrics, one would expect to find considerable obscenity, not necessarily for its own sake but rather directed toward some aim or used simply to increase the effectiveness of the desired message; Green's citation to the Ibo, quoted above, seems to be of this type. Speaking of the Gros Ventres, Flannery expresses the same point in noting that "songs at the second and third circling had words, composed by enemy-friends of the scouts, the words usually being both derisive and vulgar" (1953:91). Unfortunately, there seems to be very little information concerning obscenity in song texts. Both Williamson, for the Mafulu of New Guinea (1912:215), and Ivens, for the Lau of the Solomons (n.d.:98), refer to vulgar songs but comment no further. McAllester notes the presence of a "few obscene songs" among the Apache, and adds that "they are very few as compared with our enormous body of such material. I was able to record only one which had reference to a man who ate too many cedar berries, had diarrhea and soiled his breech clout. There were similar references in some of the clowning that goes on during almost any kind of singing" (1960:472). Malinowski, speaking of the love-making expeditions of boys in the Trobriand Islands, says:

> The adventurers would, therefore, usually steal out at night and put on their ornaments outside their village. But once on the main road, they became boisterous and defiant, for this is the proper behavior on such an occasion. There are even some special bawdy songs, called *lo'uwa* to which they keep time as they go along. (1929:264)

Finally, Demetracopoulou speaks of the use of obscene songs among the Wintu:

> The obscene songs which are sung in the Bald Hills area are probably not strictly puberty songs. They are known as *sune·* and are referred to as food-begging songs. In most sub areas of the Wintu territory they were sung only as a means of obtaining food at irregular intervals. A group from one village went visiting an-

192

other village. Upon their arrival, the visitors danced naked or raised their clothes to expose their sexual organs, singing obscene songs and making obscene gestures. They usually performed this before the houses of relatives by consanguinity or affinity. The hosts, in disgust, gave them food to get rid of them. In Bald Hills, these songs were sung at puberty ceremonies by the groups arriving from invited villages, probably because this was an occasion for receiving food. (1935:490)

It is impossible to make any sort of generalization from such a brief sampling, although it does seem probable that obscene songs are sung among almost all peoples. It is equally probable, however, that a distinction is made between pornography for its own sake and the use of obscenity in the licensed song situation to emphasize a point in a way not otherwise acceptable.

What is important in all the cases cited above is that song itself gives the freedom to express thoughts, ideas, and comments which cannot be stated baldly in the normal language situation. It appears, then, that song texts, because of the special kind of license that singing apparently gives, afford an extremely useful means for obtaining kinds of information which are not otherwise easily accessible.

One of the forms through which this is made most evident is the topical song such as the Calypso (Crowley 1959a), which has a very widespread distribution and which may well be found in almost every society. Topical songs take many forms, but in broadest application they may be characterized simply as songs of comment upon aspects of daily life. Speaking of the Chopi of East Africa, Tracey has perhaps best summarized the content of the topical song, although his reference is most frequently to a specialized variety, the song of social control:

> The subject-matter may be gay, sad, or purely documentary. In every case it is highly topical and appropriate to the locality, so much so, in fact, that most of the allusions would be caught only by those in close touch with the villagers and the district. They are often highly critical of those in authority over them, white or black, and to a large degree it may be said that the poems reflect the attitude of the common people towards the conditions of their society. High good humour is a very prominent feature of most of their poems. Sly digs at the pompous, outspoken condemnation of those who neglect their duties, protests against the cruel and overbearing, outcries directed against social injustices as well as philosophy in the face of difficulties, are all to be found in their songs. . . . (1948:3)

193

Tracey expresses a very cogent point concerning the function of such song.

> . . . it performs a highly social and cathartic function in a so-
> ciety which has no daily press, no publications, and no stage other
> than the village yard in which publicly to express its feelings or
> voice its protests against the rub of the times. It will be realized
> how important it is to keep open such a channel through which
> incidents perpetuated for a while in song express symbolically the
> plethora of similar incidents which gratify, amuse, exasperate, or
> sadden the common people—community expression through the
> self-expression of their composers. It might even be regarded as a
> form of theatre. . . . (loc. cit.)

There are a number of varieties of topical song which can be separated
on the basis both of intent and content, including, for example, songs of
insult, pure and simple. Crowley writes of the two major singing societies,
La Rose and La Marguerite, in St. Lucia, whose members practice and
parade on the appropriate day, "attending Mass in a body, parading
through the streets carrying banners and wearing fancy dress indicative
of . . . society status. The rest of the year the societies hold 'seances' or
evening meetings where the members practice their songs . . . and deride
the attributes of the opposite society.

> On the register, it is the King
>   of the water—(nickname of
>   La Marguerite)
> who is registered.
> Go to other countries, it is
>   the king of the water
> who is registered.
> La Rose cannot have that
>   because they have too much noise.

Crowley also points out that in the past "such boasting and insults led to
blows, court cases, and occasional street riots. . . ." (1957:7-8). Speaking
of the "Nail," a type of facial marking introduced among the Nigerian Tiv
in fairly recent times, Akiga reports that "the younger Tiv are split into
two factions, and there is bitter feeling between them. Those with the
lumps make up mocking songs about the Nail Men, and the Nail Men
about the Lumpy-faced" (East 1939:46).

Another broad category of topical song is the more or less "neutral"
comment on scandal; in this case there is no direct function of causing
action, but rather the song simply takes note of what is going on. Crowley

194

reports on a St. Lucian *caliso*, giving the text of a song which comments on a "recent rum bonding scandal."

> Some say they don't know at all
> Some say it was just bòbòl ("graft")
> But what I would like to know is
> How the cask get out of the Government
> bondhouse? (1957:13)

Speaking of the Australian Songman, Elkin says that songs are made up ". . . about everyday incidents, including love affairs. Frequently the patent meaning of the text is quite innocuous, but a second or latent meaning is understood by the hearers. . . . The Songman is careful that his allusions are not too direct" (1954:74). A. B. Ellis makes similar comment concerning the Tshi-speaking peoples of West Africa:

> Frequently the words have reference to current events, and it is not uncommon for singers to note the peculiarities of persons who may pass and improvise at their expense. This is particularly the case when the strangers are Europeans, as the latter do not as a rule understand Tshi, and the singers can allow themselves greater latitude than would be the case if their remarks were understood. (1887:328)

Herskovits speaks of songs of gossip and scandal in discussing the work party in Haiti.

> The *combite* songs are distinctive in Haitian music for their melodic quality. . . . At the *combite* a man not only learns all the gossip of the day, but enjoys learning and singing the songs which caustically comment on the shortcomings of neighbors, or evaluate the hospitality of those who have called *combites*, or detail scandal, phrased with sufficient directness to allow the reference of the song to remain clear, but warily, so as not to give the individual pilloried ground for direct recrimination. (1937:74)

Five texts are given, referring to "a miserly *combite* host," an affair of a first cousin with first cousin, "an impending quarrel where a suspicion of magic practices entered," a challenge of physical might, and "a composition which complains against a shirker who comes and eats, but does little work." Further information concerning the same song type comes from the Herskovitses' work in Trinidad:

> A favorite method of comment is in song. The form is not one of narrative detail, but of deft allusion, of the suggestive image. The

pattern of putting into song important happenings of the day lies deep in the tradition of the group. . . . The pattern of comment on current happenings places emphasis on the humorous, the pretentious, the malicious. An occasional note of pity, or self-pity enters; and the more frequent theme of the braggard, or the strong, boastful fellow; and the love motif. But the principal effect sought for and achieved is laughter. (1947:276-78)

The examples of song texts given include decrying "the free and easy manner of the young girls," "taunting a rival," "the elderly woman who weds a man much younger than herself," "allusion . . . to the girls who love not wisely," "variations on the theme of the young girl who finds herself with child," love for a girl, and so forth (pp. 278-84).

Clyde Mitchell, writing about the Kalela dance in the towns of Northern Rhodesia, gives as examples texts concerned with self-praise, with lampooning the modern girl who uses powder and paint, the mercenary interest of parents in marriage payments, and other topics. The Lamba preoccupation with adultery cases is commented upon in the following song:

> Mothers, I have been to many courts,
> To listen to the cases they settle:
> They settle divorce cases,
> They talk about witchcraft cases,
> They talk about thefts,
> They talk about tax-defaulting,
> And refusing to do tribute labour.
> But the things I saw at Mushili's court,
> These things I wondered at.
> From nine o'clock in the morning,
> To four o'clock in the afternoon,
> The cases were only adultery.
> Then I asked the court messenger:
> "Do you have any different matters to settle?"
> The court messenger said: "No,
> There are no other matters,
> It is just like this in Lambaland—
> There are no assault cases,
> There are no theft cases:
> These are the cases in the courts of Lambaland."
> (1956:7-8)

Topical songs such as these are a reflection of the concerns of the culture of which they are a part. While they may contribute to the correction of those aspects of behavior to which they call attention, simply through the means of putting them in the public eye, their major function seems to be one of comment on various aspects of everyday life. At the same time, such songs exhibit a keen eye for scandal and gossip, and they lead quickly to a further subgrouping of the topical song.

This song group is concerned with direct social control, that is, songs are sometimes used, through admonition, ridicule, and in some cases even more direct action, to effect actual change in the behavior of erring members of society. Such songs may be directed toward a wide variety of social ills, among them sex offenses, such as the song in Dahomey heard by Herskovits and "sung against a young woman who had been careless with her favors and had in addition been guilty of theft" (1938b:II, 323). Burrows reports that on the Pacific islands of Uvea and Futuna:

> A different kind of taunting song ridicules evildoers, particularly sex offenders. Though sexual intercourse before marriage, and even adultery, are regarded rather leniently, birth of a child to these unions is definitely a misdemeanor, as is the practice of *moe-tolo*, which is defined by Grezel as *aller a la recherche des femmes endormies pour faire le mal sur elles; faire de mauvaises actions sur des femmes endormies.*
>
> Usually it is the man who is punished. The official punishment is a fine of cooked food; but no one who has seen how Polynesians wince under ridicule can doubt that these mocking songs are punishment too. (1945:74-5)

The rectification of wrong done through thievery may also be the object of such songs. Firth says that "one way of relieving the owner's feelings, and perhaps bringing disrepute and shame upon the thief, is to compose a song about the incident and have it chanted as a dance chorus in the ordinary way. Natives say that the thief, listening to this, is made to feel shame. The song thus becomes a kind of legal mechanism by which the ridicule of the community is mobilized and launched against the offender" (1939:269).

But song can be the vehicle for legal action in a much more direct fashion than this. Bohannan (1957:142-44) recounts in detail a legal case among the Tiv directly stimulated by the use of song. The principals in the case were Torgindi and Mtswen, and Bohannan states the background of the case as follows: "Mtswen was the secondary marriage guardian of the wife of Torgindi's son, and had been guilty of some rather highhanded tactics that caused the marriage to fall through. Mtswen had then refused to act as intermediary to get Torgindi's bride-wealth refunded, and the two men exchanged angry words." Torgindi's response to the exchange

197

was to return to his compound and make up a song commenting on "what a skunk Mtswen was." That night, he sang the song as loudly as possible, within Mtswen's hearing, and this was repeated the following night with the members of his lineage joining in. Mtswen, not being skillful in composition, then hired a composer to make up similarly scurrilous songs about Torgindi, who in turn hired his own composer. Both men were active in singing the songs every night, and each gathered food and drink in order to attract others to come and sing the songs and support their cause. Bohannan says:

> There are some specific rules for these songs. Chenge told me that if an act attributed in such a song was possible of human performance, it should be true, or the slandered person could call a *jir*. However, if the act was not humanly possible anything could be said. In one of Mtswen's songs, he accused one of Torgindi's wives of stealing yams: this, by local consensus, was probably true because this particular wife was one of the Udam tribe, and widely thought to be a thief. But if it was not true, Chenge insisted, Torgindi and the wife could call a *jir* against Mtswen and the song-maker. Another song, and one of the catchiest tunes which the contest produced, told how Torgindi changed himself into a pig at night and made it unsafe for every sow in the countryside. The Shangev song-maker . . . said that since even Torgindi couldn't actually do that, such a song couldn't be the basis for a *jir*. The song-maker said that he had thought of some much worse things to suggest that it was in Torgindi's nature to do, if it were only humanly possible, but that Mtswen had stopped him saying that all he wanted to do was to win the contest, not to "spoil Torgindi's heart permanently." They were, after all, neighbors.

The singing and drumming continued every night for more than three weeks before the legal authorities took notice, but the two principals were finally informed that they were to appear at a certain time and place. Both men came with substantial groups of supporters, music instruments, and other paraphernalia, and the two groups performed for almost two hours before the authorities called for silence and announced that the case would be judged.

> The case, which was a simple marriage case, was very quickly settled, and both men—anxious to be rid of the vast expense they were incurring—concurred in the judgment. After the case was settled on its jural points, the *mbatarev* announced the winner of the song contest: Torgindi won the case, but Mtswen had better songs.

They then advised both song-makers to go home immediately and not return to MbaDuku for a couple of months until the feelings which had been aroused had died down.

An apparently similar kind of formalized legal process among the Eskimo is reported by Holm, who says that murder, theft, or destruction of another's property may be the occasion, though cases involving women are most important:

> The drum-matches are held both summer and winter. A match of this kind is not settled in one evening, but is continued for a number of years, the parties taking turns to visit one another. For each new meeting the parties prepare and practise new songs. In these songs the crimes are vastly exaggerated, and if they can find no other material, they father new crimes on their opponent, or reproach him for crimes he has merely intended but not committed. They also enumerate the faults of their opponent's family, and even of their dead ancestors. In the hands of malicious people these attacks may assume an exceedingly brutal form. . . .
>
> The opponents stand facing one another. They sing one at a time . . . the other party standing quiet and apparently indifferent in front of him. The singer mocks the other in a great number of ways, as a rule by snorting and breathing right in his face and by striking him with the forehead . . . so that he tumbles backward.
>
> The other party receives this treatment with the greatest composure, nay even with mocking laughter to show his audience his indifference to it. When his opponent is about to strike him, he shuts his eyes and advances his head to receive the blow. (1914: 127-28)

The singing may go on all night, and Holm reports that it is received with a high degree of interest by the audience. The opponents do not show hostility toward each other in the breaks between the songs.

There are several difficulties with Holm's description of these drum matches. We do not really understand why they are held, that is, what occasion arising out of the background of legal dispute causes the actual coming together of the opponents. Neither do we discover, unfortunately, what constitutes resolution of the conflict. Holm does say that "when one party dies, the other plumes himself on it and boasts over it to others," but there is no indication that any sort of judge is present or that the drum matches do anything save vent the feelings of the disputants (pp. 127-28).

Speaking of the same phenomenon, Thalbitzer gives somewhat more detail, but again does not indicate clearly the resolution of the conflict. He does say, however:

> Two men, or sometimes two women, having become enemies would once a year have a settlement with each other in a drum-fight where, in turn, they would give vent to their anger in a poetical form, one drumming and singing against the other. . . .
>
> The songs were constantly renewed, as the hostility between the two opponents only in rare instances resulted in homicide (never during the drumfight itself), but only in a continuation of the fight at the next meeting, the following summer or winter. (1923a:166-69)

These passages seem to reinforce the conclusion that the drum contests were not truly juridical, for apparently no legal solution resulted; rather, they seemed to function as a means of public expression of hostility, continuing as long as the hostility remained. That drum contests do work in this manner in some Eskimo groups is indicated by Spencer (1959:176).

Another similar procedure is found in the "halo" competitions reported for the Ewe of Ghana. Gadzekpo says:

> "Halo" is a kind of music competition in which two neighboring villages compete in making songs about each other. As a rule there are no judges at such competitions, but spectators often form their own opinion about the winners, who are determined by the effectiveness of their insult through songs. . . .
>
> Songs of insult deal with the shameful history of individuals among the opponents. . . .
>
> Often one side will invite the other to come and be insulted. They sing to each individual the songs composed about him, and he must muster courage to be able to stand the abuse in the presence of spectators. . . .
>
> "Halo" matches last for a long time—anything from two to about ten years, and are terminated by order of the chiefs, who summon the competing parties to make peace. (1952:819)

A much shorter but essentially similar notice of halo matches is given by Gbeho (1954:62), but in neither case is the means of resolution of the conflict made clear.

Finally, it may be noted in considering action songs of a legal nature that Thurnwald, speaking of the Buin of the Solomon Islands, says that although formal legal action was not taken through song, the result might well be the same, for "in the old times a fight easily ensued from the invectives of a smart song. Or a grieved woman committed suicide" (1936:6).

Song texts, then, can be used as a means of action directed toward the solution of problems which plague a community. While this can take the form of ridicule and shame, or sanctioned legal action, it is also apparent that song texts provide psychological release for the participants. Indeed, because of the freedom of expression allowed in song, texts seem clearly to provide an excellent means for the investigation of the psychological processes of the people who constitute a culture. Through the study of song texts it may well be possible to strike quickly through protective mechanisms to arrive at an understanding of the "ethos" of the culture and to gain some perspective of psychological problems and processes peculiar to it. Song texts have been used in this way by a number of authors.

Weston LaBarre has used limericks sung by American college students to make a Freudian analysis of the unconscious in a "normal" situation. The framework of his study was set in the context of obtaining materials from normal individuals in order to refute charges that Freudian analysis is too frequently based upon examples from those who are not normal. Noting that the super-ego is liquidated in ordinary drinking situations, La-Barre concludes:

> We have presented a study of the "normal" unconscious, as its content is externalized in the relaxed social context of drinking, when the force of the super-ego is weakened somewhat as in the analytic situation of formally-permitted "free association." Abundant evidence of the presence of repressed polymorphous infantile perversities has been brought. . . . The fact that this state of affairs is demonstrably the case, is clear evidence that the Freudian theory of the genesis of the unconscious through repression is applicable to "normal" as well as to neurotic or psychotic individuals. (1939:212)

It is significant to note that LaBarre sought a situation in which normal individuals would be free of certain societal restraints, and that he found it in a music context, thus emphasizing again the importance of the fact that music provides situations in which language behavior is freed from the restraints imposed in normal discourse.

A similar kind of analysis from song texts, though not couched in Freudian terms or carried out for the specific purpose of proving a theoretical point, was made by S. I. Hayakawa concerning popular songs in the United States (1955). Wendell Johnson in his *People in Quandaries* (1946) formulated the concept of the IFD disease, which

Hayakawa defines as "the triple-threat semantic disorder of Idealization (the making of impossible and ideal demands upon life), which leads to Frustration (as the result of the demands not being met), which in turn leads to Demoralization (or Disorganization, or Despair)" (p. 84). In his study he points out that popular songs emphasize the I F D, that the ideals set are basically impossible ideals, that this idealization inevitably turns out to be disappointing, and that it finally leads to demoralization. In contrast to the popular song, Hayakawa finds that the blues have "a considerable tough-mindedness . . . a willingness often absent in popular songs to acknowledge the facts of life" (p. 93), and that they do not give "a false or misleading impression of what life is likely to be. . . ." This leads him to the following conclusion:

> If our symbolic representations give a false or misleading impression of what life is likely to be, we are *worse* prepared for life than we would have been had we not been exposed to them at all. The frustration and demoralization of which Wendell Johnson writes are of necessity preceded by the expectations created by unrealistic idealization. This is not to say, of course, that idealizations are in themselves unhealthy; they are a necessary and inescapable product of the human processes of abstraction and symbolization, and without idealizations we should be swine indeed. But there is a world of difference in the semantogenic effects of *possible* and *impossible* ideals. The ideals of love, as depicted in popular songs, are usually impossible ideals. (p. 93)

Hayakawa is here concerned with a psychological situation and the possible results which may stem from it. Herskovits, on the other hand, in a particularly useful paper proposes "to indicate certain aspects of the psychology of . . . Negro cultural behavior which may be better understood when some of the broader simpler concepts of psychoanalysis are applied to their interpretation" (1934:76). Taking the concepts of repression and compensation, he points out a number of mechanisms in Negro cultures, both African and New World, and emphasizes that "there exists both a recognition of the neuroses as induced by repression, and of the therapeutic value of bringing a repressed thought into the open" (p. 77). His vehicle for the discussion rests partly upon an analysis of song and dance. He notes:

> In Dahomey, the institution of the avogan, the dance in the marketplace, is . . . recognized by the natives as affording release for suppressed emotions. At stated periods the people of each of the quarters of the city of Abomey have in turn their opportunity to stage such a dance. Crowds come to see the display and to watch

the dancing, but most of all, to listen to the songs and to laugh at the ridicule to which are held those who have offended members of the quarter giving the dance. Names are ordinarily not mentioned, for then fighting may result. In any event, the African relishes innuendo and circumlocution too well to be satisfied with bald, direct statement. However, everyone who is present already knows to whom reference is being made. Thus the song might be:

> Women, thy soul is misshapen.
> In haste was it made, in haste.
> So fleshless a face speaks, telling
> Thy soul was formed without care.
> The Ancestral clay for thy making
> Was moulded in haste, in haste.
> A thing of no beauty art thou,
> Thy face unsuited to be a face,
> Thy feet unsuited for feet. (pp. 77-8)

Such release is also given to co-wives who sing songs against each other.

The *lobi singi* of the Negroes of the coastal region of Dutch Guiana, especially of Paramaribo, is discussed at some length by Herskovits in the same article, as is the institution of *fiofio* in the same area, and he summarizes by saying:

> What has been shown is that among the . . . Negroes, both in Africa and the New World, patterned types of psychic purges are recognized as valid; what is important for a psychoanalytic approach to the understanding of these social data is the fact that, in every case, the native explanation of the particular type of behaviour, though ordinarily couched in terms of the supernatural, can be restated in terms of the unconscious. (pp. 82-3)

The points made by Herskovits, and especially the situations he describes, are strongly reminiscent of the Eskimo song-battles, the halo institution of the Ewe, and the songs of social control cited earlier in this chapter. The same points are applicable to the Mapuche of Chile, described by Titiev (1949). In this case, unaccompanied songs are improvised at social gatherings by men or women "who take advantage of these occasions to 'blow off steam,' or to call general attention to some matter of personal concern to the singer. Songs of this kind are called 'assembly songs,' and their moods may vary from naive and joyful to slanderous, bitter, or ironic" (p. 2). Examples of texts, as well as their interpretations, indicate clearly that the songs must indeed afford release for suppressed emotions. In the interpretations, we find the following examples:

203

The singer complains that her husband is rapacious and in-considerate. According to Collio, she is also implying that her spouse does not satisfy her sexual desires. . . .

In explaining this song my informant said that it is of the type sung by a young wife to call attention to the fact that her husband is sexually overactive. On hearing such a complaint, her relatives and friends try to advise her spouse to moderate his marital be-havior. Sometimes a group of elderly men will arrange to meet the husband in private, without the wife's knowledge, in order to give him the benefit of their experience. Among other things they may tell the husband not to seek sexual satisfaction daily and to ab-stain from intercourse for at least twelve hours after a meal. . . .

The husband expresses remorse for his errors and promises to mend his way at once and henceforth to keep his mind only on his wife. . . .

In these words a girl expresses her unwillingness to set a definite wedding date. Her song implies that she may yet be willing to marry her suitor, but is not interested in a casual love affair.

The Mapuche songs function as a release mechanism but, coupled with what is clearly freedom of expression, they are a means of disseminating information which leads to redress of grievances and solutions of problems.

The use of texts as a means of escape and refuge has been commented upon by Opler and Obayashi (1945) in connection with Senryu poetry studied at the Tule Lake Relocation Center for people of Japanese descent during World War II. Senryu is a form of Japanese poetry first developed as Hai-ku about two hundred years ago; it is regarded by the authors as a "folk art." At Tule Lake there developed an association of Senryu composers who met regularly; analysis of the poetic materials revealed that about forty-eight per cent were devoted to abstract ideas such as Daytime, Making Money, The Act of Thinking, Scent, and so forth, and that the rest were approximately evenly divided between Topics Expressed by a Verb, Adverb, Adjective, and Preposition (Peeping, Too, Getting Ready, Careless), and Topics Expressed by a Common Noun (Wall, Ice, Father). The authors conclude that "the members preferred as subject matter topics unrelated to life at Tule Lake," and that "they desired to forget the drab existence in the Center, and as a matter of fact sought in Senryu a method of escape from it. . . . The cultural form itself provides the refuge, the recreation, and the escape. . . . It is also . . . an instrument of community expression" (p. 7).

We are drawn closer and closer here to the point of view that song texts clearly reflect the culture of which they are a part. This has been tersely expressed by Burrows in speaking of Polynesia:

> An important function of gatherings for community singing was to emphasize the values stressed by the culture. Songs in praise of chiefs fostered political loyalty. Songs in praise of places expressed the sentiment for the homeland. In a negative way, songs of ridicule and scandal were at once a punishment to culprits and a warning to others. Such songs constituted something very like a legal sanction through public opinion. (1940:339)

This expression of general cultural values revealed in song texts can be carried further to a study of the underlying phychological set or "ethos" of a particular culture. A study of texts of social songs among the Congo Bashi, for example, indicated what appears to be a deep-seated malaise characterizing the culture. One song perhaps summarizes the general flavor of the texts: it tells of a man who is very weak, both physically and mentally; his fields are not properly cared for, he is impotent, and basically ineffectual in all he undertakes. The singer shows no sympathy for these faults or for the tragic situations which inevitably result from them; rather he is contemptuous of the man and sings of his weaknesses. It is songs of this general type which mark the Bashi text; little patience is manifested with the social weakling, and indifference is displayed toward him as a person. But more important is the tendency toward social irresponsibility, perhaps leading to eventual social breakdown. Fighting, social rejection, acts against society, the abuse of authority, and all manner of similar situations occupy the major portion of the Bashi texts. Even in those texts in which authority is commented upon, the comments take the form of protest against the abuse of power, complaints against a job, boasts of powers held; in general, excesses of authority or power form the basic line of comment. The Bashi song texts seem to reflect a preoccupation with what may perhaps be called the less attractive side of social behavior. Not only deeds of violence, but social rejection and the indifference of society toward itself and its individual members appear as dominating themes. It is significant to note that very rarely is comment made upon the obvious injustices or distortions of perspective displayed by the individuals concerned; rather, the actions or thoughts are simply detailed, with little active comment or resistance offered. The society seems almost completely passive to what goes on within its limits.

These general attitudes stand in striking contrast to those evinced in the song texts of neighboring people. The Bahutu of Ruanda, for example, express in their songs a high degree of self-confidence and pride:

> I am a brave man.
> I will not be shaken by anything.
> When we spend a day somewhere,
>   the people are happy because
>   we sing for them.

or

> Because Kayijika was a brave man,
>   they gave him Kiganda.
> All other young people must be
>   brave like him.
> Gafurafura was the one who shot best.
> Because of this, the King gave
>   him a gift.
> So let us, all young people,
>   be like him.

Further examples could be cited, drawing the texts at random; the difference between the songs of the two groups is striking.

It may perhaps be argued that the Bashi texts, rather than indicating possible social disintegration, imply instead social criticism, that is, that the singers are highly sensitive to social behavior or misbehavior and through the medium of song are attempting to bring erring members of the society back into channels of acceptable behavior. If we are to accept this view, however, we must also accept the fact that approximately eighty per cent of the social songs of the Bashi are concerned with admonition and direction to those members of the society who are not following accepted patterns of social behavior. On the face of it this does not seem likely (cf. Merriam 1954).

Similar kinds of analysis have been directed in our own culture toward the blues, by Paul Oliver (1960), and Negro spirituals, by Fisher (1953), with revealing results. There is little doubt that song texts present an extremely fruitful potential for the understanding of deep-lying values and sanctions, as well as problems, of a given group of people.

Song texts are used in a great variety of ways in addition to those noted above. In Chapter VIII we have remarked upon the use of texts as a teaching device; Best, for example, comments on the teaching of "historical incidents, traditions, myths . . . so as to familiarize children with the names of characters, incidents, etc." among the Maori (1924:II,143), and Blacking notes the use of texts as teaching devices in Venda intiation (1957:passim). Outstanding examples of how texts are used for teaching and as a vehicle of legend and mythology are found in numerous sources

206

on Polynesia (Taylor 1870; Gill 1876, etc.). Texts may also serve as a vehicle of history; although this problem will be discussed more fully in Chapter XIV of this book, a single example can be noted here. Burrows, writing in 1945 about Uvea and Futuna, says:

> Indeed, both Uvea and Futuna have songs about the World War. Several of the best remembered "ancient" Futunan songs . . . tell about the arrival of European boats, from the time when that was still a notable event. A Futunan song tells about the deposition of two kings in 1927 when their plan to control the copra beds led to conflict with the French authorities. (1945:67)

An extremely interesting use of song texts has been reported from Polynesia by Firth, who writes:

> There is also a group of terms relating to men who are industrious, properly instructed, or technically expert. . . . Men who are generally recognized as appropriately described by such terms sometimes bring such recognition to public expression by composing dance songs, lauding their own virtues and achievements. Such songs are received by the community at large as appropriate compositions and come into general currency through being chanted by groups of people while dancing. A man who is recognized by his fellows as inefficient would have to face ridicule if he ventured to extol himself in this way. (1939:152-53)

Firth gives several examples of such songs, including one by a fisherman about himself, and another, composed under the general formula, by a wife in honor of her husband. The phenomenon of boasting in song appears to be fairly widespread (see, for example, Mitchell 1956:5, 8), but in the Polynesian case, song takes the somewhat different function of a legitimate tribute which apparently cannot be challenged under normal circumstances and thus is not truly boastful in intent.

We have seen that song texts are a reflection of the culture of which they are a part and that they are also a device for relieving psychological tension and for correcting erring members of society. In all these phases, song texts are essentially *post facto*; that is, they tend to arise out of situations which already exist. But song texts may also be considered to lead the way, both in rectifying unsatisfactory conditions and in crystallizing new demands. This is seen in the United States of 1963 in which desegregation demands are often put into the form of song, as in Bob Dylan's "Blowin' in the Wind." Johen Greenway (1953) has traced "American folksongs of protest" back as far as 1800, and his work concerns the songs of Negroes, textile workers, miners, migratory workers, farmers, and laborers; actually, songs of this type could be traced back even farther in time.

Speaking of music as an agent of political expression, Rhodes points out that music has served in Southern Africa at least since 1899 as a rallying point for political expression. Thus a song composed in 1959 by Isaac Banda, "We Want Freedom Now, Just Now," proclaims the goals of the contemporary African political movement:

> Whenever you people cast your votes
> For Harry Nkumbula of Africa
> You vote for freedom now.
> For Nkumbula is the truest Moses
> This country of ours ever had,
> The destroyer of Federation.
> We pay our respects to all
> Members of the Legico (Legislative Council)
> Those members siding with Nkumbula
> In the liberation of Africa.
> A black man is busy everywhere
> Preparing himself for freedom now.
> For this is truly African time,
> Whatever happens he will be free.   (Rhodes 1962:20)

Song texts, then, provide a number of insights into questions of primary concern to students of human behavior. The area of music-language relationships is important to the ethnomusicologist and the linguist, as well as the student of poetry, for music influences language and language influences music. Given the fact that language in connection with music tends to have special features, it is not surprising to find that song texts provide a framework for permissive language behavior. One of the song forms in which this is most clear-cut is the topical song, of which there are a number of varieties. We find as well that song texts reveal a number of problems of a psychological nature, as they concern the individual and also the society at large. Texts reflect mechanisms of psychological release and the prevailing attitudes and values of a culture, thus providing an excellent means for analysis. Mythology, legend, and history are found in song texts, and song is frequently used as an enculturative device. Finally, songs lead as well as follow, and political and social movements, often expressed through song because of the license it gives, shape and force the moulding of public opinion. Song texts provide the student of human behavior with some of the richest material he has available for analysis, but their full potential remains to be exploited.

CHAPTER XI

USES AND FUNCTIONS

The uses and functions of music represent one of the most important problems in ethnomusicology, for in the study of human behavior we search constantly, as has been pointed out time and time again in these pages, not only for the descriptive facts about music, but, more important, for the meaning of music. Descriptive facts, while in themselves of importance, make their most significant contribution when they are applied to broader problems of understanding the phenomenon which has been described. We wish to know not only what a thing is, but, more significantly, what it does for people and how it does it.

The title of this chapter implies that there is a difference of meaning between "uses" and "functions" and that the difference is a significant one. Ethnomusicologists in the past have not always been careful about making this distinction, and, indeed, the problem still exists to some extent in anthropology in which the concept of function has played an extremely important theoretical and historic role. In speaking of the meaning of these two words, it must be made clear that the concepts are complementary and are applied initially as they stem from within the society. While it is the outside observer who makes the judgments, using analytical evaluation, his frame of reference is not himself but rather whatever phenomenon he is studying in its own context. In observing uses of music, the student attempts to increase his factual knowledge directly; in assessing functions he attempts to increase his factual knowledge indirectly through the deeper comprehension of the significance of the phenomenon he studies. Thus music may be used in a given society in a certain way, and this may be expressed directly as part of folk evaluation.

209

The function, however, may be something quite different as assessed through analytical evaluation stemming from the folk evaluation. The student can, for example, learn something of the values of a culture by analyzing song texts for what they express; however, he does so from the folk and analytic points of view. Thus his conclusion is not only that he has found such-and-such values in song texts, but also that song texts perform particular functions for the society through the fact that they do express values. Function, in particular, may not be expressed or even understood from the standpoint of folk evaluation—such evaluations we would group under the heading of "concepts." The sense in which we use these terms, then, refers to the understanding of what music does for human beings as evaluated by the outside observer who seeks to increase his range of comprehension by this means.

When we speak of the uses of music, we are referring to the ways in which music is employed in human society, to the habitual practice or customary exercise of music either as a thing in itself or in conjunction with other activities. The song sung by a lover to his love is being used in a certain way, as is a sung invocation to the gods or a musical invitation to animals to come and be killed. Music is *used* in certain situations and becomes a part of them, but it may or may not also have a deeper *function*. If the lover uses song to woo his love, the function of such music may be analyzed as the continuity and perpetuation of the biological group. When the supplicant uses music to approach his god, he is employing a particular mechanism in conjunction with other mechanisms such as dance, prayer, organized ritual, and ceremonial acts. The function of music, on the other hand, is inseparable here from the function of religion which may perhaps be interpreted as the establishment of a sense of security vis-à-vis the universe. "Use" then, refers to the situation in which music is employed in human action; "function" concerns the reasons for its employment and particularly the broader purpose which it serves.

The concept of function has been used in social science in a number of ways, and Nadel (1951) has summarized the various usages into four major types. First, "having a 'function' is used as a synonym for 'operating', 'playing a part', or 'being active', the 'functioning' culture being contrasted with the sort of culture archaeologists or diffusionists reconstruct." Secondly, "function is made to mean non-randomness," that is, that "all social facts have a function . . . and that in culture there are no 'functionless' survivals, relics of diffusion, or other purely fortuitous accretions." Third, function "can be given the sense it has in physics, where it denotes an interdependence of elements which is complex, intermediate, and reciprocal, as against the simple, direct, and irreversible dependence implied in classical causality." And finally, function "may be taken to mean the specific effectiveness of any element whereby it fulfills the requirements of the situation, that is, answers a purpose objectively defined; this is the equation of function with purpose which, since Spencer, has dominated biological thought" (pp. 368-69).

A. R. Radcliffe-Brown, whose theoretical orientation is closely connected with the concept of function in contemporary anthropology, tends to stress the third and fourth of these usages, but with particular application to the social system:

> By the definition here offered 'function' is the contribution which a partial activity makes to the total activity of which it is a part. The function of a particular social usage is the contribution it makes to the total social life as the functioning of the total social system. Such a view implies that a social system . . . has a certain kind of unity, which we may speak of as a functional unity. We may define it as a condition in which all parts of the social system work together with a sufficient degree of harmony or internal consistency, i.e., without producing persistent conflicts which can neither be resolved nor regulated. (1952:181)

Radcliffe-Brown stresses two further points which are of importance here. "One is that the hypothesis does not require the dogmatic assertion that everything in the life of every community has a function. It only requires the assumption that it *may* have one, and that we are justified in seeking to discover it." This, of course, negates the position subsumed in the second use of "function" as noted by Nadel. "The second is that what appears to be the same social usage in two societies may have different functions in the two. . . . In other words, in order to define a social usage, and therefore in order to make valid comparisons between the usages of different peoples or periods, it is necessary to consider not merely the form of the usage but also its function" (p. 184).

In ethnomusicology, these terms have often been used interchangeably, though usually in one or another specific sense in a given context. For example, it is often noted that music is an everyday and all-pervading aspect of life in nonliterate societies. In our own society, it is said, we tend to compartmentalize the arts; that is, we stress the differences, or supposed differences, between "pure" and "applied" art, and between the "artist" and the "commercial artist" or "craftsman" who are differentiated both in role and function. We also draw sharp distinctions between the "artist" and his "audience," with the first group tending to be small in number and limited to "gifted" individuals and the second expected to be a more or less undistinguishable mass whose perceptions vis-à-vis art are of varied and usually indiscriminating quality. In nonliterate societies in general, "It can safely be said that . . . no . . . distinctions of this order prevail. Art is a part of life, not separated from it" (Herskovits 1948:379). This does not necessarily mean that specialization is absent in the music of nonliterate peoples, but rather that relatively large numbers of people in nonliterate societies are competent to participate in music. Music is held to be functional in the sense that it draws from a large proportion of the people of any given nonliterate society and that almost everyone participates in it, thus emphasizing the lack of basic distinction between "artist" and "craftsman" or between "artist" and "audience."

When we speak of music this way, we are using "function" in the sense first described by Nadel, that is, as a synonym for "operating," "playing a part," or "being active," and perhaps even more specifically we are saying that music is "more functional" in nonliterate societies than in our own. We may note that Nadel dismisses this use of the word "function" as "an indifferent and redundant use, which can be disregarded," and it seems clear that what is really being talked about in this respect is use rather than function. But there is an equally important point here, and this is the question of whether music actually is *used* more in nonliterate societies than in our own. This seems to be a question which has never received really serious discussion; rather, it is simply an assumption.

It is quite true that in our society we tend to make a distinction between pure and applied art; in respect to music, we accept what we call "classical," or better, "art" music as pure, and such forms as movie, radio, or television music as applied. There are, however, several questions which may be raised in connection with this distinction. In the first place, is this a real distinction or merely a question of splitting semantic hairs? The lines of distinction between so-called "classical" music and much of contemporary "jazz" are difficult indeed to draw, and we tend to speak at present of certain folk music as being "art." On the other hand, is program music really divorced from "application" in the sense that it is supposed to impart specific emotions and impressions? Second, in the interpretation of whether music is pure or applied, it is of considerable consequence to know who precisely makes the application. We often tend to forget that United States society consists of a large and differentiated mass of people whose judgments and perceptions of music vary widely. In truth, the division of music into pure and applied types is made only by a certain specific segment of that society; its validity for large numbers of people is a matter for some doubt. Finally, we do not really know whether nonliterate peoples make these same sorts of distinctions. We do know that some music in such societies is used exclusively for entertainment; we do not know whether this forms the basis for judgments concerning

212

"pure" art, nor do we know whether nonliterate peoples regard songs used for medicinal purposes, for example, as a more "applied" form of music.

Taking the problem a step further, we may also inquire as to how clear-cut our own distinction is between the "artist" and the "commercial artist" or "craftsman." Certainly there are some definite cases, but it must be allowed that the man who makes modern cutlery may be described as falling on either side of the imaginary line, and the same is true of today's "third stream" composer associated with modern jazz. On the other side, it seems logical for us to assume that such distinctions are not made in nonliterate societies, but again we do not seem to have accumulated much evidence to this effect. What of the professional "wandering minstrel" found so frequently in Africa? Is his the role of the craftsman? Is there no distinction between his role and that of the journeyman chorus member? We have already seen that many societies support professional musicians in one way or another and that the composer's role is differentiated as something special; are such specialists craftsmen or artists? We do not have a clear-cut answer to this question.

The artist and audience question is similarly reft with problems. While it is true that our concert performers tend to be rather sharply differentiated from their audience, what of contemporary folk music situations in which the audience is encouraged to participate, or certain aspects of jazz in which the audience joins the musicians fully, perhaps by dancing? Again, in nonliterate societies we have had occasion to point out a number of situations in which the musician performs before an audience; true, the audience participates by clapping its hands rhythmically, or dancing, but this happens as well in our own society. And to the assertion that more people, proportionally, take part in music in nonliterate societies than in our own, one can only point to the incredible numbers of music instruments sold in the United States and to the almost overwhelming estimates concerning the numbers of people who perform some kind of music, be it for themselves or for others.

In sum, questions of this sort are not so easily answered as has often been assumed. The fact of the matter is that when we make distinctions we are speaking of special cases within our own society as opposed to assumptions made for all nonliterate societies. We speak primarily of what we call art music, but we do not consider the many other kinds of music that are also a part of our musical culture. If such distinctions have some element of truth, as they probably do, it is reasonable to ask whether the exceptions are not so significant as to vitiate any usefulness the distinctions may seem to have. In any case, describing the role of music in the manner noted here is not really to speak of function, but rather to call attention to the use of music.

213

Another kind of assertion made by ethnomusicologists about the "functions" of music concerns the oft-repeated statement that while music is used in and integrated with almost all aspects of life among nonliterate peoples, such is not the case in Western society. Thus examples such as the following, which refers to the Tutsi of Ruanda, are cited:

> . . . songs for boasting purposes, for war and greeting, songs sung when young married women meet together and reminisce about absent friends, children's songs, songs to flatter a girl, and many more. Of special importance to the Tutsi are songs dealing with cattle, and these subtypes include boasting songs called *ibiririmbo*, in which two men sing in competition with each other, alternating musical phrases; they may vie either in praising one cow or in singing of the merits of one cow against another. Special songs, not ibiririmbo, are sung in praise of cows, others to indicate the importance of having cows; there are songs for taking cattle home in the evening, for the herder when he is getting ready to take the cattle home, when he is drawing water for the cattle, when he is with other herders in the evening. Praises for the royal cattle, *inyambo*, are sung; children sing special cow songs, and other songs are sung when cattle are being shown to visitors. Special flute songs circumvent cattle thieves at night, and other songs recount historical events in which cattle have played a part. (Merriam 1959a:50)

This impressive list of song types refers to but one element of Tutsi musical culture; it could be extended dramatically if reference were made to marriage songs or other subtypes, and this is to say nothing of religious songs as a body.

Again, when we speak of music in these terms, we are dealing primarily with the usage of song, i.e., Nadel's "operating," "playing a part," or "being active." If we also emphasize, as we often do, the concept that music in nonliterate societies is "more functional" than in our own, there must be some evidence to support the contention. On the face of it, there would seem to be. United States society certainly does not have a series of songs which compares in detail with that created around Tutsi cattle, and yet we often overlook the wide variety of uses that *is* present in our music. We have love songs, war songs, sport songs, funeral songs, and working songs; we use music to stimulate activity in work and play and to lull us as we eat; housewives are supplied with special music to accompany their work; exercisers are accompanied by music, and so forth.

The crux of this problem, however, seems to lie in the fact that the word function is wrongly used in this context. When we speak of music in

214

nonliterate societies as being "more functional" than in our own, we imply that it is also of greater importance; what we really mean is that music in nonliterate societies may be used in a greater *variety* of situations than in our own society. In this sense, music in nonliterate societies may well be used more in minute and directly applied ways, but it is by no means necessarily more functional.

There is another sense in which music has been described by ethnomusicologists as being functional, and this concerns the fact that in some cultures, at least, music is not abstracted from its cultural context. Among the Basongye, for example, the total body of music is a known rather than an unknown, as in our culture, and further, individual songs are recognized instantly in terms of their use. This means that music as such does not exist apart from its context; to the contrary, the context may well determine the conceptualization of music. We shall have more to say on this matter in Chapter 13, but the use of the word function in this connection coincides with Nadel's third definition, that is, it "denotes an interdependence of elements which is complex, intermediate, and reciprocal, as against the simple, direct, and irreversible dependence implied in classical causality."

We may take this a step further, however, for the extent to which the musician and his music are functional in some nonliterate societies has rarely been commented upon. It will be recalled that among the Basongye, musicians are considered to fall low on the social scale; both musicians and non-musicians say emphatically, for example, that they do not wish their children to become musicians. At the same time, the thought of a village without musicians and their music is inconceivable, and it can almost be said that the Basongye view includes the value that life without music is not to be considered life at all.

More specifically, a major funeral cannot take place among the Basongye without the presence of a professional musician and his music. Such a funeral extends over a period of seven days, with the interment of the body usually taking place on the second day. The professional musician makes his appearance after the body has been interred and performs a number of functions which he alone can contribute. There is no other person who takes the role of the foil for aggressive pantomime carried on by the female relatives of the deceased; the pantomime serves to help establish the magical or non-magical nature of the death, allows the externalization of inner tensions on the part of the women, and publicizes their emotional and innocent involvement in the death of their kinsman. Without the professional musician, these various expressions would have to be shifted to some other person, but as the funeral is presently structured it is the musician who performs these functions. It is also the

215

musician's role to help the mourners begin to forget the tragedy of death. Upon his appearance, the entire course of the funeral is changed; people begin to smile and joke for the first time since the death; social dances, whose function is specifically that of helping people to forget, are introduced and encouraged by the musician; by acting the clown he contributes heavily to the release of tensions which to this point in the funeral have been on a high level of intensity. Again, other individuals could perform this role as well as the musician, but the point is that in Basongye society other people do not perform it. The musician is a key figure in the funeral. He is similarly a key figure in other kinds of activities, including dancing, hunting, certain religious behavior, and other aspects of Basongye life as well. Indeed, without the musician, whose numerous roles have barely been touched upon here, the structure of much of Basongye behavior would be markedly changed. The integration of the musician into the fabric of society at large is extremely important, and it illustrates Nadel's fourth use of the word function, i.e., "the specific effectiveness of any element whereby it fulfills the requirements of the situation, that is, answers a purpose objectively defined; this is the equation of function with purpose. . . ."

At one time or another, then, ethnomusicologists have used the concept of function in three of the four senses described by Nadel, but in the great majority of cases in his first sense, that is, as synonymous with "operating," "playing a part," or "being active." When employed in this way, the more precise term is "use" rather than "function"; in such cases, although we know how music is fitted in with other activities, we do not know what its purpose, or "function," may be.

Having made these distinctions, we can now attempt to obtain some idea of the various uses and functions of music in human society. Turning first to the former, it is evident that music is used as accompaniment to or part of almost every human activity. Anthropologists have devised a number of schemes for encompassing all of any given culture and at the same time dividing it into parts which can be handled with relative ease. Among these is Murdock's organizational scheme in which the materials of culture were originally subsumed under forty-six categories (Murdock *et al.*, 1945), and the title of almost every division brings instantly to mind some associated music activity. Among the Flathead Indians fourteen major types of music situation can be isolated, and each of these is subject to numerous subdivisions (Merriam and Merriam 1955). We have already cited the complexity of Tutsi music types in respect to some social songs, and an incomplete catalogue of Basongye songs reveals well over thirty types which could again be subdivided.

While it is not possible or desirable to attempt a catalogue of all the uses of music, we can at least indicate the range of music activity which cuts across all the aspects of culture. Herskovits (1948:238-40) has devised a useful set of categories for the handling of cultural materials, which will be followed here in broad outline.

His first division, Material Culture and Its Sanctions, is divided into two parts, Technology and Economics; associated music activities are numerous. Work songs seem to be found in almost every culture, including such types as canoe-paddling songs, songs to accompany the grinding of grains, the harvesting of crops, the construction of houses, the carrying of goods, and so forth. Song accompanies the technology of medicine as well as its practice, and it is used to assure a good hunt, good fishing, or a bountiful harvest. The composer, performer, and instrument-maker profit from their activities and contribute to the general economy.

Herskovits' second division is Social Institutions, which comprises Social organization, Education, and Political structures. Social organization is marked at almost every point by song: the life cycle includes birth songs, with special subdivisions for multiple births; lullabies; naming songs; toilet training songs; puberty songs; greeting songs; love and marriage songs; family, lineage and clan songs; songs of social associational groups; funeral songs; and many others of equally specific social application. We have previously noted the use of song for educational purposes and will have occasion to speak of it again. Political structures are constantly involved with song, as in praise songs for political dignitaries sung at the occasion of the investiture of office, comment on political events and desired political aims, and so forth.

Man and the Universe comprises Herskovits' third aspect of culture, subdivided into Belief systems and The Control of Power. Religious beliefs are expressed through musical prayer, myth and legend set to music, divination songs, cult songs, songs of religious functionaries, and others. The control of power is often achieved through songs of supplication; magic songs for curing, hunting, and many other activities which require supernatural assistance; songs of spirits, witches, and other superhuman phenomena; melodic invocations; and so forth. We have already had occasion to note the crucial use of music in the Plains Indian vision quest and in the Basongye funeral. In this connection special attention must be called to the enormously detailed studies of religious ceremonial and ritual among American Indian groups provided by American anthropologists in the early part of this century. These studies include minute descriptions of ceremonies and contain a wealth of information concerning the use of music. Dorsey, for example, gives a minute-by-minute account of the Ponca Sun Dance in which the participation of musicians is meticulously detailed (1905b). In describing the

217

Osage rite of vigil, LaFlesche gives an extremely tight description of the important part music plays in the ceremony (1925). Mooney describes the use of music and its important role in the Ghost Dance; its significance is emphasized by the fact that he devotes almost forty per cent of his monograph to song texts (1896). Such descriptions are among the most detailed in existence, and each contributes substantially to our knowledge of the way music is used in religious ceremonial.

Herskovits' fourth category is Aesthetics, divided into Graphic and Plastic Arts, Folklore, and Music, drama, and the dance; the relationships to music are very close. Music and the dance have an inseparable relationship, and drama, almost by definition, includes music. Folklore and music are found in conjunction with great frequency as parts of the same social gathering, when song forms a part of a folk tale, through the use of proverbs in song texts, and when praise names are sung. Songs are composed to consecrate masks, song and masking are very frequently found in conjunction, and there are special songs for woodcarvers, painters, potters, metal-workers, and other artists.

Herskovits' final category is Language, and we have devoted a chapter of this book to a discussion of song texts, which exist in the closest association with music. In addition, special kinds of language are conveyed by music devices as in drum, whistle, and trumpet languages; secret languages are also used frequently in music.

These observations comprehend but a fraction of the uses of music in human society and yet they indicate the enormous range of activity in which music plays a part, sometimes tangentially but often centrally. The importance of music, as judged by the sheer ubiquity of its presence, is enormous, and when it is considered that music is used both as a summatory mark of many activities and as an integral part of many others which could not be properly executed, or executed at all, without music, its importance is substantially magnified. There is probably no other human cultural activity which is so all-pervasive and which reaches into, shapes, and often controls so much of human behavior.

When we turn to the functions of music, the problems become more involved, for we are searching primarily for generalizations which are equally applicable to all societies. In attempting to make an initial assessment of such functions viewed as cultural universals, we are using the word "function" primarily in Nadel's fourth sense, i.e., "the specific effectiveness of any element whereby it fulfills the requirements of the situation, that is, answers a purpose objectively defined; this is the equation of function with purpose. . . ." There is, however, a broadening of this usage since we are attempting to discover the purposes, or functions, of music viewed in the widest possible sense. It must also be restated

218

that on this level we are concerned with analytical and not folk evaluations —we are searching for answers to the question of what music does for and in human society. I should like to propose ten such major and over-all functions, as opposed to uses, of music, and each will be discussed below in no special order of significance.

The function of emotional expression. There is considerable evidence to indicate that music functions widely and on a number of levels as a means of emotional expression. In discussing song texts, we have had occasion to point out that one of their outstanding features is the fact that they provide a vehicle 'for the expression of ideas and emotions not revealed in ordinary discourse.

On a more general level, however, music seems clearly to be involved with emotion and to be a vehicle for its expression, whether such emotion be special (obscenity, censure, etc.) or general. Burrows, for example, makes a special and repeated point in this connection in many of his works concerning the music of Oceania. Speaking of Uvea and Futuna, he writes:

> Characteristic of all the singing of the two islands is its social character. Solo singing is confined to leading off a chorus, or to responsive or interspersed passages. This may explain the scarcity of songs expressing more intimate emotions—for example, the absence of lullabies. Where an emotion may be either individual or collective, it is the collective aspect that finds expression in song. . . . In sum, the collected songs indicate that singing in Uvea and Futuna may express and stimulate any emotion that is shared by a group, be it household, working gang, or entire kingdom. (1945:78-9)

In another passage, Burrows lists a number of "functions" of music in the Tuamotus and again stresses the importance of emotional expression:

> Stimulating and expressing emotion in the performers, and imparting it to the listeners. The emotion may be religious exaltation, as in the creation chant and song of the sacred red bird; grief, as in the laments; longing or passion, as in the love-songs; joy in motion; sexual excitement, and a variety of other emotions, in the dances; exaltation of the ego in chants of glory; stirring to new courage and vigor, as in the enlivening chants; and doubtless others. . . .

Underlying all of these in greater or less degree is the general function of stimulating, expressing, and sharing emotion. This function is involved even in the work songs. According to the native way of thinking, something more than emotion—namely, mana or supernatural power—is conveyed in the incantations; but from the European point of view the function actually performed is still of imparting emotion. (1933:54-56)

A somewhat similar point of view, though expressed in connection with Western music, is suggested by McAllester when he notes: "With us a principal function of music seems to be as an aid in inducing attitude. We have songs to evoke moods of tranquillity, nostalgia, sentiment, group rapport, religious feeling, party solidarity, and patriotism, to name a few. Thus we sing to put babies to sleep, to make work seem lighter, to make people buy certain kinds of breakfast foods, or to ridicule our enemies" (1960:469).

Approaching his analysis from a still different direction, Freeman arrives at similar conclusions in discussing verses known as "lei Ana Ika," or "U.S.E.D.," sung in Hawaii before, during, and after World War II (1957). In this case, however, he considers three major changing functions of folksongs, two of which involve emotional expression and two of which, overlapping, involve other functions. Freeman's major hypothesis is that "the functional significance of a folksong should be revealed through its interrelationship with other aspects of the social cultural system," and that "a particular type of folk expression should be associated with a particular kind of social organization" which in changing should also "engender changes in the nature of the associated folklore" (p. 215). His conclusions are as follows:

> In the first place, social protest verses emerge when the members of a society are deprived of other mechanisms of protest. Such songs will be found in any disfranchised segment of society and will persist as long as these individuals are deprived of other more direct techniques of action. These verses represent an attempt of the members of the society to cope with inacceptable social conditions. On the other hand, they may diminish frustrations— they allow the individual to "let off steam" in a congenial group setting and thereby to adjust to social conditions as they are. On the other hand, they may accomplish social change through mobilizing group sentiment. In either case such verses function to reduce societal imbalance and to integrate the society.
>
> Secondly, when there exists a long-term frustration or conflict in personal needs or cultural demands which is tied in with the mores of society, stabilizing verses will be sung. These will describe the conflict, but they will not end in protest. Rather, they will provide the solution which is sanctioned in the mores. Thus, stabilizing

verses permit the person to "let off steam" and they tend to validate the social system.

Thirdly, when conditions allow other institutionalized modes of personal expression and when long-term moral conflicts are not predominant, verses of a purely recreational type will be evident. Such verses will serve strictly entertainment functions. (pp. 219-20)

Charles Keil, in an unpublished paper (1962), sees music as divisible into a "solidarity function" and a "catharsis," or "release function." We shall speak of his solidarity function later, but the release function he finds best expressed in jazz music. He further postulates that there is a correlation between these two general functions of music and the societies which express them; thus "a cultural tradition that lays stress on social control, moderation, quiet, 'shame' sanctions, etc. is likely to provide at least one or two musical outlets to relieve the tensions that may develop for particular individuals."

Both Freeman and Keil attempt to provide explanation for the function of music as an emotional expression, but the most detailed discussion has been offered by Devereux, who couches his work in terms of Freudian theory and applies it to all the arts (Devereux and LaBarre 1961). Devereux's major point is that art "exists because it meets a social need not gratified by other cultural activities"; this is what he calls the "safety valve function." "In addition to viewing art as a harmless safety valve," he says, "society and the artist alike consider the artistic utterance as *unrepudiable* in regard to *form*, but *repudiable* as to *content*" (pp. 368-69). Devereux continues:

In brief, art can function as a social safety valve precisely because, like wit, it is a compromise and is, moreover repudiable as to intent and content. It permits the artist to say—and the consumer to hear (or to see)—the forbidden, provided only that:

(1) The utterance is formulated in a manner which a given society chooses to call "art,"

(2) The actual content of the utterance is officially defined as subordinate to its form, and

(3) The utterance is understood to be repudiable. . . .

Having demonstrated that art provides a safety valve for the expression of that which is tabooed, we must next seek to define the tabooed subjects which find expression in art. These subjects belong to three main layers:

(1) The generally human taboos: Incest, in-group murder, etc.

(2) The culture specific taboos: Sex in puritanical society, avariciousness in Mohave society, cowardice in Plains Indian society, etc.

(3) The idiosyncratically (neurotically) tabooed: repressed wishes, etc. . . .

The artist's perception of the rules of his game and his alibi maneuvers, which turns his "obscenity," "rebellion," or "blasphemy" into art, are also significant. . . . The artist must also possess supreme skill in "skating on thin ice." Indeed, the better the skater, the thinner can be the ice (of rules of art) on which he can skate. In other words, the better an artist masters his craft, the nearer he is able to come to expressing, *without loss of affect*, the tabooed. (pp. 369, 380, 370)

We have thus far spoken of the emotional release offered through music to the individual who finds himself in particular social situations, but it must also be pointed out that the creative process itself offers emotional release. Gotshalk calls attention to this fact when he points out the importance of "the satisfaction of the will or of the drive for mastery and achievement that the public object may embody for the creative artist. A work of art for him may be, not the thin wish-fulfillment of a reverie indulged in, but the solid wish-fulfillment of a reality achieved. It may stand in his eyes as a reassuring landmark in the development of his talent, as a symbol of his power to accomplish, and as a victory of his self as a creative force over enormous obstacles and difficulties" (1947:157).

Finally, music can function as a mechanism of emotional release for a large group of people acting together. Such is the case, for example, with the Flathead Indians—and presumably many other American Indian tribes as well—who carry on traditions of certain kinds of songs and dances although the real occasion for their performance has long since vanished. The Flathead genuinely enjoy the frequent occasions on which they perform music and dance intended for war, scalping, marriage, ceremonial occasions, and so forth, although there is no opportunity whatsoever to practice the actions with which most of the songs and dances were created to be combined. Music and dance in this case serve as an expression of emotional release from the essentially hostile culture which surrounds the Flathead and through stressing cultural values it gives an opportunity in a sanctioned situation to release the hostility the Indians feel.

An important function of music, then, is the opportunity it gives for a variety of emotional expressions—the release of otherwise unexpressible thoughts and ideas, the correlation of a wide variety of emotions and music, the opportunity to "let off steam" and perhaps to resolve social conflicts, the explosion of creativity itself, and the group expression of hostilities. It is quite possible that a much wider variety of emotional expressions could be cited, but the examples given here indicate clearly the importance of this function of music.

The function of aesthetic enjoyment. The problem of aesthetics in respect to music is not a simple one. It includes the aesthetic both from the point of view of the creator and of the contemplator, and if it is to be considered as one of the major functions of music it must be demonstrable for cultures other than our own. Music and an aesthetic are clearly associated in Western culture, as well as in the cultures of Arabia, India, China, Japan, Korea, Indonesia, and perhaps some others as well. But whether the association is present in the cultures of the nonliterate world is a moot point. Involved here is the primary question of what, exactly, an aesthetic is, and particularly whether it is a culture-bound concept. These are important questions to which we will devote Chapter 13; at this point, it must be left in doubt, and it can only be said that the function of aesthetic enjoyment is clearly operative in some cultures of the world, and perhaps present in others.

The function of entertainment. Music provides an entertainment function in all societies. It needs only to be pointed out that a distinction must probably be drawn between "pure" entertainment, which seems to be a particular feature of music in Western society, and entertainment combined with other functions. The latter may well be a more prevalent feature of nonliterate societies.

The function of communication. We have had occasion to discuss music as a communication device in Chapter 1, and it will be recalled that the major problem is that while we know music communicates something, we are not clear as to what, how, or to whom. Music is not a universal language, but rather is shaped in terms of the culture of which it is a part. In the song texts it employs, it communicates direct information to those who understand the language in which it is couched. It conveys emotion, or something similar to emotion, to those who understand its idiom. The fact that music is shared as a human activity by all peoples may mean that it communicates a certain limited understanding simply by its existence. Of all the functions of music, the communication function is perhaps least known and understood.

The function of symbolic representation. There is little doubt that music functions in all societies as a symbolic representation of other things, ideas, and behaviors. We shall discuss this function of music in detail in Chapter 12.

The function of physical response. It is with some hesitation that this

223

"function" of music is put forward, for it is questionable whether physical response can or should be listed in what is essentially a group of social functions. However, the fact that music elicits physical response is clearly counted upon in its use in human society, though the responses may be shaped by cultural conventions. Possession, for example, is clearly elicited in part at least by music functioning in a total situation, and without possession certain religious ceremonials in certain cultures are considered unsuccessful (see for example, Herskovits 1938b:II, 189). Music also elicits, excites, and channels crowd behavior; it encourages physical reactions of the warrior and the hunter; it calls forth the physical response of the dance, which may be of prime necessity to the occasion at hand. The production of physical response seems clearly to be an important function of music; the question of whether this is primarily a biological response is probably overridden by the fact that it is culturally shaped.

The function of enforcing conformity to social norms. Considerable discussion has been devoted to this function of music in Chapter 10. Songs of social control play an important part in a substantial number of cultures, both through direct warning to erring members of the society and through indirect establishment of what is considered to be proper behavior. This is also found in songs used, for example, at the time of initiation ceremonies, when the younger members of the community are specifically instructed in proper and improper behavior. Songs of protest call attention as well to propriety and impropriety. The enforcement of conformity to social norms is one of the major functions of music.

The function of validation of social institutions and religious rituals. While music is used in social and religious situations, there is little information to indicate the extent to which it tends to validate these institutions and rituals. In respect to the Navaho, Reichard says that "the primary function of song is to preserve order, to co-ordinate the ceremonial symbols. . . ." (1950:288), and Burrows comments that one of the functions of song in the Tuamotus is "imparting magical potency by incantations" (1933:54). We may also recall Freeman's assertion that stabilizing verses are sung when there exists "a long-term frustration or conflict in personal needs or cultural demands which is tied in with the mores of the society"; in such a case the conflict is described and a sanctioned solution suggested. "Thus, stabilizing verses permit the person to 'let off steam' and they tend to validate the social system" (1957:220). Religious systems are validated, as in folklore, through the recitation of myth and legend in song, as well as through music which expresses religious precepts. Social institutions are validated through songs which emphasize the proper and improper in society, as well as those which tell people what to do and how to do it. This function of music, however, needs to be further studied and more concisely expressed.

The function of contribution to the continuity and stability of culture. If music allows emotional expression, gives aesthetic pleasure, entertains, communicates, elicits physical response, enforces conformity to social norms, and validates social institutions and religious rituals, it is clear that it contributes to the continuity and stability of culture. In this sense, perhaps, it contributes no more or no less than any other aspect of culture, and we are probably here using function in the limited sense of "playing a part."

At the same time, not many elements of culture afford the opportunity for emotional expression, entertain, communicate, and so forth, to the extent allowed in music. Further, music is in a sense a summatory activity for the expression of values, a means whereby the heart of the psychology of a culture is exposed without many of the protective mechanisms which surround other cultural activities. In this sense, it shares its function with others of the arts. As a vehicle of history, myth, and legend it points up the continuity of the culture; through its transmission of education, control of erring members of the society, and stress upon what is right, it contributes to the stability of culture. And its own existence provides a normal and solid activity which assures the members of society that the world continues in its proper path. We may recall the Basongye reaction to the suggestion that musicians be eliminated from their village, or cite the remark of a Sia Indian to Leslie White: "My friend, without songs you cannot do anything" (White 1962:115).

Waterman has summarized the contribution of music to the continuity and stability of Yirkalla culture in Australia in pointing out that as an enculturative mechanism, music reaches into almost every aspect of life. He writes:

> Basically, music functions at Yirkalla as an enculturative mechanism, a means of learning Yirkalla culture. Throughout his life, the Aboriginal is surrounded by musical events that instruct him about his natural environment and its utilization by man, that teach him his world-view and shape his system of values, and that reinforce his understanding of Aboriginal concepts of status and of his own role. More specifically, songs function as emblems of membership in his moiety and lineage, as validation of his system of religious belief, and as symbols of status in the age-grading continuum. They serve on some occasions the purpose of releasing tensions, while other types are used for heightening

225

the emotionalism of a ritual climax. They provide a method of controlling, by supernatural means, sequences of natural events otherwise uncontrollable. Further, some types of songs provide an outlet for individual creativity while many may be used simply to conquer personal dysphoria. In every case, the enculturative function of the music in helping to shape the social personality of the Aboriginal in the Yirkalla pattern rather than in some other, is apparent. (1956:41)

The function of contribution to the integration of society. In a sense we have anticipated this function of music in the preceding paragraph, for it is clear that in providing a solidarity point around which members of society congregate, music does indeed function to integrate society. This function has been commented upon by a number of writers. Nketia, speaking of the Yoruba musician in Accra, says, "For the Yoruba in Accra, performances of Yoruba music . . . bring both the satisfaction of participating in something familiar and the assurance of belonging to a group sharing in similar values, similar ways of life, a group maintaining similar art forms. Music thus brings a renewal of tribal solidarity" (1958:43). Elkin remarks that while the varied activities of the Australian Songman might bring him admiration, "it would not make a social institution. This arises from his function as a unifying and integrating factor in his clan and tribe" (1953:92). Freeman's remarks (1957) concerning Hawaiian folksong suggest that songs of social protest may allow the individual to let off steam and thus to "adjust to social conditions as they are," or they "may accomplish social change through mobilizing group sentiment. In either case such verses function to reduce societal imbalance and to integrate the society." We may also recall Keil's dichotomy (1962) between the "solidarity" and "release" functions of music, in which composers are "attempting to express cultural unity" in their music and inviting "the listener to identify with the collective American experience, binding every conceivable musical device to that purpose." Finally, in speaking of the Andamanese dance, Radcliffe-Brown stresses the integrative function:

> The Andamanese dance (with its accompanying song) may therefore be described as an activity in which, by virtue of the effects of rhythm and melody, all the members of a community are able harmoniously to cooperate and act in unity . . .
> The pleasure that the dancer feels irradiates itself over everything around him and he is filled with geniality and good-will towards his companions. The sharing with others of an intense

pleasure, or rather the sharing in a collective expression of pleasure, must ever incline us to such expansive feelings. . . .

In this way the dance produces a condition in which the unity, harmony and concord of the community are at a maximum, and in which they are intensely felt by every member. It is to produce this condition, I would maintain, that is the primary social function of the dance. The well-being, or indeed the existence, of the society depends on the unity and harmony that obtain in it, and the dance, by making that unity intensely felt, is a means of maintaining it. For the dance affords an opportunity for the direct action of the community upon the individual, and we have seen that it exercises in the individual those sentiments by which the social harmony is maintained. (1948:249, 251, 252)

Music, then, provides a rallying point around which the members of society gather to engage in activities which require the cooperation and coordination of the group. Not all music is thus performed, of course, but every society has occasions signalled by music which draw its members together and reminds them of their unity.

It is quite possible that this list of the functions of music may require condensation or expansion, but in general it summarizes the role of music in human culture. Music is clearly indispensable to the proper promulgation of the activities that constitute a society; it is a universal human behavior—without it, it is questionable that man could truly be called man, with all that implies.

CHAPTER XII

MUSIC AS SYMBOLIC BEHAVIOR

A good deal of the discussion of music as a meaningful part of human existence has centered upon its role and function as a symbolic device. Ernst Cassirer, for example, states flatly that "art may be defined as a symbolic language" (1944:168), and he rejects various other theories of the nature of art. He traces back to Aristotle the view that art is essentially imitative, that is, that the principal function of art is to be mimetic. Cassirer's objection to this point of view is expressed as follows: "If 'all beauty is truth,' all truth is not necessarily beauty. In order to reach the highest beauty it is just as essential to deviate from nature as to reproduce nature" (p. 139).

A second view, which Cassirer traces to Rousseau and Goethe, is that art is characteristic, that is, an overflow of emotions and passions which are shaped into a functional whole whose parts express a single feeling. But if this were the reason for art, Cassirer argues, it would not be a simple reproduction of things, as in the view which holds art to be imitative, but rather "it would become a reproduction of our inner life, of our affections and emotions" (p. 141), and art is more than this.

The impact of hedonistic theories is ascribed to Santayana, who held that art exists purely for pleasure; while Cassirer agrees that pleasure is a part of art, it is not the entire reason for its existence. Finally, art is sometimes assigned the single function of play. Cassirer comments:

> Artistic imagination always remains sharply distinguished from that sort of imagination which characterizes our play activity. In play we have to do with simulated images which may become so vivid and impressive as to be taken for realities. To define art

as a mere sum of such simulated images could indicate a very meagre conception of its character and task. . . . Play gives us illusive images; art gives us a new kind of truth—a truth not of empirical things but of pure forms. (p. 164)

For Cassirer, then, art, including music, is a symbolic device, to be distinguished from other approaches in the following manner:

Science gives us order in thoughts; morality gives us order in actions; art gives us order in the apprehension of visible, tangible, and audible appearances. (p. 168)

A similar point of view toward the arts, and in this case specifically toward music, is taken by Susanne Langer, who comments:

. . . music is 'significant form,' and its significance is that of a symbol, a highly articulated, sensuous object, which by virtue of its dynamic structure can express the forms of vital experience which language is peculiarly unfit to convey. Feeling, life, motion and emotion constitute its import. (1953:32)

There is no question that music is symbolic, but the difficulty lies in the precise nature of what is meant by symbolism. We enter here upon a troublesome area, for symbolism can be defined in a number of ways, and the distinction between signs on the one hand and symbols on the other is not always clear.

Signs seem most often to be defined as things by and of themselves. Thus Leslie White speaks of the sign ". . . as a physical thing or event whose function is to indicate some other thing or event. The meaning of a sign may be inherent in its physical form and context, or [it] may be merely identified with its physical form. . . ." (1949:27). Similarly, Langer defines the sign in terms of the fact that it ". . . indicates the existence—past, present, or future—of a thing, event, or condition" (1942:45-6).

Our reference here is that a sign is something used by human beings and is therefore inevitably associated with behavior; thus we can speak of "signing" as a process rather than simply as a thing. White notes that sign behavior establishes a relationship between a stimulus and a response, and Charles Morris defines the categories of actors and significance in signing behavior:

Any organism for which something is a sign will be called an *interpreter*. The disposition in an interpreter to respond, because of the sign, by response-sequences of some behavior-family will be called an *interpretant*. Anything which would permit the completion of the response-sequences to which the interpreter is disposed because of a sign will be called a *denotatum* of the sign. A sign will be said to denote a denotatum. Those conditions which are such that whatever fulfills them is a denotatum will be called a *significatum* of the sign. A sign will be said to *signify* a significatum; the phrase "to have signification" may be taken as synonymous with "to signify." (Morris 1955:17)

Using these distinctions in his definition of what signs are and what signing is, Morris further distinguishes among three major kinds of signs. Indexical signs are those which can denote only a single object, while characterizing signs are those which can denote a plurality of things. Universal signs are those which can denote everything, such as the term "something," which has universal implications (Morris 1938:17).

As the sign can be defined both as thing and as behavior, so apparently can the symbol, and thus White speaks of the symbol as ". . . a thing the value or meaning of which is bestowed upon it by those who use it. I say 'thing' because a symbol may have any kind of physical form; it may have the form of a material object, a color, a sound, an odor, a motion or an object, a taste" (White 1949:25). On the other hand, Langer says that "symbols are not proxy for their objects, but are *vehicles for the conception of objects*. To conceive a thing or a situation is not the same thing as to 'react toward it' overtly, or to be aware of its presence" (1942:49).

The problem here, of course, is to make a clear-cut distinction between signs and symbols, and particularly to define the latter. From White's point of view, this distinction is to be made on the basis of the degree of abstraction involved in the object or behavior functioning as a sign or symbol, as the case may be. The symbol is not, and cannot be, derived from properties intrinsic in its physical form; rather, it is the human attribution of abstract meaning which makes a thing a symbol. A word, for example, "is a symbol only when one is concerned with the distinction between its meaning and its physical form" (White 1949:26); that is, the form may in itself be a sign, but its meaning on an abstract level makes it a symbol.

Morris' terminology differs somewhat, since he sees symbols only as a particular kind of sign rather than a different level of abstraction, but essentially his distinction follows the same line of reasoning. Returning to his delimitation of three kinds of signs, we note:

> The semantical rule for an indexical sign such as pointing is simple: the sign designates at any instant what is pointed at. In general, an indexical sign designates what it directs attention to. An indexical sign does not characterize what it denotes (except

231

to indicate roughly the space-time co-ordinates) and need not be similar to what it denotes. A characterizing sign characterizes that which it can denote. Such a sign may do this by exhibiting in itself the properties an object must have to be denoted by it, and in this case the characterizing sign is an *icon;* if this is not so, the characterizing sign may be called a *symbol.* A photograph, a star chart, a model, a chemical diagram are icons, while the word "photograph," the names of the stars and of chemical elements are symbols. (1938:24)

This same degree of abstraction holds true when the symbol is defined in terms of behaving:

> Where an organism provides itself with a sign which is a substitute in the control of its behavior for another sign, signifying what the sign for which it is a substitute signifies, then this sign is a *symbol,* and the sign-process is a *symbol-process;* where this is not the case the sign is a *signal,* and the sign-process is a *signal-process.* More succinctly, a symbol is a sign produced by its interpreter which acts as a substitute for some other sign with which it is synonymous; all signs not symbols are signals. (Morris 1955: 25)

We must at this point reach some working definition of a symbol which will enable us to apply the concept to music if we are to reach an understanding of whether music can be symbolic behavior. A symbol involves, first, the abstraction level of the thing or behavior which we wish to define as symbol. That is, a symbol in the first instance seems to be the sign of a sign; if the characterizing sign itself exhibits the properties of what it denotes, then it is an *icon;* if the properties are not in themselves found in the characterizing sign, then it is a symbol: a star chart is an icon, but the name of a star is a symbol. Second, a symbol must have ascribed meaning to be a symbol, and this ascription of meaning to some thing or behavior which in itself is not descriptive of something else is a purely human phenomenon. Thus a dog, for example, can understand both signs and symbols, and can itself give signs; humans can also do these things, but only humans can make up symbols. Given the validity of these two distinctions, then, is music symbolic behavior?

Susanne Langer argues both that music is symbolic and that it is not, but the distinction she makes is more one of degree than of kind. On the one level she argues that the function of music is not "stimulation of feeling, but expression of it; and furthermore, not the symptomatic expression of feelings that beset the composer but a symbolic expression of the forms of sentience as he understands them" (1953:28). On the other hand, she argues that music cannot truly and completely be symbolic because it does not have what she calls "assigned meaning" (1942:195). That is, meaning in music is not fixed by common consent of those who create or listen to it; rather, it is emotions and general meaning sets which are expressed.

> . . . music at its highest, though clearly a symbolic form, is an unconsummated symbol. Articulation is its life, but not assertion; expressiveness, not expression. The actual function of meaning, which calls for permanent contents, is not fulfilled; for the *assignment* of one rather than another possible meaning to each form is never explicitly made. (1942:195)

In a strict sense, this is true; specific assignment of meaning to specific sets of music sound is not a feature of most music systems, and in this sense it must be agreed that music is symbolic and yet an unconsummated symbolic form. This is not true, however, of all music systems in the world, nor is it true of all music in any given system; and, further, ascriptive and thus symbolic meaning of music can and does change over time within any particular culture.

In a similar vein, Charles Morris argues that music can be, and is, symbolic on the level of general categorization. He reports:

> I have asked many persons, for instance, what kind of situation Stravinsky's *Rite of Spring* might denote (that is, what is its signification). The answers are various: a herd of wild elephants in panic, a Dionysian orgy, mountains being formed by geological processes, dinosaurs in conflict. But there is no suggestion that it might denote a quiet brook, or lovers in the moonlight, or the self's tranquility. "Primitive forces in elemental conflict"—such is the approximate signification of the music, and such conflict is presented iconically in the music itself. (1955:193)

These observations—particularly those of Morris and Langer—have been questioned by Charles L. Stevenson (1958), who feels they are of limited applicability and usefulness. Morris, he argues, has developed a system of thought which is so general that virtually everything becomes a sign of something and may even be a sign of itself. Langer, says Stevenson, uses signing in such a way that music becomes a sign for the emotions; "music quite literally *designates* an emotion . . . it stands *for* an emotion, or *represents* it" (p. 203). Stevenson reports:

> . . . the sounds of music are actually accompanied by (and *not* merely signified by) a certain feeling or mood—one that is *some-*

thing like an everyday-life emotion but not *exactly* like it. For instance, the feeling or mood that attends sad music may have a generic resemblance to that attending a bereavement, but need not resemble it in provoking tears, or in being uncontrollable, etc. Our application of the term "sad" to music is then explained . . . by our tendency to extend the term to this otherwise unnamed feeling or mood. . . . (p. 214)

Given this position, Stevenson argues with considerable cogency that the application of a theory of signs to the arts in general becomes more and more difficult as the art becomes more and more abstract. Thus "such arts as pure music and non-objective painting appear to have no aesthetically relevant symbolic function at all" (p. 202), and music, as such, while it may resemble emotions, does not at all necessarily signify them.

This problem of whether the theory of signs and symbols is truly applicable to music is a serious one, and it is further emphasized when application is sought on a cross-cultural basis. In these conditions, it is questionable whether a true distinction can be made between the sign and the symbol, and it seems more likely that we deal here with a continuum in which the sign melts imperceptibly into the symbol on higher and higher planes of abstraction.

In any case, whether we treat signs and symbols as rigidly separable or as a continuum, music does seem to function as a "symbolic" part of life, at least in the sense that it does represent other things. There are four ways in which this relationship is manifest in human experience, and each of these can be related to concepts of signs and symbols on an ascending order of abstraction.

The first of these is perhaps closest to a "level of signing"; in this case, art is symbolic in its conveyance of direct meanings. This level is most easily expressed through arts other than music; some dance is mimetic, and some visual art is representational. In this sense such behavior is probably signing rather than symboling, for the nature of the product directly represents human action. Erotic movements in the dance are the same or nearly the same movements used in actual behavior, and a sculptured bust is a direct though by no means identical representation of the person involved.

In dealing with music the problem is more involved, for it is difficult to see how music sound itself can ever be a direct representation of anything. Morris argues that Western program music is essentially iconic and uses as an illustration Stravinsky's *Rite of Spring* in the sense of general categorization. It will be recalled, however, that an icon, by definition,

234

exhibits in itself the properties an object must have to be denoted by it, and in these terms it is difficult to see how music can be iconic. At the same time, certain kinds of music in the Western sphere approach this more closely than do other kinds, and the most specific examples are found in radio and television cue music and in motion picture music. Even in these examples, the connection between the music sound and what it is supposed to represent can only be made through ascription of meaning which is culturally defined, and thus we move immediately from the signing to the symboling level. Radio and television cue music and scoring for motion pictures come close to iconic signing in music, but they do not fulfill all the requirements necessary to make it so.

A more direct example is found in those compositions in Western art music which utilize bird song, cannon shots, or other direct representations. The difficulty here, of course, is that such sounds can only be admitted as music on highly contestable grounds, and, further, cannon shots, for example, are not really iconic but are the actual sounds themselves. At the same time, they do represent more than the cannon shot as such; they are a sign from which the imagination is expected to draw its cues for wider visualizations. One or two examples from nonliterate societies seem to fall within this same general category, although they too raise similar problems. Thus Howard and Kurath note for Plains Indians that:

> Their Sun dance is performed to call the thunderbird to bring rain and thus provide grass for the buffalo (or, today, cattle and crops), and to induce this rainmaker to stop and "rest" in their territory where a "nest" is provided for him in the fork of the Sun dance pole. . . . The dancers are dressed to represent baby thunderbirds and their piping on eagle bone whistles imitates the chirpings of nestlings. (1959:2)

Very similar is Wachsmann's point that among the Ankole of Uganda "there are long low notes sung by the chorus that represent noises made by cattle. . . ." (1953:55) in songs apparently associated with herding. In neither of these cases is it made clear whether the sounds produced are considered to be music or imitations of sounds of daily life, yet both are clearly part of the music performance. The question remains, then, whether these are music sounds of an iconic nature or whether they are practical intrusions into music.

Of a somewhat different, although related, nature is the short melodic section which identifies the class of song being sung. Burrows has described such a melody in connection with the *bwarux*, or serenade, on Ifaluk in Micronesia, where each song of the general class uses the same

235

short melodic line as part of the presentation (1958:17, 20). In this case the characterizing melody stands as a sign for a type of song, but Burrows intimates that identification is not based completely upon what he calls the "little tune," but rather upon a constellation of factors. Thus he adds:

> Fully as distinctive of *bwarux* as "the little tune" is the manner of singing. When the pitch rises, at the point written as the beginning of the second measure, the voice is carried up in a slur or *portamento*, maintaining a "chest tone," so that some versions sound as much like shouting as singing. The final descent in pitch is similar, sometimes a downward *portamento* without definite pitch. (p. 17)

Burrows also notes that "little melodic formulas" characterize "most of the main kinds of songs," and suggests that since there is a constellation of identifying factors, one must deal more with style than with a single characteristic. This suggests, in turn, that style itself may be considered iconic in a loose sense, that is, that either the characteristics of an identifiable group of songs or the peculiarities of individual performance are in themselves signs. Of these, the latter seems to be closer to the concept of what is iconic; it is perhaps illustrated most clearly from the Western jazz idiom, where an extremely high value is placed upon the individuality of style created by the musician. Whether this is truly iconic is a moot point, but it seems reasonably clear that it at least approaches what is usually meant by the iconic sign.

A phenomenon similar to the Ifaluk "little tune" occurs in those cultures in which recognized tunes act as signals for some particular activity. Meek writes:

> In the same way among the Jukun there are recognized tunes for summoning the people to war or to work. Thus there is a special tune for summoning men for roadwork. There is another tune for summoning maidens to repair the king's palace, to fetch water for a Government rest house, or to greet distinguished visitors. (1926:460)

Although the problem of whether it is the tune or its context which is important is one which we shall have to discuss at some length later, something does operate meaningfully in such a connection to signal a particular kind of activity, and this seems to be essentially signing behavior.

A final example of interest is given by Waterman for the Yirkalla. Speaking of the *karma*, or sacred but non-secret ceremonial songs, he writes:

It is the pattern formed by these melodic tones in relation to the pitch of the drone-pipe that makes each *karma* song-cycle distinctive. Thus, if we take the note of the drone-pipe as an octave or two below the first of scale, a *karma* cycle of the *ridajigo*-speaking lineage uses the first, the flatted second, and the flatted third of scale; a cycle of the *komaitt*-speaking lineage uses the natural second and flatted third of scale, and one of the *magkalili*-speaking lineage the flatted third and the fourth. . . . This permits them to be identified at a distance even when the words are indistinguishable. (1956:46)

Music can perhaps also be the vehicle for signing in its use of song texts. That is, texts themselves make certain statements which have specific and direct meaning—"I love you," "The child sleeps in his cradle." The problem here is that language is itself a symbolic mechanism, and thus in dealing with song texts which are expressed through the vehicle of music sound we are clearly dealing with symbolic behavior. If we accept song texts in this particular context as an integral part of music, we come close again to the level of symbolic behavior with which we are dealing, but at the same time texts are not music sound and, though shaped and modified by music, they are inevitably linguistic rather than music behavior as such.

On the level of signing, then, the most obvious examples are found in arts other than music—mimetic dance and representational visual art. Music sound, however, lies on such a high level of abstraction that it appears always to be more in the nature of symboling than signing, although some of the examples noted here are close to the latter.

On a second level, the arts in general—and music specifically in this case—are symbolic in that they are reflective of emotion and meaning; we can refer to this as "affective" or "cultural" meaning, and here we are on much stronger and more obvious ground, for the symbolism is distinct and culturally defined.

In Western music, for example, we assign the emotion of sadness to what we call a minor scale; certain combinations of music instruments playing together suggest certain physical or emotional phenomena, and selections of particular combinations of notes can and do symbolize particular states of being. In addition, individual music instruments are characterized as expressive of particular emotions, and instruction in the relationship between instrument and emotion is a part of standard textbooks of instrumentation and orchestration. In speaking of the woodwinds, for example, Rimsky-Korsakow writes:

a) Flutes.—Cold in quality, specially suitable in the major key, to melodies of light and graceful character; in the minor key, to slight touches of transient sorrow.

b) Oboe.—Artless and gay in the major, pathetic and sad in the minor.

c) Clarinet.—Pliable and expressive, suitable, in the major, to melodies of a joyful or contemplative character, or to outbursts of mirth; in the minor, to sad and reflective melodies or impassioned and dramatic passages.

d) Bassoon.—In the major, an atmosphere of senile mockery; a sad, ailing quality in the minor.

In the extreme registers these instruments convey the following impressions to my mind:

	Low register	Very high register
a) Flute—	Dull, cold	Brilliant
b) Oboe—	Wild	Hard, dry
c) Clarinet—	Ringing, threatening	Piercing
d) Bassoon—	Sinister	Tense

(Rimsky-Korsakow n.d.:19)

Thus there is an ascription made on the cultural level to the particular sound of music instruments even before they are sounded. It is noteworthy here that Rimsky-Korsakow expresses these meanings in individualistic terms: "these instruments convey the following impressions to my mind." That is, he seems to indicate that others may hear these instrumental sounds in different ways, thus emphasizing Susanne Langer's point that "the assignment of one rather than another possible meaning to each form is never explicitly made." At the same time, however, texts such as Rimsky-Korsakow's and Forsyth's (1946) have been used by generations of students in the West, and thus the particular orientations and interpretations of these scholars have tended to become standardized in Western musical culture. This is particularly true where, as in this case, the standard works on the subject both reflect and reinforce preceding traditions of interpretation.

A similar ascription of meaning to music in the Western art tradition is found in connection with particular devices; in a discussion of chromaticism and its meaning, for example, Lowinsky writes:

Chromaticism always represents the extraordinary. . . . Again and again we find chromatic treatment given to such highly emotional concepts as crying, lamenting, mourning, moaning, inconsolability, shrouding one's head, breaking down, and so forth.

238

In the Italian madrigal the same concepts find expression through the medium of chromaticism. There they represent man as entangled in his earthly passions, while in the music of the Netherlands they symbolize the devout believer struggling with the burden of sorrow which God has laid upon him to test his faith. (Lowinsky 1946:79)

A similar formulation has been proposed for the visual arts by Longman, who divides the symbolic nature of visual art into two categories, "form meaning" and "symbolic meaning" (1949:9-12). Longman defines form meaning as "meanings which may be read in the form itself, apart from representation" (p. 9), and he treats such meanings as universals, holding that they are inherent in form. Thus horizontal lines represent "repose, peace, quiet, equilibrium," circles represent "completeness and finality, but instability because of tendency to roll," and colors such as red, orange, and yellow are "exciting, magnetic, buoyant, and open," while those such as blue and green are "soothing, quiet, reserved, inhibitory," and so forth. It must be stressed that these designations of form meaning, which Longman considers basic, are held to be universal and inherent in the shapes and colors themselves, although no evidence of cross-cultural universality is given.

Contrasted with form meaning is symbolic meaning, which refers to what we have called here cultural or affective meaning, that is, what is read into the form in an extrinsic representation of what the art is or stands for. Thus in chart form the following equations are given:

Color	Form-meaning	Symbolic meaning
pale green	exquisite delicacy or lyric joy	sea foam
red	warmth, excitement, buoyancy	flames
golden yellow	richness, well-being, radiant satisfaction	gold or sunflowers
dark purple	aristocratic dignity, pride, affluence	a king's robes
a vertical rectangle	symmetry and dignity	a window or door (p. 12)

Such distinctions between form meaning and symbolic meaning would be difficult to maintain on a cross-cultural basis, for there is no reason to assume, for example, that "dark purple" represents "aristocratic dignity" in any culture other than our own. At the same time, the designations given to forms and colors parallel Rimsky-Korsakow's designations for the

239

sounds of particular music instruments. The parallel, however, is not quite exact, for Longman has ascribed meanings to particular parts of the internal structure of art as a form; to be exactly parallel, we should have to find similar ascriptions to music form such as particular intervals or kinds of rhythm. Descriptively we do this in our use of intersense modalities, and Lowinsky's remarks concerning chromaticism are quite similar, but it appears that in music ascription of cultural meanings does not penetrate as deeply as it does in the visual arts.

Perhaps the most direct expression of affective or cultural meaning in Western music is found in radio and television cue music and the music of motion pictures. In these media music is used very specifically to induce emotions in the audience, and in order to be successful it must use certain tested clichés proved to be evocative of the emotion desired. Radio or television cue music must establish mood and emotion in extremely short passages; the technique and rationale of such scoring has been made explicit in a number of manuals and texts.

George Davis, for example, writing on the techniques of radio cue music, has supplied a considerable background for the dramatic purposes of music:

> Music reflects emotional states. It can arouse in the listener similar emotional states. Hence:
>
> Where the emotional quality of dramatic action is *explicit*, the music matching this quality will *heighten* its intensity.
>
> Where the emotional quality is *implicit*, but not expressed, the music can *clarify* it.
>
> Music underscoring a narration can *foreshadow* for the listener the *mood* of the scene to follow. It can *supply those nuances of thought* which on the stage or screen are revealed by action and facial expression.
>
> The music is an exciting *commentator* on the emotional state of characters and ideas in the play, *inviting* the audience to participate vicariously in this emotion. . . .
>
> N.B. In serialized Radio-drama occurs opportunity to create musical themes by which characters will be identified. The appearance of these themes will announce the characters, suggest their influence, etcetera. (Davis 1947:19)

This general delineation of what music can do in suggesting emotions in radio cue music can be made much more explicit. Frank Skinner, in a text concerned with writing motion picture music, points out the various attributes of music instruments. It is no accident that his delineation of the sound of the flute, for example, is very similar to that of Rimsky-

240

Korsakow: "A FLUTE can be gay in the upper register, but lonesome and rather cold in the lower register" (Skinner 1950:49). Skinner also gives music examples and says:

There are many types of love stories, such as sincere love, which has a little sorrow and a tear behind it; a light, gay romance; a teen-age puppy love, which is sweet; a sophisticated love; and a very intense, dramatic love.

For example, a theme for a sincere love scene, with a feeling of sadness, could be . . .

This theme has a certain amount of pleading and anxiety in its character.

A theme for a light, gay romance could be . . .

This theme can be transformed into a gay waltz . . .

(Skinner 1950:33)

Skinner sketches out themes applicable to "teen-age puppy love," an intense, dramatic love scene, menace, comedy, sophistication, and so forth, and in some instances suggests a variety of ways in which the theme could be effectively developed (pp. 32-9). This use of music in radio, television, and motion pictures is a sharp example of the affective or cultural meanings which may be assigned to music in a given culture, as well as the use of music in situations in which heavy reliance is placed upon the ascribed symbolism.

Music can be assigned even broader symbolic roles in society and culture, roles in which the music itself is taken to symbolize values and even passions of the most specific yet most general nature. A case in point is jazz which, during a period from approximately 1920 to 1940, was under constant attack by the public press. In this period, a substantial segment of American society assigned to jazz a role of almost unmitigated evil, and it was used as the symbol for a wide variety of ills which were supposed to afflict the society as a whole. Dr. M. P. Schlapp, Professor of Neuro-pathology at the New York Post Graduate Hospital, quoted in *Etude* in 1925, laid down a general background:

> We are headed for a smash in this country, if we keep on the way we are going. There is a curve in the emotional stability of every people which is an index of their growth and power as a nation. On the upswing the nation expands and prospers and gains in power with the normal development of emotional life. Then comes a time when emotional instability sets in. When it reaches a certain point there is a collapse. We have almost reached that point. This emotional instability causes crime, feeble-minded-ness, insanity. Criminal conduct is a pathological matter, just as are these other orders.
>
> Our emotional instability is the product of immigration, auto-mobiles, jazz and the movies. (Anon. 1925b:6)

The editor of *Etude* commented: "The sociological significance of music at this time, when regarded from certain aspects, is horrific. . . . We know that in its sinister aspects, jazz is doing a vast amount of harm to young minds and bodies not yet developed to resist evil temptations. Perhaps this is the explanation of America's enormous crime rate at present" (Anon. 1925b:5-6).

Jazz, then, was associated with crime, insanity, feeble-mindedness, and other ills as a co-symbol of the degradation of a nation; but it was also looked upon as the symbol and instrument of individual physical collapse. Mr. Charles A. Newcomb, a dietitian, warned restaurant owners that irritating music spoils the appetite and that jazz is irritating music (Anon. 1927a:22). One "Coach Knox" of Harvard reported that "jazz parties" give boys "spindle legs and hollow chests" (Anon. 1924:18), and the Salvation Army in Cincinnati became exercised over the fact that a theatre in which jazz was played had been located near a maternity hospital, for ". . . we are loathe to believe that babies born in the maternity hospital are to be legally subjected to the implanting of jazz emotions by such enforced propinquity to a theatre and jazz palace" (Anon. 1926a:4).

In this period, too, jazz came to be regarded as the symbol of barba-rism, primitivism, savagery, and animalism. Professor Smith of Boston suggested that "jazz music . . . is turning modern men, women and children back to the stages of barbarism. . . ." (Anon. 1925a:22), and the Reverend Dr. A. W. Beaven of Rochester commented: "Jazz may be analyzed as a combination of nervousness, lawlessness, primitive and savage animalism and lasciviousness" (Anon. 1922b:15). The composer, Sir Hamilton Harty, worried that future historians "will see that in an age which considers itself musically enlightened we permit groups of jazz barbarians to debase and mutilate our history of classical music and listen with patience to impudent demands to justify its filthy desecration" (Anon. 1929:24), and a Dr. Reisner added that "Jazz is a relic of barbarism. It tends to unseat reason and set passion free" (Anon. 1926b:30).

It is not surprising that, given its supposed reversion to barbarism, jazz was also attacked as an anti-Christian symbol. As early as 1921, Zion City, Illinois, threatened to burn all jazz records found in the city as ". . . the chief item in a new program put under way today for the further salvation of Zion" (Anon. 1921:9). Archbishop Beckman, speaking in New York, said: "We permit, if not endorse by our criminal indifference, 'jam sessions,' 'jitter-bugs' and cannibalistic rhythmic orgies to occupy a place in our social scheme of things, wooing our youth along the primrose path to hell!" (Anon. 1938:20), and Monseigneur Conefrey saw a sinister plot in jazz: "Jazz was borrowed from Central Africa by a gang of wealthy international Bolshevists from America, their aim being to strike at Christian civilization throughout the world" (Anon. 1934b:IV,2).

The symbol of jazz as an inherently evil force was so prevalent and so intensely felt that as responsible a newspaper as the New York *Times* began to identify almost any unpleasant sound as jazz and to attribute evil influence to jazz no matter how distant the connection. Thus on April 7, 1922, it ran an article under the headline "Musician is Driven to Suicide by Jazz"; in the body of the article, it turned out that Mr. Melville M. Wilson, the musician in question, was seventy-two years old and played the cello, an instrument not remotely connected with jazz at the time (Anon. 1922a:1). In another article, titled "Jazz Frightens Bears," the *Times* solemnly reported that bears had been a nuisance in Siberia and that the people beat kettles in an attempt to drive them away; "beating kettles" was apparently synonymous with jazz in the mind of the writer (Anon. 1928a:16). And in 1927, the same paper, in an editorial, reported: "Now comes the report from Arizona that a prehistoric jazz band has been found, including drums and an instrument which may be said to be toward the saxophone of today what the Neanderthal man is to the modern New Yorker" (Anon. 1927b:III,4).

The extent of the vision of jazz as a symbol of evil throughout the Western world is emphasized by its being banned in countries outside the United States. In 1934 in Ireland, the Gaelic League branded jazz as a menace to and enemy of civilization (Anon. 1934a:IV,3); in Russia in 1928, it was announced that "anyone importing and playing American jazz is liable to fine of 100 rubles and imprisonment for six months" (Anon. 1928b:VIII,8); and in Mexico in 1931, a Students' League

". . . declared American jazz music is used as a means for developing the dominion of the United States over Mexico," and promptly decided to ban it, at least among themselves (Anon. 1931:7).

The degree to which jazz served as a symbol of culturally defined evil in the United States, and in other countries as well, may seem incredible to us today, but it was a real fact in the 1920's and 1930's. It is an extremely clear illustration of how music, and in this case not individual sounds but an entire body of sound, can be used symbolically on the level of affective ascribed cultural meaning. The very fact that views of this sort concerning jazz are not nearly so prevalent today illustrates as well how symbolism on the cultural level can be transferred to and from a particular music style over time; our fears and hostilities today are directed toward rock and roll.

When we turn from the music of the West to that of other cultures, examples of music as symbolic mechanisms on the affective or cultural level are less easy to find. This is probably not so much because music is not used symbolically in other cultures, but rather that we have not paid this particular aspect of music much attention. In respect to the music of the Near and Far East, however, the symbolic connections between music and other aspects of culture are striking, and considerable information is available.

In the music of India, for example, musical tones are organized into *ragas* which correspond most closely to our concept of modes, and *ragas* are symbolic in a very wide sense. Arnold Bake reports, for example, that each *raga* can be depicted as divine or human beings, situated in particular surroundings which suggest the moods they are intended to evoke. *Ragas* are considered to be masculine, while *raginis* are feminine, and each has connections with times of day and night and seasons of the year. In northern India, especially, the *ragas* are personified in paintings and, quoting from Sanskrit writings, Bake describes the *raga Megha* (cloud) as follows:

> *Megha* is heptatonic, having *dha* in the three functions of *graha, amsa,* and *nyasa,* in the *murcchana uttarayata* (the third of the *sa-grama*), to be sung with the altered (*vikrta*) *dha*. A gush of erotic sentiment.
>
> *Raga Megha,* the Youth, having a body like the blue lotus, with garments like the moon, dressed in yellow, implored by thirsty *cataka*-birds (who drink only raindrops), with a smile sweet as nectar, is resplendent among heroes, in the midst of clouds. (1957:214)

A. H. Fox Strangways further sees a musical set of criteria upon which major distinctions among modes and their associated cultural meanings can

244

be made (1914:153), and Raffe presents a detailed discussion of the philosophy and aesthetics of the *raga*, with considerable attention to symbolism (1952).

The situation in respect to music symbolism is much the same in China (Picken 1954). Here, for example, the *Huang chung*, or foundation tone, was formerly considered to be "a sacred eternal principle (probably as an image of the divine will)," and even as the actual basis of the state; it was "vitally important to find the correct foundation tone for each dynasty," and if the foundation tone was not correct, or if it was disturbed, serious consequences would ensue (p. 225). The actual tones of the pentatonic scale, reached through alternate ratios of 2:3 and 3:4, were symbolically related to many other elements of Chinese culture. The numbers used in the ratios themselves had cosmological significance, and the number 5, represented in the five notes of the scale, was fundamental in Chinese philosophy. The five scale tones were linked with the five virtues—benevolence, righteousness, propriety, knowledge, faith—and with various other elements such as season, element, color, direction, and planet. In the Chinese system, music on the level of ascribed cultural meanings was and is extremely important as a symbolic mechanism.

Among nonliterate peoples, the use of music as a symbolic device on the affective or cultural level has been little commented upon. What few studies have been made are concerned primarily with music instruments, although the symbolic meanings discussed are primarily those concerned with the decoration of instruments rather than with meanings assigned to the instruments themselves (Boone 1951:81-6). There are a few exceptions, however.

In Ruanda, among the Abatutsi people, the drum is the symbol of political power, and no other than the *Mwami* and the Queen Mother may, theoretically, possess sets of drums. "Le symbole de la royauté etait Kalinga, le tambour sacré. Posseder ce tambour signifiait être roi" (Maquet 1954:147). Père Pages notes:

Il [Kalinga] est le tambour sacré par excellence, l'emblème de la souveraineté et le palladium du royaume. On ne le frappe pas habituellement. En principe, il doit suivre le roi dans ses déplacements. Il est porté dans un hamac et les autres tambours battent en son honneur. Il a droit aux mêmes égards que le roi et les gens frappent trois fois les mains l'une contre l'autre quand ils défilent devant lui. On l'ouint de temps à autre, pour le conserver, de beurre et de sang de boeuf dont les entrailles ont "blanchi", c'est-à-dire dont le sacrifice a été reconnu favorable par les devins-sacrificateurs. (1933:371-72)

245

Among the most detailed descriptions of the symbolic aspects of a music instrument is that given by Viviana Paques for the *ngoni* among the Bambara.

L'anthropomorphisme de la harpe. ngoni, est très net dans la pensée des usagers.

La caisse rectangulaire de l'instrument représente le masque de Koumabana, l'ancêtre qui a reçu la parole; les deux éclisses latérales sont ses yeux, l'ouïe, son nez et sa respiration, le cordier, sa bouche et ses dents, les cordes au nombre de 8, ses paroles. Elle est aussi l'image de sa tombe et les deux baguettes qui la traversent représentent le deuxième et le troisième ancêtre qui l'accompagnèrent dans la mort. La caisse représente aussi la face du devin et sa tombe, les deux baguettes étant les deux tiges de mil mises en terre avec le cadavre. A l'extrémité du manche, des sonnailles de cuivre ont les même rôle, à la fois technique et religieux, que celles fixées au tablier du tambour décrit plus haut.

Chaque son donné par chacune des 8 cordes est une prière. Les cordes sont pincées séparément par le devin, suivant leur rang et en fonction de la qualité du consultant et des questions qu'il pose. . . .

[L'harpe] préside aux sacrifices, aux rites cathartiques ou de médication, aux purifications, aux rites apotropaïques, aux méditations solitaires. Ses notes hautes sont célestes et symboles de plénitude; les basses connotent les choses terrestres et l'incomplétude. Son jeu commande les arrivées et les départs, les proliférations et les amenuisements, les rappels à l'ordre; sa présence au bord d'une mare où elle a été deposée en silence, est gage d'apaisement.

L'harpiste, avant de commencer son office, place sa bouche devant l'orifice de la caisse et murmure au mâitre du Verbe: "Maintenant c'est ton tour, organise le Monde." (1954:106-07)

There is no question but that music serves a symbolic function in human cultures on the level of affective or cultural meaning. Men everywhere assign certain symbolic roles to music which connect it with other elements in their cultures. It should be emphasized that on this level we do not expect to find universal symbolism ascribed to music; rather, this symbolic level operates within the framework of individual cultures. The ascription of certain symbolic values to the harp among the Bambara would not necessarily be found among their neighbors or among peoples of other world areas; this is culturally defined symbolism, the particular expression of particular groups of people. It should also be noted that studies on this level, particularly among nonliterate peoples, are seldom

246

found in the literature, despite the fact that music and music instruments are probably assigned culturally defined symbolic roles in every culture. One exception is Leonard Meyer's *Emotion and Meaning in Music* (1956) in which problems such as these are discussed fully for Western music and some approach is made to the music of other cultures as well. But it does not seem to have occurred to most students of the music of nonliterate peoples to investigate this particular problem, and quite possibly the difficulty of knowing the culture well enough to learn symbolic meanings has contributed to this lack.

The third level upon which we can approach the study of music in its symbolic aspects is through the ways in which music reflects other cultural behavior, organization, and values. It is here somewhat more difficult to apply the defined sense of the symbolic, for we speak primarily from an understanding of the integration of culture rather than of concentration of ideas or behavior which stand for other things.

Anthropologists have long stressed the concept of the integration of culture, for it is clear that no body of learned behavior can exist as a whole if its parts exist as independent entities. Thus there are interrelationships among the elements of culture, and it is usually assumed that changes in one element produce changes in other elements as well, that is, that culture is itself a system. Further, various psychological approaches to the problem of the integration of culture have indicated basic themes, configurations, sanctions, or patterns which tend to run through an entire culture bringing holistic unity to it (see Herskovits 1948:214-26).

We would expect, therefore, that any aspect of any given culture would reflect other parts of it, and this is certainly the case with music. All societies, for example, make distinctions between the social roles of children and adults, which are reflected in music. In almost all cultures, there are special songs sung by children, and these are not ordinarily employed by adults. Game songs, counting songs, language songs, and many others are specific to children, although as he grows older the child gives up these songs special to age and moves either abruptly or gradually into the sphere of adult music. Herskovits reports that in Dahomey a child is taught a special song to be sung with his playmates on the loss of his first tooth (1938b:I,275), and Nketia reports that the Ashanti of Ghana have a special song of insult for the habitual bed-wetter (1961b:7), though it is not made clear whether this is sung by children to the errant child, or by adults to children. On the opposite side of the picture, there are of course many songs for adults, some or most of which are prohibited to children, either by direct sanction or simply through acceptance of the child-adult relationship.

Similarly, music reflects the sex distinctions made in all societies; some

247

songs are reserved for men and some for women. Examples might include hunting songs for men and corn-grinding songs for women among some American Indian groups, or palm-nut-pounding songs in Africa for women. Again the division may be made on a restrictive basis or simply through acceptance of the fact that men do not sing women's songs, and vice versa. This distinction on the basis of sex is also reflected through music where the sex groups themselves are at the basis of certain aspects of religious ritual. Among the Congo Basongye, for example, it is the women who are the primary singers for the village fertility figure, but the men who are the true professional musicians. Thus music reflects, and in a sense symbolizes, male-female roles.

Kinship may be another basis on which music reflects other elements of culture. Clan songs are found in many societies, and in those which support a moiety system it is often the case that each of the two divisions supports its own songs. Even lineages sometimes have songs specific to their own social grouping.

Associational groups may also support special music practice. In some societies, for example, associations of hunters have their distinctive songs. Warrior organizations, various political groupings, religious associations, economic work groups, and other like organizations almost always support their distinctiveness through the mechanism of music. On broader levels, people draw distinctions between their own village and neighboring ones, or between Africans and Europeans, through music. Thus music reflects the social and political organization, economic behavior, religious activity, and other structural divisions of society, and in this respect it is, in a sense, symbolic of the formal aspects of the culture.

The reflection of cultural behavior can extend also into the deeper realm of values, and this problem has been attacked by McAllester in his study of music and values among the Navaho, *Enemy Way Music* (1954). In his introduction, McAllester summarizes the purpose of his study as ". . . an attempt to explore cultural values through an analysis of attitudes toward music and through an analysis of the music itself" (p. 3). In so doing, McAllester organizes his study on the integrational level; that is, he takes cognizance both of the values expressed in and through music and of those expressed in and through other elements of Navaho culture. Between the two, he finds a marked correspondence and thus tacitly reaches the conclusions that the general values of the culture are found in music, that these general values shape attitudes toward music as they shape other aspects of cultural behavior, and that since music embodies the general values of the culture, it reinforces them and thus in turn helps to shape the culture of which it is a part. Here the integration of culture is again expressed: values in the culture at large are transferred to music as

248

well and thus help to shape the music system. At the same time, this is a question of mutual interaction, for music, in expressing the general cultural values, also shapes the culture. The two are not mutually exclusive, but rather jointly conceived as a single broad pattern of behavior.

Working along these lines, McAllester found a number of Navaho music values which are reflections of general values as well. Thus, individualism is a strong Navaho sanction in that "authority has traditionally rested in the family or extended family group, a situation which usually gives the individual a maximum of personal autonomy. In ownership of property, which includes possession of songs . . . and even in manner of singing, Navaho individualism is clearly expressed" (p. 87). Provincialism and conservativism are also important Navaho values, and McAllester finds the same values expressed in music. Protective formalism is important in the culture, and for music "There is a right way to sing every kind of song" (p. 88). Indeed, "the structural analysis of the songs was rewarding in that it revealed a formalism, even in the most informal songs, highly consistent with the Navaho approach to life. Kluckhohn's formula: '*Maintain orderliness in those sectors of life which are little subject to human control,*' seems to extend beyond ritual behavior, poetry, and ceremonial music, to include even Squaw Dance songs" (*loc. cit.*).

McAllester's study, then, is essentially one of functional integration which points up the reflection of general cultural values in music, as expressed both in attitudes toward and about music, and in music sound and organization itself. As such, it gives us a number of clear-cut leads for further investigation—not only of how music reflects cultural values but of how it leads in their formation.

A more recent study by Alan Lomax follows somewhat the same lines but with a differing emphasis (1959). Lomax sees music as a reflection of the values and behavior in culture as a whole and, in this respect, as fulfilling a social function: ". . . the primary effect of music is to give the listener a feeling of security, for it symbolizes the place where he was born, his earliest childhood satisfactions, his religious experience, his pleasure in community doings, his courtship and his work—any or all of these personality-shaping experiences" (p. 929). But more important for Lomax is that music sound ". . . symbolizes a fundamental and social-psychological pattern, common to a given culture" through his belief that "the sexual code, the position of women, and the treatment of children" are the social patterns most commonly reflected in a music style (p. 950).

In a similar vein, Charles Seeger has indicated a potentially fruitful approach in which he holds the view that music reflects not only man's experiences within a particular culture but also basic biosocial life. Seeger speaks of "paradynamism," by which he means:

249

> . . . the incorporation, in sound, of dynamic tensions, tonicities and detensions that parallel, reflect or reconstitute those experiences in the individual biological-social life and in the collective social continuum characteristic of a culture.

This process, he says, takes place

> . . . in a manner of which man is in control, in contradistinction to biological-social life in which man has little or no control. In a particular song, or instrumental piece, there is a selection of particular tensions, tonicities and detensions; in the total practice of a culture-area, an established and potential aggregate of selection. (1961a:40-41)

It is evident that Lomax and Seeger are approaching the same problem in somewhat different ways; where Lomax tends to make specific attributions, Seeger's approach is as yet more general.

Each, however, as well as McAllester, is essentially interested in how music reflects the culture of which it is a part and, in the case of Lomax and Seeger, how it reflects the biosocial background out of which it arises. In terms of the definition of symbols noted at the beginning of this discussion, it is somewhat unclear as to whether we should regard this as symbolic use of music. Certainly from the standpoint of the performer, it is not symbolic; from that of the outside observer, we may consider it symbolic or not depending upon the particular point of view. That is, if we take the functional and integrative approach, then music is no more symbolic of culture as a whole than culture is of music, for music is simply an integral part of culture and thus inevitably reflects its general structures and values. If, on the other hand, we look at music as an entity separable from the rest of culture, then it obviously reflects or symbolizes the general patterns of that culture. McAllester tends toward the first point of view, while both Lomax and Seeger apparently tend toward the second. However, it does not seem to matter which point of view is stressed, for it is clear that music is an integral part of culture and, like all other aspects of it, is bound to reflect the general and underlying principles and values which animate the culture as a whole.

This general point of view has been further expressed by Armstrong in connection with Javanese arts (1963). Taking as his premise the Javanese concern with "avoiding three dimensionality," which he describes as a "cultural motif," he makes application of this deep-lying organizational principle to dance and, in less detail, to the other arts including music.

> In the dance, as in the shadow puppet plays, action is presented in relief. Hand and head movements, the positioning of the torso,

250

the extension of the limbs—these are all executed two-dimension-
ally. The body is never foreshortened, with movements directed
from the actor toward the audience. It is never presented at right
angles to the plane of the viewer's face, but always parallel with it.
It seems as though population density were more than mere
statistics to the dancers. (p. 8)

Armstrong also points out that folk paintings are always done in two
dimensions, as are batiks, and that bas relief on temple walls "offer a not
very interested or convincing illusion of three dimensions. . . . And the
same flatness is to be found in the music of the gamelan, which,
predominantly eurhythmic, fails to display any concern with dynamic
melodic development." (*loc. cit.*)

Harap approaches the relationship between music and the culture of
which it is a part from a Marxian standpoint:

> In our own time music is also sharply divided into two groups,
> popular and sophisticated, each of which in its special way pro-
> vides psychological reinforcement of bourgeois values and attitudes.
> The sophisticated tends to be experimental with an aridity or
> thinness of emotional content, and is on the whole lacking in
> vitality. For the composer has lost his anchorage in the masses of
> men, in their lives and interests, and reflects rather the hopelessness
> and disillusionment of the sensitive bourgeois. . . . The malad-
> justment of the bourgeois composer's relation to society is reflected
> in his music. . . . But a great part of contemporary bourgeois
> music reflects the rootlessness, pessimism and barrenness in the
> outlook of fine sensibilities in our society. . . . The result is a
> negation of vital emotional content.
>
> The second grand division of contemporary music, the popular,
> is a more direct, deliberate manipulation by the movies, radio,
> phonograph, and sheet music enterprises . . . toward a content
> that deflects the masses from a realistic understanding of their
> problems. . . . Thus the monopolistic owner of the mass music
> media achieves a dual interrelated purpose: he imposes on the
> mass audience an inferior, sentimentalized product which sells in
> large quantities by virtue of its escapist quality, and he diverts the
> emotional life of the masses from a serious, realistic approach to
> their problems and hence helps to prop declining capitalism.
> Thus the connection between popular music and its ideological
> function is close. (1949:101-02)

Although further examples concerning music could be cited, among
them McLeod's analysis of the relationship between music and occasion

251

structure (1957), there are also excellent illustrations of the reflection of culture in arts other than music. In discussing the Kaguru of Tanganyika, for example, Beidelman finds in the folk tale of Rabbit and Hyena ". . . a social problem of great concern to the Kaguru . . . presented in simple and relatively innocuous form. The problem is that of conflict and division within a matrilineage, the most important social unit in Kaguru society." Beidelman analyzes the significance of the tale in considerable detail (1961). Similarly, Devereux points out the importance of cultural reflections in visual art when he notes:

> Needless to say, the culturally prescribed distortion (style) glaringly reflects the tensions and problems of the artist's milieu. . . . The African, Melanesian, Maori, Marquesan, Kwakiutl, Aztec, Maya or Inca artist distorted his figures intentionally and in accordance with cultural rules governing artistic utterances. Moreover, as regards certain African, Melanesian and medieval gargoyle carving artists, their nightmare vision of the human body—reflected in its artistic distortion—is closely related to what I, for one, view as their nightmare vision of the universe and of life. (1961:366)

Although it does not concern music, J. L. Fischer's discussion (1961) of the relationship between art and society opens up lines of investigation which might well be exploited by ethnomusicology. Fischer works from the premise that form in the "expressive aspects of culture . . . is social fantasy, that is, the artist's fantasies about social situations which will give him security or pleasure," and that thus, no matter what the overt content, there will always be expressed "some fantasied social situation which will bear a definite relation to the real and desired social situations of the artist and his society." He establishes his problem by defining two kinds of societies, the authoritarian, in which "social hierarchy is positively valued," and the egalitarian, in which "hierarchy as a principle of organization is rejected." On the basis of this dichotomy, Fischer establishes the four following hypotheses:

> 1) Design repetitive of a number of rather simple elements should characterize the egalitarian societies; design integrating a number of unlike elements should be characteristic of the hierarchical societies.
>
> 2) Design with a large amount of empty or irrelevant space should characterize the egalitarian societies; design with little irrelevant (empty) space should characterize the hierarchical societies.
>
> 3) Symmetrical design (a special case of repetition) should

characterize the egalitarian societies; asymmetrical design should characterize the hierarchical societies.

4) Figures without enclosures should characterize the egalitarian societies; enclosed figures should characterize the hierarchical societies. (p. 81)

Using a sample of twenty-eight societies, Fischer found his hypotheses borne out to a high degree of probability, and he applied similar methods to investigate such problems as those concerning the sex of the artist, the presence or absence of straight and curved lines, and complexity and non-complexity in art.

This interesting study might well be used as a model for a similar approach in ethnomusicology, granting the relative simplicity of the authoritarian-egalitarian dichotomy and the many problems it implies. Would the repetitive monotone, or some other repetitive element characterize egalitarian societies? Does music with a wide tonal range and large leaps reflect the hierarchical organization, and does music with substantial numbers of rests (empty spaces) correlate with the egalitarian? The difficulty in formulating such problems, as so often seems to be the case in music, lies in delimiting units; that is, at what point do we say that a certain kind of music is "empty" rather than "full," or "symmetrical" rather than "asymmetrical"? Despite such difficulties, a problem of this kind in music does not seem to be insoluble, and it is almost certain that fruitful results indicating the relationship between music on the one hand and culture and society on the other would emerge.

The fourth and final level upon which we can approach the problem of music as symbolic behavior involves still deeper and more fundamental aspects of human behavior. In this case, instead of looking at music as indicative of behavior in a particular culture, we search for broad principles of universal application. That is, does music as such symbolize human behavior? Can we find underlying expressions, of whatever nature, about man and his behavior through symbolic expression in music symbols? Approaches to this kind of problem have been few.

One approach was taken by Curt Sachs (1937:181-203; 1943:30-43), who divides melodic materials into three major types: logogenic (word-born), pathogenic (motion-born), and melogenic (music-born). These three melodic types, which Sachs feels are of universal application, are correlated with other phenomena of human behavior. Thus logogenic melodies are of narrow range and use small intervals, and where this occurs Sachs also finds dances which are tight, controlled, and expressed through narrow steps. Pathogenic melodies, on the other hand, are of wide range with bold and dramatic melodic leaps; the corresponding dances are also bold and the physical motions large. Similarly, the two contrasting melodic forms are the symbolic expression of masculinity and femininity:

The same contemplative, patient, imperturbable, introvert disposition which through the ascendancy of female characteristics creates a predominantly feminine culture and leads from the food-gatherer to the planter level, makes itself felt in dance and music through close movement and through an urge towards the static and the symmetrical. The alert, impatient, vivid, and impulsive extrovert disposition which leads to the dominance of the masculine qualities in a culture and to hunting and cattle-breeding, is reflected in dance and music through expanded movement and through the urge towards the dynamic and the asymmetrical. (1937:203)

There seems to be some hint in Sachs's discussion of a relationship between melodic type and anatomical types in that pygmoid peoples are supposed to use small intervals, while taller people use larger intervals. It is intimated, too, that small intervals in music are used generally by peaceful peoples, while the larger intervals are the property of those who tend toward war.

Bruno Nettl (1956:55-6) has criticized this approach on several grounds, primarily from the point of view that the correlations suggested by Sachs do not hold true in an examination of examples from various parts of the world. In addition, a major problem exists in the nature of the categories chosen for discussion. It is extremely difficult, if not impossible, to define what a "warlike" or "peaceful" people is, except in the most general of ways, and further it is clear that while the music style of the Plains Indians, for example, who use pathogenic melodic types, has not changed basically since those styles have been defined, their way of life has changed, and drastically. Less than one hundred years ago, the Plains Indians could perhaps have been described as warlike in a general sense; yet today, when outside pressures have removed this cultural complex, at least in its manifest form, the melodic style associated with it remains.

The quarrel we may have with formulations such as this is not so much with the exploratory nature of the ideas as with the means chosen to reach them. It seems almost certain that there are broad correspondences of music type and cultural considerations and that these principles may well be expressed in human rather than individualistically cultural terms; but the particular kind of illustration proposed by Sachs is simply not acceptable.

Similar kinds of formulations have been made by other writers. Marius Schneider says that "music is the seat of secret forces or spirits which can be evoked by song in order to give man a power which is either higher than himself or which allows him to rediscover his deepest self. . . . Every being has its own sound or its own song, the timbre and rhythm of which embody the mystic substance of the owner" (1957:42). This analysis is carried to considerable lengths by Schneider; unfortunately, the conclusions are almost totally unacceptable because of the author's insistence on approaching the problems from a racial standpoint. For Schneider, the so-called primitive peoples represent almost a separate species of mankind, and he treats race and culture as dependent variables. Races are held to have special and mystic abilities, and what the anthropologist attributes to learning and to culture, Schneider attributes to race and says specifically that certain music characteristics are "rooted in men's constitution. In fact, the innermost essence of the more intensely specialized types of song cannot be transmitted at all . . . since the dynamic and vocal timbre which is inseparably bound up with it cannot be acquired by learning" (1957:27). While Schneider brings many potential insights to his material which may well point to possible human music symbolism, the nature of his arguments is so clouded in mystic race-culture confusions as to be almost meaningless.

A second major approach to music as indicative of human symbolism has been through Freudian formulations. This is clearly expressed in discussions of music instrument symbolism, and Curt Sachs writes:

> Tubular wind instruments, straight and elongated like a man's organ, belong to man, and a mixture of symbols arises when a flute is globular instead of tubular, or when a trumpet is made out of a conch shell which is connected with water. . . .
>
> Sound, also, is a factor as well as form in these connotations. Most of the instruments reserved for men have a harsh, aggressive, indeed ugly tone; most instruments preferred by women have a muffled timbre. (Sachs 1940:52)

In another passage Sachs speaks of the East African drum as symbolically feminine, basing his analysis upon information from the Banyankole and the Wahinda, among whom, he feels, drums are equated with ". . . round, domed enclosure, earth, night, moon and milk, which, in the primitive mind, are connotations of woman and female sex" (p. 36). He further feels that the drumstick is a phallic symbol, and makes a particular citation to East African drums ". . . struck with sticks made of human tibias, which likewise have a phallic significance" (*loc. cit.*). Similar points have been made by Kunst (1958:12).

Psychoanalytic analysis has by no means been confined to studies of music instruments. Margaret Tilly proposes that masculine and feminine

255

principles are indicated in a composer's music through his individual personality. She writes:

> Jung's theory shows man's feminine side (or Anima) to be usually suppressed, remaining for the most part in his unconscious. When the Anima is overstrong, and not projected onto a woman, a neurotic condition is caused and results in a homosexual personality. Much of the Anima is likely to be projected through the creative work of the individual, in which we then recognize a strongly neurotic feminine flavour, while in the better integrated man, his feminine side will show as merely part of a well-balanced whole, for the Anima then serves rather than dominates him. (1947:477)

Working from this premise, Tilly argues that we respond most favorably to music "in which the strength of the Anima approximates that in ourselves," and she analyzes the work of several Western composers on the basis of masculine and feminine qualities in music.

Masculine Qualities	Neurotic Feminine Qualities (As found in the man)
Form	Mood
Impersonality	Personal approach
Direct approach	Indirection
Drive	Sentimentality
Rhythmic power	Rhythm subservient to melody and harmony
Sustained thought and emotion	Quickly shifting emotions
Superior thinking	Love of decoration, per se
Greater output of large works	Small output, with short works predominating

(*loc. cit.*)

Tilly finds the feminine principle predominant in the music personality of Chopin, Tschaikovsky, and Liszt, and the masculine principle in the personalities and music of Bach, Handel, and Beethoven.

Angelo Montani explains the quality of sadness or sorrow in the minor mode in Western music in essentially Freudian terms. Arguing that the number 3 is symbolically associated with the phallus, that in ancient Italian the semantic symbolism of major and minor is respectively "hard" and "soft," which correlates in turn with "virile, masculine, and powerful," and "feminine, weak, diminished," he concludes as follows:

> With the ideas of "less strong, weaker, etc.," are associated the unconscious feeling of suffering, chastisement, pain, all of

which in Psycho-analysis is attached to the "Complex of Castration" which generates the feelings of "sadness, melancholy and death." These "strange" denominations . . . appear as literary versions of more primitive censured thoughts.

Thus the mysterious feeling of sadness developed by the Minor Mode can be explained. We are confronted with still one more of those tortuous paths which the "ID" takes with the purpose of surpassing the "Ego." (1945:227)

The problems posed by analyses such as those of Tilly and Montani are considerable. Given the assumption of psychoanalysis as probing universal symbols, we can assume properly that the two analyses are meant to be applicable to all mankind. Such speculations, however, are not subject to empiric proof, and since no such analysis has been broached in respect to music of non-Western peoples, its applicability is in serious doubt. If, indeed, these are considered to be universal principles, there will surely be difficulty in making their cross-cultural application, for the Major as opposed to the minor mode is not a dichotomy expressed or, so far as we know, even considered in cultures other than our own. Further, except by its own internal logic, is there any means for proof of the assumption that "form," for example, represents a masculine quality, while "mood" is essentially feminine? As in the case of Freudian interpretation of instrument symbolism, it can only be said that it is not the exploratory nature of the ideas with which we must quarrel, but rather with the categories and interpretations chosen.

It may be noted briefly that psychoanalytic techniques have been applied more widely to the content of oral literature than they have to music, perhaps primarily because in oral literature the analyst can work with spoken texts which have semantic meaning. Thus Ernest Jones argues for the presence of primitive impulses which may come into consciousness normally or abnormally; in the latter case they may give rise to neurotic symptoms, dream life, and folklore. Folklore, in turn, reflects such unconscious impulses as omnipotence of thoughts, disregard of reality, and symbolism, of which "an astonishing number certainly the large majority," he says, are sexual symbols (1951:12). Franz Ricklin has argued that fairy tales, specifically, are mechanisms of wish fulfillment, saying ". . . the human psyche produces at all times and in all places . . . a symbolism, which is chiefly constructed from the unconscious . . ." Thus fairy tales are filled with ". . . means to look into the future and to attain one's wishes, apples of life and water of life for rejuvenation and the preservation of this otherwise all too short existence" (1915:2-3, 14). Jung, of course, argues for the existence of archetypes which are common to man. These archetypes represent the constellations

257

of the collective unconscious, and they appear out of the unconscious especially in a state of reduced consciousness as in dreams. Since, he argues, the so-called primitive mind always operates in a state of reduced consciousness, the archetypes come easily to the fore. Myths are invented by primitive people because of this reduced state of consciousness, and they reflect the archetypes which are suppressed more successfully in "higher" human beings who are in better control of the conscious (Jung and Kerenyi 1949:99-103).

The problems of folklore analysis closely parallel those of music. On this level, symbolism is interpreted in the broadest possible terms in the hope that application can be made to men everywhere rather than to men in specific cultures. The search for such symbolism is extremely important, and when removed from the intracultural and analytic biases evident in the work published thus far, may quite conceivably result in a better understanding of the drives which impel man toward music-making.

Symbolism in music, then, can be considered on these four levels: the signing or symboling evident in song texts, the symbolic reflection of affective or cultural meaning, the reflection of other cultural behavior and values, and the deep symbolism of universal principles. It is evident that the approach which sees music essentially as symbolic of other things and processes is a fruitful one; and stressed again here is the kind of study which seeks to understand music not simply as a constellation of sounds, but rather as human behavior.

CHAPTER XIII

AESTHETICS AND THE INTERRELATIONSHIP OF THE ARTS

One of the most important aspects of the study of music concerns the concepts of aesthetics and the interrelationship of the arts. This is dangerous and tricky ground trod by a number of aestheticians most of whom have concerned themselves with strict application of these concepts to Western art alone. In Western art, the subject is of major importance because it is an avenue of understanding which leads toward the aims and purposes of art, as well as the attitudes taken toward it; given this importance, it is surprising that so few attempts have apparently been made at cross-cultural application and understanding. It is not the purpose here to discuss the history of aesthetics or the application of aesthetics in Western culture, for these problems have been covered in detail (Gilbert and Kuhn 1939; Munro 1951). Rather, it is to attempt to discover whether Western aesthetic concepts can be transferred and applied to other world societies.

One of the major problems encountered here is that despite the enormous literature devoted to aesthetics, it is extremely difficult to discover precisely what an aesthetic is. While various of the arts or individual works of art are described, usually in affective terms, as *being* aesthetic, it often seems that what is aesthetic is reflected from the art or the individual object rather than being something applied to it. Thus it is particularly difficult to use the concept cross-culturally, since we cannot make such application if we do not know clearly and concisely what it is that we are applying. The challenge, then, is first to seek an understanding of what is meant by an aesthetic, and second, to attempt to discover whether other societies have and use it in the same manner as ourselves. In

259

order to do this, we shall have to lay down several postulates and assumptions which will form the basis for discussion.

In the first place, it is held that the aesthetic is a concept used in Western and certain Middle and Far Eastern cultures to denote something about the arts. It derives from philosophies which are traceable in history to the Greeks in Western culture and even further back in time in Eastern cultures. It is also held that, while they differ in matters of content and detail, the Eastern and Western aesthetic philosophies are essentially alike. There will be no further attempt to base discussion on Eastern aesthetic philosophy; rather, the arguments will derive from and apply to the Western concept of the aesthetic alone.

Second, it is held that in the West we have surrounded the aesthetic concept with a torrent of ideas, a verbal jungle which tends to obscure rather than to clarify the essential ideas contained in the philosophy of the aesthetic. What is aesthetic has become primarily a matter of words, a semantic, which culminates in an almost intuitive feeling for what is and what is not considered to be aesthetic.

Third, in discussing the aesthetic, Western aestheticians have made it primarily applicable to but one kind of art. In so doing, they have strengthened the division made in our culture between "fine art" as opposed to "applied art," or the "artist" as opposed to the "craftsman." Thus Munro, for example, can say, ". . . the word 'art' in itself implies an aesthetic function. Thus any skill or product which is classed as an art is by definition 'fine' or aesthetic" (1951:518). Apparently, then, folk or popular music cannot, by definition, be aesthetic, since it is not, also by definition, "fine" art. The concept of the aesthetic for Americans applies only to a particular kind of music and excludes other kinds; it is a culture-bound concept applied by us to those particular forms which we call fine art.

Fourth, it is held that no object or action is, in itself, aesthetic; that is, what is aesthetic comes from the creator or the observer who attributes something aesthetic to the object or action. Thus the aesthetic implies an attitude which includes values held, and if this be true then the Western attribution of an aesthetic to a non-Western object is of no value to analysis, except in that it sheds light upon our own aesthetic concept. In order to demonstrate that Western aesthetic concepts apply to other cultures, it must be shown that similar concepts are held by people in those cultures and that they are applied to objects or actions.

In sum, the object is to attempt to discover what is meant by the aesthetic in Western culture, and to attempt to apply this meaning to other cultures and thus to determine whether it is, indeed, applicable on a scale greater than that involved in a single culture. If it is found that the concept is applicable, then we have taken another step in the search for universal elements of culture that demonstrate a degree of unity in the behavior of all mankind. If, on the other hand, it is found that the concept is not applicable to other cultures, the discovery is equally important, for two reasons. First, it means that people are not alike in this respect, and negative information is often as important as the positive. More important, however, is the indication that people in other cultures must view their arts in ways that differ from ours, and in ways that have yet to be clearly understood. This would not denigrate the arts in other cultures; rather, it would simply indicate a difference of attitude, and perhaps of use and function as well.

In order that there be the least possible chance for misunderstanding, it must be repeated that the assumption here is that we are dealing specifically with a Western concept viewed strictly from the Western point of view. The problem is to attempt to ascertain whether this specific Western concept is reduplicated in any societies other than our own. In order to do this we will attempt to isolate those factors which appear to be prerequisite to the aesthetic and to apply them to specific cases in societies other than our own. For the latter purpose, we shall use the Basongye and Flathead societies upon which we have drawn so heavily throughout this book.

In looking at the aesthetic in Western society, there appear to be six factors which, taken together, comprise the concept. It seems impossible to determine which of these is the most important, if any one of them is, or whether the absence of one, two, three, or more indicates a lack of an aesthetic. If, however, the six factors are correctly adduced, their limited attribution or their absence in another society would seem to indicate serious question as to the presence of an aesthetic, defined always in Western terms.

The first of these factors is what has been called *psychic* or *psychical distance*. As used by Bullough (1912) the term was applied primarily in the sense of "objectivity," but it has also been used in the senses of "absence of utility or purpose," "feeling of unreality," and "repose or complete participation in the object" (Longman 1949:14). The sense in which it is used here has also been suggested previously; this is the sense of "detachment and isolation" (*loc. cit.*). What is meant is the ability of the person interested in music to remove himself from it, to hold it at arm's length as it were, and to examine it for what it is. In Western culture, those who are involved with art on an aesthetic level are constantly in the process of doing this; we tend to stand away from our own "art" music and look at it as an object by and of itself, examining it critically not only for its form but for what it expresses.

261

We take this process a step further in that we can and do isolate music as a thing in itself and look at and analyze it as an object quite apart from its context. For example, we can turn on the radio, hear a piece of music being performed, and listen to it without having to know who the composer is, what period he represents, or what the function, if any, of the music is. We can take music out of any other context and treat it objectively or subjectively as something which exists for itself. We do this not only in the listening process, but in our analysis of music; the student of music form looks at it as an objective entity which can be divorced both from himself and from its context.

Neither the Basongye nor the Flathead do this. For the Basongye, to the contrary, every song depends heavily upon its cultural context and is conceptualized in this relationship. This derives from two Basongye approaches to music. The first is that while theoretically infinite, the Basongye corpus of music encompasses a limited number of songs which is a known in the culture rather than unknown as it is in our own culture. While we can turn on the radio and listen to a piece of music without having precise knowledge of what it is, and can divorce ourselves from it to regard it as an object in itself, the Basongye know precisely what any given song is about and recognize and label it immediately. If the individual cannot do this himself, he has available around him a number of people who have the requisite knowledge and, because it is a part of cultural practice, will do so. The thoretical question of whether, given an unknown song but one of Basongye origin, a Musongye could recognize and categorize it, is of little utility when posed to the Basongye, for it is not really conceivable that any Basongye song could be unknown.

The second point is that the Basongye not only know the corpus of music, but that individual songs are recognized immediately in terms of their use. Each song is conceptualized and recognized for what it is: a war song, a birth song, a social dance song, a death song. In other words, the Basongye do not abstract music from its cultural context; indeed their conceptual system simply does not allow them to do so, and music *cannot* be abstracted from context. This, of course, is neither "good" nor "bad"; it is simply a fact of Basongye existence that music is an integrated part of life which does not exist as an abstraction outside its context.

The situation among the Flathead Indians is almost identical and thus does not require more than passing comment here. Music is again a known rather than an unknown, and songs are conceptualized in terms of the categories into which they fall. It is virtually inconceivable that an "unknown" Flathead song could exist, but if it did, most informants are quite sure that it could be identified in terms of use-category. Some difference does exist between Flathead and Basongye, however, due to

262

differential degrees of acculturation. The Flathead have had substantially more Western contact than the Basongye, and over a considerably longer period of time. Thus, abstractibility from context is conceptualized by the Flathead, but only in respect to Western music. Many Flathead "like" cowboy songs, not for their use-value or because they are *cowboy* songs, but because they enjoy the music. This divorce from context does not apply, to the best of my knowledge, to Flathead songs except in rare instances. On one or two occasions I have heard individuals singing quietly to themselves in the tipi; in later conversation, such people have remarked that they were singing "for fun" because they "liked it." This seems to argue that on such occasions music is abstracted from context, but as will be noted at some length later, it is impossible to determine whether it is the music or the context that provides the pleasure.

Neither the Basongye nor the Flathead, then, seem to meet the criterion of the first factor in the Western aesthetic, although the Flathead may approach it slightly. Music is not abstracted from its cultural context as a normal procedure; it does not seem to be regarded as a thing apart, but rather is conceptualized only as a part of a much wider entity. It must be re-emphasized here that the standard we are taking for the aesthetic is the Western; if psychic distance can be accepted as one of the factors in the Western aesthetic, neither the Basongye nor the Flathead hold aesthetic attitudes in this respect.

The second factor which, in conjunction with the others, contributes to the total Western concept of the aesthetic is the *manipulation of form for its own sake*. This is a strong part of Western music culture where change is a value, and it seems logical that where music is treated as an abstract thing in itself the manipulation of form almost automatically follows. Indeed, the manipulation of form for its own sake might almost be regarded as a criterion of the presence or absence of abstractibility. We may assume that in order to manipulate form there must be concepts of elements of form; in Western terminology these would include such things as intervals, melody, rhythm, meter, harmony, and so forth. We have seen in Chapter VI that the Basongye do have some formal verbalized concepts: singers speak of the characteristics of a good voice, musicians discuss matters of pitch, rudimentary over-all structure, rhythm, and so forth. Similarly, the Flathead verbalize at least some aspects of over-all structure and rhythm. However, there is no apparent verbalized concept of such things as intervals, polyphony, melodic lines, melodic range, tonics, and so forth, in either culture.

If there is relatively little recognition of formal elements of music, it seems doubtful that music form can be consciously manipulated, for manipulation implies a juggling of the elements of music structure in

263

order to arrive at a fresh form. Two problems are apparent here. The first is that if it is assumed that music is culturally shaped but at the same time is created by individuals who work within the cultural framework, then those individuals and that culture must recognize form. If this is not the case, then either there could be nothing called music, or no two musics would be different and no member of culture A could distinguish his music from that of culture B. The answer to this problem is that there is a substantial difference between a style and the conscious manipulation of elements of that style. Among the Flathead we must assume that songs obtained in the vision quest are in actuality created by the individual undergoing the quest. We must further assume that the songs are within the over-all Flathead style but that they are altered sufficiently to mark them as separable entities. Among the Basongye where, it will be recalled, individuals do not admit to individual composition but state that all songs come from God, the situation is much the same. New songs appear; they fall within the Basongye style; but they are individually separable as songs. In both cases, however, the source of music is superhuman, and the situation is quite different from that in Western culture, for the human individual does not sit down and consciously recombine elements of structure into a new song; rather he is the "unconscious" agency through which music is given to man by superhuman beings. Attention must again be called to the fact that we are here deliberately contrasting situations in different cultures against the yardstick of a Western concept. In Western art music, the composer sits to his task, deliberately selects aspects of music structure which serve his purpose, and strives to compose something which is a recombination of elements of form; his deliberate attempt is to create something new out of old materials. While it is perfectly acceptable to say that both style and individuality are present in Basongye and Flathead music, this is a far different concept from that of the deliberate manipulation of form for its own sake which is part of the Western aesthetic.

The second problem concerns the fact that what constitutes elements of form in Basongye and Flathead society may well be markedly different from such concepts in Western music. As a corollary, it may be that the Basongye and Flathead concepts differ so markedly as to be missed or simply not understood by the Western investigator. This is always a possibility in research, but in view of the fact that attention was concentrated on this specific problem among both Basongye and Flathead, it does not seem highly likely. There does remain, however, the possibility that the whole conceptual approach to music is so different from our own that it remains inaccessible or at least is not understood.

In any case, neither Basongye nor Flathead society manifests the extreme attention paid to manipulation of form for its own sake in Western society. Although both groups more closely approach our position in this aesthetic factor than in that of psychical distance, neither one seems really close at all, and we are forced to conclude that in this respect, again, neither society views music aesthetically in the Western sense.

The third factor which contributes to the core of assumptions in Western aesthetics concerns the *attribution of emotion-producing qualities to music conceived strictly as sound*. By this is meant that we in Western culture, being able to abstract music and regard it as an objective entity, credit sound itself with the ability to move the emotions. A song in a minor key is sad and makes the listener sad; certain kinds of music can be gay or pathetic or produce any one of a number of other emotions. We may disregard here the question of intersense modalities discussed in Chapter V, as well as that of physical responses discussed in Chapter VI. What is germane is that we consider that music, by itself, creates emotions, or something like emotions, and that emotion is closely bound up with the aesthetic. The aesthetic person is also considered to be an emotional person, moved by the art he surveys; it must be stressed that he is moved not by the context in which the art is perceived, but directly by the art itself.

It will be recalled that this problem was discussed briefly for the Basongye in Chapter IV, where it was pointed out that Basongye musicians agree on three things concerning the emotions of the performing individual. The musician is happy; he concentrates so heavily upon his music that any other emotion may be blocked out; yet conflicting emotions may be present in performance. In respect to emotions evoked by music in persons other than the performer, the Basongye are almost unanimous in saying that music sound itself can induce emotions. Thus a funeral song out of context makes the listener sad; a birth song out of context makes him happy.

The difficulty here harks back to Basongye conceptualization which makes it impossible to abstract music from its context. While in Western society we can state flatly that a minor mode or a particular key induces emotion, it seems doubtful that the Basongye can. In the first place, so few elements of music structure are isolated that it would be difficult to find anything analagous to a "mode" or a "key" which could be correlated with emotion. Equally important is the fact that Basongye music is not abstracted from its context; a piece of music always has a set of social and cultural associations which automatically go with it. Given this, how can we distinguish the impact of the music sound from the impact of the associations? Is the Musongye moved by the sound of music,

265

or by the context in which it is performed or with which it is associated? On hearing a funeral song, do people weep because of the music or because it is a funeral? The answer to such questions might possibly be reached, but only through such an abstract and theoretical process that it seems doubtful whether significant results would emerge. If a song could be composed in the Basongye style by someone outside the culture in order to be sure that it would have no prior association, and then played for the Basongye who could be questioned as to the emotions elicited, some light might be shed upon the matter. But this is a problem fraught with difficulties; while it may be accepted that such a song could be successfully composed by an outsider, it would have to be composed in some sub-style characteristic of children's, or hunting, or funeral songs. If it were successful, it seems clear that it would be accepted as, say, a hunting song, and immediately vested with the associations that go with this kind of music.

The situation among the Flathead is again very similar. People are definitely moved emotionally by music, as when a woman sings her mother's love song and can barely proceed because of her own tears, but again we are vexed with the question of whether it is the music sound or the recollection of the mother that stirs the singer. In such a case it is doubtless both, acting in conjunction with one another, but if so we are no further toward our solution to the problem.

There may be danger here of splitting hairs, but the crucial fact remains that in the Western aesthetic it is music sound itself which is considered to be capable of stirring the emotions. The minor key, in no matter what context, has itself this capability; it is not that we use the minor key exclusively for funeral songs. There is brought into play again the enormous importance of the abstractibility or non-abstractibility of music from its cultural context. Neither Basongye nor Flathead view music as abstractible; therefore the outside observer is at a loss to disentangle music sound from music context and it is impossible to determine the emotional effect of music sound on the listener. We cannot positively assess the applicability of the third aesthetic factor, though the fact of non-abstractibility in itself suggests strongly that neither group views music aesthetically in the sense of the attribution of emotion-producing qualities to music sound.

The fourth factor involved in the Western aesthetic is the *attribution of beauty to the art product or process*. This statement is not meant to imply that art and beauty are the same thing, that art is always beautiful, or that beauty is always artistic. However, the concept of beauty as applicable to the art product or process is an integral part of the Western aesthetic; beauty is irrevocably tied up with art.

The Basongye have three verbal concepts which may in some way bear upon beauty. The first of these is *bibuwa,* but on close examination this appears to refer more precisely to "goodness" than to beauty as such. The specific reference is, first, to non-human things, and second, to the inherent quality of goodness in the thing referred to. Thus the sun is inherently good in the view of some, because it provides warmth and because an association is made between it and the production of crops. A palm tree is *bibuwa* because it provides food. This is clearly not beauty in the sense of its Western aesthetic application.

Bibuwa has its counterpart in a second concept, *biya,* which refers to humans or to human actions rather than to non-human things, but which also has reference to the inherent quality of goodness. Thus a child is *biya,* not in the sense of being a good as opposed to a bad child, but in the sense that children are inherently a good thing in themselves. Again this concept is not beauty in the Western aesthetic sense.

The third term with possible application here is *kutaala,* and this comes closest of any of the three to paralleling our concept of beauty as such. It is germane to note, however, that *kutaala* is a relatively rare word in Kisongye; when he first thought of it after much cogitation, my interpreter, a young man, was so uncertain of the word and its meaning that he went off to check it with older members of the society. Further, *kutaala* does not equate precisely with the Western concept of beauty. When asked to illustrate to what things *kutaala* might be applied, the Basongye almost invariably answer "water." On further investigation, it is clear that this applies only to special kinds of water and not, for example, to water standing in a pan. The most specific reference is to water in the river and, by extension, to the river itself. The river, as it flows past the village, is calm and reasonably deep, and the association is further equated with coolness and calmness, which is expressed in another term, *kwikyela.* *Kwikyela,* in turn, is an expression of an emotional ideal in the society which stresses that each individual would *like* to be calm, cool, almost self-contained. In fact, Basongye life is anything but withdrawn, for every individual lives in intimate contact with his kinsmen and his neighbors; he is often enough immersed in some sort of struggle with them, and, as a matter of fact, one of the overt cultural values says that he must not keep to himself—"the man who eats alone is a man to be suspected," say the Basongye.

We have come a long way from what on the surface might have been taken as a simple expression of beauty, for, as it turns out, beauty leads us to a deep underlying ideal principle of freedom to withdraw into oneself, which is almost an exact opposite of what the culture really demands of the individual. But in any case, *kutaala* cannot be applied to music; the

267

idea that the two concepts might be combined is surprising, and almost shocking, to the Basongye. *Bibuwa* can be and is a word associated with music, but it does not refer to the quality of the music performance or sound; rather, what is meant is that music has within itself an inherent quality of something good, not beautiful. *Biya*, of course, is out of the question because it can only apply to human beings.

Among the Flathead Indians, the situation is surprisingly similar although the information is not so detailed. The Flathead also appear to have three words which may apply in some sense to beauty. *Suenu* seems to mean "pretty," but is applicable to a human being. *Kwamkompt* seems to be applicable to inanimate objects such as beadwork; it is usually translated as "beautiful." Finally, *nhastsi* is translated either as a "beautiful" or a "good" voice, and it is difficult to make a distinction between the two. Again it is the case that none of these three concepts can be applied to music as such; the idea of combining any of these words with that for song strikes the Flathead as highly amusing.

Returning to the Basongye, it should be noted that attributions of beauty are not made in other areas which we consider aesthetic. For example, until its introduction by Europeans, perfume was unknown to the Basongye. The odors which are objectified are generally the strong and unpleasant ones—body odors, the unpleasant smell of a newborn child, a skunk, and so forth; flowers do not have an odor for the Basongye. In the visual arts, judgments tend to follow functional or technical lines rather than being aesthetic *per se*.

In sum, neither Basongye nor Flathead attribute the idea of beauty to music or make a clear-cut connection between the two. While it must be repeated that art and beauty are by no means identical, the Western aesthetic inevitably makes this a very strong association.

The fifth factor in the Western aesthetic is the *purposeful intent to create something aesthetic*. While this is somewhat similar to the manipulation of form for its own sake, the difference lies in the word "aesthetic." The Western artist sets out with the deliberate intention of creating an object or sound which will be aesthetically admired by those who view or hear it, and this element of conscious striving reemphasizes the abstractibility of art from its cultural context. The importance of purposeful intent has been commented upon by other students of the art of nonliterate societies, among them Boas (1955:11) and Crowley (1958); the latter notes: "To the student of society however, creativity and aesthetic experience must be conscious activities, . . ."

Among the Basongye and the Flathead, the absence of the first four factors of the Western aesthetic makes it very doubtful that there can be purposeful intent, and in the Basongye culture this is emphasized by

268

further points. The Basongye, including even professional musicians, are almost unanimous in *saying* that they prefer to listen to music rather than to create it. This may be referrable to the Basongye value, previously noted, that individualism is undesirable behavior. Marriage partners should match physically; people should not act alone but rather in consort with their fellows; and this principle alone helps to account for the value placed on listening, which is a group activity, as opposed to the value placed on creating, which is an individual activity. But further, people do not listen so much to enjoy as they do to learn—and those who say they would rather create music (in the sense of performing it) give as their reason not aesthetic ends but the accumulation of wealth. We refer again to the refusal of the musician to admit to composing songs in Basongye society and the marked reluctance to do so among the Flathead. Thus neither culture seems to have a pattern of purposeful intent to create something aesthetic.

The final factor in the constellation of traits making up the Western aesthetic is the *presence of a philosophy of an aesthetic*, and in a sense this factor is a summary of the five that precede it. We have indicated time and time again that no verbal concepts exist for this or that among the Basongye or the Flathead, and we have also referred to the possibility that such concepts have simply been missed by the ethnographer. While the latter is conceivable, it does not seem likely, and there is in any case a more important point to be pressed. The contrast between these two societies and Western society in respect to an aesthetic is precisely most noticeable in the verbal sphere. The Western aesthetic *is* primarily verbal; while gesture and bodily attitude complement the verbal, it is the latter which is most characteristic. Reference is made again to the "verbal jungle" which has grown up around the aesthetic, the plethora of terms and descriptive adjectives, the verbal play which surrounds the central concern. Indeed, what distinguishes the Western ideas and ideals of form and beauty is a definite "language of the aesthetic," and it is precisely this which is lacking in both Basongye and Flathead societies. We may pose the crucial question, then, of whether an aesthetic exists if it is not verbalized; the answer seems clearly to be that it does not, at least *if we use the Western concept of the aesthetic, which is exactly what has been done in these pages.* By Western definition and practice, then, neither Basongye nor Flathead have an aesthetic. Both societies engage in activities which lead to what we would call artistic ends; both societies clearly make evaluative judgments; but neither society has the Western aesthetic.

This conclusion has a number of implications. It may well indicate that the Western aesthetic is a special product of a special culture and that it is

269

not a universal in human society. On the other hand, while some non-Western societies, at least, do not practice the special aesthetic of the West, attitudes about something similar to that aesthetic may be present but unrecognized by the outside observer. It is possible as well that Basongye and Flathead societies, while surprisingly similar, are atypical. Finally, it may be suggested that the Western aesthetic is but one manifestation of a broader set of principles which surrounds the topic of art, and that it may be the exception to the general rule.

Relatively little information of the kind presented here is found for societies other than our own, and what does exist is devoted primarily to the visual arts rather than to music. We can with profit, however, refer briefly to four such studies in order to reemphasize the difficulty of cross-cultural application of the aesthetic concept.

In attempting to reach what is called "a structural approach to esthetics," Warren d'Azevedo (1958) concludes that art and the aesthetic are separable entities, with the latter referring specifically to "the qualitative feature of the event involving the enhancement of experience and the present enjoyment of the intrinsic qualities of things" (p. 706). Thus what is aesthetic in d'Azevedo's terminology is an attitude rather than the action involved in creating the art product. This is quite similar, in a broad sense, to the summatory result of the six factors presented here as being characteristic of the Western aesthetic; that is, the aesthetic attitude involves attribution of beauty, psychic distance, and so forth. The difficulty here is that the Liberian Gola society on which d'Azevedo bases his work seems to be quite different from either the Basongye or the Flathead in one important respect: there is apparently intense verbalization about form, purposeful intent, and emotion, expressed in a situation of psychic distance and leading to a philosophy of the aesthetic (pp. 705-06). It appears, then, that Gola society is very similar to Western society in respect to the aesthetic, and that d'Azevedo finds a clear-cut Gola aesthetic because of this close parallel. The aesthetic attitude of which he speaks is observable and actually present because it is verbalized, or, conversely, it may be verbalized because the Gola have these particular attitudes. Thus it is suggested that d'Azevedo finds firm evidence of an aesthetic among the Gola precisely because the Gola concept does recognize and affirm the factors of the Western aesthetic. But what of Basongye and Flathead societies, where these factors do not seem to be present, where there is no verbalized "philosophy of the aesthetic"?

The importance of d'Azevedo's work is that it attempts to make a distinction on a structural basis between art and the aesthetic, and that it contributes significant and sensitive knowledge about aesthetics in another culture. At the same time, because of the similarities between that culture and our own in aesthetic matters, it probably does not reach the final cross-cultural definition of the aesthetic which is sought.

The problem of the aesthetic is approached in a somewhat different way by Sieber, who has coined the concept of the "unvoiced aesthetic" which he has applied specifically to African visual art (1959). The reasoning which lies behind the concept is expressed roughly as follows: African art symbolizes security and "lies at the center of a hard core of beliefs." Thus there is no need for the African to analyze and dissect his art, for "it is taken for granted that art, almost without exception, reinforces the positive aspect of his world view, participates actively in the fulfillment of his needs however these may be defined." In any given cultural framework, such goals are "known, understood, assumed, shared," and they form the basis for the African's view of art. Therefore the African does not need a complex voiced aesthetic; rather, all these assumptions lie behind art and constitute the unvoiced aesthetic.

This view contrasts with d'Azevedo's, for among the Gola the aesthetic is clearly voiced. It also presents a concept of the aesthetic which differs from the Western view, for it omits the crucial factor of the verbalized philosophy of the aesthetic. In this respect, Sieber's approach may be of more universal application than is the Western concept, but unless we are willing to alter our understanding of the meaning of the word aesthetic, it seems that a new term must be coined. The phrase "unvoiced aesthetic" is a contradiction in terms within the normal Western usage of the word "aesthetic."

A similar difficulty is found in McAllester's use of the phrase "functional aesthetic." Speaking of the Western Apache, McAllester notes:

> There is little esthetic discussion in our sense. Appreciation of a song is nearly always phrased in terms of understanding it—of knowing what it is for. One or two informants did speak of preferring songs with long choruses and short verses since these are easier to learn, but the usual preference was for the important healing songs or the sacred songs in the puberty ceremony. This "functional esthetic" is found very widely among preliterate peoples. (1960:471-72)

The juxtaposition of the words "functional" and "aesthetic" seems to be a contradiction in semantic usage. If our attitude is aesthetic, can it at the same time be functional? There is no question that a building, for example, can be functional and can at the same time be viewed aesthetically by the observer, but in this case it is not the object which is both. The building can only be functional; it is the observer's *attitude*

271

which is aesthetic, for it is only he who can supply the aesthetic factor. Similarly, in Western Apache music, the music can be functional while the attitude of the observer is aesthetic, but McAllester says that his informants did not take an aesthetic attitude toward their music. Therefore, working always within the Western sense of the term, there is not only a semantic but a logical contradiction in the use of the phrase "functional aesthetic."

A different case and problem is discussed by Harold K. Schneider in reference to the Pakot of Kenya (1956). Here, the term *pachigh* "(which refers to a state of being, a condition of a thing)" can be applied to two classes of objects. The first includes "those things which are considered beautiful but are not made by the Pakot," such as objects of nature and of foreign manufacture, and here again is stressed the "aesthetic attitude" which has run so strongly through our discussion. The second class consists of objects made or obtained by the Pakot "which are added to utilitarian objects by Pakot themselves." These include such things as paint, colored beads, cowry shells, designs, and so forth, and the important point is that anything which can be called "beautiful" (*pachigh*) is additive rather than the object itself. A milk pot for the Pakot is not beautiful, but an added pouring lip is.

The result of this Pakot concept is cogently expressed by Schneider:

> This discussion would be incomplete if it were not said that although it may be useful for purposes of ethnography to isolate according to a universal definition the particular area of life of the Pakot that may be called "art," a classification of this kind is liable to be very misleading if not qualified by Pakot concepts of beauty. Pakot do not recognize anything called art as such. There is mere *pachigh* and non-*pachigh* whether man-made or occurring in nature. Our attempts to separate the two for purposes of this paper were highly artificial, in some cases dubious, and a violation of Pakot conceptualization of the universe. In short, we might argue that analysis of Pakot culture would proceed more adequately with a category of "beautiful" or "aesthetic" things than with a category of "art." (p. 106)

The constant theme of our discussion has been the point of view that the aesthetic, as conceived in Western terms, involves a conscious and verbalized special attitude toward certain objects as reflected in the six factors noted above. There is more than a suspicion that this applies in some societies other than our own, but it is equally clear that it does not in some other societies.

272

There remains one point in connection with the aesthetic, and this concerns the difference between the aesthetic, on the one hand, and "making evaluative judgments" or "doing things with a flair" on the other. It is clear that people in all cultures do make evaluative judgments in the sense of "better" or "worse," and that probably people do some things with a flair as well. Judgments of better and worse do not necessarily imply an aesthetic, for an evaluation is simply an evaluation, a choice of alternatives involved in innumerable situations in every society. Neither is doing things with a flair necessarily aesthetic, although it may well in the end reveal an aesthetic attitude. What differentiates these actions from the necessary implication of the aesthetic is the fact that neither indicates by itself the presence of a philosophy of the aesthetic.

We can turn now to the problem of the interrelationship of the arts, although our discussion will be briefer than that devoted to aesthetics since the subject has already been approached in Chapter 5. As an idea, the interrelationship of the arts goes hand in hand with the concept of the aesthetic. Reference is not made here to the integration of the arts, that is, the way the arts can be put together in performance as in drama, for example, where visual art, music, literature, dance, and even architecture are fused. Rather, the interrelationship of the arts refers to the point of view that the arts stem from the same sources, that all the arts are really just one Art differently expressed because their materials are different.

Susanne Langer gives a useful summary of this point of view, noting that those who hold it agree ". . . that the several arts are just so many aspects of one and the same human adventure, and almost every recent book in aesthetics begins with the statement that the customary distinctions among the arts are an unfortunate result of our lives" (1957:76). Langer continues: "Before long this one universal interrelation is described either as an original identity or as an ideal ultimate union. . . . It ends much as it began, with quotations from many authorities denouncing the customary separation, but heightened by the positive advice that art schools should take cognizance of the sister arts, painting, poetry, and drama" (p. 77).

According to Langer, the question is posed as follows: if art is a universal, and all aspects of it are functions of the same thing, why does it go under so many names? The answer given is that artists work with different materials and thus they *seem* to be doing different things. Langer is not satisfied with this answer and holds the difficulty to be simply that the basic unity of the arts is assumed and not demonstrated: "what we begin with is not what we arrive at—discover, clarify, or demonstrate" (p. 78).

She handles the problem as follows:

My approach to the problem of interrelations among the arts has been the precise opposite: taking each art as autonomous, and asking about each in turn what it creates, what are the principles of creation in this art, what its scope and possible materials. Such a treatment shows up the differences among the several great genera of art—plastic, musical, balletic, poetic. Pursuing these differences, rather than vehemently denying their importance, one finds that they go deeper than one would expect. . . .

But if you trace the differences among the arts as far and as minutely as possible, there comes a point beyond which no more distinctions can be made. It is the point where the deeper structural devices—ambivalent images, intersecting forces, great rhythms and their analogues in detail, variations, congruences, in short: all the organizing devices—reveal the principles of dynamic form that we learn from nature as spontaneously as we learn language from our elders. These principles appear, in one art after another, as the guiding ones in every work that achieves organic unity, vitality of form or expressiveness, which is what we mean by the significance of art.

Where no more distinctions can be found among the several arts, there lies their unity. (pp. 78-9)

While Langer seems certain of a basic and underlying unity of the arts, the problem is that if we wish to establish cross-cultural evidence for its presence we must assume one of two positions: either the arts are interrelated because they do spring from the same, single source of human creativity, or it is human beings who say the arts are interrelated and thus themselves create a unity which does not really exist. If we take the first point of view, it would seem logical to assume that a universal principle of this striking a nature would be widely recognized by artists everywhere; if we take the second, we would assume that the concept is Western, tied directly with the Western concept of aesthetics, and demonstrable in other cultures only through analytical evaluation and not discernible in folk evaluation. These are not simple problems and they will not be solved here, but the evidence available from Basongye and Flathead societies does indicate that there is little or no recognition of the interrelationship of the arts on the part of individuals of those cultures.

It will be recalled that Hornbostel (1927) supports his argument for the unity of the arts partly, at least, on the evidence of intensense modalities. That is, we transfer linguistic descriptions of one sense area to the description of the products of other sense areas; brightness, for example, is a linguistic concept applied to several sense areas. It will also be recalled that the Basongye do not do this except in the most isolated cases; neither do the Flathead. Both Basongye and Flathead consider questions and discussion concerning the relationship, if any, between color and music highly amusing and barely rational. In uncounted hours of discussion with Basongye and Flathead artists, no comparability was ever discovered between music and sculpture, art design and odor, dance movements and shapes of buildings, or any other combination, at least so far as the artists themselves were concerned. Basongye and Flathead cultures may be exceptions in this case; Waterman, for example, says that among the Yirkalla "within the largest musical category almost every song has a painted iconographic design or hard-wood carving, a story, a dance, and a segment of ritual associated with it" (1956: 40-41).

Gbeho, speaking of the former Gold Coast, says: "May I make clear that when I talk about music I am referring to drumming, dancing and singing? They are all one thing and must not be separated. If we speak of a man being musical we mean that he understands all the dances, the drums and the songs" (1952:31). Nketia, though speaking of the integration of the arts in performance, may have interrelations in mind when he writes:

> Observation of the attitudes and behaviour of the participants in the drama of the possession dance shows that the possession dance is not only something to be done to fulfill the requirements of belief. It also has aesthetic merits for the communities in which it is staged. Accordingly the integration of the elements of the drama—ecstatic behaviour, music and dancing—and details of the routine of action, forms of appearance, gracefulness of movement, expressiveness of action and so on, receive attention. (1957: 6)

All these comments, however, are made by outside observers who have received training in the Western tradition; we still do not know whether the artists conceive of their arts in the same way.

It is easy to say, especially in questions of the arts, that something is there which the artist does not see, but this can be dangerous, particularly in the cross-cultural situation. Analytical evaluation is fitting and proper and a necessity for the understanding of human phenomena, but its successful application depends upon the demonstrability of clear-cut evidence from which conclusions are drawn. Neither the applicability of the Western concept of the aesthetic nor the evidence for the concept of the interrelationship of the arts has been demonstrated in clear enough fashion to allow us to admit the postulate that either is a universal in human society. On the other hand, the evidence to the contrary from but two societies—the Basongye and the Flathead—is not enough to convince

275

us that the two concepts may not be more widely distributed than we can presently envisage. Certainly d'Azevedo's description of the Gola indicates an aesthetic formulated in a way that shows a striking parallel to the aesthetic of the West; it is equally possible, although d'Azevedo does not discuss the question, that the Gola do envisage the arts as being interrelated. In any case, these questions are of enormous interest and concern to the ethnomusicologist who, almost by definition a comparative scholar, is in a superb position to contribute to our further understanding of them.

CHAPTER XIV

MUSIC AND CULTURE HISTORY

The use of music as a technique for the understanding and reconstruction of culture history has long been a part of ethnomusicology as students of the discipline applied various methodologies borrowed from evolutionary and diffusionist theories of anthropology. Such studies gradually dropped out of fashion as the theoretical framework on which they were based was shown to be faulty or lacking, but within the past few years there has been some resurgence of interest. This has taken place primarily in the Africanist field where the problem of culture history has been of special interest because of newly arisen political, theoretical, and empiric aims. Students of African history have begun to employ a much wider variety of tools of analysis than is commonly used in studying the history of those areas for which written records exist: some of these include archaeology merged into historic record, oral literature, ethnographic distributional analysis, linguistic relationships, botanical evidence, visual art, and, perhaps most recently, music. The last interest has, of course, renewed a number of questions on whether and how music can contribute to studies of culture history.

A primary question here concerns what is meant by the phrase "reconstructing culture history" and how music can be used to do so, for the use of any special tool of investigation involves at least three separate possibilities. In the first place, part of the culture history of any group of people consists of a description of a way of life; that is, at any particular point in time the culture inventory of a people contains certain items which tell us something about the people and their way of life. Such descriptions, whether broad or narrow in terms of the number of items described, can be reached either through the use of historic accounts or through archaeological excavation, in which the time depth is usually considerably larger. From such an approach we learn certain things about a way of life, subject to the limitations to be noted below in the case of music.

But inevitably, in considering the reconstruction of culture history, there is implied a dynamic which involves the wider framework of development through time. In this case we look at culture change, and thus history, as a process of time, and we are interested in any theory which implies process and which enables us to reconstruct what has happened in the past. Again music can be used this way, though within certain limitations.

Finally, in using a specific tool—in this case music—we must inevitably raise the question of whether there is anything unique, or special, about the tool which makes it particularly applicable in attempting to solve the problem of reconstruction of history.

Each of these approaches will be considered in turn, but first it must be made clear that the potential importance of music in this kind of problem varies widely due to some of its special characteristics. So far as is known, no nonliterate culture has independently developed a notational system for its organization of culturally-defined music sound, and this means there is relatively little hope of reconstructing the aural shape of music with any great accuracy. As will be noted below, some attempts have been made along this line, either through special archaeological techniques or through the application of *a priori* anthropological theory, but such attempts do not seem particularly effective or reliable. Thus the tracing of music sound to any substantial time depth does not appear to be very fruitful in reconstructing culture history as a whole.

At the same time, music is represented not only by sound but by music instruments as well, and some of these instruments do persist over considerable time spans. Thus in dealing with music as a tool for historic reconstruction, we must consider two aspects and be prepared to use either or both as the possibilities present themselves.

Finally, music sound as an entity in itself has three major characteristics (to be noted below) which seem to make it potentially of particular value in the reconstruction of culture contact. These characteristics, which culminate in the reliability of the reduction of sound to statistical terms, may in the future give us a particularly sharp tool for analysis.

One of the approaches to the culture history of a group of people consists of a description of that culture at any given point in time. The question is whether this can be done for music, and, if so, what kinds of things it tells us.

278

Although our focus is not primarily on historic documentation from written records, this source of understanding cannot be overlooked. Nketia has made an ethnohistorical study of West African music, using written materials to assess the "factors which appear to have influenced the main lines of change in musical organisation." These he lists as the following: "political factors, such as those which governed or facilitated the creation and administration of states and empires, . . . the pursuit of trade, and . . . religion" (n.d.:5). Kirby has used historic documents to trace the xylophone in East Africa back to 1586 (1953:47), and considerable numbers of references since that time give us rather remarkable information concerning African instruments over the past four centuries.

In respect to music sound, the time depth is much shorter, though fragments of notated songs appear from time to time in the accounts of early travelers, explorers, missionaries, and others. The validity of these transcriptions, however, is in doubt, and it is not until much more recent times that large and reliable samples of music transcribed from phonograph records begin to appear. In 1917, for example, Hornbostel transcribed and analyzed songs collected in 1907-09 by the Deutschen Zentral-Afrika-Expedition headed by the Duke of Mecklenburg (1917), and various other bodies of song from a similar time period are available to us now.

The question is whether such materials help us markedly in reconstructing culture history and, if so, how. It seems clear that we do not profit greatly from knowing that the Ruandaise had music in 1907, or even precisely what form that music took when reduced to notation by a European expert, though this is of considerable significance when cast in the framework of the theory of culture change. Yet if we were to find an instance in which such early materials differed drastically from those which we can record today, we would be faced with a problem of great importance, for we should be forced to the conclusion that historic events of considerable impact had taken place in the meantime, whether through internal or external influence. To the best of my knowledge, no such sharp differences exist between past and present music sound systems, but neither have really detailed comparative studies of such materials been undertaken.

Much of the same sort of information is available from the study of historic records of music instruments. We should expect and, so far as I know, find cultural continuity in music instrument form, but again the studies have not been exhaustive.

This kind of reconstruction from historic account tells us certain kinds of things about the history of the people involved. The information gleaned is obviously primarily directed toward the history of music and

279

music instruments, as things in themselves; that is, music is a part of culture, culture moves through time, and thus through music we can approach certain kinds of history. Further, as pointed out above, we expect the processes of change to proceed in a more or less orderly fashion; when the available record shows discontinuities, in this case in the course of music, we should expect to find reasons for them. In sum, where documents are available, they must be used, employing the careful methods worked out by historians and ethnohistorians.

Where there are no documents, however, other methods may prove useful; among these is the use of song texts. We have had occasion to discuss texts as records of history in Chapter 10, but some further remarks are here in order. Waterman and Bascom (1949:21), for example, in commenting on the topical song in Africa, write:

> . . . the topical songs have been known to persist for generations when they commemorate some historic event or when they treat with some incident of lasting interest. Thus, songs referring to battles of the 18th century are still current in Nigeria, much as calypsos were composed in Trinidad deriding certain slave overseers or commemorating the first visits of The Graf Zeppelin or The Duke and Duchess of Kent.

Similarly, Herskovits notes the historic usages of song in Dahomey:

> Songs were and are the prime carriers of history among this non-literate folk. In recounting the ritual associated with the giving of offerings to the souls of those who were transported into slavery, this function of song came out with great clarity. The informant at one point could not recall the sequence of important names in the series he was giving. Under his breath, to the accompaniment of clicking finger-nails, he began to sing, continuing his song for some moments. When he stopped he had the names clearly in mind once more, and in explanation of his song stated that this was the Dahomean method of remembering historic facts. The role of the singer as the "keeper of records" has been remarked by those who visited the kingdom in the days of its autonomy. (Herskovits 1938b:II, 321)

Nketia has used the content of song texts as one factor in investigating a problem of culture history among the Ga of Ghana (1962), and Buck speaks of the use of texts as history on the Polynesian island of Mangareva:

> As intellectuals, the rogorogo took within their field of study the native history . . . and genealogies. At social gatherings, the

rogorogo were called upon to recite the appropriate genealogy, and they composed and sang the chants which lauded the nobility. The *rogorogo* supplied the accepted versions of myths, legends, traditions, historical narratives, and genealogies; and there can be little doubt that it was they, as a class, who added local details to the mass of oral literature. (1938:305)

Further examples could be cited, though the study of song texts from the standpoint of culture history has not been frequently undertaken. There is a further problem in this connection, and this refers to the authenticity of the texts in terms of the accuracy of the message or description they convey. The problem is similar to that involved in the acceptance or rejection of the authenticity of oral literature, but we have one example at least of a song text which has remained unchanged over the past sixty-four years. This is "Nkosi Sikelel' iAfrica" first sung publicly in 1899 at the ordination of Reverend M. Boweni, a Shangaan Methodist minister, and more recently adopted unofficially as the national anthem of Central and South Africa, as reported by Rhodes (1962:16-17). It appears, then, that song texts are capable of existing unchanged in the folk idiom over substantial periods of time, though we do not know for how long. A study and analysis of this problem might well lead the investigator into some relatively important areas of historic information, though there is some doubt whether the time span would be long, despite the Waterman and Bascom claim of a period of approximately 200 years. At the same time, historic reconstruction of relatively recent periods is in its way as valuable as that of great epochs of history and, given the limitations of the song text, it appears that music may be useful in this way.

Another approach to the reconstruction of culture history in terms of the description of a culture at any given point in time and through the use of music, depends upon the findings of archaeology. Two kinds of problems have been approached using this method.

The first has been carried on primarily by European scholars who weld together interests and talents in antiquarianism and music instrument studies, and it is best illustrated through reference to Egyptian studies. Research on Egyptian music instruments is particularly rich, it has been pointed out, because of

> the extreme aridity of the desert soil and the Egyptian belief in the magic power of painting and sculpture. Aridity has preserved hundreds of instruments from decomposition, and many musical scenes are depicted on tomb walls. . . .
>
> . . . Egyptian art works are explained by short, naive texts written between the human figures wherever an empty spot is left.

281

"He is playing the harp," they read, or, "He is playing the flute." Thus, we know the authentic names of practically all Egyptian instruments. (Sachs 1940:87)

Because of these two factors, it has been possible to reconstruct the instrumentation of the early Egyptian orchestra and, with some limitations, the kinds of scales and possibly even the orchestral sounds produced. Instruments provide the student with measurable acoustic quantities which can give a high degree of precision, and where instruments are not available, scholars such as Sachs and Hickmann, among others, have reconstructed both forms and probable musical sounds from finger positions .of harpists, for example, as these are depicted in a substantial number of paintings and bas-reliefs (Sachs 1921, 1940, 1943; Hickmann 1952, 1955a&b).

The archaeological record is not always so rich, since most music instruments are made of wood and since the aridity of Egypt does not everywhere prevail. But notable exceptions are present, and among the best examples are the iron gongs and rock gongs of Africa; the latter will be discussed briefly here, while the former will be discussed below.

A considerable number of publications have been devoted recently to what is sometimes called the "Rock Gong complex" of Africa (see, for example, Fagg 1956, 1957; Conant 1960; Vaughan 1962). These are ringing rocks characterized by so-called "chatter marks," which are small cuplike depressions caused by repeated nonrandom striking of the rock with a hammerstone. Rock gongs have been located in Nigeria, the Northern Cameroons, Uganda, the Sudan, Portugal, Brittany, Wales, and England.

Interpretations of the rock gongs, and rock slides and rock paintings which are sometimes assumed to be associated phenomena, vary widely. Fagg, for example (1957), characterizes them as a megalithic, prehistoric complex, and calls attention to the common interpretation that stone instruments are among man's earliest musical modes of expression (1956:42), while Conant argues for a more limited interpretation:

. . . may the use of rock gongs represent a substitution of abundantly available ringing rock for the double hand gong made of iron, a much more scarce material? The quality of notes produced by both instruments is so similar that it is sometimes difficult to tell them apart. . . . In other words, it would be most suggestive if rock gongs and iron gongs eventually prove to have roughly the same distribution. The significance of rock gongs then might be largely in terms of the diffusion of iron metallurgy in

Africa, associated by some prehistorians with the spread of Bantu-speaking peoples. (1960:161)

Given the current state of uncertainty as to the antiquity of the rock gongs, it is clear that only further research will establish their usefulness in reconstructing Africa's culture history, but there now appears to be some tendency to attempt to solve the puzzle of the uses to which rock gongs have been put in the past through description of current practice. Thus Vaughan (1962) describes contemporary use of the rock gong complex among the Marghi of Nigeria, and holds that the parts of the complex "should be viewed as distinct variables in a much larger behavioural context—rites of passage." He lists the following patterns (p. 52) which he feels may characterize the complex: social rebellion, symbolic death to childhood; birth into adulthood; fertility rites; and publicity, and he concludes his discussion by noting:

> Extrapolation from the Marghi materials to all other rock paint-
> ings in Nigeria would be unwise, but these data are suggestive
> of possible behavioural bases to rock paintings and gongs. More
> importantly they indicate that a shift in emphasis from anti-
> quarian studies of material traits to studies of rites of passage may
> lead to new discoveries of paintings, gongs and associated phe-
> nomena, and could certainly lead to a broader understanding of just
> what these non-behavioural artifacts mean. (p. 52)

Two major kinds of information emerge from materials of this sort. The first relates to the history of music itself, and in this case the emphasis is upon a single aspect of culture and its development through time. The second relates to music as being descriptive of one phase of culture at any given point in time and, primarily through extrapolation, its relationship to other aspects of culture. The last is a reconstructive process which depends upon evidence but also upon controlled comparative analysis and logical deduction.

The second major approach to the reconstruction of culture history involving the possible use of music is through the establishment of theories implying grand processes which operate throughout the course of time. Anthropology has seen the rise and fall of many such theories in the past and some of them will be discussed here for a number of reasons. First, theories of evolution and of *kulturkreis* form a part of the history of ethnomusicology. Second, such theories have all left their imprint, though we may be unwilling and unable to accept them as originally phrased. And third, though the broader patterns of such theories are now rejected, there remain some truths and some speculations which are clearly not without merit.

Least acceptable today are evolutionary theories of the development of music, particularly those which, through the use of what is now regarded as an invalid comparative method, arrayed facts from cultures around the world into systems which "proved" the deductively-formulated theory. We need not consider such formulations, which led to systems of stages of culture through which mankind must inevitably move.

Of equal difficulty are theories of the particular and ultimate origin of individual music styles or instruments. Balfour, for example, held that the African friction drum originated from the stick-and-membrane bellows and found the two to have a roughly coterminous distribution in the continent (1907). While he may conceivably be correct, it is probably as logical to suppose that the stick-and-membrane bellows developed from the friction drum, and there seems to be little that is useful in this kind of search for origin.

A more controlled but still largely speculative kind of evolutionary analysis is found in the work of Kirby, who postulates a developmental sequence for the musical bow but restricts himself primarily to applying his analysis to the Bushmen. Thus he speculates that the hunting bow is probably at the origin of a number of stringed instruments. The first stage is the twang emitted by the bow-string when the arrow is fired; the second appears when it occurs to the hunter "to tap his bow-string with an arrow, thus applying a new method of sound-production to the string." The third stage comes when a number of bows are placed together on the ground and are tapped by a single person, and further evidences of evolution are postulated as the performer learns to use his own body as a resonating chamber, adds outside resonators, and so forth. It also should be pointed out that a Bushman rock painting exists in which the third stage is illustrated, according to Kirby (1953:193-95). Similar sorts of formulations have been made for music sound, as for example in the case of Phillips (1953), who postulates a series of stages in the development of music in general and attempts to apply them to Yoruba music in particular.

One of the more recent formulations in this same direction, though applied in a more cautious manner, is that of Nettl in respect to the music of the Shawnee Indians of North America. In this case, Nettl has put together historic data and music structural materials to reach conclusions about the history of the Shawnee. Basic to his work, however, and basic to all evolutionary schemes, is the assumption that culture works from the simple to the complex in point of view of time, and thus Nettl postulates that the simplest songs are the oldest, simplest in this case being those with "small range, simple form, and two or three tone scales" (1953a:284). Younger in style are more complex songs, still younger are

284

those whose style appears to make it possible to postulate that they were borrowed from Southern Plains tribes, and newest are the Peyote songs whose origin in time is known.

Nettl's study works from the basic fact that Shawnee style is internally diverse, with some songs showing certain constellations of traits and others showing other constellations. In the particular case of the Shawnee, the facts of the diversity of the style give clues to the influences which have shaped it, and these in turn can be coupled with historic records of the migrations of the Shawnee to help fix the history of these people.

The major problem in this kind of study is the assumption of a simple-old syndrome. While there is a great deal of archaeological evidence to indicate that technological developments proceed from the simple to the more complex through time, and while it is logical to assume that the same applies to music, the assumption is extremely difficult to apply in cases where there is no real documentation. Thus it might be pointed out that the music system of India is extremely complex and at the same time very old, while American rock and roll is quite simple and yet relatively new. We might argue as well that because a style is simple it must perforce be new because there has not been sufficient time for elaboration. The question of simplicity as a criterion of age has been much discussed, and it does appear to be useful in the study of technological process (Sapir 1916:13); whether it applies to music structure or to concepts about music as well as to tool-making remains a moot point.

Those who were interested in the study of evolution as a theory of culture also tended to place much emphasis on the ultimate origins of aspects of human culture, and this preoccupation has also characterized certain periods and approaches in ethnomusicology. Theories of this sort have been summarized by Nettl (1956:134-37), who takes as his own point of view "the assumption that an undifferentiated method of communication existed in remote times, one which was neither speech nor music but which possessed the three features that they hold in common: pitch, stress, and duration," and that from this early method of communication, through a long series of gradual stages of differentiation, "the two specific media, language and music, developed" (p. 136).

Anthropologists have long eschewed the search for ultimate origins of aspects of culture for the simple reason that they appear to be unrecoverable. Stone tools persist in time and can be compared and placed stratigraphically in relation to other kinds of tools, but ideas leave no concrete residue behind. While the ultimate origin of music may provide material for interesting and even logical speculation, the theories can only remain theories.

The possible use of evolutionary schemes in reconstructing culture

285

history is not particularly hopeful. In order to use such schemes, we should have to make assumptions which do not seem tenable, i.e., if one finds the stick-and-membrane bellows in one location and the friction drum in another, it must follow, according to Balfour, that the culture of the first people is older than that of the second. Similarly, the culture of people who use the simple hunting bow as a musical bow must be older than that of people who use instruments of several strings. Or, people who use two- or three-note melodies have older cultures than those who use six- and seven-note melodies. We can follow the logic of such propositions without difficulty; the problem is that logic and deductive theory are not substitutes for empiricism.

The same kind of criticism can be applied to *kulturkreis* theories of the origin and history of various elements of culture, but because music played such a large part in formulations of this kind, some discussion must be entered into here.

It was Friedrich Ratzel who established the first step in a series of speculations by drawing attention to the similarities between West African and Melanesian bows in the cross section of the bow shaft, in the material and fastening of the bow string, and in the feathering of the arrow. Leo Frobenius, however, took the idea a step further in calling attention to various other culture elements which he considered to be similar in the two areas; in at least one source Frobenius used the drum as a primary piece of evidence:

Our investigation of culture-anatomy may begin with African drum forms. By far the larger part of African drums consist of a log scooped out, one or both ends covered with hide. We need not enter into details here, and I do no more than state the fact that the Indonesian method of bracing drums reappears on the West African coast. Besides these commonest drum forms, others occur made entirely of a log, hewn round or with angles; in the latter case usually wedge-shaped, the broad surface resting on the ground. The logs are hollowed out within through a cleft, made always on the broad side. Often the cleft is enlarged at its ends, the enlargement forming a round aperture in the drums of the Congo, an angle in those of the Cameroons. The famous signaling or telegraph drums of the Cameroons belong to this class. The drums covered with hide are found throughout the whole of Africa, with the exception of its southernmost part, but the wooden drums occur only in the Congo Basin and in Upper and Lower Guinea. The hide-covered drums are a development of the famous millet mortar, which points to East India. The civilization of the Mediterranean shores has similar drums made of clay, and related to those found in Persia and in prehistoric tombs of Germany. Now, the wooden drums belong to the Malayo-Negrito elements of African culture. They recur in Melanesia and frequently in Polynesia. Their home obviously must be the same as that of the lofty bamboo cane, for these drums are developed from the bamboo. (1898:640-41)

Using music instruments as one of his criteria for resemblance, Frobenius developed four culture circles in Africa: the Negrito, Malayo-Negrito, Indo-Negrito, and Semito-Negrito. In like order, each of these included the following music instruments: 1) staff as music instrument; 2) bamboo lute, tangola and drum, wooden kettledrum, and marimba; 3) violin, guitar, earthenware bass drum, iron kettledrum, and tambourine; 4) gubo, gora, hide as drum, mortar drum, and pot drum (1898:650). Similar uses of music instruments were made by others, among them Ankermann (1905).

Once established, the idea of the Melanesian-West African relationship, as well as that of culture circles, was elaborated by other theorists, and music instruments almost always formed part of the schemes. George Montandon (1919) devised a system of ten culture circles, postulated an original development in and near the Himalayan region which led through Oceania to Africa, and as usual cited music instruments as a major part of the reconstruction.

For Africa, specifically, he arrived at a series of five circles, as follows: 1) africaine primitive (15,000-20,000 ans et plus avant notre ère) [including boomerangs, bullroarers, whistles, trumpets, and other idiophones as instruments]; 2) nigritienne (dès 15,000 ans ou plus avant notre ère) [Pan pipes, primitive xylophones, wooden drum, musical bow]; 3) protokamitique (dès 10,000 ans ou plus avant notre ère) [music instruments developing out of 1 and 2]; 4) kamito-sémitique (dès 8 a 7,000 ans avant notre ère) [same instruments plus those of India]; 5) néosémitique (dès l'an 700 de notre ère) [instruments of Western Asian origin including the rebab, various lutes, etc.] (1919:93).

These developments in turn led to the postulation of further schemes involving similar principles but devoted exclusively to music instruments. In his *Geist und Werden der Musikinstrumente* published in 1929, Curt Sachs, using the *kulturkreis* theory, laid out a worldwide theory of the history of all music instruments which involved the creation of twenty-three strata; this was later to be "corroborated" by André Schaeffner among the African Dogon (1956:29-30), and it formed the basis for an extended study of African music instruments by Hornbostel (1933).

Hornbostel gave considerable attention to the comparison of his "groups" with Sachs's "strata," and found that they agreed in general though there was difference in particular points. Using apparently the single criterion of extent of distribution of instruments, and assuming that the instruments with the widest distribution were necessarily also the oldest, Hornbostel arrived at a total of twelve groups, arranged as follows: "I. *Earliest Cultures.* 1. Universal: strung rattles, bull-roarer, bone-flute, scraped idiophones; 2. Universal-sporadic in Africa: end-blown conch trumpet; 3. Sporadic everywhere it occurs: percussion-rod. II. *'Ancient Sudan.'* Extensive but not universal: gourd rattle? Cylindrical drum, mouth bow. III. *'West African.'* W. and Central Africa, S. and E. Asia, South America: slit-drum, globular-flute, log-xylophone, nose-flute. IV. *'Mid-Erythraean.'* E. Africa, S. and E. Asia–S. America: Pan-pipes, stamping-tube, central-hole flute, (gourd drum), single-skin hourglass-drum. V. *'Pan-Erythraean, Early,'* Indonesia-Africa: gourd; xylophone, iron bell, cup-shaped drum. VI. *'Pan-Erythraean, Late.'* India–Africa: bow with gourd resonator, harp-zither with notched bridge. VIa. *'Hova.'* Indonesia–Madagascar: flat-bar zither, tube-zither. VII. *Ancient SW. Asia–Ancient Egypt:* 1. Proto-Hamitic? Animal horn. 2. Pre-Islamic. Bow-harp. 3. Post-Islamic. Double clarinet, tanged lute. VIII. *Buddhism.* Buddhist Asia, sporadically in NW. Africa: double-skin hourglass-shaped drum. IX. *Pre-Christian, West Asiatic.* Arabia, E. Asia, Sudan: bowl-lyre. X. *Post-Christian, Pre-Islamic.* W. Asia–Indonesia, W. Africa: hooked drumstick. XI. *Islam.* NE. Africa, W. Asia–Indonesia: tanged fiddle with lateral pegs, kettledrum (1933:299-301).

Finally, Sachs later (1940:62-4) gave a concise explanation of his "method" and reduced his twenty-three strata and Hornbostel's twelve groups to three major ones. In respect to the method used both by himself and by Hornbostel, he noted as the chief axioms:

1) An object or idea found in scattered regions of a certain district is older than an object found everywhere in the same area.

2) Objects preserved only in remote valleys and islands are older than those used in open plains.

3) The more widely an object is spread over the world, the more primitive it is. (p. 62)

In his three-part scheme derived from these principles, he reached the following conclusions:

The early stratum comprises those instruments which, prehistorically, occur in paleolithic excavations and, geographically, are scattered all over the world. These are:

IDIOPHONES	AEROPHONES	MEMBRANO- PHONES	CHORDO- PHONES
rattles	bull-roarer		
rubbed shell?	ribbon reed		
scraper	flute without		
stamped pit	holes		

No drums and no stringed instruments appear in this early stratum.

The middle stratum comprises those instruments which, prehistorically, occur in neolithic excavations, and, geographically, in several continents, though they are not universal. These are:

slit-drum	flute with	drum	ground-harp
stamping tube	holes		ground-
	trumpet		zither
	shell trumpet		musical bow

The late stratum comprises those instruments which, prehistorically, occur in more recent neolithic excavations, and, geographically, are confined to certain limited areas. These are:

rubbed wood	nose flute		friction
basketry rattle	cross flute		drum
xylophone	transverse trumpet		drum stick
jaws' harp			

This rough chronology, though established on the objective data of distribution and prehistory, gives satisfaction also to the mind concerned with workmanship and cultural level. (pp. 63-4)

How useful are theoretical formulations such as these? There seems, first of all, little reason for accepting the propositions forwarded by Frobenius and Montandon, partly because factual information is now available which did not exist some sixty years ago and which makes certain of their assumptions untenable, but mostly because both appear to have been dealing with *a priori* schemes for which they were intent upon supplying facts. The severest criticism must be directed toward assumptions of "layers of time." Nevertheless, the relationships between Africa and other parts of the world, in terms of migrations of peoples or of cultures, have never been clearly proven false or acceptable, and the criteria of form and quantity proposed by the *Kulturhistorische Schule* remain to be well used in studying diffusion problems of more restricted scope.

The same criticisms may be applied to the work of Hornbostel and

Sachs, and yet it is clear that their formulations are based upon more reliable information more cautiously applied. In both cases, one is struck by the extraordinary range of knowledge of music instruments brought to the theories and it seems clear that the results may well be reasonably accurate in the broadest perspective. Logic is on their side, and in this case it is more carefully buttressed by fact; the major difficulty is in accepting the three premises regarding the diffusionary process, and if we cannot accept them on the scale proposed by Sachs, then the theory must fall. In sum, the approaches taken by Hornbostel and Sachs appear more reasonable than those advanced by Frobenius and Montandon; they represent a step in the direction of greater control of materials within the framework of diffusion studies.

There is no need to summarize the increasing restrictions placed upon the study of diffusion and the reconstruction of culture history through the application of more and more rigorous methodology. But the result has been a controlled use of distribution and diffusion based upon certain principles which have been succinctly expressed by Herskovits:

> It would seem, all things considered, that the effort is worth the return, provided 1) *that the area selected for analysis should be one whose historic unity can be assumed,* and 2) that *the probability, not the absolute fact of historic developments,* be *recognized as the aim.* (1948:521)

Under these conditions, we can examine some of the diffusion studies of music instruments which have been made more recently, and assess their value in the reconstruction of culture history.

The concept of culture clusters as a taxonomic device for ordering cultures was suggested by P. H. Gulliver (1952) and further discussed by Merriam (1959a) in relation to the cultures of the former Belgian Congo. In the latter article, the cluster was contrasted with the concept of culture area, and it was noted that:

> The cluster concept, however, adds a dimension lacking in the area concept in that it *suggests* generic relationship on the basis of historic fact and in what we have called commonality. In a culture area, diffusion from one or more centers is assumed and can often be traced, but in a cluster, by definition, we find not only diffusion but also the factor of commonality. Thus, for example, the fact that the Mongo say they are all related and have myths and other means to "prove" it, makes them quite different from the Flathead and Sanpoil Indians who are grouped together in the same Plateau area of North America but who deny any

290

relationship to each other. The cluster involves an acknowledged historic unity, while an area shows unity, but of a descriptive nature only.

In these terms, then, our primary goal is a taxonomic description of peoples in the Congo whose cultures can be grouped together in small units on the basis of common traits and complexes and, most important, a recognized unity. The implication involved is that of generic relationship because of the factor of commonality. (1959a:374-75)

If the existence of the culture cluster can be accepted, and if it is further realized that music instruments may be among the material traits characterizing a cluster, then it follows that we should expect instrument and cluster distributional boundaries to be roughly the same. This, in fact, turns out to be the case in the Congo, where J. S. Laurenty has attempted to map the distribution of some of the music instruments (1960). In reviewing Laurenty's work, the present writer attempted to draw attention to the correlations between clusters and instruments.

In the first place, he [Laurenty] finds that in instrument distribution the peoples to the north of the Congo River and to the east of the Lualaba River are quite sharply differentiated from those in the Congo basin whose area is south of the Congo and west of the Lualaba: the differences are found in the form of affixing the drum head; the fact that the xylophone, zither and harp are found together in the north and somewhat to the east and not in the basin; and that the pluriarc is found in the basin and not to the north and east. Thus the boundary formed by the rivers makes a sharp distinction between harps and zithers on the one hand, and pluriarcs on the other. On the basis of ethnic divisions, this distinction is not particularly surprising; the pluriarcs are found among the Mongo peoples of the basin who form an enormous cluster of interrelated groups . . . , while the harp, zither and xylophone belong to such well-defined clusters as the Mangbetu-Azande and the related Mamvu-Lese. . . .

It is generally felt that the Mamvu-Lese were pushed into their present location from the northwest probably before the 17th and 18th centuries, while the Mangbetu established themselves about 1750-1800 and the Azande about 1830, both coming from the northwest and north. On the other hand, it appears that the Mongo have been in their present location for "several hundred years," having come from the northeast. The Mongo, then, must have moved through the present Mangbetu-Azande and Mamvu-

291

Lese areas before the two latter clusters had arrived there, and thus the instrument distribution accords with what we know of the history of some, at least, of the peoples involved. . . .

M. Laurenty's second conclusion is that there are some sharp distinctions between the Equator region north of the Congo River in the great bend of the Uele River, and those of Lake Leopold II; again evidence from the study of culture clusters accords with this conclusion. Further, Laurenty sees Ruanda-Urundi, the Lower Congo, and the Katanga as generally separated from each other and as distinct from all other populations as well in terms of musical instruments; again this is not surprising in view of what we know of populations and population movements. Ruanda-Urundi seems clearly to be East African in origin and affiliation, and thus separate from the Congo itself; the Kongo people in the Lower Congo are one of the earlier groups in the Congo region, having reached the Kasai about 500 AD, and thence moved into their present location by about 1150 AD; the Luba of the Katanga came into the area from the northeast while the Lunda peoples came from roughly the same area but before the Luba.

I am not trying to argue a necessary racial or even tribal correlation with musical instruments, of course, but it does seem logical that migrating groups would carry with them their musical instruments, which may or may not be like those of the earlier neighbors, and that thus we should expect some correlation to exist. But such correlation, it seems to me, can best be expected where culture clusters are involved, and not so much where we deal only with culture areas or even ecological areas. Thus the distribution of instruments noted by Boone and Laurenty and brought together by Laurenty, seem clearly to accord with what we already know about clusters in the Congo. . . . (Merriam 1962b:48-9)

We have cited here at some length in order to make two points: first, the culture cluster seems to be a valid concept which gives us much more precision than the older area concept in handling distribution of culture traits and the movements of peoples; and second, it appears that the presence and distribution of music instruments is predictable within the cluster. Reversing the latter point, it would then seem feasible to predict that the distribution of music instruments within limited areas can be used both to help establish clusters and to help trace, preferably in conjunction with other pieces of evidence, the movements and history of the particular people involved. The proposition as presented here seems to accord well with the restrictions on distribution and diffusion studies noted by Herskovits.

A second example of the use of music instruments in distribution and diffusion studies as applied to the reconstruction of culture history concerns iron gongs; this is a study better known to prehistorians interested in African studies than to ethnomusicologists.

The first of a series of articles concerning iron gongs was published by James Walton (1955) and in it he established three gong classes, "double gongs joined by an arched link, single gong suspended from both ends, single gong with handle" (p. 20). He found these gongs archaeologically distributed at Zimbabwe, Imnukwana, and Dhlo Dhlo in Southern Rhodesia, and from their distribution and development postulated that:

> Stratigraphical evidence at Zimbabwe shows that the arrival of these double gongs in Southern Rhodesia took place after the foundation of the Monomotapa Empire by Hima invaders at the end of the fourteenth century. The distribution pattern indicates that they spread from the Congo along the Kasai to Kazembe and thence southwards to Zimbabwe, and the Kazembe peoples, according to their own traditions, migrated from Mwato Yanwo on the Kasai to Kazembe. (p. 22)

Barrie Reynolds raised some questions in a later article (1958) concerning Walton's descriptive typology and dating, as well as the diffusion route, and on the basis of this and other evidence Walton changed his formulation both about the date and the means of introduction of the gongs into the Rhodesias.

> Studies subsequent to the publication of my original paper confirm that the iron gongs were introduced into Northern Rhodesia and further south by peoples who migrated from the Congo basin. This introduction took place sometime after A.D. 1500 when the first peoples began to migrate from the Congo into Northern Rhodesia and iron gongs may well have reached Southern Rhodesia by the middle of the sixteenth century. . . . The people concerned could not have been the Lunda unless the gongs did not reach Southern Rhodesia until after A.D. 1740. (Walton 1959:68)

Further studies on the problem were carried out by Brian Fagan (1961a&b), particularly in Northern Rhodesia, and he reached roughly the same conclusions.

The Lusitu gongs open the question of the ultimate origin of these instruments, and the date of their arrival in Northern Rhodesia. It seems that they were introduced from the Congo by some reasonably early settlers, such as the Chewa-Maravi groups,

293

who arrived in Northern Rhodesia from the Southern Congo about A.D. 1500 or earlier. . . . It seems probable that gongs were introduced into Southern Rhodesia from the Congo by elements which entered the country around A.D. 1500-1600. (1961b: 204, 206)

Finally, using the gongs as well as other iron implements, Fagan was able to establish three phases of iron-working in Northern Rhodesia.

1) The Earliest Period (c. A.D. 0 to ? A.D. 1000).
2) The Middle Period (c. ? A.D. 1000 to A.D. 1740). . . . and a few ceremonial objects including gongs are rarely found; at Lusitu and in Southern Rhodesia, they are more common. The Chewa/Maravi migration brought in new ideas and tool forms around A.D. 1500.
3) The Late Period (A.D. 1740-1900). [The source here is the Luba who came in repeated migrations.] (1961b:209)

In the case of iron gongs in Central Africa, then, a music instrument recovered from archaeological sites and analyzed in stratigraphic and distributional terms has assisted materially in establishing dates and phases or periods of iron-working. Again the criteria proposed by Herskovits—for working in limited areas where historic unity can be assumed, and for taking the probability rather than the absolute fact of history—have clearly been met.

Quite a different kind of correlation of evidence has been used by Elkin in tracing the diffusion of song and ideas concerning music in Australia (1953). He holds that "the routes along which songs and chants are heard or passed on are the normal 'trade' routes. Groups and individuals travel along them to visit one another, to take an initiate on his 'round' of clans and tribes, to exchange goods, to hold dances and ceremonies and to arrange marriages. The routes are well known" (p. 103). Using these routes as the basis of his investigation, Elkin is able to present an impressive and well-documented study of the diffusion of music among the Australian aborigines.

Nettl (1958b) has used a particular trait of music style as the basis for some speculations concerning diffusion; this is the use of transposition as a composition technique. He postulates:

There seems to be a broad belt of "transposing cultures" stretching from Western Europe across Northern Asia into North America. Some peoples outside this belt, such as the Torres Straits Islanders, are represented in our examples as well, but on the whole the area given includes those cultures most obviously characterized by transposition. Furthermore, some cultures near the center of this area, including the Czechs, Hungarians, other Finno-Ugric peoples living in Russia, and Mongols, make more use of this technique than the others. Thus it is possible that transposition as a specific technique originated at one point, perhaps in Central Asia, and became diffused in all directions, affecting some cultures more than others but decreasing in intensity from the center of distribution. On the other hand, the notion of transposition is so simple and so widely encountered . . . that multiple origin also seems likely. (pp. 61-2)

We begin to return here to a somewhat broader use of principles of diffusion as the studies center on single items and postulate possible diffusion over wider world areas. This is not to say that such studies are invalid, but the kinds of evidence presented in such work as that of Kunst for relations between the Balkans and Indonesia (1954), Collaer on Carib-Mayan-Indonesia correlations (1956b), or Izikowitz for the relative age of South American music instruments (1935) do raise again questions of the supportable use of materials in diffusion studies.

While it is neither possible nor desirable to enter here into a detailed exposition, some mention may be made of the cautions which have been entered concerning diffusion studies. Outstanding among these was the detailed study of Sapir, previously cited (1916), but in addition Kroeber (1948), Wissler (1917, 1923), Dixon (1928), Herskovits (1948:505-22), and Hodgen (1942), among a number of others, have outlined the difficulties which beset diffusion studies. Of central concern in all such discussions is the question of what causes the similarities viewed between two cultures, or in what way such similarities can be explained. Thus, for example, two similar cultures may have had a common ancestor in the past and have drawn apart through physical migration; they may have been two distinct cultures which were thrown together at one period and then separated again; the similarities may be due to internal dynamisms which have coincidentally developed. The problems of successful application of diffusionist theory are by no means simple, and we may recall once more the cautions entered by Herskovits that "the area selected for analysis should be one whose historic unity can be assumed," and that "the probability, not the absolute fact of historic developments, be recognized as the aim."

Some mention must be made at this point of the establishment of music areas, since they are derived from the anthropological concept of culture areas so intimately connected with diffusion studies. Only two attempts to delimit music areas have been made, for North American

Indians by Nettl (1954a), and for Africa by Merriam (1959a). The difficulties in establishing music areas are numerous. In the first place, their sheer validity is questionable, for it is difficult to distinguish whether they are truly made up of similar musics or whether the similarities are more apparent than real. The problem depends ultimately upon the units selected for comparison, and there is considerable doubt as to what these units should be in connection with music. Both attempts thus far have been based upon factors of music style, but music instruments have not figured prominently, nor have concepts and behaviors associated with music style. Nettl himself points out that no specific consideration has been given music instruments, complexity or simplicity of style, or traits concerning "the cultural background of the music," and it is significant to note that the music areas thus delimited do not coincide with the established culture or linguistic areas (pp. 36-41). The conclusion seems inescapable that music is a different genre from language, or at least that the two are not irrevocably interconnected and that neither is of the same nature as culture taken as a whole. The difference may lie in two considerations: first, while the culture area concept attempts to group together a large number of unrelated facts which are organized into a complex whole, the music area, as used thus far, centers upon a single aspect of culture; and second, while the culture area concept was developed using traits and complexes of material culture, the music area is concerned primarily with ideation. Further, it seems apparent that the constellation of ideas we call music sound, structure, or style must diffuse independently of other aspects of culture, since music areas do not necessarily coincide with culture or linguistic areas, and that it can also diffuse independently of music instruments, since music and music instrument areas do not necessarily coincide. Why these facts should be so we do not as yet know, and the most we can say is that the study of diffusion and areas in connection with music is far more complex than is often assumed.

To this point three major applications of music in reconstructing culture history have been discussed, the first of which is the reconstruction of the history of music and music instruments through the utilization of various historic and archaeological techniques. It is assumed that such reconstruction for a particular aspect of culture is of value to the general historic picture since the analysis of a single complex such as music reveals patterns of change indicative of the culture as a whole. Second is the use of music and music instruments as an adjunct to other kinds of investigations, and third is the role of music and music instruments which, in given situations such as the archaeological, may point the way toward hypotheses which can be corroborated by additional information. All of

296

these techniques are essentially additive, that is, they contribute to our knowledge of culture history through analysis by methods which are basically non-musical, i.e., historic documents or archaeological techniques. The question is whether music or music instruments in themselves present us with any unique method for the reconstruction of culture history. The answer is that music does seem to offer one extremely precise way of reconstructing contacts between peoples as well as the migrations of cultures through time.

It was noted previously that music seems to have three special attributes which make it particularly valuable in the reconstruction of history. The first of these was suggested by Herskovits (1941), who phrased it as follows: "The peculiar value of studying music . . . is that, even more than other aspects of culture, its patterns tend to lodge on the unconscious level" (p. 19). This means that while the patterns of music do not seem to be objectified by most members of most cultures, including our own, they are thoroughly learned. It apparently makes no difference that most of us cannot make sharp definitions of consonance and dissonance, or speak with real knowledge of the perfect cadence; we recognize what is consonant and what is dissonant in our music, and we have learned our music patterns well enough to know when the closing measures of a composition are brought to a satisfying or to an "unfinished" end. We learn what kinds of sounds are satisfactorily fitted into our music without necessarily having any technical knowledge about it; music structure is carried subliminally and, since it is not objectified in most individual cases, it is resistant to change.

This does not mean that music does not change; it does change, but with the exception of cultural accident, it changes within what seems to be a culturally determined framework. In other words, barring unusual exception, we can expect music over time to retain its general characteristics, and this is borne out in studies, for example, of New World Negro cultures whose music differs from the original African but retains what seem to be the characterizing traits of African music (Merriam 1951; Merriam, Whinery, and Fred 1956; Waterman 1943).

The second attribute of music which makes it especially useful in studying culture contact is the fact that it is a creative aspect of culture which, through recording, can be frozen as it happens. This in turn means that it can be repeated over and over and studied in detail.

Finally, and perhaps most important, music is one of those relatively rare aspects of culture whose structure can be transcribed to paper and expressed precisely through arithmetic and statistical means. While some questions remain to be answered in this connection, a number of such studies have been carried out with the result that there is a strong

297

possibility of obtaining extremely fine and precise measurements of music pitches, as well as reducing the song structure to a series of arithmetic measures which are subject to statistical analysis.

One of the earliest such studies was carried out by Hornbostel (1911), who made comparisons between the absolute pitches of music instruments in Burma and Africa, and in the Solomon Islands and Brazil. In approaching the problem, Hornbostel set up three necessary criteria for significant comparison; these he refers to as exact determination, absence of purpose, and variability. Since the rate of vibration of various tones can be set out with what appears to be absolute precision, the first criterion, exact determination, is fulfilled simply in music. The criterion of absence of purpose is met by the fact that what is important in music is not the absolute pitch of any given note, but rather the intervallic relationships among the various steps of the scale. That is, it does not matter whether the first tone of a scale is at 236 or 250 vibrations per second; the human ear distinguishes both, and comparison on a world basis indicates that almost every possible absolute pitch is used by one or another culture. Therefore, absolute pitch seems to fulfill the requirement of absence of purpose. Finally, since pitch is infinitely variable theoretically, the criterion of variability is met. In sum, any single pitch is an extraordinarily complex matter since pitch in general is theoretically infinitely variable; and since it is intervallic relationship rather than any single pitch which is of vital concern in different musical systems, the possibility of coincidence, convergence, or parallel invention is very slight.

Hornbostel used the tones of four Burmese xylophones and two African xylophones, one from the Bavenda and one from the Mandingo. It is not necessary here to indicate the various computations made, but the result is a series of three figures, expressed in terms of vibrations per second, which represent the Burmese, the theoretical, and the Bavenda figures. These are as follows: 672, 669, 675; 738.5, 739, 735; 408, 408, 408; 450, 450, 453. These figures are almost incredibly close, and given the complexity of the event, as well as the coincidence of absolute pitch, type of instrument, and character of scale, the relationship is difficult to contravene. Similar coincidences, it may be noted, were reached for Melanesian and Brazilian pan pipes. The difficulty, of course, is represented by the enormous distances which separate the cultures compared, and this disparity of the evidence cannot be resolved at present.

More recently, A. M. Jones has made a similar study in which a somewhat broader range of music characteristics has been used (1960). Jones, too, notes the almost exact similarity of beginning absolute pitch in comparing xylophone pitches of the Chopi, Malinke, and Bakuba in Africa, with xylophones of Cambodia and Java. At one point he charts the pitches of the scale of six xylophones from these regions and finds that in all cases the octave is divided into equitonal steps which are almost precisely the same size, and that the variations in no case exceed the smallest fraction of a semitone. Again, he notes the two Javanese scales: the pelog, which is the seven-toned equidistant-stepped, and the slendro, an artificial pentatonic scale whose steps are either equitonal or nearly so. A comparison of Javanese with Ngbandi, Malinke, and Baganda xylophones shows a similar arrangement and correspondence. Finally, Jones adds information and comparisons of other kinds, i.e., the distribution of the techniques of singing in thirds as opposed to singing in fourths, fifths, and octaves; correspondence of physical form of music instruments found only in Java and West Africa; linguistic evidence; decorative patterns; game forms; and others. Jones closes his argument by saying:

> The thesis we have propounded alters our perspective of Africa; it calls for a map with the Indian Ocean in the center—a basin whose rim is Indonesia on the east, Madagascar in the south, and Africa on the west, all, to a greater or less extent, sharers in a common sphere of influence. The theory calls for the collaboration of scholars working all round this rim. Perhaps African studies have tended to be too much confined to Africa, . . . Let us all come into the open with evidence for or against. We would welcome discussion and criticism, but, as a musician, with one *caveat*, that those who would demolish the non-musical evidence must at the same time account for the musical phenomena if their argument is to stand.
>
> Perhaps all this is mere coincidence: but if so, will someone tell us what has to be its coefficient of frequency before coincidence changes overnight to become positive evidence? (p. 46)

The problems which arise in connection both with the Hornbostel and Jones formulations center about the difficulty of distance and the lack of a clear-cut possibility of assuming a known historic connection between the areas cited. Yet the kind of evidence presented is extremely difficult to dismiss. One possible approach which might indicate the extent to which such materials can be accepted is an extremely simple one. To the best of my knowledge, similar studies have not been carried out on the music pitches of instruments of two cultures where an historic unity *can* be assumed. If such a study showed that similar correspondences do exist, then at least the feasibility of the approach might be strengthened; if no correspondences were found, the mystery would be deepened, for we would be faced with two possible explanations: coincidence, or a remarkable exception to the rule which demands corroboration of other than musical evidence.

We have previously indicated that precision of technique and result can characterize either music pitch or music structure as a whole; the studies of Hornbostel and Jones have used the former, but the latter is of equal potential importance.

The analysis of a music style depends upon breaking down a structure into its component parts and understanding how these parts fit together to form a coherent whole. Some thirty to forty different parts can be isolated, measured, and expressed in arithmetic terms: for example, tonal range; melodic movement; melodic level; ascending vs. descending intervals; proportions of wide, medium, and narrow intervals; proportions of kinds of intervals used; and so forth. Given the assumption that such measurements are significant, it is clear that precise comparisons can be made between music styles. For example, the following figures were reached in a study in which Gêge (Dahomean-derived music of Brazil), Rada (Dahomean-derived music of Trinidad), and Ketu (Yoruba-derived music of Brazil) were compared, and in which the three groups were contrasted with Cheyenne Indian music which was used as a control group. The figures below refer to the proportionate use of the intervals named, expressed as a percentage of the total number of intervals.

Total	Gêge	Rada	Ketu	Cheyenne
Minor second			1.3%	
Major second	31.5%	25.3%	39	33%
Minor third	35.5	39.6	22	28
Major third	12.3	14.3	13.5	10
Perfect fourth	13.5	14.3	21	15
Perfect fifth	4.4	3.9	2.3	5

(Merriam, Whinery, and Fred 1956:170)

It does not take a practiced eye to see that for this small number of measurements taken alone, the differences between the samples are almost precisely what one would expect. That is, Cheyenne music stands apart in almost every respect, falling either above or below the African-derived figures. Further, the Gêge and Rada groups, both of which are Dahomean-derived, place themselves together in almost all respects, and are opposed to the Ketu (Yoruba-derived) music.

If we can express a music style with this precision, and if the style does have individual integrity, then we should be able to use the technique for the reconstruction of culture history. That is, given an unknown body of song in the New World, for example, we should be able to tell whether it

300

is American Indian or African in derivation—common sense would tell us this, but through the application of this kind of analysis we can be certain of it. But more important, it is apparently possible, once we know that the song body is African-derived, for example, to know that it is Dahomean or Yoruba or Bakongo. Similarly, if the method is correct, we should be able to take a Mongo group in the Congo, for example, and given the requisite quantity of comparative material, trace its antecedent forms in other parts of Africa, providing those still exist. And still further, given all the suppositions of the reliability of method and assuming refinement of technique, we should be able to disentangle the component parts which have contributed to the establishment of any given music style.

Two major problems arise in connection with this use of music. The first is that while features of music style may indicate a relationship, we do not necessarily know the nature of the relationship, i.e., whether two cultures were one in the past, whether music ideas have diffused independently of other ideas, and so forth. This difficulty can be met, in part at least, by the use of other aspects of culture and other techniques of the reconstruction of culture history in conjunction with music studies.

The second problem is somewhat more complex. In Chapter XIII attention was called to Fischer's discussion of the relationship between particular kinds of societies and certain stylistic aspects of visual art (1961). If Fischer is correct, it is evident that structurally similar art styles may arise not because of historic connections but because of similar internal organization. Fischer is aware of this problem, noting:

> If art style is determined primarily by current social factors this does not invalidate the study of relatively trivial technical details as evidence for historical connection between cultures. . . . It does, however, cast strong suspicion on the use of general features of art style to establish historical connections, or on the use of known historical connections alone to explain the similarities of art styles of two distinct cultures. (p. 89)

These strictures apply equally to music, with perhaps the added problem that in music it would not be easy to make a clear distinction between "trivial technical details" and "general features of . . . style." In broad perspective we might hold that melodic contour is a general feature while percentages of intervals used is technical, but the problem quite probably cannot be so easily resolved.

In sum, the study of music contributes in a number of ways to the reconstruction of culture history. In certain ways it is corroborative, that is, its own history contributes to the knowledge of history in general, and both music sound and music instruments can be handled through techniques of historic documentation and archaeological investigation. It has reflected anthropological theory and history in that it has been widely used in evolutionary and diffusionist theories and, as in the case of other culture complexes, it can be used in diffusion and distribution studies and to establish a specific type of area. Its greatest potential contribution, however, may well lie in the fact that both music sound and music instruments are subject to analysis of an extremely precise nature through the use of statistics.

CHAPTER XV

MUSIC AND CULTURAL DYNAMICS

The statement that "culture is dynamic" is a commonplace in anthropology, and it is equally applicable in ethnomusicology. No matter where we look, change is a constant in human experience; although rates of change are differential from one culture to another and from one aspect to another within a given culture, no culture escapes the dynamics of change over time. But culture is also stable, that is, no cultures change wholesale and overnight; the threads of continuity run through every culture, and thus change must always be considered against a background of stability.

Culture change can be viewed from two vantage points. It can be observed either as it has occurred in the past or as it is occurring in the present. The former is usually subsumed under the rubric of diffusion, defined as "achieved cultural transmission," while the latter is approached under the heading of acculturation, defined in this frame of reference as "cultural transmission in process" (Herskovits 1948:525). Change can also be viewed as it originates from within a culture, or internally, as opposed to change which comes from outside a culture, or externally. Internal change is usually called "innovation" while external change is associated with the processes of acculturation.

Murdock has reduced the phenomena of culture change to a set of four simple processes (1956). "Culture change," he says, "begins with the process of *innovation*," in which an individual forms a new habit which is subsequently learned by other members of his society. Types of innovation include variation, invention, tentation, and cultural borrowing. An innovation remains an individual habit, however, until a second process occurs, that of social acceptance, in which the innovation spreads from the originator to other persons until it may become universally practiced by all members of the society. But every socially accepted innovation must also undergo the process of selective elimination in which it enters into "a competition for survival"; here the rewards associated with it are weighed against the rewards given by alternative behaviors, ideas, or things. Finally, the socially accepted innovation which has withstood the process of selective elimination is integrated with other elements of the culture and becomes an accepted part of the functioning whole.

This version of the processes of culture change is enormously simplified, but it covers the essential points in the anthropological approach. In ethnomusicology, some but by no means all of these points have been discussed. While it is not possible to call attention to all such studies, it may be noted that discussion of culture change in ethnomusicology has tended to follow three major lines of orientation. Our emphasis here will not be upon descriptions of change in music as it is viewed around the world, but rather on the theoretical suggestions concerning both the causes and results of music change as these have been advanced by ethnomusicologists. We have already discussed points of view relating to achieved cultural transmission in Chapter XIV; we shall concentrate our attention here on the processes of cultural dynamics in music as these are at present observed and observable.

One of the major ideas concerning the dynamics of culture which has been applied in a reasonably consistent fashion by ethnomusicologists is the assumption of the continuity and general stability of music. Ethnomusicologists make frequent reference to the idea that music is considered to be one of the most stable elements of culture, although the reasons for this assumption are seldom clarified or documented. There is some evidence, however, which points dramatically to the stability of music over time. Densmore, for example, writing of the Teton Sioux, records the following experience:

> In 1912 the writer recorded four songs of the Creek Women's Society of the Mandan, from Mrs. Holding Eagle, one of its members. In 1915 Mrs. Holding Eagle recorded the songs a second time, and on comparison it was found that the pitch and metronome speed of all the songs was the same in the second as in the first records. In two of the songs there was no difference in the slightest respect. . . . Another and similar instance occurred among the Chippewa. Odjibwe . . . recorded certain songs in August, 1909, and March, 1910, the two recordings showing the same pitch of the song as a whole. (1918:60-61)

A similar kind of occurrence is reported by Fletcher and La Flesche:

> . . . the writers have phonographic records of the same song
> sung by different groups of singers, the records having been taken
> at an interval of more than ten years, yet the songs show no varia-
> tion. An interesting instance occurred some ten years ago. An old
> Ponca was visiting the writers, when, in a period of silence, he was
> heard to hum a familiar Omaha song. He was asked, "Where did
> you learn the song?" "Among the Omaha," he replied. "When did
> you learn it?" "When I was a lad." "Have you always sung it as
> you sing it now?" With a look of astonishment he replied: "There
> is but one way to sing a song!" As he was a man then more than
> 70, his version of the song must have been of full fifty years'
> standing. On comparison of his rendition of the song with three
> other records of the same song from different singers in the posses-
> sion of the writers, no variation was discovered. This incident, so
> far as it goes, indicates a fair degree of stability. (1911:373)

We have previously had occasion to cite Herzog's remarks concerning the
importance of absolutely accurate rendition in Navaho rituals (1936b:8),
as well as McLean's emphasis on the importance of absolute accuracy
among the Maori (1961:59), and Densmore adds further material
concerning the Seminole and Chippewa (1954b:155).

This assumption that music has a basic internal stability seems to be
reasonable when viewed against the general theory of culture. It is
assumed that every culture operates within a framework of continuity
through time; while variation and change inevitably occur, they do so
within that framework unless the culture is disturbed by some form of
what has been called historic accident (Herskovits 1948:588-93). Put
crudely, this simply means that under normal circumstances it is not
reasonable to assume that at some point in time West Africans will
suddenly begin singing Chinese opera. We cannot account for such a
happening by reference to the internal dynamics of culture change; it is
only reasonable—if at all—by reference to culture contact.

At the same time, it is evident that the music of some cultures changes
more rapidly and markedly than that of others when viewed from the
standpoint of internal change. Some explanation for this difference has
been pointed out in our discussion of the concepts upon which music is
based, in Chapter IV, the process of composition, in Chapter IX, and at
various other points. It has been hypothesized that change and receptivity
to change will be more frequent in those cultures which stress the
importance of the individual composer as opposed to those which receive
their music materials from a fixed superhuman source. We also find that

305

some cultures simply stress the value of change in music more than do others, and further such hypotheses have been advanced throughout the course of this book. Internal change, then, derives not from chance but in great part, at least, from the concepts held about music within the culture, and it is to these sources, which provide the broad background for thinking about music, that we must turn for a fuller understanding of why music changes more in some cultures than in others. We shall have occasion to return to this point in subsequent discussion.

While the assumption of internal continuity and stability is usually taken for granted in ethnomusicology, there is a substantial potential for empiric studies of this problem. Ethnomusicology has reached the point at which a considerable amount of material having a time depth of some fifty years is available for comparison with contemporary music. Thus Hornbostel's work (1917) on materials collected in Ruanda in 1907 provides a baseline for the study both of stability and change over a period now of fifty-six years. The work of Herzog, Densmore, Fletcher, Bartok, and many others is available for similar use. An example of such a study is that by Burrows on the music of Ifaluk (1958), in which comparison is made of materials collected in 1947-48 and 1953 with those gathered on the German Expedition of 1908-10 and studied by Herzog some twenty-five years later (Herzog 1936a). Burrows remarks that "most of Herzog's generalizations are confirmed, so far as Ifaluk is concerned" (p. 20), but that "the most conspicuous showing of this account—that little melodic formulas characterize most of the main kinds of song, or perhaps more precisely, most of the main occasions for singing—does not appear in Herzog's material." Burrows does not have any clear-cut explanation for the differences; while he suggests that the original Sarfert recordings were made on occasions which did not demand the use of the melodic formulae, he advances this only as a possible hypothesis. He also notes "that such changes should occur within 50 years is no surprise," which indeed it is not (pp. 20-21). Burrows' study seems to confirm the assumption that there is continuity of style over a substantial period of time but that change does occur, though it is not made clear whether Burrows felt the change to be the result of internal or external factors. We cannot generalize from this single study, but its importance as a model cannot be minimized.

Thus far we have spoken only about the assumed internal stability of music over time, but what of situations in which culture contact occurs? Again ethnomusicologists have assumed the essential stability of music in such a situation but documentation of the hypothesis has remained sketchy. That music is stable in the contact situation seems to be borne out in the case of New World Negro music which has persisted in virtually unchanged major form over periods of time ranging up to four hundred years' duration. The only explanation for such tenacity has been offered by Herskovits (1941), who postulates that music is particularly stable in the contact situation because it is carried subliminally, thus making it resistant to direct attack. The difficulty here, however, is that while the hypothesis appears plausible when applied to the New World Negro situation, it does not appear to be applicable in other parts of the world. Most students of the music of Polynesia comment both upon the rapidity with which Polynesians took over Western forms, and the striking extent to which traditional music was abandoned. If we assume that the hypothesis concerning the subliminal nature of music should apply equally well to Polynesians and Africans, it is evident that it does not suffice to explain the two contact situations. While subliminality appears to be a reasonable hypothesis, its inapplicability to the Polynesian situation makes it clear that other factors must be at work, and this brings us to the second major constellation of ideas and problems of music change which are of central concern to ethnomusicology.

We have seen that explanations both for internal and external music change as they apply to the problem of stability and continuity in music do not in themselves seem satisfactory. While the conditions for stability and change are provided by the culture, and while other explanations may give us partial explanations for these processes, no single explanation fulfills all requirements. It is clear that ethnomusicology needs a theory of change which will apply both to internal and to external factors, either separately or in conjunction with each other. Given the present state of our knowledge of music change, it is not possible to present such a unified theory, but a number of suggestive approaches have been made which at least give us some idea of the directions in which our search may proceed. Let us turn first to internal change and examine some of these possibilities.

We can begin by repeating, first, that the degree to which internal change is possible in a culture depends to a major extent upon the concepts about music held in the culture. That is, ideas about the sources of music, composition, learning, and so forth, provide the cultural framework within which change is encouraged, discouraged, or allowed.

A second point which has gained frequent acceptance, but which has yet to be demonstrated clearly, is that within a music system different kinds of music are more or less susceptible to change; thus it is assumed that less change can be expected in religious than in social or recreational music. The basis for the assumption is apparently that religious ritual depends upon music, while recreational music, for example, is used simply as accompaniment to other activities. This seems to argue for different

307

degrees of integration of music into other aspects of society; the argument is that religious music is so much a part of general religious practice that it cannot be altered without altering other aspects of ritual, while recreational music fulfills other needs which are not highly rigidified. There may be truth in this assumption about differential change in music, but conclusive demonstration remains to be carried out. If it were found acceptable, questions of stability such as that of African cult music in the New World might well be substantially clarified.

A third contributory theory to the explanation of the processes of internal music change is found in the concept of cultural variability. Internal variation is a constant in human behavior; no two people behave in exactly the same ways in any given situation and thus there always exists an almost infinite series of deviations from the norms of the society. Ideal and real behavior differ as well, and no society exists which does not offer its individual members behavioral alternatives organized around what is considered "normal." As such variation exists in society as a whole, so does it exist in music, and we should expect that the examples cited above from Densmore, Fletcher and LaFlesche, and others, regarding the exact repetition of music, would tend to be the exception rather than the rule.

One of the most careful studies of variation in music was carried out by Roberts in connection with Jamaican folk song (1925). Her basic problem was to "discover what are the limits of variation within a restricted, fairly homogeneous population,—what indeed are the ranges of fluctuation with even one individual," and although she did not succeed in making precise delimitations of the boundaries of allowable variation, her study did indicate clearly some possibilities for the better understanding of what parts of music are allowed to vary. Using variation in a single song by the same singer and variation in a single song by several singers. Roberts reached both general and more specific conclusions:

> Therefore probably it may be said with truth that individual players and singers follow in the main a rather fixed form, each of his own, which might be called an individual habit-form, which, however, is modified slightly, either to suit a whim, to vary monotony, or unconsciously, in countless little ways, especially melodically, although rhythmic changes are also favored. . . . Given average conditions, however, most singers were fairly constant in tempo and pitch. . . . a certain tempo, especially, seems to belong with a certain song. . . .
>
> In the matters of "doubling" and the point at which to begin or end a song there is the greatest leniency. It is largely a matter of mood with the singer. (pp. 167, 168)

In addition, song was "never" stopped in the middle of a phrase. In a final summary, Roberts writes:

> . . . very few individuals were able to reproduce strict repetitions of their tunes time after time. There would be minor shifts in rhythm, melody, words, and even phrases, and sometimes relative order. . . . The majority of persons who were made to wait between repetitions of their songs . . . were found to be more liable to slight variations. . . . But all persons were seen to have one special form of their own to which, on the whole, they closely adhered, but this was generally not shared by others, even by members of the same immediate family. (pp. 214-15)

What we learn from Roberts' study is that variation does exist in the Jamaican music she studied, and that the rendition of a song tends to be idiosyncratic. Equally important, however, is her finding that some aspects of music structure tend to remain more stable than others. Thus tempo appears to be a constant, perhaps a stable, factor in Jamaican music, as is the unity of the phrase. Pitch is apparently almost equally stable, while rhythm is much less so. Doubling and the point at which the singer begins or ends a song appear to be least stable. Again it is impossible to generalize from a single sample in a single culture, but there is a suggestion here that different elements of music structure may be more or less subject to variation and hence to change. If similar results are found in other cultures, it may be possible to postulate a theory of differential change in aspects of music structure and thus, by extension, to predict the kind of change which can be expected in a given situation.

Although he is speaking of a situation in which external change has been operative, Kolinski's analysis of Coastal and Bush Negro songs in Suriname is suggestive of the validity of this approach (1936). In comparing the structures of the two groups, Kolinski states that "the most striking fact is the difference in proportion of entirely or almost entirely anhemitonic songs, this being 63% in the Bush and only 10% in the city." Further, Kolinski found a marked difference in the use of wide melodic skips and the combinations of such skips, with the Bush Negroes using more and wider skips than the Coastal Negroes. Kolinski discusses various other features of melodic change as well, but it is significant to note that his only comment on rhythm and meter is the single statement that "the development toward the European manifests itself in the gradual supplanting of songs with free rhythm by songs with a strict rhythm" (pp. 517-20). Again, we cannot generalize on the basis of a single piece of evidence, but the suggestion may be made that if one investigator (Roberts) finds the greatest internal variation in melody in one culture,

309

and another investigator (Kolinski) finds that in a situation of culture contact the most "striking" changes have been melodic, we may have the basis for an hypothesis concerning change in music structure.

This question can be taken one tentative step further by referring to the suggestion that there are certain elements of music structure which, because of acoustic or physiological principles common to mankind, tend to be common factors and resistant to change. Wiora apparently has held this point of view, as reported by Wachsmann: "Wiora, especially, saw something in the equality of these ratios that gave them greater fitness for survival than could be found in other intervals" (1961:143). Collaer argues that the physiological structure of the vocal apparatus among all men accounts for the special importance of the interval of the fourth (1956a:45-46). The primacy of the octave has long been held to be paramount in music as a genre, and there may be further such arguments. The point is clear; if there are acoustic or physiological criteria of music production which affect certain of the elements of music structure, they may well have a specific effect on music change. So little appears to be known about such matters, however, that they can only be advanced as potentially interesting speculations.

We have attempted to point out in the preceding pages that any theory of music change, particularly as it applies to internal dynamics, must consider the possibilities of reaching an understanding of differential aspects of music structure. In suggesting, however, that melody may be more susceptible to change than rhythm, we have omitted detailed discussion of why this may be so for the simple fact that no really clear-cut explanations seem available. We are led here to a further set of possible explanations of change in music, and this concerns the human factor which has thus far not entered the discussion. That is, if it is true that melody tends to vary more than rhythm, for example, and if we cannot explain it directly, it is at least certain that whatever changes appear are due to some kind of human action. Thus whatever we can learn about human actions in conditions of music change will of necessity contribute to our understanding of the process.

One of the most important of human actions is individual idiosyncratic behavior. Roberts found that each Jamaican individual has his own version of a song to which he closely adheres and which, under normal circumstances, is shared by no one else; this, in itself, is a human source of variation and, hence, of potential change. But individual idiosyncratic behavior can widen variation and stretch the limits of what is considered to be normal. This factor apparently has not been the subject of direct study in ethnomusicology; but in folklore, where the situation is very similar, Benedict has contributed a striking study which may be cited here (1935).

In her work with Zuni mythology, Benedict set up a special situation in which her informants 3 and 6 were brother and sister, residents by virtue of the Zuni kinship system in different households, but members of the same religious group and tied together by the Zuni matrilineal bonds. Informant 4 was their mother, and informant 8, their father, who had been a resident of the clan household for some forty years. Thus all members of this group had heard the same tales told around the same fireside, and the differences in their versions could be attributed only to individual handling of folklore materials. On the other hand, informant 7 was of a rival faction, and a man who was something of a psychological social deviant. He had considerable self-reliance and individualism, and was a person of outstanding ability, commanding presence, with a great need for achieving personal eminence. The questions discussed by Benedict were first, whether there were significant differences in the tale versions told by informants 3, 4, 6 and 8, and second, whether their tales as a group showed any cohesion as opposed to those told by informant 7. As might be expected, the answers to both questions were strongly in the affirmative, and Benedict concluded that the individual personality has a considerable effect on the way the tale is told as well as on the tales selected for telling (pp. xxxviii-xl).

We should expect that what is here true for folklore would also be true for music. Individual variation has been demonstrated in the Jamaican material and there is every reason to suppose that it is present in all music systems; the factor of the individual personality and its impact on variation, and hence change, is a very important one.

A further suggestion concerning mechanisms of change in music has been made by Roberts, as cited by Nettl (1955b). This is the phenomenon of patterning which "involves a tendency in some cultures to have great stylistic similarity among musical items of the same function." Roberts describes how diverse materials are changed in order to make them conform to a unified style, as well as the elimination of materials which do not fit the style. Thus patterning has the effect of decreasing the number of elements in a style. Communal re-creation, discussed previously in Chapter IX, is another agent of change, but it would hold the opposite effect from patterning, tending to contribute to the multiplication of stylistic elements and song variations.

Finally, in connection with jazz Neil Leonard (1962) has proposed an over-all pattern which he feels summarizes the mechanics of acceptance of innovation, at least in this particular music form. Leonard holds that a new art form or style usually provokes controversy as it is opposed by "traditionalists" in the culture and supported by "modernists." The struggle between the two causes a group of "moderates" to arise who try to bridge the gap between the two extremes.

> With the passage of time the controversy cools and the moderate viewpoint gains while both the traditionalist and modernist sides lose strength. . . . The more basic the innovation, the more slowly opposition to it dissolves and the more numerous the successive modifications. Promoted chiefly by moderates with close ties to the traditional culture, early modifications (refined and symphonic jazz, for example) tend to dilute the innovation in ways which diminish its esthetic value. Later modifications (like swing) are usually the work of moderates who are less tied to traditional values and who restore many of the techniques first associated with the innovation and much of its former esthetic value. . . .
>
> By this time the moderate viewpoint begins to lose adherents as the audience increasingly recognizes the weaknesses of the early modifications and begins to question the value of some of the later ones. Eventually, the innovation begins to be widely adopted in its original state (popularity of reissues of early jazz records is a case in point), or in a state similar to the original (for instance, the music of the Dixieland revival). But by now many of its characteristics have become so formalized and static that they no longer satisfy many modernists who feel compelled to create further innovations (e.g., bop). At this point the earlier innovation has become the basis or rallying point for the resistance to further innovation. Then the pattern of social response to esthetic novelty may begin anew—often before the earlier innovation has become a fully accepted part of the dominant complex of values. (pp. 155-56)

This explanation of trends in style change fits the jazz case so perfectly that there is some suspicion it has been tailored too finely to the particular example to generalize easily from it. However, Leonard's statement of the case has clear possibilities of application to other music situations.

To this point we have spoken primarily of studies made by ethnomusicologists suggestive of procedures which shed light upon the processes of internal innovation in music. Study in this area is, however, subject to much wider exploitation than has been the case in the past, and it is apropos to suggest some of the possibilities which might be derived from anthropological investigation and theory.

H. G. Barnett, in what has become a classic work in anthropology (1953), has investigated the processes of innovation in detail, and the application of his formulation to ethnomusicology is clear. Barnett points out that while all innovations are initiated by individuals, all individuals must of necessity work out of a cultural background which provides them with certain potentials for innovation and certain conditions within which they must operate. This organization of culture and the potentials it offers for change has been described by Barnett in a series of nine points (pp. 39-95). Thus under the heading "the accumulation of ideas," he points out that the size and complexity of the available cultural inventory establishes the limits within which the individual must function; that is, the state of knowledge, the degree of its elaboration, the range and kind of artifacts, the techniques and instruments that the individual has available for use, all contribute toward making some new developments possible and some impossible. The likelihood that a new idea will develop is enhanced if there is a "collaboration of effort," in which several individuals are simultaneously and cooperatively exploring the same possibility. Innovation flourishes where there is an "expectation of change"; on the other hand, where there is "dependence upon authority" innovations are not so likely to appear.

While the culture, then, provides the framework within which innovations are stimulated or suppressed, there is also a variety of internal incentives to innovation (pp. 97-151). Thus there are "credit wants," which refer to the desire of some individuals to bring credit to themselves by initiating change. There is the drive to creativity itself, expressed as "creative wants." "Relief and avoidance wants" refer to changes in existing conditions desired because the individual experiences physical or mental discomfort under given conditions. Some changes are welcomed because existing mechanisms do not provide enough of something that is valued, and Barnett calls this "the desire for quantitative variation."

Finally, there are innovative processes (pp. 181-266), some of which we have discussed in Chapter IX; Barnett notes configuration, recombination, identification, substitution, discrimination, gain and loss, and their various ramifications.

It is not suggested that all these possibilities apply equally well to music, but it is clear that there are a considerable number of fruitful suggestions for ethnomusicology to be derived from the study of innovation. Internal change in music is little understood although the materials for its study are readily available; the problem is a particularly vital one for ethnomusicology.

Let us turn at this point to the theories advanced by ethnomusicology in respect to external change, or the dynamic processes which mark the occasions of culture contact. This area, known as acculturation, and previously defined briefly as the study of "cultural transmission in

313

process," has received somewhat greater direct attention from ethnomusicologists than has the study of internal change though the approaches which are available represent only a beginning.

The greatest amount of theoretical attention has been focused upon one aspect of the process of music change in the acculturative situation; this is syncretism, which is defined as one aspect of reinterpretation. Reinterpretation refers to "the process by which old meanings are ascribed to new elements or by which new values change the cultural significance of old forms" (Herskovits 1948:553), and syncretism is specifically that process through which elements of two or more cultures are blended together; this involves both changes of value and of form.

One of the most important studies of music syncretism, made by Waterman (1952), concerned the blending of European and African stylistic characteristics in the music of the New World Negro. Waterman contends that "there is enough similarity between African and European music to permit musical syncretism" (p. 207), and bases the contention upon the relative homogeneity of the music of the Old World land mass (taken to include both Europe and Africa) and the presence of similar concepts of harmony and basic scale construction (pp. 207-10).

This same problem was later expressed as an hypothesis by the present writer, who attempted to expand it by further generalization: "When two human groups which are in sustained contact have a number of characteristics in common in a particular aspect of culture, exchange of ideas therein will be much more frequent than if the characteristics of those aspects differ markedly from one another" (Merriam 1955:28). The hypothesis was worked out in connection with the differential acculturation present in African and Flathead Indian cases, and it was contended that the syncretism of African and European styles was due to a considerable number of music characteristics held in common which facilitated exchange and blending, while the lack of syncretism between European and Flathead Indian styles was due to the absence of common characters and, specifically, the opposition of several characteristics of music style.

A third approach to the same problem has been taken by Nettl (1953b), who contends that "the amount of change, and the nature of it, in a folk song is not determined (at least primarily) by individual tempers, moods, etc., but rather that it is determined by the musical styles of itself as well as of the repertory which it is entering" (p. 216). Nettl feels that three possibilities exist in considering "the stylistic correspondence between a musical item and a repertory it is entering . . . .: 1) the styles may be identical; 2) the styles may be similar; and 3) they may be completely unrelated." Thus, "the amount of differences between the two styles determines the amount of change which a song will

314

undergo . . . and the amount of change which a song undergoes in entering a new repertory indicates the amount of original stylistic difference" (p. 218). As an example of two unrelated styles, Nettl cites Western European folk music and North American Indian music; as an example of similar but not identical styles, he cites Western European folk music and the music of Africa.

While no specific objection has been made to this "mass" theory of syncretism in music, so far as is known, some reservations have been entered to its underlying assumptions. Thus Spicer proposes alternatively that "the social structure of contact situations is an important determinant of the culture change which goes on when two societies with differing cultures come into contact," and that given this, it is no longer possible to generalize that "traits from one culture which are incompatible with traits in another are resisted by participants in the latter" (1958:433). While social structure certainly plays an important part in the processes of culture change, nothing in Spicer's further discussion indicates that questions of compatibility and incompatibility should be abandoned as irrelevant. The question does not seem to demand an either-or answer so much as a fuller understanding of how both processes operate in the contact situation.

A concept closely related to that which considers compatibility and incompatibility as a contributing factor in the process of change is compartmentalization, which stresses the fact that in some situations of acculturation peoples tend to absorb and use two culture systems which are kept separate from one another. Dozier (1958) has discussed an example of this phenomenon in respect to the religion of the Rio Grande Pueblo, but no discussion of it as such seems available in the ethnomusicological literature. Compartmentalization is known to exist, however, among the Flathead Indians where individuals are skilled both in Western European and traditional music systems but do not mix or confuse the two. In school, the Flathead child may learn to play the clarinet in a Western marching band situation, while at the same time he may be learning to be a traditional musician either through the encouragement of members of his family or, more likely, through participation in group music activities. In this dual situation the Flathead have kept the two kinds of music learning and activity apart, so that no traces of traditional music appear in Western performance, and no traces of the Western idiom appear in traditional performance. Again this may be traceable, in part at least, to the incompatibility of the two music systems, and at this point in time there is nothing in the situation to indicate that compartmentalization will eventually break down; rather, it is to be expected that future Flathead will insist on one or the other of the forms.

315

Other theoretical approaches have been taken to the problem of the processes of acculturation in music. Cray, for example, has proposed an acculturative continuum for Negro folk song in the United States which attempts to trace the relationships between Negro and White music as evidenced in folk, popular, and classical forms through the period from 1900 to the present (1961). Nettl proposes a post-acculturative theory of "strong versus weak features" (1956:132-33), and says that "a trait that defies acculturation is strong; it will persist in the behavioral conditions of its original cultures and is evidently essential to that culture." Thus he postulates that hot rhythm and antiphonal and responsorial techniques are strong features in African music while polyphony and scale types are weak features; this analysis reminds us again of the results of Roberts' study of variation in Jamaican folksong. Nettl has also postulated that in music acculturation "the currents nearly always move from the advanced to the primitive [sic] group," (1956:120), but this is open to considerable doubt in the face of numerous examples to the contrary, among them jazz. Connected with this hypothesis is the further postulate that "the more complex style tends to influence the simpler one" (1958a:523), but here again we face the extreme difficulty of deciding which criteria differentiate simple and complex styles. Of more direct interest is the suggestion that neighboring styles tend to become similar: "an area in which there is little contact among groups is likely to have diverse styles, but one in which the contact is great is likely to have a more unified style" (1958a:524).

While all these formulations represent approaches to the study of acculturation in music, it is clear that they are but a beginning to the theory of change in music that we are seeking. Again we may call attention to the complexity of anthropological theory, in this case in respect to acculturation. Herskovits (1938a) has summarized an extraordinary number of situations in which acculturation occurs. Selectivity is widely held to be an important feature of culture change, that is, no group accepts innovations from other cultures wholesale, but rather accepts some items and rejects others. Barnett (1953) has discussed the problems of acceptance and rejection from the point of view of the advocates of change, advocate assets, novelty characteristics, novelty values, and acceptors and rejectors (pp. 291-410). Herskovits has proposed a theory of cultural focus to account for selectivity in borrowing, and has also discussed the problems of reinterpretation, retention, and syncretism (1948:542-60). Attention has been given by many students to the results of acculturation, often summarized within the framework of acceptance, adaptation, reaction, and rejection. Indeed, the accumulation of materials in anthropology concerning acculturation provides one of the largest single bodies of literature in the discipline; acculturation is a complex and

316

difficult subject of which ethnomusicologists have but recently begun to take real cognizance.

The third broad area of interest evidenced by ethnomusicologists in connection with the dynamics of music change has been in the documentation of such change. Rhodes has written on acculturation in the music of North American Indians (1952), Bose on Western influences in contemporary Asian music (1959), and there have been many others. These however are primarily descriptive rather than theoretical works; as such they tell us what has happened but not necessarily why or how they happened. Especially important are those studies in which music change has been documented as it occurs, a relatively rare experience. Demetracopoulou, for example, speaks of the introduction of singing at funerals among the Wintu, and is able to date it to 1923. He also notes that a particular accompaniment to funeral song, the waving of dandelion puffs to represent spirits of the deceased which float away, was introduced at a particular time by a particular individual (1935:486).

Field workers who have returned to a group previously studied are in a particularly good position to document change. Among the Flathead, which the author studied in 1950 and again in 1958, a number of small changes occurred in the eight-year interval. Most of them were explicable through the concept of cultural drift as propounded by Herskovits (1948:580-88), but more important were the major changes attributable to a single individual whose motives included gaining credit for himself, the importance of stress on traditional values, and the accumulation of financial reward. This individual, LT, returned to the Flathead Reservation about 1955 after an absence of several years, and proceeded to organize a group known as the Flathead Ceremonial Dancers. Claiming research into the past "history" of the tribe, he deliberately organized his group in traditions more closely approximating modern American show business. In doing this, the major problem was to introduce variety into a group of songs and dances which, for the non-Indian audience, tend to be dull and repetitive. Special dances based upon traditional steps but not traditional choreography were created, and special "song types," claimed as traditional by LT, were introduced. Among these were the so-called Dance of the Forked Stick, the Round Dance, the Thunderbird Dance, and the Novelty War Dance, none of which is found in traditional culture, but each of which was introduced with appropriate "ethnographic information." The troupe was a considerable success and traveled rather extensively to perform at rodeos, fairs, pageants, and so forth, and the financial gain to the participants was multiplied literally by hundreds of per cent. The potential changes wrought in Flathead musical culture were substantial: new dance steps, new types of song, new "ethnographic

317

explanations" for music and dance phenomena, and a new appreciation of the earning power to be derived from music and dance were all the result of the activities traceable to the impetus of a single individual.

The importance of observation and analysis of change in process is substantial because of the opportunity it gives for understanding not only changing forms but the processes and reasons for change. A number of laboratory situations in which change is occurring at present exist in today's world, but they have not as yet been fully exploited. One of the most interesting falls within the framework of studies of changing occupations in contemporary Africa; in connection with music, the problem is twofold: first, what happens to musicians who move from the traditional to the urban culture; second, of those who remain musicians under the new conditions, what kind of organization, both social and musical, is created. There is no available information concerning the first, but a rather substantial body of materials is appearing in relation to the second.

Kenneth Little, writing of West Africa, points out that a number of Ewe drumming companies are being formed in Ghanaian towns and that they retain much of their traditional character in the urban situation (1962). Usually organized on a ward basis, they are divided into three kinds of groups: children, young men under thirty, and "elders" over thirty. Both men and women belong to the companies, though the leaders are always men. "Leadership of a senior drumming company usually rests in the hands of two or three men, who are always among the oldest members. The leaders of the middle company are selected from the senior company, while the junior company in turn selects leaders belonging to the middle company." Drumming is used on public occasions and occasions of crisis in the individual life cycle, and there is competition among the various companies. "While their 'traditional' functions have to some extent been retained, the companies at this stage resemble voluntary associations of semi-professional entertainers who travel about the country in search of engagements" (pp. 206-09).

A similar phenomenon has been noted by Nketia for groups of Yoruba musicians organized in Accra, Ghana (1958). In these companies, there is similarly a structural organization which constitutes a chain of leadership and which is rewarded by a larger proportion of earnings. Nketia notes that ". . . all drummers form a voluntary association and are organized for their functions in the apportioning parts. . . ." (p. 36).

Writing of the Kalela Dance teams on the Rhodesian copperbelt, Mitchell (1956) pays particular attention to the social structure of the group. He lists the members of the team, their ages, occupations, and so forth. Almost all members come from a particular rural chiefdom, and all

318

except one from the same tribe. "No one in the dancing team is over the age of thirty. Most are under the age of twenty-five. . . . Another striking regularity is that all the dancers live in the single quarters" (p. 4). The organization is headed by a "king" who is older than other members of the team and who is made socially outstanding by a number of social and personal attributes.

Descriptions of similar organizations of traditional musicians in urban areas are given by Nadel for Nigeria (1942:301-03), Balandier for Brazzaville in the Congo Republic (1955:143-45), and Rycroft for Johannesburg (1959), among others. Very few of these descriptions of change in process treat of change in the music *per se*, though Rycroft is an exception, giving examples of music style and concluding that "in the new 'town music' of Johannesburg, African and non-African elements tend to mingle and produce hybrid styles in which indigenous practices become weakened and new, imported techniques are adapted and over-simplified" (p. 29). The phenomenon of the organization of music companies along traditional African lines but in the urban settings represents an extremely fruitful situation for the study of acculturation both in terms of music sound and social and cultural behavior.

A similar laboratory situation in the United States is presented by jazz, a music phenomenon old enough to have time depth and also constantly in the process of change. A number of studies of jazz have been carried out from this point of view (see Merriam and Mack 1960), but the potential of the situation has by no means been fully exploited. Of particular contemporary interest is the recent appearance of "soul" music, an almost ideal situation for a case study of a contra-acculturative movement (see Hentoff 1961: 60-74).

The study of the dynamics of music change is among the most potentially rewarding activities in ethnomusicology. Change in music is barely understood, either as concerns music sound as a thing in itself or the conceptual behavioral activities which underlie that sound. Indeed, the challenge of ethnomusicology today lies not so much in understanding what has been done in the past as in blazing the way in the future toward a better understanding of the study of music in culture.

REFERENCES CITED

Alakija, Oluwole Ayodele
1933   Is the African musical? Wasu 3 (Apr.-June): 26-30.

Andersen, Johannes C.
1933   Maori music with its Polynesian background. Journal of the Polynesian Society 42:Memoir No. 10.

Ankermann, B.
1905   Kulturkreis und Kulturgeschichten in Afrika. Zeitschrift für Ethnologie 37:54-90.

Anonymous
1921   Voliva bans jazz records. New York Times, Jan. 11, 9:2.
1922a   Musician is driven to suicide by jazz. New York Times, April 7, 1:2.
1922b   Primitive savage animalism, preacher's analysis of jazz. New York Times, March 3, 15:7.
1924   He sees a change for the worse. New York Times, Oct. 13, 18:5.
1925a   Condemns age of jazz. New York Times, Jan. 27, 22:8.
1925b   Is jazz the pilot of disaster? Etude 43 (no. 1): 5-6.
1926a   Enjoin "jazz" palace to protect new born. New York Times, Feb. 4, 4:3.
1926b   Praises Broadway music. New York Times, Jan. 11, 30:6.
1927a   Jazz music and digestion. New York Times, May 13, 22:5.
1927b   Sufferers before our time. New York Times, Nov. 20, III, 4:6.
1928a   Jazz frightens bears. New York Times, Nov. 24, 16:5.
1928b   The Soviet cult—jazz outlawed. New York Times, Jan. 8, VIII, 8:8.
1929   Composer sees jazz as feverish noise. New York Times, Sept. 3, 24:6.
1931   Mexican students ban jazz as aid in spreading our rule. New York Times, April 20, 7:2.
1934a   Ban against jazz sought in Ireland. New York Times, Jan. 7, IV, 3:4.
1934b   Says jazz threatens Christian civilization. New York Times, Dec. 16, IV, 2:7.
1938   Warns of effects of "swing" on youth. New York Times, Oct. 26, 20:8.

Armstrong, Robert P.
1963   Notes on a Java year. Tri-Quarterly (Northwestern University) 5 (Winter):3-11.

Bake, Arnold
1957   The music of India. In Egon Wellesz (Ed). Ancient and Oriental music. London: Oxford University Press, pp. 195-227.

Balandier, Georges
1955   Sociologie des Brazzaville Noires. Paris: Librairie Armand Colin, Cahiers de la Fondation Nationale des Sciences Politiques 67.

Balfour, Henry
1907   The friction-drum. Journal of the Royal Anthropological Institute 37:67-92.

Barnett, H. G.
1953   Innovation: the basis of cultural change. New York: McGraw-Hill.

Barry, Phillips
1939   Folk music in America. New York: Works Progress Administration, Federal Theatre Project, National Service Bureau, Publication No. 80-S.

Bartholomew, Wilmer T.
1942   Acoustics of music. Englewood Cliffs, N.J.: Prentice-Hall.

Bartok, Bela, and Albert B. Lord
1951   Serbo-Croatian folk songs. New York: Columbia University Press.

Basden, G. T.
1921   Among the Ibos of Nigeria. Philadelphia: J. B. Lippincott.

Beidelman, Thomas O.
1961   Hyena and Rabbit: a Kaguru representation of matrilineal relations. Africa 31:61-74.

Bell, F. L. S.
1935   The social significance of amfat among the Tanga of New Ireland. Journal of the Polynesian Society 44:97-111.

Benedict, Ruth
1922   The vision in Plains culture. American Anthropologist 24:1-23.
1935   Zuni mythology. New York: Columbia University Contributions to Anthropology, Vol. XXI. 2 vols.
1948   Anthropology and the humanities. American Anthropologist 50:585-93.

Bérenger-Féraud, Dr.
1882   Étude sur les griots; des peuplades de la Sénégambie. Revue d'Anthropologie 5:266-79.

Best, Elsdon
1924   The Maori. Wellington: Memoirs of the Polynesian Society, Vol. V. 2 vols.
1925   Games and pastimes of the Maori. Wellington: Dominion Museum Bulletin No. 8.

Bingham, W. V.

1914   Five years of progress in comparative musical science. Psychological Bulletin 11:421-33.

Birket-Smith, Kaj.
1935   The Eskimos. New York: E. P. Dutton.

Blacking, John
1957   The rôle of music amongst the Venda of the Northern Transvaal. Johannesburg: International Library of African Music.
1959   Problems of pitch, pattern and harmony in the ocarina music of the Venda. African Music 2 (2):15-23.

Boas, Franz
1948   Race, language and culture. New York: Macmillan.
1955   Primitive art. New York: Dover.

Bodiel, Thiam
1949   Hierarchie de la société Ouolove. Notes Africaines 41 (Janvier):12.

Bohannan, Paul
n.d.   The social life of man. Unpublished draft of: Social anthropology. New York: Holt, Rinehart and Winston, 1963.
1957   Justice and judgment among the Tiv. London: Oxford University Press.

Boone, Olga
1951   Les tambours du Congo Belge et du Ruanda-Urundi. Tervuren: Annales du Musée du Congo Belge, Nouvelle Serie in-4°, Sciences de l'Homme, Ethnographie, Vol. 1.

Bose, Fritz
1959   Western influences in modern Asian music. Journal of the International Folk Music Council 11:47-50.

Boulton, Laura
1954   The Eskimos of Hudson Bay and Alaska. New York: Folkways Records, Album Notes for FE4444.

Bowers, Raymond V.
1954   Research methodology in sociology: the first half-century. In Robert F. Spencer (Ed). Method and perspective in anthropology. Minneapolis: University of Minnesota Press, pp. 251-70.

Bright, William
1963   Language and music: areas for cooperation. Ethnomusicology 7:26-32.

Buck, Peter (Te Rangi Hiroa)
1938   Ethnology of Mangareva. Honolulu: Bernice P. Bishop Museum Bulletin 157.

Bullough, Edward
1912   Psychical distance as a factor in art and an aesthetic principle. British Journal of Psychology 5:87-98.

Burrows, Edwin G.
    1933   Native music of the Tuamotus. Honolulu: Bernice P. Bishop Museum
            Bulletin 109.
    1936   Ethnology of Futuna. Honolulu: Bernice P. Bishop Museum Bulletin
            138.
    1940   Polynesian music and dancing. Journal of the Polynesian Society 49:
            331-46.
    1945   Songs of Uvea and Futuna. Honolulu: Bernice P. Bishop Museum
            Bulletin 183.
    1958   Music on Ifaluk Atoll in the Caroline Islands. Ethnomusicology 2:9-22.

Carrington, John F.
    1949a   A comparative study of Central African gong-languages. Bruxelles:
            Institut Royal Colonial Belge, Section des Sciences Morales et Po-
            litiques, Memoires, Collection in-8° Tome XVIII, fasc. 3.
    1949b   Talking drums of Africa. London: Carey Kingsgate.

Cassidy, Harold Gomes
    1962   The sciences and the arts: a new alliance. New York: Harper.

Cassirer, Ernst
    1944   An essay on man. New Haven: Yale University Press.

Chase, Gilbert
    1958   A dialectical approach to music history. Ethnomusicology 2:1-9.

Clough, Shepard B.
    1960   Basic values of Western civilization. New York: Columbia University
            Press.

Coleman, James S.
    1961   The adolescent society. Glencoe: The Free Press.

Collaer, Paul
    1956a   État actuel des connaissances relatives à la perception auditive, à
            l'émission vocale et à la mémoire musicale. In Paul Collaer (Ed). Les
            Colloques de Wégimont. Bruxelles: Elsevier, pp. 37-55.
    1956b   Musique caraïbe et maya. In Studia Memoriae Belae Bartok Sacra.
            Budapest: Academiae Scientiarum Hungaricae, pp. 125-42.

Conant, Francis P.
    1960   Rocks that ring: their ritual setting in Northern Nigeria. Transactions
            of the New York Academy of Sciences, Ser. II, Vol. 23, No. 2:155-62.

Cowles, John T.
    1935   An experimental study of the pairing of certain auditory and visual
            stimuli. Journal of Experimental Psychology 18:461-69.

Cray, Ed
    1961   An acculturative continuum for Negro folk song in the United States.
            Ethnomusicology 5:10-15.

Crowley, Daniel J.
    1957   Song and dance in St. Lucia. Ethnomusicology Newsletter No. 9
            (January):4-14.

1958   Aesthetic judgment and cultural relativism. Journal of Aesthetics and Art Criticism 17:187-93.
1959a   Toward a definition of "Calypso." Ethnomusicology 3:57-66, 117-24.
1959b   Review: Music from oil drums. Ethnomusicology 3:33-4.

Cudjoe, S. D.
1953   The techniques of Ewe drumming and the social importance of music in Africa. Phylon 14:280-91.

Culver, Charles A.
1941   Musical acoustics. Philadelphia: Blakiston.

Cushing, Frank Hamilton
1891-92 Outlines of Zuni creation myths. Washington: Thirteenth Annual Report of the Bureau of American Ethnology, pp. 321-447.

Davis, George
1947   Music-Cueing for radio-drama. Boosey & Hawkes.

d'Azevedo, Warren L.
1958   A structural approach to esthetics: toward a definition of art in anthropology. American Anthropologist 60:702-14.

Demetracopoulou, D.
1935   Wintu songs. Anthropos 30:483-94.

Densmore, Frances
1910   Chippewa music. Washington: Bureau of American Ethnology Bulletin 45.
1918   Teton Sioux music. Washington: Bureau of American Ethnology Bulletin 61.
1922   Northern Ute music. Washington: Bureau of American Ethnology Bulletin 75.
1923   Mandan and Hidatsa music. Washington: Bureau of American Ethnology Bulletin 80.
1926   The American Indians and their music. New York: Womans Press.
1929   Pawnee music. Washington: Bureau of American Ethnology Bulletin 93.
1930   Peculiarities in the singing of the American Indians. American Anthropologist 32:651-60.
1954a   Importance of rhythm in songs for the treatment of the sick by American Indians. Scientific Monthly 79:109-12.
1954b   The music of the American Indian. Southern Folklore Quarterly 18:153-56.

Devereux, George, and Weston LaBarre
1961   Art and mythology. In Bert Kaplan (Ed). Studying Personality Cross-Culturally. Evanston: Row, Peterson, pp. 361-403.

Diserens, Charles M.
1926   The influence of music on behavior. Princeton: Princeton University Press.

Dixon, Roland B.
1928   The building of cultures. New York: Scribner's.

Dodge, Richard Irving
  1882   Our wild Indians. Hartford: A. D. Worthington.

Dorsey, George A.
  1903   The Arapaho Sun Dance: the ceremony of the offerings lodge. Chicago:
          Publication 75 of the Field Columbian Museum, Anthropological
          Series Vol. IV.
  1904   Traditions of the Arikara. Washington: Carnegie Institution of Wash-
          ington Publication No. 17.
  1905a   The Cheyenne. II. The Sun Dance. Chicago: Field Columbian
          Museum, Anthropological Series, Vol. IX, No. 2.
  1905b   The Ponca Sun Dance. Chicago: Field Columbian Museum, Anthro-
          pological Series, Vol. VII, No. 2.
  1906   The Pawnee: Mythology (Part I). Washington: Carnegie Institution
          of Washington Publication No. 59.

Dozier, Edward P.
  1958   Spanish-Catholic influences on Rio Grande Pueblo religion. American
          Anthropologist 60:441-48.

East, Rupert (translator)
  1939   Akiga's story. London: Oxford University Press.

Edmonds, E. M., and M. E. Smith.
  1923   The phenomenological description of musical intervals. American
          Journal of Psychology 34:287-91.

Elbert, Samuel H.
  1941   Chants and love songs of the Marquesas Islands, French Oceania.
          Journal of the Polynesian Society 50:53-91.

Elkin, A. P.
  1953   Arnhem Land music. Oceania 24:81-109.
  1954   Arnhem Land music. Oceania 25:74-121.

Ellis, A. B.
  1887   The Tshi-speaking peoples of the Gold Coast of West Africa. London:
          Chapman and Hall.

Ellis, William
  1833   Polynesian researches. New York: J. & J. Harper. 4 vols.

Fagan, Brian
  1961a   A collection of nineteenth century Soli ironwork from the Lusaka area
          of Northern Rhodesia. Journal of the Royal Anthropological Institute
          91:228-43.
  1961b   Pre-European ironworking in Central Africa with special reference to
          Northern Rhodesia. Journal of African History 2:199-210.

Fagg, B. E. F.
  1956   The rock gong complex today and in prehistoric times. Journal of the
          Historical Society of Nigeria 1:27-42.
  1957   Rock gongs and rock slides. Man 57:No. 32.

326

Farnsworth, Paul R.
1958   The social psychology of music. New York: Dryden.

Firth, Raymond
1939   Primitive Polynesian economy. London: George Rutledge & Sons.
1940   The work of the gods in Tikopia. London: London School of Economics and Political Science, Monographs on Social Anthropology Nos. 1 and 2. 2 vols.

Fischer, J. L.
1961   Art styles as cultural cognitive maps. American Anthropologist 63:79-93.

Fisher, Miles Mark
1953   Negro slave songs in the United States. Ithaca: Cornell University Press.

Flannery, Regina
1953   The Gros Ventres of Montana. Part I. Social life. Washington: The Catholic University of America Press.

Fletcher, Alice C.
1907   Music and musical instruments. *In* Frederick Webb Hodge (Ed). Handbook of American Indians North of Mexico. Washington: Bureau of American Ethnology Bulletin 30, Pt. 1.

Fletcher, Alice C., aided by Francis LaFlesche
1893   A study of Omaha Indian music. Cambridge: Archaeological and Ethnological Papers of the Peabody Museum, Vol. I, No. 5, pp. 231-382.

Fletcher, Alice C., and Francis LaFlesche
1911   The Omaha tribe. Washington: Twenty-Seventh Annual Report of the Bureau of American Ethnology, 1905-06.

Forsyth, Cecil
1946   Orchestration. New York: Macmillan, Second Edition.

Fox Strangways, A. H.
1914   The music of Hindostan. Oxford: Clarendon Press.

Freeman, Linton C.
1957   The changing functions of a folksong. Journal of American Folklore 70:215-20.

Freeman, Linton C., and Alan P. Merriam
1956   Statistical classification in anthropology: an application to ethnomusicology. American Anthropologist 58:464-72.

Frobenius, L.
1898   The origin of African civilizations. Annual Report of the Board of Regents of the Smithsonian Institution, Vol. I. Washington: Government Printing Office, 1899, pp. 637-50.

Gadzekpo, B. Sinedzi
1952   Making music in Eweland. West African Review 23:817-21.

Gamble, David P.
1957   The Wolof of Senegambia. London: International African Institute, Ethnographic Survey of Africa, Western Africa, Part XIV.

Gbeho, Philip
1951   Beat of the master drum. West African Review 22:1263-65.
1952   The indigenous Gold Coast music. African Music Society Newsletter 1 (June):30-33.
1954   Music of the Gold Coast. African Music 1:62-4.

Gilbert, Katharine Everett, and Helmut Kuhn
1939   A history of esthetics. New York: Macmillan.

Gill, William Wyatt
1876   Myths and songs from the south Pacific. London: Henry S. King.

Gillin, John
1948   The ways of men. New York: Appleton-Century-Crofts.

Gilman, Benjamin I.
1909   The science of exotic music. Science 30:532-35.

Gorer, Geoffrey
1935   Africa dances. London: Faber and Faber.

Gotshalk, D. W.
1947   Art and the social order. Chicago: University of Chicago Press.

Green, Margaret M.
1947   Ibo village affairs. London: Sidgwick and Jackson.

Greenway, John
1953   American folksongs of protest. Philadelphia: University of Pennsylvania Press.

Grottanelli, Vinigi L.
1961   Asoŋu worship among the Nzema: a study in Akan art and religion. Africa 31:46-60.

Gulliver, P. H.
1952   The Karamajong cluster. Africa 22:1-22.

Haag, William G.
1960   The artist as a reflection of his culture. In Gertrude E. Dole and Robert L. Carneiro (Eds). Essays in the science of culture in honor of Leslie A. White. New York: Thomas Y. Crowell, pp. 216-30.

Handy, E. S. Craighill
1923   The native culture in the Marquesas. Honolulu: Bernice P. Bishop Museum Bulletin 9, Bayard Dominick Expedition Publication Number 9.

Hanson, Howard
1942   A musician's point of view toward musical expression. American Journal of Psychiatry 99:317-25.
1944   Some objective studies of rhythm in music. American Journal of Psychiatry 101:364-69.

Harap, Louis
1949   Social roots of the arts. New York: International Publishers.

Harich-Schneider, Eta
1959   The last remnants of a mendicant musicians' guild: the *Goze* in Northern Honshu (Japan). Journal of the International Folk Music Council 11:56-9.

Hartmann, George W.
1933a   The increase of visual acuity in one eye through illumination of the other. Journal of Experimental Psychology 16:383-92.
1933b   Changes in visual acuity through simultaneous stimulation of other sense organs. Journal of Experimental Psychology 16:393-407.
1934   The facilitating effect of strong general illumination upon the discrimination of pitch and intensity differences. Journal of Experimental Psychology 17:813-22.
1935   Gestalt psychology: a survey of facts and principles. New York: Ronald.

Hayakawa, S. I.
1955   Popular songs vs. the facts of life. Etc. 12:83-95.

Heinlein, C. P.
1928   The affective character of the major and minor modes in music. Journal of Comparative Psychology 8:101-42.

Hentoff, Nat
1961   The jazz life. New York: Dial.

Herskovits, Melville J.
1934   Freudian mechanisms in primitive Negro psychology. *In* E. E. Evans-Pritchard *et al* (Eds). Essays presented to C. G. Seligman. London: Kegan Paul, Trench, Trubner, pp. 75-84.
1937   Life in a Haitian valley. New York: Alfred A. Knopf.
1938a   Acculturation: the study of culture contact. New York: J. J. Augustine.
1938b   Dahomey. New York: J. J. Augustine. 2 vols.
1941   Patterns of Negro music. Transactions, Illinois State Academy of Sciences 34 (Sept.):19-23.
1944   Drums and drummers in Afro-Brazilian cult life. Musical Quarterly 30:479-92.
1948   Man and his works. New York: Alfred A. Knopf.
1950   The hypothetical situation: a technique of field research. Southwestern Journal of Anthropology 6:32-40.
1952   Economic anthropology. New York: Alfred A. Knopf.
1954   Some problems of method in ethnography. *In* Robert F. Spencer (Ed). Method and perspective in anthropology. Minneapolis: University of Minnesota Press, pp. 3-24.
1956   On some modes of ethnographic comparison. Bijdragen Tot de Taal-, Land- en Volkenkunde 112:129-48.

Herskovits, Melville J., and Frances S. Herskovits
1947   Trinidad Village. New York: Alfred A. Knopf.
1958   Dahomean narrative. Evanston: Northwestern University Press.

Herzog, George
1935   Special song types in North American Indian music. Zeitschrift für vergleichende musikwissenschaft 3 (1/2):1-11.
1936a   Die musik der Karolinen-inseln aus dem phonogramm-archiv, Berlin. In Anneliese Eilers. Westkarolinen. Hamburg: de Gruyter, Ergebnisse der Südsee-Expedition, 1908-10, Part IIB, Vol. 9, pp. 263-351.
1936b   Research in primitive and folk music in the United States. Washington: ACLS Bulletin No. 24.
1942   Study of native music in America. Washington: Proceedings of the Eighth American Scientific Congress, Vol. II, pp. 203-09.
1945   Drum-signaling in a West African tribe. Word 1:217-38.
1946   Comparative musicology. The Music Journal 4 (Nov.-Dec.):11 et seq.

Hevner, Kate
1937   The affective value of pitch and tempo in music. American Journal of Psychology 49:621-30.

Hewes, Gordon W.
1955   World distribution of certain postural habits. American Anthropologist 57:231-44.

Hickmann, Hans
1952   Miscellanea musicologica. Annales du Service des Antiquités de l'Égypte 52:1-23.
1955a   La flûte de Pan dans l'Égypte ancienne. Chronique d'Égypte 30:217-24.
1955b   Le problème de la notation musicale dans l'Égypte ancienne. Bulletin de l'Institut d'Égypte 36: 489-531.

Hodgen, M. T.
1942   Geographical distribution as a criterion of age. American Anthropologist 44:345-68.

Holm, G.
1914   Ethnological sketch of the Angmagsalik Eskimo. In William Thalbitzer (Ed). The Ammassalik Eskimo, Meddelelser om Grønland 39:1-147.

Homans, George Caspar
1961   The humanities and the social sciences. ACLS Newsletter 12 (March): 3-7.

Hood, Mantle
1957   Training and research methods in ethnomusicology. Ethnomusicology Newsletter No. 11:2-8.
1961   Institute of ethnomusicology. Los Angeles: University of California.

Hornbostel, Erich M. von
1905   Die probleme der vergleichende musikwissenschaft. Zeitschrift der Internationale musikgesellschaft 7:85-97.
1911   Über ein Akustisches Kriterium für Kulturzusammenhange. Zeitschrift für Ethnologie 3/4:601-15.
1917   Gesänge aus Ruanda. In Jan Czekanowski. Ethnographie-Anthropologie I. Leipzig: Wissenschaftliche Ergebnisse der Deutsche Zentral-Afrika-Expedition 1907-1908, Band VI, Erster Teil, pp. 379-412.

1925   Die Einheit der Sinne. Melos 4:290-97.
1927   The unity of the senses. Psyche 7 (April):83-9.
1933   The ethnology of African sound-instruments. Africa 6:129-57, 277-311.

Howard, James H., and Gertrude P. Kurath
1959   Ponca dances, ceremonies and music. Ethnomusicology 3:1-14.

Ivens, Walter G.
n.d.   The island builders of the Pacific. Philadelphia: J. B. Lippincott.

Izikowitz, Karl Gustav
1935   Musical and other sound instruments of the South American Indians.
        Goteborg: Goteborgs Kungl. Vetenskapsoch Vitterhets-Samhalles
        Handlinger, Femte Foljden, Ser. A, Band 5, No. 1, pp. 1-433.

John, J. T.
1952   Village music of Sierra Leone. West African Review 23:1043-45, 1071.

Johnson, Wendell
1946   People in quandaries. New York: Harper.

Jones, A. M.
1959   Studies in African music. London: Oxford University Press.
1960   Indonesia and Africa: the xylophone as a culture-indicator. African
        Music 2:36-47.

Jones, Ernest
1951   Psycho-analysis and folklore. *In* Essays in applied psycho-analysis II.
        London: Hogarth Press, pp. 1-21.

Jung, C. G., and C. Kerenyi
1949   Essays on a science of mythology. New York: Pantheon Books, Bol-
        lingen Series XXII.

Karpeles, Maud (Ed)
1958   The collecting of folk music and other ethnomusicological material: a
        manual for field workers. London: Interational Folk Music Council.

Karwoski, Theodore F., and Henry S. Odbert
1938   Color-music. Psychological Monographs 50 (2).

Keil, Charles
1962   Sociomusicology. Unpublished Ms.

Kerr, Madeline, and T. H. Pear
1932-33 Synaesthetic factors in judging the voice. British Journal of Psychology
        23:167-70.

King, Anthony
1961   Yoruba sacred music from Ekiti. Ibadan: Ibadan University Press.

Kirby, Percival R.
1953   The musical instruments of the native races of South Africa. Johannes-
        burg: Witwatersrand University Press.

Kolaja, Jiri, and Robert N. Wilson
1954   The theme of social isolation in American painting and poetry. Journal of Aesthetics and Art Criticism 13:37-45.

Kolinski, Mieczyslaw
1936   Suriname music. In Melville J. and Frances S. Herskovits. Suriname Folk-Lore. New York: Columbia University Contributions to Anthropology, Vol. XXVII, pp. 489-758.
1957   Ethnomusicology, its problems and methods. Ethnomusicology Newsletter No. 10:1-7.

Kroeber, A. L.
1900   Cheyenne tales. Journal of American Folk-lore 13:161-90.
1948   Anthropology. New York: Harcourt, Brace.

Kunst, Jaap
1954   Cultural relations between the Balkans and Indonesia. Amsterdam: Koninklijk Institut voor de Tropen, Mededeling No. CVII.
1958   Some sociological aspects of music. Washington: The Library of Congress.
1959   Ethnomusicology. The Hague: Martinus Nijhoff, Third Edition.

LaBarre, Weston
1939   The psychopathology of drinking songs. Psychiatry 2:203-12.

LaFlesche, Francis
1925   The Osage tribe: the rite of vigil. Washington: Thirty-Ninth Annual Report of the Bureau of American Ethnology, pp. 31-636.

Lane, M. G. M.
1954   The music of Tiv. African Music 1:12-15.

Lange, Charles
1959   Cochiti: a New Mexico pueblo, past and present. Austin: University of Texas Press.

Langer, Susanne K.
1942   Philosophy in a new key. New York: Mentor.
1953   Feeling and form. New York: Scribner's.
1957   Problems of art: ten philosophical lectures. New York: Scribner's.

Laurenty, J. S.
1960   Les cordophones du Congo Belge et du Ruanda-Urundi. Tervueren: Annales du Musée Royal du Congo Belge, Nouvelle Série in-4°, Sciences de l'Homme, Vol. 2. 2 vols.

Leonard, Neil
1962   Jazz and the white Americans. Chicago: University of Chicago Press.

Lewis, Albert B.
1951   The Melanesians: people of the South Pacific. Chicago: Chicago Natural History Museum Press, Third Printing.

Lewis, Oscar
1953   Controls and experiments in field work. In A. L. Kroeber (Ed). Anthropology Today. Chicago: University of Chicago Press, pp. 452-75.

1961 Comparisons in cultural anthropology. *In* Frank W. Moore (Ed). Readings in Cross-Cultural Methodology. New Haven: HRAF Press, pp. 55-88.

Licht, Sidney
1946 Music in medicine. Boston: New England Conservatory of Music.

Linton, Ralph
1936 The study of man. New York: D. Appleton-Century.

List, George
1963 The boundaries of speech and song. Ethnomusicology 7:1-16.

Little, Kenneth L.
1951 The Mende of Sierra Leone. London: Routledge & Kegan Paul.
1962 Some traditionally based forms of mutual aid in West African urbanization. Ethnology 1:197-211.

Lomax, Alan
1959 Folk song style. American Anthropologist 61: 927-54.
1962a The adventure of learning, 1960. ACLS Newsletter 13 (February):10-14.
1962b Song structure and social structure. Ethnology 1:425-51.

Lomax, Alan, and Edith Crowell Trager
1960 Phonotactics in folk song. Unpublished Ms.

Longman, Lester D.
1949 History and appreciation of art. Dubuque: Wm. C. Brown.

Lowie, Robert H.
1910 The Assiniboine. New York: Anthropological Papers of the American museum of Natural History, Vol. IV, Pt. I, pp. 1-270.

Lowinsky, Edward E.
1946 Secret chromatic art in the Netherlands motet. New York: Columbia University Press.

McAllester, David P.
1954 Enemy Way music. Cambridge: Peabody Museum, Harvard University.
1960 The role of music in Western Apache culture. *In* Anthony F. C. Wallace (Ed). Selected papers of the Fifth International Congress of Anthropological and Ethnological Sciences, pp. 468-72.

McLean, Mervyn Evan
1961 Oral transmission in Maori music. Journal of the International Folk Music Council 13:59-62.

McLeod, Norma
1957 The social context of music in a Polynesian community. London School of Economics and Political Science: Unpublished M.A. thesis.

McPhee, Colin
1935 The "absolute" music of Bali. Modern Music 12:163-70.
1938 Children and music in Bali. Djawa 18:1-14.

Madumere, Adele
1953   Ibo village music. African Affairs 52:63-7.

Malinowski, Bronislaw
1925   Complex and myth in mother-right. Psyche 5: 194-216.
1929   The sexual life of savages in north-western Melanesia. New York: Eugenics Publishing Co.
1944   A scientific theory of culture and other essays. Chapel Hill: University of North Carolina Press.
1950   Argonauts of the Western Pacific. New York: E. P. Dutton.

Malm, William P.
1959   Japanese music and musical instruments. Rutland, Vermont: Charles E. Tuttle.

Maquet, Jacques J.
1954   Le système des relations sociales dans le Ruanda ancien. Tervueren: Annales du Musée Royal du Congo Belge, Sciences de l'Homme, Ethnologie, Vol. I.

Masson, David I.
1949   Synesthesia and sound spectra. Word 5:39-41.

Mauny, Raymond
1955   Baobabs—cimetieres a griots. Notes Africaines 67 (Juillet):72-6.

Mead, Margaret
1930   Growing up in New Guinea. New York: Mentor.
1940a   The arts in Bali. Yale Review 30:335-47.
1940b   The mountain Arapesh. II. Supernaturalism. Anthropological Papers of the American Museum of Natural History 37, Pt. 3, pp. 317-451.
1941-42 Community drama, Bali and America. American Scholar 11:79-88.
1950   Sex and temperament in three primitive societies. New York: Mentor.

Meek, C. K.
1926   A Sudanese Kingdom. London: Kegan Paul, Trench, Trubner.

Merriam, Alan P.
1951   Songs of the Afro-Bahian cults: an ethnomusicological analysis. Northwestern University: Unpublished doctoral dissertation.
1954   Song texts of the Bashi. Zaire 8:27-43.
1955   The use of music in the study of a problem of acculturation. American Anthropologist 57:28-34.
1957   The Bashi Mulizi and its music: an end-blown flute from the Belgian Congo. Journal of American Folklore 70:143-56.
1959a   African music. In William R. Bascom and Melville J. Herskovits (Eds). Continuity and Change in African Cultures. Chicago: University of Chicago Press, pp. 49-86.
1959b   The concept of culture clusters applied to the Belgian Congo. Southwestern Journal of Anthropology 15:373-95.
1960   Ethnomusicology: discussion and definition of the field. Ethnomusicology 4:107-14.
1962a   The Epudi—A Basongye ocarina. Ethnomusicology 6:175-80.

1962b   Review: J. S. Laurenty, Les cordophones du Congo Belge et du Ruanda-Urundi. Ethnomusicology 6:45-7.

Merriam, Alan P., and Warren L. d'Azevedo
1957   Washo Peyote songs. American Anthropologist 59:615-41.

Merriam, Alan P., and Raymond W. Mack
1960   The jazz community. Social Forces 38:211-22.

Merriam, Alan P., and Barbara W. Merriam
1955   The ethnography of Flathead Indian music. Missoula: Western Anthropology, No. 2.

Merriam, Alan P., Sara Whinery, and B. G. Fred
1956   Songs of a Rada community in Trinidad. Anthropos 51:157-74.

Messenger, John C.
1958   Reflections on esthetic talent. Basic College Quarterly (Michigan State University) 4:18-24.

Meyer, Leonard B.
1956   Emotion and meaning in music. Chicago: University of Chicago Press.
1960   Universalism and relativism in the study of ethnic music. Ethnomusicology 4:49-54.

Migeod, Frederick William Hugh
1926   A view of Sierra Leone. London: Kegan Paul, Trench, Trubner.

Mitchell, J. Clyde
1956   The Kalela dance. Manchester: Rhodes-Livingstone Papers Number Twenty-seven.

Mockler-Ferryman, A. F.
1892   Up the Niger. London: George Philips.

Montandon, George
1919   Le généalogie des instruments de musique et les cycles de civilisation. Archives suisses d'anthropologie général 3, No. 1:1-120.

Montani, Angelo
1945   Pychoanalysis of music. Psychoanalytic Review 32:225-27.

Mooney, James
1896   The Ghost-Dance religion and the Sioux outbreak of 1890. Washington: Fourteenth Annual Report of the Bureau of American Ethnology, Pt. 2.

Morey, Robert
1940   Upset in emotions. Journal of Social Psychology 12:333-56.

Morgan, John J. B.
1936   The psychology of abnormal people. New York: Longmans, Green, Second edition.

Morris, Charles
1938   Foundations of the theory of signs. International Encyclopedia of Unified Science 1 (no. 2).
1955   Signs language and behavior. New York: George Braziller.

Mueller, John H.
1951   The American symphony orchestra: a social history of musical taste. Bloomington: Indiana University Press.

Munro, Thomas
1951   The arts and their interrelations. New York: Liberal Arts Press.

Murdock, George Peter
1956   How culture changes. In Harry L. Shapiro (Ed). Man, Culture, and Society. New York: Oxford University Press, pp. 247-60.

Murdock, George Peter et al
1945   Outline of cultural materials. New Haven: Yale Anthropological Studies Vol. II.

Nadel, S. F.
1942   A black Byzantium. London: Oxford University Press.
1951   The foundations of social anthropology. Glencoe: Free Press.

Nash, Dennison J.
1956-57 The socialization of an artist: the American composer. Social Forces 35: 307-13.
1961   The role of the composer. Ethnomusicology 5: 81-94, 187-201.

Nettl, Bruno
1953a   The Shawnee musical style: historical perspective in primitive music. Southwestern Journal of Anthropology 9:277-85.
1953b   Stylistic change in folk music. Southern Folklore Quarterly 17:216-20.
1954a   North American Indian musical styles. Philadelphia: Memoirs of the American Folklore Society, Vol. 45.
1954b   Notes on musical composition in primitive culture. Anthropological Quarterly 27:81-90.
1955a   Aspects of primitive and folk music relevant to music therapy. In E. Thayer Gaston (Ed). Music Therapy 1955. Lawrence, Kansas: Proceedings of the National Association for Music Therapy, Vol. V, 1956, pp. 36-9.
1955b   Change in folk and primitive music: a survey of methods and studies. Journal of the American Musicological Society 8:101-09.
1956   Music in primitive culture. Cambridge: Harvard University Press.
1958a   Historical aspects of ethnomusicology. American Anthropologist 60: 518-32.
1958b   Transposition as a composition technique in folk and primitive music. Ethnomusicology 2:56-65.

Nikiprowetzky, Tolia
1961   La musique de la Mauritanie. Paris: SORAFOM.
1962   Les griots du Senegal et leurs instruments. Paris: Radiodiffusion Outre-Mer OCORA.

Nketia, J. H. Kwabena
1954   The role of the drummer in Akan society. African Music 1:34-43.
1957   Possession dances in African societies. Journal of the International Folk Music Council 9:4-9.

1958   Yoruba musicians in Accra. Odu 6 (June):35-44.
1961a   African music (Part I). AMSAC Newsletter 3 (Jan.-Feb.):3-6.
1961b   African music. AMSAC Newsletter 3 (Mar.-Apr.):4-8.
1962   Historical evidence in Ga religious music. Unpublished MS: Presented
         to the IVth International African Seminar organized by the Interna-
         tional African Institute.
n.d.   History and the organization of music in West Africa. Unpublished Ms.

Odbert, H. S., T. T. Karwoski, and A. B. Eckerson
1942   Studies in synesthetic thinking: I. Musical and verbal associations of
         color and mood. Journal of General Psychology 26:153-73.

Oliver, Douglas L.
1955   Solomon Island society. Cambridge: Harvard University Press.

Oliver, Paul
1960   Blues fell this morning: the meaning of the blues. New York: Horizon.

Omwake, Louise
1940   Visual responses to auditory stimuli. Journal of Applied Psychology
         24:468-81.

Opler, Marvin K., and F. Obayashi
1945   Senryu poetry as folk and community expression. Journal of American
         Folklore 58:1-11.

Osgood, Cornelius
1940   Ingalik material culture. New Haven: Yale University Publications in
         Anthropology No. 22.

Pages, Révérend Père
1933   Un Royaume Hamite au centre de l'Afrique. Brussels: Institut Royal
         Colonial Belge, Section des Sciences Morales et Politiques, Memoires,
         Vol. I.

Paget, Violet (Pseud. Vernon Lee)
1933   Music and its lovers. New York: E. P. Dutton.

Paques, Viviana
1954   Les Bambara. Paris: Presses Universitaires de France, Monographies
         Ethnologiques Africaines, Institut International Africaine.

Parker, William R.
1961   The relationship between the humanities and the social sciences: report
         of discussion. ACLS Newsletter 12 (March):14-18.

Parrish, Carl
1944   Criticisms of the piano when it was new. Musical Quarterly 30:428-40.

Paul, Benjamin D.
1953   Interview techniques and field relationships. In A. L. Kroeber (Ed).
         Anthropology Today. Chicago: University of Chicago Press, pp. 430-41.

Phillips, Ekundayo
1953   Yoruba music. Johannesburg: African Music Society.

Picken, Laurence E. R.
  1954   Chinese music. *In* Eric Blom (Ed). Grove's Dictionary of Music and
          Musicians. London: Macmillan, Fifth Edition, pp. 219-48.

Quain, Buell Halvor
  1948   Fijian village. Chicago.

Radcliffe-Brown, A. R.
  1948   The Andaman Islanders. Glencoe: Free Press.
  1952   Structure and function in primitive society. Glencoe: Free Press.

Radin, Paul
  1926   Crashing Thunder: the autobiography of an American Indian. New
          York: D. Appleton.
  1933   The method and theory of ethnology. New York: McGraw-Hill.

Raffe, W. G.
  1952   Ragas and raginis: a key to Hindu aesthetics. Journal of Aesthetics and
          Art Criticism 11:105-17.

Railsback, O. L.
  1937   A chromatic stroboscope. Journal of the Acoustical Society of America
          9:37-42.

Rasmussen, Knud
  1931   The Netsilik Eskimos: social life and spiritual culture. Copenhagen:
          Report of the Fifth Thule Expedition 1921-24, Vol. VIII, No. 1-2.

Rattray, R. S.
  1923   Ashanti. Oxford: Clarendon Press.
  1954   Religion and art in Ashanti. London: Oxford University Press, Second
          Impression.

Reichard, Gladys A.
  1950   Navaho religion: a study of symbolism. New York: Pantheon Books,
          Bollingen Series XVIII. 2 vols.

Reichard, Gladys A., Roman Jakobson, and Elizabeth Werth
  1949   Language and synesthesia. Word 5:224-33.

Reynolds, Barrie
  1958   Iron gongs from Northern Rhodesia. Man 58:no. 255.

Rhodes, Willard
  1952   Acculturation in North American Indian music. *In* Sol Tax (Ed).
          Acculturation in the Americas. Chicago: Proceedings of the 29th Inter-
          national Congress of Americanists, Vol. II, pp. 127-32.
  1956   On the subject of ethnomusicology. Ethnomusicology Newsletter No.
          7:1-9.
  1962   Music as an agent of political expression. African Studies Bulletin 5
          (May):14-22.

Richards, Audrey I.
  1956   Chisungu. London: Faber and Faber.

Richardson, Jane
    1940   Law and status among the Kiowa Indians. New York: Monographs of the American Ethnological Society, I.

Ricklin, Franz
    1915   Wishfulfillment and symbolism in fairy tales. New York: Nervous and Mental Disease Monograph Series No. 21.

Riggs, Lorrin A., and Theodore Karwoski
    1934   Synaesthesia. British Journal of Psychology 25:29-41.

Rimsky-Korsakow, Nicolas
    n.d.   Principles of orchestration. Scarsdale: E. F. Kalmus Orchestra Scores, Inc.

Roberts, Helen H.
    1925   A study of folk song variants based on field work in Jamaica. Journal of American Folklore 38:149-216.
    1931   Suggestions to field-workers in collecting folk music and data about instruments. Journal of the Polynesian Society 40:103-28.
    1936   Musical areas in aboriginal North America. New Haven: Yale University Publications in Anthropology Number 12.

Roberts, Helen H., and Morris Swadesh
    1955   Songs of the Nootka Indians of Western Vancouver Island. Philadelphia: Transactions of the American Philosophical Society, New Series, Vol. 45, Part 3.

Rout, Ettie A.
    1926   Maori symbolism. London: Kegan Paul, Trench, Trubner.

Rycroft, David
    1959   African music in Johannesburg: African and non-African features. Journal of the International Folk Music Council 11:25-30.

Sachs, Curt
    1921   Die Musikinstrumente des alten Aegyptens. Berlin.
    1929   Geist und Werden der Musikinstrumente. Berlin.
    1937   World history of the dance. New York: W. W. Norton.
    1940   The history of musical instruments. New York: W. W. Norton.
    1943   The rise of music in the ancient world east and west. New York: W. W. Norton.
    1946   The commonwealth of art: style in the fine arts music and the dance. New York: W. W. Norton.
    1962   The wellsprings of music. The Hague: Martinus Nijhoff.

Sapir, E.
    1916   Time perspective in aboriginal American culture: a study in method. Ottawa: Canada Department of Mines, Geological Survey, Memoir 90, No. 13, Anthropological Series.

Schaeffner, André
    1956   Ethnologie musicale ou musicologie comparée. *In* Paul Collaer (Ed). Les colloques de Wégimont. Bruxelles: Elsevier, pp. 18-32.

Schapiro, Meyer
   1953   Style. *In* A. L. Kroeber (Ed). Anthropology Today. Chicago: University of Chicago Press, pp. 287-312.

Schneider, Harold K.
   1956   The interpretation of Pakot visual art. Man 56: No. 108.

Schneider, Marius
   1957   Primitive music. *In* Egon Wellesz (Ed). Ancient and Oriental music. London: Oxford University Press, pp. 1-82.
   1961   Tone and tune in West African music. Ethnomusicology 5:204-15.

Seashore, Carl E.
   1938a   Color music. Music Educators Journal 25 (October): 26.
   1938b   Psychology of music. New York: McGraw-Hill.

Seeger, Charles
   1941   Music and culture. Proceedings of the Music Teachers National Association for 1940 64:112-22.
   1951   An instantaneous music notator. Journal of the International Folk Music Council 3:103-06.
   1957   Toward a universal music sound-writing for musicology. Journal of the International Folk Music Council 9:63-66.
   1958   Prescriptive and descriptive music writing. Musical Quarterly 44:184-95.
   1961a   Music as communication (abstract). *In* Abstracts American Anthropological Association, 60th Annual Meeting, Philadelphia, Nov. 16-19, 1961, pp. 10-11.
   1961b   Semantic, logical and political considerations bearing upon research in ethnomusicology. Ethnomusicology 5:77-80.

Seligman, C. G.
   1910   The Melanesians of British New Guinea. Cambridge: University Press.

Sieber, Roy
   1959   The esthetic of traditional African art. *In* Froelich Rainey (Ed). 7 Metals of Africa. Philadelphia: The University Museum, n.p.

Skinner, Frank
   1950   Underscore. Los Angeles: Skinner Music Company.

Smith, Carleton Sprague
   1941   Musicology as a means of intercultural understanding. Proceedings of the Music Teacher's National Association for 1940 64:54-57.

Smith, Henry Clay
   1927   Music in relation to employee attitudes, piecework production, and industrial accidents. Stanford: Applied Psychology Monographs No. 14.

Spencer, Robert F.
   1959   The North Alaskan Eskimo. Washington: Bureau of American Ethnology Bulletin 171.

Spicer, Edward H.
   1958   Social structure and cultural process in Yaqui religious acculturation. American Anthropologist 60:433-41.

Stevenson, Charles L.
1958   Symbolism in the nonrepresentational arts. *In* Paul Henle (Ed). Language, thought, and culture. Ann Arbor: University of Michigan Press, pp. 196-225.

Strechow, Wolfgang
1953   Problems of structure in some relations between the visual arts and music. Journal of Aesthetics and Art Criticism 11:324-33.

Taylor, Richard
1870   Te ika a maui: New Zealand and its inhabitants. London: William Macintosh.

Thalbitzer, William
1923a   Language and folklore. *In* William Thalbitzer (Ed). The Ammassalik Eskimo, Second Part, Meddelelser om Grønland 40:113-564.
1923b   Social customs and mutual aid. *In* William Thalbitzer (Ed). The Ammassilik Eskimo, Second Part, Meddelelser om Grønland 40:569-739.

Thompson, Laura
1940   Southern Lau, Fiji: an ethnography. Honolulu: Bernice P. Bishop Museum Bulletin 162.

Thuren, Hjalmar
1923   On the Eskimo music in Greenland. *In* William Thalbitzer (Ed). The Ammassalik Eskimo, Second Part. Meddelelser om Grønland 49:1-45.

Thurnwald, Richard C.
1936   Profane literature of Buin, Solomon Islands. New Haven: Yale University Publications in Anthropology No. 8.

Thurow, Donald
1956   The Baoule of the Ivory Coast. New York: Folkways Records, Album Notes for EFL P456.

Tiffin, Joseph, and Frederic B. Knight
1940   The psychology of normal people. Boston: D. C. Heath.

Tilly, Margaret
1947   The psychoanalytical approach to the masculine and feminine principles in music. American Journal of Psychiatry 103:477-83.

Titiev, Mischa
1949   Social singing among the Mapuche. Ann Arbor: University of Michigan Press, Anthropological Papers Museum of Anthropology, University of Michigan No. 2.

Tracey, Hugh
1948   Chopi musicians: their music, poetry, and instruments. London: Oxford University Press.
1949   Editorial. African Music Society Newsletter 1 (March):2-3.
1954   The social role of African music. African Affairs 53:234-41.

Vaughan, James H., Jr.
1962   Rock paintings and rock gongs among the Marghi of Nigeria. Man 62:No. 83.

341

Vernon, P. E.
    1930   Synaesthesia in music. Psyche 10 (April) :22-40.

Voth, H. R.
    1903   The Oráibi Oáqöl ceremony. Chicago: Field Columbian Museum, Publication 84, Anthropological Series Vol. VI, No. 1.

Wachsmann, K. P.
    1953   Musicology in Uganda. Journal of the Royal Anthropological Institute 83 (Jan.-June) :50-57.
    1961   Criteria for acculturation. In Jan LaRue (Ed). Report of the Eighth Congress New York 1961. Kassel: Barenreiter for the International Musicological Society, pp. 139-49.

Walton, James
    1955   Iron gongs from the Congo and Southern Rhodesia. Man 55:No. 30.
    1959   Iron gongs from Northern Rhodesia. Man 59:No. 92.

Waterman, Richard A.
    1943   African patterns in Trinidad Negro music. Northwestern University: Unpublished doctoral dissertation.
    1952   African influence on the music of the Americas. In Sol Tax (Ed). Acculturation in the Americas. Chicago: Proceedings of the 29th International Congress of Americanists, Vol. II, pp. 207-18.
    1956   Music in Australian aboriginal culture—some sociological and psychological implications. In E. Thayer Gaston (Ed). Music Therapy 1955. Lawrence, Kansas: Proceedings of the National Association for Music Therapy, Vol. V, pp. 40-49.

Waterman, Richard A., and William R. Bascom
    1949   African and New World Negro folklore. In Maria Leach (Ed). Dictionary of folklore, mythology and legend. New York: Funk and Wagnalls, pp. 18-24.

Weman, Henry
    1960   African music and the church in Africa. Uppsala: Studia Missionalia Upsaliensia, 3.

Werner, Heinz
    1948   Comparative psychology of mental development. Chicago: Follett, Revised Edition.

White, Leslie A.
    1949   The Science of Culture. New York: Farrar, Straus.
    1962   The pueblo of Sia, New Mexico. Washington: Bureau of American Ethnology Bulletin 184.

Whorf, Benjamin Lee
    1951-52 Language, mind, and reality. Etc. 9:167-88.

Williamson, Robert W.
    1912   The Mafulu Mountain people of British New Guinea. London: Macmillan.
    1939   Essays in Polynesian ethnology. Cambridge: University Press.

Willmann, Rudolph R.
  1944   An experimental investigation of the creative process in music. Psychological Monographs 52 (1).

Wissler, Clark
  1912   Ceremonial bundles of the Blackfoot Indians. New York: Anthropological Papers of the American Museum of Natural History, Vol. VII, Part 2, pp. 65-298.
  1917   The American Indian. New York: McMurtrie.
  1923   Man and culture. New York: Thomas Y. Crowell.

Abatutsi, 245
Abstractibility of music from cultural context, 262-263, 265-266
 problem of, 215-216
Acculturation, 303
 studies of in ethnomusicology, 313-317
 syncretism, 313-315
 theory of, 316
 See also under Culture change
Aesthetic, functional, 271-272
 unvoiced, 271
 Western, cross-cultural applicability of, 269-273
Aesthetics, 33, 48, 259-273, 275-276
 a matter of words, 260
 a Western concept, 260, 261
 as applicable to one kind of art, 260
 as to what is aesthetic, 260
 assumptions held, 260-261
 difficulties in studying, 259-260
 importance of for ethnomusicology, 259-261
 purpose of studying in ethnomusicology, 260-261
 relation to intersense modalities, 99
Aesthetics, Western, factors in, 261-269
 attribution of beauty to art product or process, 266-268

attribution of emotion-producing qualities, 265-266
 manipulation of form for its own sake, 263-265
 psychic distance, 261-263
 presence of a philosophy of an aesthetic, 269
 purposeful intent to create something aesthetic, 268-269
Akan, 67, 69, 77, 125-126, 131, 133, 143, 149, 150, 157-158
Alakija, O. A., quoted, 68
Analysis of music style, 300
 use in reconstructing culture history, 300-301
Anang Ibibio, 67-68, 131
Andamanese, 175, 226-227
Andersen, J. C., quoted, 167
Ankermann, B., cited, 287
Ankole, 235
Apache, 99, 117, 147, 151, 192, 271-272
Applied ethnomusicology, 42-43
Apprenticeship in music learning, 157-158
 among the Basongye, 158
Arapesh, 83
Arapaho, 76, 83, 178
Arikara, 76
Arioi society, 140
Armchair ethnomusicology, 38-39
Armstrong, R. P., quoted, 250-251

357